HISTORIES OF THE UNEXPECTED

The Vikings

By the same authors

Histories of the Unexpected

In the same series

Histories of the Unexpected: The Tudors
Histories of the Unexpected: World War II
Histories of the Unexpected: The Romans

STATISTICAL QUALITY CONTROL

A Loss Minimization Approach

SERIES ON APPLIED MATHEMATICS

Editor-in-Chief: Frank Hwang
Associate Editors-in-Chief: Zhong-ci Shi and U Rothblum

Series on
Applied Mathematics
Volume 10

STATISTICAL QUALITY CONTROL

A Loss Minimization Approach

Dan Trietsch

MSIS Department
University of Auckland
New Zealand

World Scientific
Singapore • New Jersey • London • Hong Kong

Published by

World Scientific Publishing Co. Pte. Ltd.

P O Box 128, Farrer Road, Singapore 912805

USA office: Suite 1B, 1060 Main Street, River Edge, NJ 07661

UK office: 57 Shelton Street, Covent Garden, London WC2H 9HE

Library of Congress Cataloging-in-Publication Data
Trietsch, Dan.
    Statistical quality control : a loss minimization approach / by
Dan Trietsch.
        p.   cm. -- (Series on applied mathematics; v. 10)
    Includes bibliographical references and index.
    ISBN 9810230311
    1. Quality control -- Statistical methods.   I. Title.   II. Series
TS156.T75   1998
    658.5'62--dc21   98-10545
                                                               CIP

British Library Cataloguing-in-Publication Data
A catalogue record for this book is available from the British Library.

Printed in Singapore by Uto-Print

Dedicated to my parents

Preface

This book originated as part of a proposed textbook in Total Quality (TQ). The main theme was that TQ should be studied as a system. By now it's almost universally agreed that TQ should be applied as widely as possible, i.e., to the whole system, but looking at TQ *itself* as a system is less prevalent. My own premise is that TQ is a system whose aim is to maximize quality by continuously increasing it. Therefore, once we define quality, we should be able to judge what tools and philosophies belong to the TQ system. The test is simple: does it support the system aim (increase quality)?

But unless we define quality broadly, maximizing it may cause suboptimization. Some definitions of quality are not wide enough for this purpose. For example, defining quality as conformance to specifications implies that conformance should be sought without regard to cost. Further, it suggests that the design to which we try to conform is necessarily good. *Fitness for use,* Juran's definition, implies both good design and good conformance, but neglects the cost element. Deming -- who inspired me more than any other quality teacher -- wrote in his last book: "A product or service has quality if it helps someone and enjoys a good and sustainable market." This includes fitness for use and economic cost. As such it is less amenable to suboptimization. But it may still happen that third parties will suffer as a result of a deal that is good for both seller and buyer (a classic example is pollution). To capture the interests of third parties, known as externalities in economics, I adopted the following definition: *Total Quality is the pursuit of maximal net utility to society*. Another side of the same coin is: ***Total Quality is the continuous reduction and elimination of any waste, including waste of opportunities***. Thus quality is net utility to society -- *value*, if you will. Since intangibles also have utility, this two-sided definition takes into account the value of leisure, culture, etc. Furthermore, it is practically impossible to measure societal utility -- at least not without destroying it! -- so we'll have to assume that societal utility is the sum of the individual utilities of the members of society. And we'll try to increase societal utility by methods that demonstrably increase that sum, rather than by transferring monies within society -- a respectable endeavor, perhaps, or maybe not, but strongly outside our scope.

Having said that, we must recognize that within the sub-field of statistical quality control (SQC) quality *is* measured by the degree to which design objectives are achieved.

That is to say, quality is measured by conformance. But conformance no longer means merely falling within preset tolerances. Rather, conformance is measured by the distance between the design ideal and the actual performance. More than anyone else, Taguchi was instrumental in making this point. The Taguchi loss function, often a quadratic function, measures quality (of conformance) by the loss imparted to society by deviating from the ideal design. One objective of SQC, then, is to minimize this loss. But in addition to the loss to society, we have to take into account the cost of production, which is also part of societal net utility. While Taguchi definitely recognized that production costs and conformance loss are equally important, he chose to define quality by loss to society alone. The definition adopted here is wider, and considers both elements as part of quality. Often, however, the cost of production is not a direct function of the conformance, and in such cases decreasing Taguchi's loss function is operationally equivalent to increasing quality.

While many texts on quality today espouse the Taguchi loss function, they rarely draw the conclusions from this endorsement. Furthermore, many consider reducing this loss to be a higher priority than reducing production costs. These deficiencies motivated me to take a closer look at established SQC methods. It turns out that using the Taguchi loss function implies some changes in the way we practice SQC, and sheds new light on questions relating to SQC. One example is the correct relationship between statistical capability and tolerance setting. An economical tolerance setting technique suggested by Taguchi highlights this connection. Another example is a myth according to which Taguchi's loss function approach calls for perfect centering. We'll discuss process adjustment issues and show that the myth is false. While doing so we'll also extend Taguchi's tolerance setting technique to processes with drifts that cannot be designed away economically. Deming devoted a lot of energy to eradicating improper adjustment methods that cause tampering and increase losses due to inferior centering. But he did not spell out how to adjust properly. I attempt to do so here, and it's one of the issues on which I had to go against Deming's teachings, at least as they are usually presented.

The book covers other issues that are usually neglected in the SQC literature, and come to light when we look at SQC as a (sub)system -- rather than a mere collection of techniques. Minimizing loss, or maximizing quality, is the driver of the system, but it has many interactions that need to be discussed explicitly, e.g., measurements, determining how many points to sample to obtain reliable control charts, and more. We also examine Deming's kp rule -- a clear economic loss reduction application -- and discuss appropriate ways to inspect incoming lots when the rule is not applicable. Also, where conformance is measured by a continuous loss function, the kp rule has to be changed: we outline how.

Taguchi's most famous contribution is the use of Design of Experiments (DOE) to reduce the loss function. Unfortunately, Taguchi's techniques leave much to be desired, and this created much controversy. Western statisticians, led by George Box, have shown that there are better ways to achieve his ends. In particular, his use of external arrays and signal-to-noise ratios have been criticized. Dorian Shainin developed yet other alternatives. Personally, I acknowledge Taguchi as a leader in terms of where to go, but not necessarily how to get there. DOE itself, although fascinating, is outside our scope. So are many other engineering techniques that are indispensable today. Chief among them are poka-yoke (error-proofing) and setup reduction techniques devised by Shigeo Shingo. All these vital methods are concerned more with breakthrough than with control. And they can easily fill another book of this size.

* * *

The book is intended for both practitioners and theoreticians, and it can also be used for teaching. To gain full benefit, however, readers should have at least an introductory level knowledge of probability and statistics. The aim to serve practitioners led me to concentrate on basic techniques, and to organize the coverage so that some mathematical details can be skipped without loss of continuity. The service to theoreticians, therefore, is not by reviewing complex models, but rather by coverage of the theoretical underpinnings of the basic ones in more detail than the norm. The service to both communities is by addressing the issues in a systemic way, stressing connections and interactions, and covering key subjects that are missing in practically all other SQC books.

Nine chapters and seven supplements provide the coverage. In general, supplements are attached to chapters, and they either discuss optional material or deal with mathematical details that are not necessary for practitioners. Some smaller mathematical expositions that are not vital for practitioners are given in unnumbered boxes ("Technical Notes"), which may be skipped without loss of continuity. In contrast, numbered boxes are used occasionally to facilitate cross-reference.

The first chapter introduces classical control charts, *Shewhart charts,* which generally follow Shewhart's concepts. Since this text concentrates on statistical control methods, and not on graphic improvement tools and so on, control charts are our main focus. Chapter 2 discusses measurements. Supplement 2 elaborates on some technical details associated with calibration and efficient measurement. Chapter 3 introduces loss functions, and covers Taguchi's economical tolerance setting method. It also shows how to change the kp rule where the quadratic loss function applies. Supplement 3 discusses asymmetrical loss functions. Chapter 4 presents economical adjustment methods that avoid tampering. It also extends Taguchi's tolerance setting technique to processes with drift. Chapter 5 is the first in a block of four that present various aspects of classic control charts. It deals with control charts for attributes. Motivated by Deming's vehement objections to doing so, Supplement 5 compares control charts with hypothesis testing, and concludes that the only major difference is that with control charts we should not claim we know the statistical risks exactly. Chapter 6 is devoted to charting continuous variables. Three supplements to this chapter deal with mathematical details: Supplement 6.1 compares the efficiency of various dispersion statistics, and shows that a recommendation made by Shewhart should be reversed; Supplement 6.2 shows how control chart constants are derived; Supplement 6.3 discusses optimal subgroup size when we want to detect a process deviation of a given size by $\pm 3\sigma$ control limits. Chapter 7 deals with pattern tests that apply to control charts. Some results in this chapter correct prevalent errors in the literature. Supplement 7 briefly discusses SQC extensions to processes with statistical dependence. Chapter 8 introduces a new graphic tool, *diffidence charts*, that can help determine how many items we should sample to establish a reliable control chart (it's more than many authorities claim). Another classic SQC subject -- inspection -- is presented in Chapter 9.

A traditional coverage of SQC could be limited to Chapters 1, 5, 6, 7, and 9. I hope readers will find that even these chapters are not completely conventional. Chapters 2, 3, and 4 provide necessary parts that are *not* covered traditionally. As for Chapter 8, I believe that studying diffidence charts is highly conducive to understanding variation. As Deming said, understanding variation is imperative. Thus, even if diffidence charts will not become part of the tool-kit of every SQC practitioner, the chapter is still useful in a practical sense.

Acknowledgement

While I'm responsible for the results, I did not work in a vacuum. Many helped me generously with their time, advice, and more. Some reviewers of the material that found its way into this book were anonymous, but their impact is considerable. In contrast, quite a few of those I know by name are also my relatives or good friends. As such, they'll understand how difficult it is to draw the line after naming a finite number of people. Thank you all, and please forgive me for taking the easy way out.

Table of Contents

STATISTICAL QUALITY CONTROL

A Loss Minimization Approach

". . . a phenomenon that can be predicted, at least within limits associated with a given probability, is said to be **controlled.** *"* (Shewhart)

Chapter 1
Introduction to Shewhart Control Charts

Invented by Walter Shewhart, control charts have been at the core of statistical quality control since the twenties. Control charts depict the performance of a process over time, and help decide whether the process should be investigated. When using *Shewhart control charts,* many experts recommend that the process should not be interfered with unless there is statistical evidence that it is misbehaving. Without such evidence, the process should not be tampered with. This does not imply that it should not be *improved*, to create better quality consistently, but such improvement is achieved by changing the design of the process rather than by tampering. Experts also recommend process design changes only after reaching *statistical control* -- i.e., once the process runs consistently without statistical evidence of lack of stability. This stems from the observation that bringing a process to a state of control improves its performance almost always, and it is then much more amenable to sustainable additional improvements. Deming, who was one of the major proponents of Shewhart control charts, reportedly said, "A state of statistical control is not a natural state for a process; it is an achievement."[1] But Deming was also on record that process improvements should be undertaken subsequently.

In Chapters 5 through 8 we study in detail particular types of control charts and how they behave. Chapters 2 through 4 are also strongly connected to control charts: Chapter 2 discusses measurement -- a crucial element for control charting. Chapter 3 introduces loss functions; the theme of the book is to study statistical quality control with the aim to minimize loss, so this is a central issue for us. Chapter 4 tells how to adjust processes without tampering: avoiding tampering is a key benefit of using control charts but we should also know how to adjust when we have to. In a sense, the present chapter is the introduction to the next seven; Chapter 9 is the only one that is not strongly tied to control charts.

---

[1]As quoted by Cortada, James W. and John A. Woods (1994), *The Quality Yearbook,* McGraw Hill.

1.1. What is "Statistical Control" and What is it Good for?

What do we mean when we say "statistical control"? The quote from Shewhart at the top of the chapter gives the general flavor, but the practical picture is more restricted: the operational definition (i.e., the practical test) of statistical control is perhaps best described as "not showing signs of being *out of control* on Shewhart control charts." Roughly speaking, statistical control, as operationally defined by conforming to Shewhart control charts, implies two things: (i) that the process that we monitor is not currently subject to any large *unusual* influence; (ii) that the major characteristics of consecutive items produced by the process belong to the same statistical distribution, but are statistically independent of each other (i.e., they are *i.i.d.* -- which stands for *i*ndependent and *i*dentically *d*istributed).

When these conditions are met we have a process that is *predictable*. More precisely, we *may* feel comfortable enough about it to gamble that it will *continue* to be under statistical control, and subject to this gamble we can predict the outcome in a statistical sense. For instance, we may be able to predict that the level of defects in the next 1000 items will be about 2% and almost certainly neither above 3.33% nor below 0.67%. In a more mature quality environment we might be able to predict that the fraction defective will almost certainly not exceed 1/10000, and will likely be much less than that. But such statements can only be made based on reliable data, and they always presume that the processes that prevailed during the collection of that data will not be allowed to deteriorate.

Such a presumption must be backed by a system that has some mechanism to either prevent deteriorations or control against them. Continual monitoring of key processes by control charts is often the method by which this is done. But not every process must be monitored forever: A process that shows unwavering control for a long time need not be monitored with the same zeal as one that goes out of control frequently. As much as possible, we should "wean" stable processes from being charted. We may then inspect them much more rarely, perhaps on a random basis. In a mature quality control environment many processes will have been weaned in this way. And some focusing is required: we should devote more attention to key measurements of key processes.

The first assumption -- lack of any large unusual influence -- speaks to the major use of control charts: to identify when the process *is* under the influence of a *special cause* that should be investigated. When the second assumption -- i.i.d. process outputs -- is met, there is no correlation between items, so unless we have evidence that the process distribution changed, we cannot use information from one item to make predictions about another. To clarify, we can always use many items to estimate parameters that apply to all items, but we cannot assume that the next item will be like the last. The second assumption is inherent in simple control charts, but advanced techniques may be used when items are statistically dependant, and it is either uneconomical or undesirable to remove the dependance.[2]

Statistical control is sufficient to achieve *consistent* results, but not necessarily *satisfactory* results. Therefore, statistical control does not imply excellence. Furthermore, when we don't know how to adjust our process to target accurately, we can still achieve statistical control by a consistent adjustment, so statistical control implies consistency, but not necessarily accuracy. A biased process that produces items that are off-target on average may still be in statistical control, as long as it is *always* subject to the same *predictable* bias. In contrast, if the bias changes with time, we no longer have the same distribution, so we don't have statistical control. Table 1.1 summarizes these distinctions.

Statistical control implies	But not necessarily
Statistically predictable results	Good results
Consistent and stable adjustment	Good adjustment

Table 1.1

Usually, control charts involve collecting data on a periodic basis by checking *subgroups* of items. For each subgroup, one or two statistics are calculated and charted. All the items in the subgroups compose the *sample*. Control charts show how the process varies from one subgroup to the next. This information would be lost if we simply commingled all the individual items to one group and investigated its distribution. Chapter 7 investigates special patterns that the subgroups may reveal (which would be lost without their use): in general, any strange pattern that can be observed in a chart, especially if it can be shown to repeat itself *after* being identified, may provide valuable clues to the analysis of the process that no other approach could provide. This is perhaps the main advantage of control charts over many other statistical methods.

---

[2]In page 6 of his landmark book Shewhart defined statistical control more broadly: "For our present purpose *a phenomenon will be said to be controlled when, through the use of past experience, we can predict, at least within limits, how the phenomenon may be expected to vary in the future. Here it is understood that prediction within limits means that we can state, at least approximately, the probability that the observed phenomenon will fall within the limits.*" [his italics]. While, as discussed above, the practical interpretation of statistical control is usually much narrower, there is a relatively modern movement to go back to Shewhart's words (as cited here) rather than to his deeds (as manifested by the use of control charts to judge control). We discuss this further in Supplement 7.

1.2. Types of Control Charts

There are three major types of basic control charts (and uncounted less basic variations). Two are associated with attributes, and one with continuous variables.

The first two types -- covered in Chapter 5 -- are used to monitor the incidence of particular occurrences, or attributes. Examples of attributes are: "defective," "red," "with triplicate paperwork," "has exact change," "vegetarian," etc. To devise and use control charts for such attributes, we may take subgroups periodically, count the incidence of the attribute in each, and compare it to control limits. These control limits, in turn, are based on an initial sample of similar subgroups. Similarly, we may use a control chart that counts attributes, e.g., the number of typos in a manuscript.

np charts monitor the number of occurrences in subgroups of constant size. *p* charts are very similar, but they monitor the *fraction* of the attribute instead: they are slightly less convenient, but they are necessary when subgroups sizes vary. We may also want to monitor occurrences that can take place more than once on each item, e.g., the number of typos in various papers. This leads to the second type: control charts that are concerned with the total count but not as a fraction of the number of items under study. For this purpose we have, again, two options: *c* charts count occurrences in a constant area of opportunity; *u* charts allow the areas to vary.

The third type of control chart -- mainly covered in Chapter 6 -- monitors continuous variables. When the fitness-for-use of an item is a function of one or more numerical dimensions, then by translating the result to an attribute (e.g., "acceptable" versus "defective") we lose much information that the sample could provide. *Continuous variable control charts* -- variable charts, in short -- monitor such crucial measurements. Usually, each crucial measurement has a separate chart. Advanced schemes exist to monitor more than one measurement on the same chart, but they are rarely utilized in practice, and as such they are beyond our scope (see Shewhart, 1931; Ryan, 1989). In mature quality control environments variable charts dominate. Attribute charts are then reserved for pure attributes -- e.g., "red" versus "white" -- but they are also useful for monitoring overall performance. We cover them first because they are simpler than variable charts.

Most variable control charts are based on taking periodic subgroups, and charting the subgroup averages, $\bar{x}$ (read "x-bar"), and a dispersion statistic associated with the within-subgroup variation. For the latter purpose the two prevailing statistics in use are R -- the range between the largest and smallest item in each subgroup -- and s, the square root of the unbiased estimate of σ^2, s^2. The resulting combinations are $\bar{x}$ *and R control charts* and $\bar{x}$ *and s control charts*. It is also possible to use s^2 directly, instead of its square root, s. We will see that the latter alternative is the most efficient, but it lacks robustness. Therefore, the best combination, and the one that Shewhart recommended most, is usually the $\bar{x}$ and s chart. The $\bar{x}$ and R combination is much more popular, and has a distinct advantage when computations are done manually. In computerized environments, however, R charts should be retired. In addition, there is also a chart for variable data that is not based on subgroups, called *individuals control chart*, or *x chart*. It is usually specified in combination with a *moving range* chart for dispersion.

The charts we mentioned are called *Shewhart control charts*: they were either created by him or follow his template closely. Chapter 6 discusses very briefly two extensions (*CUSUM* and *EWMA* charts), designed to detect small process shifts faster than variable Shewhart charts. Among other alternatives we may mention *precontrol*, which may be fairly described as a *non*-Shewhart control chart. Precontrol is not concerned with statistical control at all, but rather it focuses on creating conforming products. As such it can be said to control *capability* (Shainin and Shainin, 1988). It belongs to a family of charts known as *narrow gauge* charts, which are predicated on product specification limits rather than process-dictated limits. When combined with an adjustment rule such as the *five/ten* rule (Chapter 4), precontrol may be recommended for short runs, where it is, arguably, not practical to use Shewhart charts.[3] The main problem with precontrol, in our context, is that it is not conducive to reducing quadratic loss: its objective is limited to staying within the tolerance limits. But it should be stated that insisting on statistical control under all circumstances is not always economical, so sometimes capability control is in order (Bhote, 1991).

Before we embark on the technical details associated with control charts, we should note that although we usually talk about time as the source of variation between subgroups, the principle is also applicable to other sources of variation.

1.3. The Role of Control Charts in Improvement Projects

The main philosophy behind control charts is that variation stems from two distinct types of causes: *common causes* and *assignable causes* (also known as *special causes*). Common causes are assumed to work all the time, and are part of the system as it was designed (but not necessarily as it was *intended*). Special causes are not part of the system as it was designed, and it is possible to remove them (when they are detrimental) or use them to improve the system (when they happen to yield improved results). Thus, the results of special causes can be assigned to these causes (hence the terminology "assignable cause"),

---

[3]The five/ten rule was originally devised to replace the adjustment method incorporated in precontrol, since the latter does not yield centered results (Trietsch, 1997–98).

while the results of common causes cannot be assigned to any individual part of the system.

Often, assignable causes are *local* and common causes are *global*. Thus, common causes belong to the "larger system," which is the responsibility of management. At the level where most of us work, we can often control those causes that are assignable (e.g., a tool is not sharpened properly, a machine needs adjustment, a worker needs better glasses), but we are saddled with causes that we cannot control, which can only be improved at the initiative of upper management. (An excellent way to approach such larger problems is by an interdepartmental team, because what cannot be controlled locally can only be improved through interdepartmental efforts. But it is still management's responsibility to create and facilitate the work of such teams.) Thus, a problem that is common at one level is often assignable at a higher level, it's just a question of whether the subsystem we work within contains the causes or they are outside its limits. Nonetheless, sometimes common causes are improvable at the local level -- but they will not change unless the process is changed (redesigned).

Ideally, the results of assignable causes will show as "out of control" points on Shewhart charts, while the results of common causes will show "in control." One may say, then, that the purpose of Shewhart control charts is to sort results to common causes and to assignable causes. When an assignable cause is suspected, we should identify it and do something about it. When a common cause is suspected, we may need to improve the process, but investigating the causes of each individual defect is futile.

1.3.1. *"Fix the Process, Not the Blame!"*

Organizations that produce quality products and services regularly look for ways to improve processes. Organizations that produce scapegoats regularly look for ways to blame individuals. What's the connection to control charts? If the problems are due to common causes, it's impossible to assign blame fairly! Even if laying blame would be a productive way to manage humans, it would simply be impossible to do it correctly in such cases. Quality experts argue that 85% (Juran) to 94% (Deming) of all quality problems are due to common causes, so it is management's responsibility to deal with them *by improving the system*. The remainder are due to special causes that *may (or may not)* be the responsibility of individuals.

In companies that practice SQC, it is the responsibility of individuals to monitor quality and correct detrimental special causes. For instance, if a machine is out of adjustment, the operator is supposed to adjust it. If it is likely to drift out of adjustment, then until such time that this drift can be prevented the operator has a responsibility to monitor it and adjust it periodically. Recall that for a machine to be out of consistent adjustment is "out of control."[4]

Even if an individual *is* personally the source of a detrimental special cause, there are constructive ways to deal with the problem, and destructive ones. It is constructive to send a worker who produces many defects to an optometrist to fit her with glasses, a method that helps in a surprising number of cases. Punishing individuals, however is destructive. The common result is that rather than pursue quality, individuals exercise defensive and evasive actions: fear reigns (Deming's Point 8).

1.3.2. *The Two-Steps Process Improvement Procedure*

Most quality experts, including practically all proponents of Shewhart control charts, recommend that process improvement projects should be pursued in two consecutive steps: (i) removing special causes; (ii) improving the system of common causes. (See Bhote, 1991, for a different "non-Shewhart" approach.) First, then, assignable causes should be identified and (if detrimental) removed, with steps taken to ensure that they will not repeat. For example, if we identify the use of supplies from two (good) suppliers as an assignable cause of variation, we should either move towards using a single supplier for each part number (Deming's Point 4), or make adjustments whenever supplies are switched. If we find that a particular worker produces more than her share of errors, we should investigate. If her performance, when observed separately from the others, is in statistical control, she may have internalized bad habits that are difficult to change. This indicates flawed training (management's responsibility). In such cases, claimed Deming, it is highly unlikely that she can be retrained at reasonable cost. He recommended finding her a new assignment and making sure that she receives competent training there. But we may also find that the workstation assigned to her was designed for workers who are at least 5'3" tall, while she is 5'1". A design change in the work station may do the trick, but this is already an example of a process re-design. The latter example, taken from real-life experience (as recounted at a Deming seminar), may also serve to highlight an important point: even assignable causes do not justify laying blame. After all, in such cases we might be able to prove that the worker's performance was not "part of the system of common causes," but most of us would hesitate before chiding her for being short! Unfortunately, the real cause (short stature) can only be identified *after* we find that this worker is the source of too many errors to be considered "part of the system." Furthermore, in the final analysis it's the system that was defective from an ergonomic point of view. Deming observed that most managers do not

---

[4]Drift is discussed in Chapter 4.

realize that the business system is much more than machinery and data processing: "Few of them know that recruitment, training, supervision, and aids to production workers are part of the system" (1986, p. 366). Thus, any problems due to these issues is "part of the system," and within the responsibility of management.

A similar example, recounted by Myron Tribus, involves a GM worker whose anti-perspirant interacted adversely with wet paint. As a result, his work included assignable blemishes. But most readers will agree that he was not at fault! The anti-perspirant case may not be typical, but it pays to remember that such things can happen. Thus, even *with* statistical evidence we should not rush to judge. Instead, we should rush to solve the problem.

Sometimes a special cause is identified or suspected, but it is beyond our power to change it. For instance, large variation in the viscosity of raw materials that a big vendor supplies to a small customer may not be controllable at the customer's site, but since the changes are not frequent the variation is detectible by control charts. When the vendor either cannot or doesn't want to reduce this variation, the customer must then accept it as part of the system, and find a response that will make the best of the situation. Thus, occasionally a cause that is identifiable by Shewhart charts is still part of the system as it was designed, however much we'd like to change this particular design feature.

The second step -- improving the system of common causes -- often implies redesigning the whole system or important parts of it. A good approach to this problem is to try to identify the major causes of variation, and remove or improve them.

1.4. Establishing Control Limits

By design, Shewhart charts separate short-term variation from long-term variation. New assignable causes are not likely to enter the system within a relatively short period, so the variation between consecutive units is likely due to common causes. In contrast, when we compare units that were produced far apart, it is more likely that changes will have occurred in the process between them, and, by definition, such changes are assignable.

Usually, when creating or using control charts, we collect data about subgroups, each produced within a short period, and use it to estimate the process mean and dispersion. This provides information about the short-term behavior of the process. Such subgroups, however, are collected repeatedly (say 10 to 15 times a day for one process, but once a week for another), and differences between subgroups can then serve to judge whether there is excessive long-term variation, which would suggest that special causes have entered the picture.

Assuming our control chart has been established already, whenever we take a new subgroup we calculate its relevant statistic, and plot the result in the control chart. If the statistic falls between the control limits, we usually assume that the process is in control. Otherwise, we declare that the process is out of control. Sometimes, specifically in variable control charts, this involves more than one statistic and one chart. For instance, we usually have one chart for dispersion and a parallel one for the mean. In such cases it's enough that one chart be out of control for the process to be declared out of control.

When a control chart has not yet been established, we face a conceptual problem. To establish control limits we need to measure the parameters of the process distribution. This is usually done by taking subgroups from the process and estimating the parameters based on the sample. But without a control chart, how can we tell whether the data we use for this purpose is, indeed, representative of the process as it is supposed to run? Maybe a special cause was active while we collected the data. The main use of control charts is to identify special causes, but during the initial data collection period we don't yet have a control chart to guide us! Furthermore, during this period we are likely to find potential process improvements that may change the process while we are trying to document it. What can we do then?

Unfortunately, we must use the same data both to create the control chart and to verify it's representative and "in control." But the control limits we obtain are not considered permanent: they are treated as *trial* limits. Often, one of the first special causes we should remove is unintentional tampering (see Chapter 4). To avoid tampering, we should avoid strong adjustments during the data collection. While a process is studied, it's best not to adjust at all. It is particularly important not to adjust within a subgroup, because this renders it completely useless. Adjustments between subgroups are slightly less damaging (because their effect may be traced later), but they too should be avoided. When strong adjustments are unavoidable, it may be necessary to start the data collection afresh.[5]

After collecting, say, 25 or 50 subgroups, we can construct a trial control chart, and determine whether the points used for that purpose are "in control" (as defined operationally by the trial limits). If they are, we may use the chart to verify the validity of any additional data we may want to collect before finalizing the chart. As discussed in Chapter 8, such additional data may be necessary to increase the reliability of the chart.

---

[5]During regular production, however, it is often advisable to adjust processes periodically by a small fraction of the current deviation (Chapter 4). This introduces negligible variation into the process adjustment, but in the long run it assures that the adjustment will tend to be close to center. It is not tampering, because we only compensate for a small fraction of the current deviation.

Often, instead of collecting more data, the trial chart is analyzed to improve the process. In such cases it is not imperative to rely only on points that are "in control," since the main objective is to remove the special causes. But our actions change the process, so the trial chart is no longer valid, and we have to collect new data. Then we enter an iterative cycle of improvements and recalculations of trial control charts. Box 1.1, based on AT&T (1958), describes an example of such a process improvement project (also known as an *engineering study* or a *process capability study*).

=-

Box 1.1

A particular switch, manufactured on a machine with 12 heads, exhibited a large variation between heads, and a large fraction of defective products. A quality control team embarked on a process improvement project. They decided to concentrate on one head only, assuming it will provide data that would be useful for all heads. They collected 50 subgroups of 5 switches each, and measured the "operate value" of the switch (in Ampere Turns units). The machine setter was instructed to collect the data, at a rate of 10–15 subgroups per day, and note all known changes in the process during the study. The data he collected was plotted on $\bar{x}$ and R charts, shown in Figure 1.1. The R chart, at the

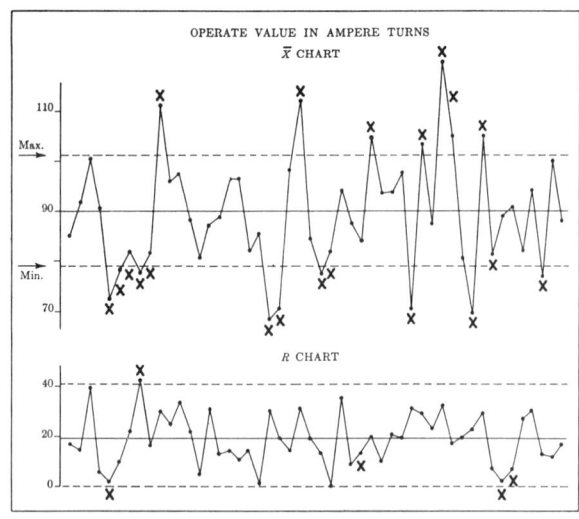

Fig. 1.1. First $\bar{X}$ and R chart in a process capability study.
(Reprinted with permission from AT&T)

bottom, monitors dispersion by the difference, or range, between the largest and smallest value in each subgroup. The $\overline{x}$ chart monitors the process mean. The x's that are marked on the charts denote out-of-control signals. Many of these have to do with exceeding the control limits, but some are associated with pattern tests (Chapter 7). For our purpose here, however, the technical details are less important. The important point is that many points show out of control. This is quite typical at the initial stage of an engineering study, because such projects focus on problematic processes.

Due to the large number of points out of control, it is clear that the problem is *not* mainly due to individual assignable causes. So it makes no sense to investigate each x individually. But there is a generic cause at work here: tampering. Tampering, unless done in the middle of a subgroup, does not impact the R chart as much as it does the $\overline{x}$ chart. In this case the team suspected tampering because the $\overline{x}$ chart is more chaotic than the R chart. Indeed, it was found that the operator adjusted a meter periodically to prevent process drift. New data were collected, without such adjustment. The results are depicted in Figure 1.2.

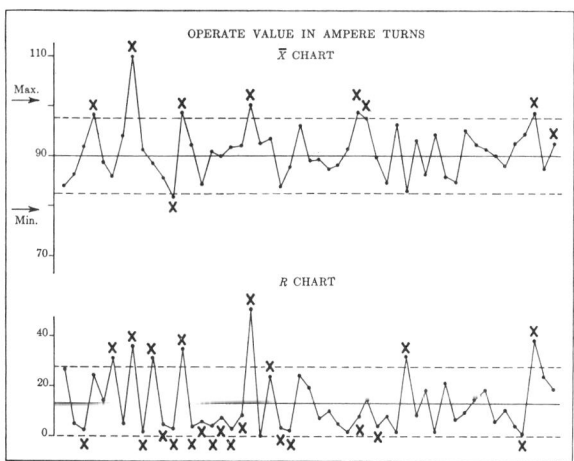

Fig. 1.2. Second $\overline{X}$ and R chart in a process capability study.
(Reprinted with permission from AT&T)

Now, although the process is still badly out of control, the control limits are tighter -- which indicates reduced variation. Since tampering increases variation, this is not a surprising result. There are now, however, many more signals on the R chart. These problems must have existed before as well, but were masked. Such dispersion chart problems are often due to loose fixtures or unreliable holding devices. In this case, one of the fixtures was replaced and new data were collected, depicted in Figure 1.3.

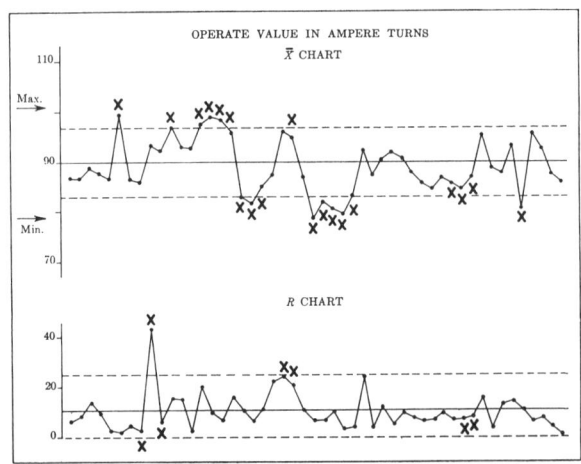

Fig. 1.3. Third $\overline{X}$ and R chart in a process capability study.
(Reprinted with permission from AT&T)

The R chart is indeed better behaved now, but the $\overline{x}$ chart shows cyclical behavior (groups of points above the limits followed by groups below the limits. Investigation showed that these cycles were related to the cooling time allowed. Specifically, when parts

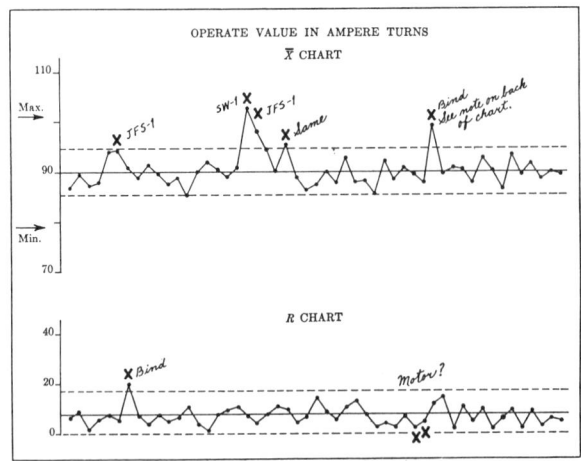

Fig. 1.4. Fourth $\overline{X}$ and R chart in a process capability study.
(Reprinted with permission from AT&T)

were removed too soon problems were caused. The "freaks" in the data (single points far outside the control limits) were found to coincide with subgroups taken immediately before or after rest periods. (Stopping and starting a process often creates special points.) As a result of this analysis, an automatic timer was installed, to prevent removing the work before sufficient cooling has taken place.[6] The results are shown in Figure 1.4.

The control limits are significantly tighter, yet more points are in control. Some of the points that are out of control are associated with an assignable cause: a condition of binding in the head's moving parts (solved by a design change). One more data collection and charting cycle yielded Figure 1.5. With the exception of clear assignable causes that were relatively easy to resolve, both charts are now in control, with much tighter limits than those prevailing originally. The process, which was far from adequate at first, proved more than capable to hold the necessary tolerances. Incidentally, in all the figures the tolerances are marked next to the $\bar{x}$ chart. This practice is *not* recommended, because the variance of $\bar{x}$ is smaller than that of the process output ($\sigma_{\bar{x}} = \sigma_X/\sqrt{5}$ here), so even when it looks as if the process is within the tolerance limits, it may produce many defective items.

The results were then applied to the other heads as well. Yet only one head was studied, for a reason. The question here was not whether there is difference between

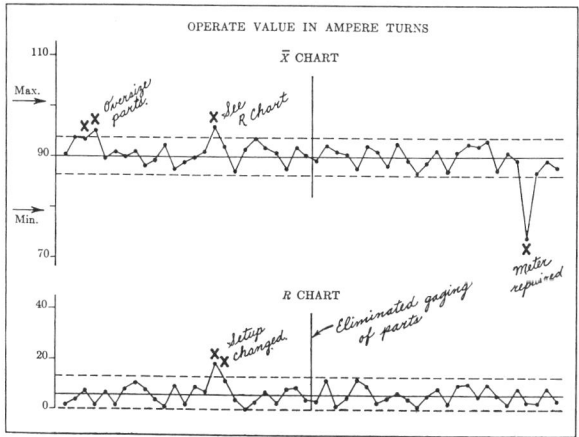

Fig. 1.5. Fifth $\bar{X}$ and R chart in a process capability study.

(Reprinted with permission from AT&T)

---

[6]Starting in the seventies, under JIT, the Japanese promote *poka-yoke* (error-proofing), which often involves *autonomation*. Autonomation is a low level of automation designed to prevent defects (Shingo, 1986). Here we have an example of autonomation in America, dating back to the fifties.

heads -- which would have necessitated sampling separately from several heads (preferably on an alternating basis to enhance tell-tale patterns) -- but rather what caused the problems in some heads. By not mixing data from several heads, a major cause of variation was intentionally designed away from the study, to make the diagnosis of the remaining causes much easier. Of course, any problems on other heads that may remain require further study.

This example is perhaps not representative in terms of complexity: many cycles were necessary, and the analysis effort was not trivial. Yet it also shows the power of control charts to provide clues for improvement.

=-

1.5. Ways and Means to Abuse Control Charts

The basic theory of control charts is older than most readers of this text (and the author). Therefore, cynics and realists should not be surprised that many bad habits have been ingrained in the culture since then. Thus, many control charts do more harm than good. While we defer the technical discussion to other chapters, it is appropriate to mention a few instances here.

A generic way to abuse any statistical method, including control charts, is to "ignore the fine print." Good statisticians always predicate their statements by necessary assumptions that are valid for the use at hand. Some overcautious theoreticians tend to stress limitations that are not really important; but hacks are much more dangerous, because they tend to ignore important caveats.

It turns out that some of the ubiquitous assumptions used for variable control charts are practical: reasonable violations are not sizably detrimental. For instance, the assumption is often made that the process being monitored is normal, but variable control charts are surprisingly robust against deviations from this assumption. Nonetheless, most texts, including this one to some extent, stress this assumption as if it is really important in practice. Unfortunately, not all assumptions are equally benign, nor equally stressed. All too often the very same sources that devote a few paragraphs to the normality assumption do not mention the more serious ones at all! For instance, in attribute control charts we usually assume that the incidence of the attribute in consecutive items is stationary (does not vary as a function of time), and mutually statistically independent (a defect now does not change the probability of a defect in the next item). These assumptions are often met; but when they are not, the impact on the control chart may be very large (i.e., control charts are not robust against deviations here). For example, if we monitor the fraction of defects we produced by a p chart, but our product mix changes continually, the stationary assumption is not met, and the control chart is likely to produce more than its share of false signals. These false signals lead to frustration as we look for special causes where none exist. Box 5.5 recounts such an instance, where the end result was that people lost all confidence in statistical control methods.

Another abuse of control charts is recalculating the limits when they should be left alone. Too many practitioners and consultants recommend re-computing the parameters of control charts periodically, to be sure that they reflect the current process. As one successful consultant told me in 1994: "I consider data that is older than about a month and a half as totally useless for quality control. Things change on the factory floor all the time." [Do you see anything wrong with this statement?] Furthermore, they often use samples of about 125 items (which are usually divided to 25 subgroups of 5) to do so; for instance, the same consultant recommends 30 subgroups of 5. This practice is also described in quality control books, and typical readers may think that this description implies endorsement. Nonetheless, this practice is badly flawed for two reasons: First, recalculating the control chart parameters without evidence that the process changed *or without a deliberate decision to accept an evident change*, is blatant tampering by Funnel Rule 4 (Chapter 4). As a result, the process is likely to drift away from its original control state. Second, even if we accept the recent performance of the process as the benchmark against which to judge its future performance, the use of such small samples is likely to produce large variation in the rate at which charts generate out-of-control signals (Chapter 8). This often causes excessive false signals (when the process is running well), and it is equally likely to reduce the power of the chart to provide true signals (when the process is misbehaving).

Some practitioners even use the data that they are supposed to check while recalculating control limits. Correct application of control charts is by comparing new data with existing limits: we use the same data to establish trial limits only when we have no choice. This additional abuse also found its way into the professional literature, and readers may be misled to believe that it's appropriate. When this is done, the control limits tend to "adapt" to the data, and therefore the control chart loses power to detect special causes within that data.

In conclusion, the main problem with the consultant's statement is that the purpose of control charts is to monitor *against* such changes (unless they are declared as *desirable* or *intentional*). Another problem is that variations in the control chart estimation are not stressed enough, so too few data are sampled. Using the same data to generate control limits adds insult to injury.[7]

Basing the chart on too few data is associated with another pitfall. Generally speaking, control charts are nothing more or less than a measurement instrument. They measure statistical control, if you will. And, like any other measurement instrument, control charts suffer from measurement errors (Chapter 2). Often, and especially when the chart is based on too few data, the measurement errors can be large relative to the process variation. Thus, the measurement they provide is not "clean." Users, all too often, are not aware of the problem, so they accept the measurement without question and look at the process as the only source of special causes. Alternatively, they automatically assume the process is okay if the control chart does not show an out-of-control signal. But the control chart itself may be the common source of what looks like a special cause (too many points out of control). A process that rarely shows out of control may, in fact, be measured by a flawed control chart. Basing control charts on much more data than the current practice may resolve these problems in most cases (Chapter 8), but it is not a cost-free solution.

---

[7]In the spirit of fixing the problem instead of fixing the blame, I will refrain from naming the erroneous publications, or the consultant I quoted. But it's only fair to say that in all these cases I found other points they made quite useful, and I learned a lot from them. This implies that even good sources are subject to such errors all too often. Accordingly, I urge the readers to apply scrutiny to this text too: I am not immune from similar errors.

In God we trust. All others must have data. (Snee's Corollary. Mistakenly attributed by some to Deming.)

The most important figures are unknown and unknowable. (Deming)

Not everything that counts can be counted; and not everything that can be counted counts. (Einstein)

Chapter 2
On Measurement

Quality and measurement are so intertwined that it's almost useless to discuss the former without clarifying the latter. In a nutshell, measurements have to be:

♦   *relevant to quality* (and, therefore, to real needs)

♦   *defined operationally* (so they'll have a clear meaning)

♦   *accurate and precise* (without bias and with small variance)

♦   *cost-effective.*

We devote one section to each of these issues. Some technical details about calibration -- which is necessary for accuracy -- are relegated to Supplement 2. Before embarking on this coverage, Box 2.1 provides realistic background to the issue of managing one's life with the help of questionable measurements.

=-

Box 2.1

In 1993, I helped a relative select an electronic blood pressure monitor. The product was well-established, with many models and a wide price range. Since all electronic monitors are easy to operate, we decided to focus on accuracy and precision.

Due to economic considerations, we decided to try the inexpensive (and most popular) models first. Our benchmark was a commercial machine provided as a public service on the floor, but we had no evidence about its accuracy. We hoped the measurements would agree to the degree in which consecutive blood pressure readings can agree.

Blood pressure is very volatile. Differences of 10 to 20 points for readings taken closely are common. It can and does change measurably between two heartbeats. Over the day, it can easily vary by 20 to 30 points. Even when taking readings from both arms at the same time, the results may vary (because the readings are not perfectly synchronous), but they should be relatively close. We measured her blood pressure at the same time with the store's machine and with the one we were considering. The difference was 32 points (the store machine showed 148, the other showed 180). Three other sets of measurements, this time using the same arm and alternating between the machines, showed an average difference of about 30 points (all in the same direction). My own blood pressure was lower on both machines, but it too showed a difference of 24 points. Furthermore, my pulse seemed lower than all my previous measurements, so I checked it again, this time comparing to a count with a stop watch. At least in terms of pulse measurement, it was clear that the instrument we were considering was very inaccurate.

Next, we tried an expensive instrument built in another country for another maker (too often the difference between expensive and inexpensive is merely in packaging and cosmetics, but when the maker *and* the brand are different this is less likely). It showed the correct pulse, but indicated an average blood pressure about 10 points *higher* than the former one -- both for my relative and for me. In her case, it showed about 40 points above that of the store machine, and well in the "red zone." Although we could not be *sure* which instrument was more accurate (the store's machine or the two instruments), we knew we had accuracy problems on our hands, so we could not buy yet.

Subsequently, we conducted a comparison of several public service machines in neighboring stores, and found statistical evidence that at least two of them had biases of about 16 points in the systolic pressure, one of those two, and a third, had significantly different diastolic readings, but they all probably read the pulse correctly. So store machines could not be trusted either, unless one was ready to accept errors of up to 20 points. The readings of the instruments we wanted to buy, however, were both significantly above the ones obtained from the public ones. The public model at the first store gave readings that agreed with the average of the other four public machines, so altogether we had evidence that the instruments we wanted to purchase were not accurate. Incidentally, such instruments provide readings with a discrimination of two points, which misleads people to believe that they are accurate enough to make such small discriminations.

The moral? There must be many thousands of people measuring their blood pressure at home with similar instruments, and getting results that are probably very inaccurate. The same applies to people who use public instruments at some drug stores. These people are likely to use the readings to make decisions such as whether to visit a doctor, increase the dose of a medicine, stay in bed, etc. Last but not least, if the readings err on the high side, people may become worried, and as a result their blood pressure may increase further (measurements *always* change what's being measured).

In this particular case we solved our immediate problem by purchasing an old-fashioned manual model, which is a little more complex to operate but provides much more trustworthy results. The results we obtained with the manual model agreed with (read: could not be discerned from) the three public service machines that we believed were most accurate.

=-

2.1. Measurements That Are Relevant

The story about the man who looked for a lost coin under the street lamp, in spite of having lost it elsewhere, applies to the art of selecting relevant quality measurements. Often we measure what's easy to measure (look where there is light), regardless of relevance. But how can we find such a coin? Looking under the street lamp is convenient, but it won't achieve the purpose. A rational answer may be to give it up, and think about loss-prevention for the future. Alternatively, we might illuminate the area where the coin was really lost (which may, or may not, be cost-effective). The latter is analogous to finding a relevant measurement.

For example, let's look at measuring the output of a teaching process. Traditionally, teachers administer various tests (written and oral). After comparing the responses of the students to those determined to be correct, teachers evaluate the fit, and describe it by grades. Thus grades are the measurement. But it is highly unlikely that a test can be devised to measure learning in a fully objective way. This does not imply that testing should necessarily be abolished, but it leaves the challenge to find more relevant measurements for learning open. We need a measurement that will really show how much the students gained by the class experience, not to what extent they could "read" what the instructor considers important. It is quite likely that the amount of learning is an unknowable quantity.

Be that as it may, students are customers of instructors, and under most TQ programs, customer satisfaction is measured routinely. Usually, at the end of the term, the students get to evaluate the instructor, using a questionnaire, which includes several questions about various aspects of the class experience for which the instructor is held accountable. Students rank the instructor on a scale (usually one-to-five or one-to-seven) on each question. The results are processed by a computer that calculates the mean and standard deviation of each response. Schools differ on how they use the results, but too often they are used to measure the "quality" of the instructor. Are these measurements relevant to the quality of teaching? It depends on what we call quality of teaching. If we consider school to be a place to relax and enjoy instructors who provide a good show, the measurement might work well for all concerned. If the objective is to learn, it is arguably a very misleading measurement. A better measurement will be obtained by asking several years after the course was given (Deming, 1986, p. 174). It's not always necessary to wait for years, but some perspective is usually required. For instance, instructors of advanced courses depend on others to prepare their students. At Naval Postgraduate School, students of a particular visiting professor required extensive rework at a subsequent class. When consulted whether to invite him again, they said it would be a major mistake. But they had given him a remarkably high evaluation one quarter before!

Research on the value of student opinion questionnaires is notoriously inconclusive: some show relevance, others show none, yet others even show negative results. Read (1979) shows by a careful statistical analysis that these measurements favor personable instructors regardless of the knowledge they possess, and teaching easy subjects helps as well. He also identified a class effect that has nothing to do with the instructor. According to Read, students (at least at Naval Postgraduate School) did not prefer teachers whom they themselves judged to be knowledgeable, i.e., they did not care about knowledge. Thus, instructors can teach error and still excel in this measurement; others may teach highly advanced concepts effectively, and receive low evaluations. Ware and Williams (1975) discuss a case where a talented actor taught a class of medical students a subject *he knew nothing about,* and got raving reviews!

Let's leave the shaky ground of academia, for a while, and go to the production floor. Here we should be able to find relevant measurements with ease, right? Wrong! Translating customer needs to meaningful measurements is difficult. Unfortunately, it looks easy to the uninitiated. They may think that design engineers have a well-grounded methodology by which they determine important tolerances, and production just needs to follow the blueprint. But even the best design engineers are far from knowing all there is to know about translating customer needs to technical specifications. Deming wrote, "A vice-president in charge of manufacturing told me that half his problems arise from materials that met the specifications" (1986, p. 140). Furthermore, quite often items that do not meet specifications perform well, while others that do, don't. As we say about areas we don't know enough about, translating customer needs to valid technical specifications is an art. According to Ishikawa mastery of this art distinguishes excellent manufacturers from mediocre ones.[1] Take the case of a pencil. The customer wants a pencil that marks clearly, does not smear, does not need frequent sharpening, is comfortable to hold, and does not roll off the table. Try submitting these requirements to production technicians and ask them to produce a pencil that measures up. No, what production people want is a set of technical specifications (length, shape, type of wood, type of graphite), some of which can be broken down even further. If we can find a set of measurable specifications that, when adhered to, produce a pencil the customer will call "a quality pencil," we found relevant quality measurements, and we're half way to satisfying our customer (we know what to do and how to measure it). If we cannot find such a set, the best measurement instruments in the world, and the best analysis tools, won't help much.

The need to specify relevant measurements establishes a strong connection between quality measurement and product design: "Tell me how you measure and I'll tell you what I'll do," goes the saying. Or, here, tell me what are the measurements of a quality product and I'll design my product to excel in these measurements. Therefore, if we have no idea how to translate real quality to such measurements *we should not measure at all!* At least this allows people to do what they think is right (manage the unknowable). In contrast, by measuring the wrong things we promote the wrong reaction. For instance, measuring instructors by student feedback promotes good showmanship over other criteria that are much more difficult to measure: continuously developing profound knowledge, challenging the students, and willingness to teach receive little attention, while instructors perfect their presentation skills and provide students with evermore (paralyzing) structure -- a proven pacifier. Incidentally, students are poor judges of knowledge: most of them gauge it by the instructor's self-assurance -- which is not always relevant. Similarly, the wrong testing methods can promote studying by rote over real learning. No wonder Deming opposed grading as well as asking students to evaluate instructors (1972; 1986, pp. 173–174).

2.2. Defining Measurements Operationally

Take a simple question: How many people are there in Mr. Trent's class? Does it have a numerical answer? Many will say yes. But the question is meaningless until we define "people." Do we count only students, or include Mr. Trent himself? Do we count Sally who went for a Coke and will be back in ten seconds? Or Jim, who's sick today? Only after we

---

[1]The Japanese developed an elaborate methodology, called Quality Function Deployment (QFD), that structures the process of translating customer needs to measurable quality specifications for products and for processes. QFD, however, is labor intensive, and often we cannot tell in advance whether the results will justify the investment of effort and time. Also, by its nature QFD is easier for new models of existing products than for really novel products.

provide a detailed answer to all these questions will it be possible to get a meaningful answer. Only with such specificity will two persons be likely to come up with the same answer. Such a detailed clarification is called an *operational definition*. Other examples follow.

Deming gave another example: "The fabric includes 50% wool and 50% cotton." Does it mean that half the area will be pure cotton and half will be wool? Does it mean that the total length of the wool fiber and of the cotton fiber should be equal? Is it okay if the amount of wool exceeds the amount of cotton by 0.1 percent? By 10 percent? We cannot answer this question offhand because the statement is not defined operationally. An operational definition may be, "If we sample five squares of two by two inches from different locations chosen at random on the fabric, the percent of wool, by weight, in each of them will be between 48 and 52." Another operational definition, clarifying what "chosen at random" means, may also be necessary. Even this may not be enough, since ambient conditions may influence the relative weight of cotton and wool, and a full operational definition may have to be even more specific to eliminate such sources of confusion. Thus, the operational definition must include clear instructions how to measure, and what the tolerances are. Similarly, it's meaningless to say that a customer needs a "round" part. To have meaning, a measurement system and tolerances must be agreed upon (e.g., "Measurements of the diameter will be taken at six evenly spaced locations around the circumference, and the difference between the smallest and largest of them should not exceed 0.001""). Formally, we also need to define operationally what we mean by "evenly spaced locations around the circumference," which can serve as an example how difficult it can be to provide a truly rigorous operational definition. In practice, this can perhaps be left unspecified, or, better, assured by training to the satisfaction of the customer. Clearly, we need to seek balance between the clarity of the operational definition and its own length and complexity.

Often an operational definition can be presented in a very simple way; e.g., by example or by a gauge. For instance, one can specify that a color will not be lighter than one specimen, and not darker than another. This may be appropriate as long as the specimens are not allowed to fade (i.e., they have to be checked or replaced periodically). Or a critical tolerance is checked by a go/no-go gauge, and it is defined to be okay if it passes through the "go" and not through the "no-go." But sometimes it is important to be very specific in unexpected details. For instance, the weight of a yarn is sensitive to humidity, and may have to be specified at a particular humidity. Metals (and other materials) are subject to thermal expansion, and may have to be measured at a specified temperature. (In precision machining, just the act of opening a door can change critical dimensions due to temperature differentials, so thermal expansion is a serious design and specification issue sometimes.) Other measures are sensitive to pressure, and so on.

The importance of operational definitions was stressed by Ishikawa and by Deming (the terminology is the one used by Deming). Deming claimed that it was the most important concept the Japanese learned in his early seminars. It is always necessary to be able to distinguish between acceptable and defective items and to establish a common language between vendors and customers. Without operational definitions inspection is subjective and arbitrary, and efforts to achieve quality are much less likely to succeed. It is equally important not to specify too much, because that may cause waste too. Attempts to foresee every contingency get good reviews, but seldom succeed. For some customers, notably government and other bureaucratic organizations, over-specification is a much more serious quality problem today than under-specification. When customers attempt to ensure quality by rigid specifications, complete with operational definitions to the last iota, the vendor is only responsible to meet the specifications. Problems almost always arise after the specifications are found wanting (or even harmful). Most defence contractors make their profits at this stage only. In addition, consider the waste involved in creating these specifications and in meeting them (including the ones that are not relevant to real quality). The solution, in this case, is to specify performance and reliability criteria, and let the expert vendor determine how best to deliver them.

2.3. Accuracy and Precision

An operational definition is not enough to ensure consistent measurements: it's also necessary to use accurate and precise measurement instruments. When two people measure the same items, following the same operational definition, their results will often differ. Discrepancies arise due to differences between people, measuring instruments, ambient conditions, and more. Even two different measurements by the same person, on the same item, and with the same instrument can disagree (especially if the instrument has a high discriminating power). Measurements have variation, and thus they cause error. Perfect precision -- an ideal that does not exist -- implies no such variation. Perfect accuracy implies no bias, i.e., that at least on average measurements should be exact. "Exact," therefore, means both accurate and precise.

Measurement is a process analogous to, say, fabrication. A process may be centered, which means that *on average* it creates the desired result exactly. Otherwise, we may say that the process is off-center, or *biased*. Likewise, measurements that are centered have no bias. But in both cases there might still be -- and in this world there *will be* -- variations around the center. Such variations are referred to as *variance, dispersion,* or *imprecision.*

Perfect accuracy is defined as lack of bias. A perfect measurement will not only be accurate, but also absolutely *precise,* i.e., without variation. Thus, an ideal measurement instrument has no bias and no imprecision: its measurements are centered on the real value, and there is no dispersion around it. In reality, we should expect some bias and some imprecision. Sometimes we can reduce the bias until it becomes negligible: this is called *calibration.* In contrast, unless there is a special cause that can be removed, it is more difficult to reduce imprecision below a threshold that is associated with the instrument and the technology it utilizes.

An analogy with sharpshooting may clarify this further. A sharpshooter is a person who can shoot bullets close to each other. Preferably, the bullets should also hit the center of the target, but if they miss consistently (bias), all we need to do is adjust the sights (i.e., calibrate), and now the sharpshooter will hit the target consistently, even if it is relatively small. A less talented shooter may or may not have a bias (again, correctable by adjusting the sights), but once trained in the techniques of steady shooting (and equipped with corrective lenses if necessary) it will be difficult to improve his precision. His bullets will be more dispersed, and therefore many of them will miss the target, especially if it is small. As the military knows, some people can be trained to be sharpshooters, and others cannot. There is a limit to the precision of people, and it differs from person to person. Likewise, there is a limit to the precision of measuring instruments, especially when combined with variation induced by the persons who operate them.

Therefore, measurement errors -- particularly imprecision -- are here to stay. As much as I'd like to, I can't please readers who don't like this message (except, perhaps, if I say that I understand their frustration). But what's important is to keep measurement errors from dominating the result of the measurement. Let's look at a few numerical examples to clarify this statement. In all our examples we will assume that we measure a population, say X, distributed with a mean, μ, of 1000 units and a standard deviation, σ_X, which will vary between 1 and 100 units. Our measurements will have a standard error (i.e., *their* standard deviation), σ_E, of 10 units. For convenience we'll assume that there is no measurement bias (i.e., the average measurements will be close to 1000 units, as in the population). This assumption implies that the instrument is calibrated perfectly. We'll also assume that the distribution of the population and the measurement error are independent statistically -- a realistic assumption for measurement errors.

Denote our measurements by Y, then $\mu_Y = \mu_X$ (no bias), and $\sigma_Y^2 = \sigma_X^2 + \sigma_E^2$ (statistical independence). Table 2.1 shows σ_Y for various σ_X values between 1 and 100 (for $\sigma_E = 10$). The last column shows σ_Y/σ_X-1, in percents; i.e., it measures by how much the standard deviation of the measurements is larger than that of the population, thus providing a measure for additional error due to measurement. As the table shows, when σ_E/σ_X grows from 1/10 to 10/1 (a ratio of 100), the additional error grows from 0.5% to 905% (a ratio of over 1800). Note that the additional error really "takes off" for $\sigma_E/\sigma_X > 1/3$ ($\sigma_X = 30$).

σ_E	σ_X	σ_Y	$\sigma_Y/\sigma_X - 1$
10	100	100.5	0.5%
10	90	90.55	0.6%
10	80	80.62	0.8%
10	70	70.71	1.0%
10	60	60.83	1.4%
10	50	51.00	2.0%
10	40	41.23	3.1%
10	30	31.62	5.4%
10	20	22.36	11.8%
10	10	14.14	41.4%
10	9	13.45	49.9%
10	8	12.81	60.1%
10	7	12.21	74.4%
10	6	11.66	94.4%
10	5	11.18	123.6%
10	4	10.77	169.3%
10	3	10.44	248%
10	2	10.2	409.9%
10	1	10.05	905.0%

Table 2.1

Thus, if the standard deviation generated by the real data is at least three times higher than the standard deviation generated by the measurement instrument, the accuracy of our results will deteriorate by 5.5% or less. For a ratio of 5 the relative measurement error is 2% -- usually quite acceptable. For a ratio of 7 and above, our relative error drops below 1%. As a rule of thumb, we can say that a ratio of 7 or better is excellent, a ratio of 5 is usually good, and a ratio of 3 is usually acceptable. Often, the purpose of measurement is to determine whether an item is within tolerance or not. In such a case, we should judge the size of the measurement error in relation to the tolerance range rather than the process variation. To this end, we multiply the ratios by six, and round to the nearest multiple of five. Thus we say that a ratio of 40 and above between the tolerance range and the standard error is excellent, a ratio of 30 is usually good, and a ratio of 20 is often acceptable. We elaborate on the technicalities of these rules in Supplement 2.[2] A rule of thumb often used by practitioners is that the instrument should be capable of dividing the tolerance range to ten parts. For many well-designed instruments the discrimination of the scale is such that at least two standard errors fit between successive readings. This assures that the instrument will not *appear* to have more accuracy than it actually does. For such well-designed instruments the requirement to divide the tolerance range to ten implies that σ_E fits into the tolerance range at least 20 times. Thus, this rule is similar to ours. Nonetheless, not all instruments on the market are well-designed in this sense (see Box 2.1), hence the need for our more specific rules. But note that once the ability of the instrument to divide falls below a threshold of about six or seven, this *in itself* will raise σ_E above our recommendation. Thus, we can rephrase the practitioners's rule of thumb as a necessary but not sufficient condition: If the instrument cannot divide the tolerance range to six or seven parts it is inadequate.

These are merely rules of thumb, and a lot depends on the circumstances. When the process is highly capable to meet the requirements we can get away with less accuracy in measurements, but a (tolerance range)/σ_E ratio of 20 (which we said was often acceptable) combined with an inadequate process will make a bad situation much worse. Generally, because it is the process that is inadequate, we should improve the process (and not the measurement). But there may be cases where it is more cost-effective to improve the measurement first. This will reduce the number of items rejected by error as well as the number of items accepted by error, and inadequate processes provide many opportunities for such errors. (In statistical terms, rejecting good items is a "type I" error, and accepting bad items is "type II.") With rejection exceeding 1%, we should consider improving both the process and the measurement. On the one hand, if we improve the measurement without improving the process, the combined variance will decrease, and therefore the number of rejects will also decrease, i.e., the *observed* performance of the process will improve. Our costs will decrease, so we'll have an economic return for the improved accuracy. Furthermore, one cannot completely separate the measurement from the rest of the process, so in a sense the process will actually improve. On the other hand, if we improve the process without improving the measurement, the number of rejects will decrease, the number of bad

---

[2]A process is often called *capable* if its standard deviation fits at least six times within the tolerance range. This motivates the choice we made here to multiply by six.

items will decrease (and thus there will be less danger of type II errors) and the *real* costs of poor quality cannot help but decrease. So process improvements should be always welcome. Thus our usual priority, to start with the process, is sensible. But depending on the economies involved there may be equally good reasons to opt for improved measurements first. Furthermore, if we improve the measurement system first, this will provide better discrimination (reduced type I and type II errors), and will facilitate data-based process improvements later.

2.3.1. *Measuring the Quality of Measurements*

To be able to tell where we stand on the issue of measurement quality, we need to know the standard error of our instrument and compare it to the necessary discrimination we require. One way is to test our instruments against standards (i.e., are they centered? is their scale correct?). We should also test whether the performance is repeatable (i.e., what is the measurement error due to variation). If there is reason to believe that the instrument's error is not influenced strongly by the particular item that is being measured, such experimentation is often done as part of regular calibration of instruments. Sometimes, however, the measuring error cannot be disassociated from the interaction of the measuring tool and the item it measures. Supplement 2 discusses how to test an instrument's performance for a given type of item.

2.3.2. *A Possible Remedy for Imprecise Measurements*

In Table 2.1 take, for example, the case where $\sigma_X = 7$. The variance is mainly due to measurement errors. Suppose now we want to measure with relative accuracy such as the one associated with $\sigma_X = 20$. This implies that we have to reduce σ_E by a factor of about 3. This can, perhaps, be done by a much better measuring instrument. To make do without a new instrument, we can take 9 independent measurements and use their average. The standard deviation of such an average, for n repeat measurements, is $\sigma_E / \sqrt{n}$. (It may be advisable to ask different people to take the measurements, thus reducing bias and dependence between measurements. It can certainly become a hassle, but jobs requiring great precision may justify it.)

Shewhart and Tippett -- independently -- studied the problem of optimizing the number of repeat measurements per item. Their objective was to find the true population average, $\overline{x}$, accurate to within ε with a prescribed probability, P. They wanted to achieve this objective at minimal cost. In 1931 they each published the following formula:

$$n^* = \frac{\sigma_E}{\sigma_X} \sqrt{\frac{a_1}{a_2}} \tag{2.1}$$

Where n^* is the optimal number of repeat measurements, a_1 is the cost of selecting and retrieving a unit for measurement, a_2 is the cost of each measurement. Since the result is not likely to be an integer, it can either be rounded or the two integer values above and below n^* can be compared. The equation does not specify how many items, N, to sample, but this can be found separately, by the following formula,

$$N \geq \frac{9\left(\sigma_X^2 + \dfrac{\sigma_E^2}{n}\right)}{\varepsilon^2} \tag{2.2}$$

where the multiplication by $9 = 3^2$ is as per Shewhart's convention. (Using the fact that for large N values $\bar{x}$ is distributed normally, a more general approach would be to use a normal table to select a multiplier that will reduce the probability of error below a required threshold. With the conventional choice of 3^2 this error is 0.27%. Choosing 1.96^2 instead -- which is also a popular selection -- would yield a much higher probability of error, 5%, but would also reduce N by more than half.) See Supplement 2 for the theoretical derivation of these results. Here, let us look at two numerical examples.

In our first example let $\sigma_X = 9$, $\sigma_E = 3$, $a_1 = \$1.00$, $a_2 = \$0.02$, and $\varepsilon = 1.5$. Our first step is to calculate n, using (2.1), and we obtain

$$n^* = \frac{\sigma_E}{\sigma_X} \sqrt{\frac{a_1}{a_2}} = \frac{3}{9} \sqrt{\frac{1.00}{0.02}} = 2.357$$

This means that we should either round to 2, or check the results for 2 and for 3. In our case, for demonstration, we'll try $n = 1$, 2, 3, and 4. Plugging n in (2.2), we calculate N. $n = 2$, for instance, yields

$$N \geq \frac{9\left(\sigma_X^2 + \dfrac{\sigma_E^2}{n}\right)}{\varepsilon^2} = \frac{9\left(9^2 + \dfrac{3^2}{2}\right)}{1.5^2} = \frac{769.5}{2.25} = 342$$

which happens to be integer, and therefore no rounding is necessary. In general, because of the inequality we must round *up*. The readers can verify that by substituting $n = 1$, 3, and 4 we obtain $N = 360$, 336, and 333 respectively. It remains to calculate the costs of these solutions. In general the cost is obtained by the following formula

$$TOTAL\ COST = N \cdot a_1 + N \cdot n \cdot a_2 = N(a_1 + n \cdot a_2)$$

Substituting $n=1$, 2, 3, and 4 we obtain \$367.20, 355.68, 356.16, and 359.64 respectively. The difference between $n=2$ and $n=3$ is really small, but 2 is the best choice. The values below 2 and above 3 are clearly inferior. In general, the total cost is quite flat near n^*, which explains the small difference between 2 and 3. This indicates that rounding is not likely to cause a large error.

In this example we started with a ratio $\sigma_X/\sigma_E = 3$, which is often acceptable, as we said above. But by taking two readings on each item we changed this ratio to about 4.2. How come we had to do that? The answer is that additional measurements on the same item are significantly cheaper than the cost of selecting and fetching a new item to measure. To illustrate this point let's look at a similar example where σ_E is relatively larger, but because a_2 will also be relatively larger no multiple readings will be specified. To this end let $\sigma_E = 6$, let $a_2 = 0.5$, and let all the other data remain intact. Again, to calculate n we use (2.1),

$$n^* = \frac{\sigma_E}{\sigma_X}\sqrt{\frac{a_1}{a_2}} = \frac{6}{9}\sqrt{\frac{1.00}{0.50}} = 0.943$$

Since $n \geq 1$ is also required, it is clear that in this case we should pick $n=1$, and thus we'll settle for a relatively large error and *not* compensate for it by repeated measurements. To continue with the example, to calculate N we compute

$$N \geq \frac{9\left(\sigma_X^2 + \frac{\sigma_E^2}{n}\right)}{\varepsilon^2} = \frac{9\left(9^2 + \frac{6^2}{1}\right)}{1.5^2} = \frac{1053}{2.25} = 468$$

Again, no rounding is necessary. The total cost of the program is \$702.

We can get additional mileage from these examples if we now investigate the value of improving the measurement instrument such that, say, σ_E will be reduced by 30%. That is, in the first case we'll obtain $\sigma_E = 2.1$, and in the second case $\sigma_E = 4.2$. For the first case we obtain $n^* = 1.65$, which means that we should either go with 2 (again) or compare 1 and 2. We'll use $n=2$ (the readers may wish to compare the result to $n=1$). Recalculating N with the new σ_E value we obtain $N \geq 332.82$, i.e., 333 (instead of 342 with $\sigma_E = 3$). Thus, the improvement in σ_E saves us \$9.36, or 2.6%. For the second case, $n=1$, while $N \geq 394.56$, i.e., 395. Thus our cost drops from $702 to $592.5, or a cost reduction of 15.6%. Note how much more valuable it is to reduce the error in this case, where we started with a very high relative value. This is an example of a general rule in economic variance reduction:

> **Variance Reduction Rule #1:** Other things being equal, always concentrate on relatively large variance elements.

In general, reducing small variance elements does not make much of a difference, but large ones dominate the picture. Chapter 3 discusses this phenomenon in more detail.

2.3.3. *The Danger of Using Highly Biased Measurements*

Some things are difficult to measure. Customer satisfaction is a quintessential example. The most popular way to try to measure such intangibles is by questionnaires which the customers are asked to answer by a scale of, say, one-to-five or one-to-seven (as with instructor evaluations). Customers are also often asked to compare competitors. Or people are polled about what they think is important in a product, or who they'll vote for.

While sometimes there is no better way to measure what customers think, we should be aware that these methods are highly unreliable. They suffer from several potential biases. For instance, in 1948 pollsters predicted with certainty that Dewey will win the presidency from Truman. But they conducted their poll by phone, and people who did not have phones gave the majority to Truman! Furthermore, it is widely recognized that publication of poll results strongly influences the vote itself. It may very well be that phone-less voters who knew of the predictions about Dewey's victory decided to vote *because* they realized their votes were necessary.

Another prevalent reason for biased responses is due to the way the questions are worded and presented. Skillful operators know how to ask questions to get the response they want. Why worry about this? Because too often people do abuse such instruments for their interests. This may be the source of the painful joke that there are three progressive types of dishonest people: liars, damn liars, and statisticians.

With widely distributed questionnaires similar biases may occur due to *adverse selection*. Only customers who are highly satisfied and those who have an ax to grind will elect to respond. In contrast, customers who are neither highly satisfied nor disappointed will usually not respond. But they're the ones who might have provided the most objective assessment. A non-industrial example of the same nature is recounted in Box 2.2

=-

Box 2.2

The Hite Report was a sensational best-seller study, by reporter Shere Hite, about the sexual behavior of American women in the eighties. Among other results, Hite reported that most American women were dissatisfied in their relationships, and most married women engaged in extramarital affairs at least once. The book influenced the thoughts, and perhaps even the behavior, of millions all over the world. But barely 4% of the (already preselected) group that received questionnaires responded! From the opinions of this self-selected group, Hite extrapolated conclusions that implicitly applied to all women in America. Subsequent research (potentially also flawed, since it is impossible to measure these things accurately) found very different results: over 90% of American women are essentially satisfied with their relationships, and less than 10% ever engaged in extramarital affairs. Believe whoever you wish, but arguably the truth is unknown and unknowable.

=-

People often believe that they can use the results of such questionnaires to concentrate on weak points, by comparing the answers for various questions and identifying the ones that are lowest as indicative of problem areas. One difficulty with this is that satisfied (dissatisfied) customers tend to give high (low) grades in *all* questions! Not surprisingly then, the difference between highest and lowest questions may not be statistically significant, so if we concentrate on the "weak" points we may be chasing phantoms (tampering). These potential difficulties may be ameliorated by careful analysis, but usually managers use them without the benefit of sound statistical knowledge, in which case they might have been better off not using them at all.

People often believe they can compare instructors, departments, agencies, or companies by comparing their numerical results on such questionnaires. This is highly dangerous, because it ignores not only the question whether the differences are significant statistically, but also other system differences. For instance, instructors who teach difficult and unpopular subjects often get lower evaluations. Or try to compare those teaching elective courses with those teaching mandatory ones. Not to mention the fact that different classes provide significantly different mean levels of responses (depending on their cohesiveness, informal leadership, and group dynamics). A colleague of mine, who taught a particularly difficult subject, got low reviews from a tough class. The chairman -- a well-meaning and reasonable person -- called her to his office and admonished her. Later, he taught the same class and received low reviews too. (Perhaps he learned something by this experience.)

It is especially dangerous to use the numerical results of such questionnaires as if they have an absolute meaning (as opposed to relative meaning). A 4.4 out of 5 may mean a lot at one situation, and not much at another. At best these numbers can provide evidence over time if a pattern can be shown (Chapter 7).[3]

In conclusion, questionnaires may be our best measurement instruments sometimes, but their results should be interpreted with great care. One would be better off not using such methods at all than using them carelessly, as is unfortunately the prevalent practice.

Take measurement of students by testing. Does testing provide a meaningful measurement of knowledge? The answer depends on many factors, but even if the test questions really represent the material taught *and* the material taught represents what should be taught, the measurement is subject to many sources of irrelevant variation, including luck (tests *always* sample the material, and studying, likewise, does not usually cover the full material with the same degree of care and understanding), cool nerves, efficient test-taking techniques, and, last but not least, honesty (including the honesty of those around you, whose "achievements" create a standard *you* have to meet). All these inject a large standard error into the testing environment. This is true when the teacher does not yet have an opinion about the students. More ominously, once such an opinion is formed a strong bias is introduced into the picture. This is due to a phenomenon known as the *Pygmalion effect*, where prophecies/expectations tend to fulfil themselves. It is likely that the many cases where moving a student to a new school transforms him into a significantly better (or worse) performer than before is simply due to the luck of the first test he takes, which then creates expectations that fulfil themselves, for better or for worse. It's important to state, however, that the Pygmalion effect does not show that teachers are *bad*: just that they are human. It applies to virtually all of us, not just teachers, and while we may not be able to eradicate it, we will do better, perhaps, once we realize what we are doing.

---

[3]Attempts to make the numbers more objective and meaningful by stipulating grading rules -- e.g., that one should only give a "5" to an instructor who is at the top 5% and a "4" to the top 20% -- only add confusion and increase the variation in the responses. In a related example, the vast majority of naval officers officially belong to the top 10% (and you thought the air is rarified at the top!). The explanation is simple: only the top 10% are considered promotable, but the Navy cannot afford to discourage 90% of its officer corps by blocking them from promotion. To achieve this remarkable result, commanding officers manipulate the numbers by many means available to them. The bright side is that by doing that they nullify a lot of the damage that the naval performance evaluation system *might* cause had it been run as officially designed. The main victim is the integrity of a surprisingly large percentage of officers.

2.4. Cost-Effectiveness in Measurement

A true measure of quality will encompass all costs, including the cost of measurements. Without doubt some things cost more to measure than they are worth to know. Or it may be enough to sample them infrequently, just to make sure that our processes remain adequate to ensure fitness-for-use without continuous measurements. A quality company will always strive to measure the right things, at the right frequency, with a view to serve the customers' quality needs. Thus, processes and products that cause significant waste will be measured both to weed out bad parts (inspection) and to improve the processes. But once a process has achieved a sufficient level of consistent quality we should reduce, or eliminate, our measurements of this process or its output.

A particular point relating to cost-effectiveness is also connected to accuracy. The act of measurement, in and as of itself, changes the measure! This is true in quantum physics (where it was articulated by Werner Heisenberg as the *principle of uncertainty*), and it is especially true in the social sciences (e.g., take the influence of polls on actual voting). In human systems the fact we measure things has an effect on the participants. Sometimes this effect is good (as was the case in the famous Hawthorn experiments where productivity rose simply because it was measured and workers received attention), but all too often it is harmful. Thus, a major cost of measurement is that it may be counterproductive through unexpected human complexities. For instance, measuring students by grades, even when accurate, may discourage those students whom many call "underachievers." Underachievers, some contend, are simply people who consider the game lost in advance. What they need is a new game, without a limit on the number of winners. Furthermore, some recognized "winners" are also victims of the system. Originally, they studied for fun, but now they have to keep up their good grades to justify the high expectations placed on them. (But not to worry, the Pygmalion effect is on their side, making it unlikely that teachers will change their minds about them easily. It's easier to keep up than to move up.)

2.5. Conclusion

We've seen that good measurements have to fulfil four conditions: relevancy, clarity (operational definition), accuracy and precision, and cost-effectiveness. Although we discussed these four conditions separately, it is quite clear that it is impossible to disassociate them from each other completely. As in any non-trivial system (and measurement can be viewed as a system designed to provide data), important relationships between parts are often present.

Specifically, we may observe that issues that are difficult to measure with relevance are also subject to lack of accuracy, and that achieving appropriate accuracy and insisting on full operational definitions to the last iota may violate the cost-effectiveness requirement. Thus, even with respect to facts that are really measurable, not every bit of data is always useful.

The statements at the top of the chapter are all correct, even though they seem contradictory. As Snee's corollary suggests, we *should* insist on data-based management when it makes sense. And it often does. But not everything is measurable, much less *economically* measurable, so we have to learn to manage the unknowable without wasting resources on denying its nature. It is very easy to spend huge resources of time and money and come up with measurements that only harm the system. Stressing the knowable not only ignores a crucial part of the system; it also causes us to violate the rules of measurement in order to "solve" the problem of ignoring the unknowable. In short, we now convince ourselves that the unknowable can be measured, and the results can be catastrophic.

Supplement 2
More on Precision and Calibration

In this supplement we discuss further the rules of thumb requiring a ratio of 40 (excellent), 30 (usually good), or 20 (often acceptable) between the tolerance range and the measurement standard error, σ_E. Then, we'll derive the Shewhart/Tippett formula.

For our first objective, we define the *process capability index, C_p,*

$$C_p = \frac{tolerance \ range}{6\sigma_X} = \frac{USL - LSL}{6\sigma_X}$$

Where USL denotes the *upper specification limit* and LSL the *lower specification limit*. For a normally distributed and perfectly centered process, $C_p = 1$ implies that 99.73% of the items should fall between the specification limits, and it is then considered "capable." If $C_p < 1$, the process is not fully capable. If $C_p > 1$, the process is even better. We discuss the process capability index in more detail in Chapter 3.

S2.1. Analyzing the Rules of Thumb for $C_p = 1$

To assess our rules, we need to estimate the economic waste involved in measurement errors. Good rules will minimize, or at least reduce, the sum of this waste and the cost of achieving accuracy. But rigorous analysis is surprisingly difficult here. As we often do when we cannot analyze a problem fully, we resort to studying a special borderline case. The borderline case we propose to investigate is when the process is centered and capable in terms of σ_X, i.e., $C_p = 1$. We *should* then reject about 0.27% of the items, but because our measurements are distributed with a larger standard deviation, σ_Y, we are going to reject more. Furthermore, we'll reject some acceptable items and accept some bad items (type I and type II errors). When $C_p = 1$, many items are potentially in danger of type I error (being rejected wrongly), but only a small minority are susceptible to type II error. Therefore we'll concentrate on the probability of type I errors as a function of σ_E / σ_X.

The analysis is summarized in Table S2.1. The first three columns of Table S2.1 are the same as those in Table 2.1, the fourth shows the fraction of items that will be rejected in the borderline case, and the fifth shows the ratio between the latter fraction and the correct one, 0.0027. To check the calculations, note that the rejection will be based on σ_Y

35

instead of σ_X. For instance, in the sixth row we find that $\sigma_Y=51.00$ and $3\sigma_X=150$. $150/51=2.94$, and by a normal table we find that 0.9983 of the population fall below $z=2.94$. Therefore, the tail area is 0.0017, and since we reject on two such tails, our probability of rejection, P_R, is 0.0034 -- the value recorded in the fourth column. Division by 0.0027 yields 1.26, as recorded in the fifth column.

σ_E	σ_X	σ_Y	P_R	$P_R/0.0027$
10	100	100.5	0.0028	1.05
10	90	90.55	0.0029*	1.07
10	80	80.62	0.0029*	1.08
10	70	70.71	0.0030	1.10
10	60	60.83	0.0031	1.14
10	50	51.00	0.0034	1.26
10	40	41.23	0.0036	1.33
10	30	31.62	0.0044	1.63
10	20	22.36	0.0074	2.74
10	10	14.14	0.0340	12.6
10	9	13.45	0.0456	16.9
10	8	12.81	0.0614	22.7
10	7	12.21	0.0854	31.6
10	6	11.66	0.1236	45.8
10	5	11.18	0.1802	66.7
10	4	10.77	0.2670	98.9
10	3	10.44	0.3890	144.1
10	2	10.20	0.5566	206.1
10	1	10.05	0.7656	283.5

Table S2.1

*The fourth column of the second and third rows is reported as equal, and yet the fifth column is different. This is because these calculations were performed with five significant digits, and they appear the same only after rounding to four digits.

Again we see a takeoff when σ_E/σ_X exceeds 1/3 or so, which is the reason for the rule of thumb that a ratio of three to one is acceptable. The fifth column provides a very crude measure of the waste involved in over-rejection. As long as the item is near the tolerance limit it does not make much of a difference whether we reject it or not. This is especially true if the tolerance limits are determined based on the real economical damage exceeding them might cause. But as σ_E/σ_X grows, more and more items that are *far* from the limits get rejected erroneously. And on the other side of the same coin, more and more items that are far outside the limit get accepted erroneously. One might say that under the borderline scenario there are not many of those to begin with, but remember that the main purpose of the measurement under our scenario is to identify these items correctly!

These figures need to be multiplied by six -- the size of the tolerance range in units of σ_X when $C_p = 1$. As we rounded to the nearest 5, our "often acceptable" case was rounded from 18 to 20. This would yield a value of 1.50 in the fifth column. Had we rounded down, we would settle for 15, which would yield a value of 1.99 in the fifth column.

S2.1.1. *The Implications of the Borderline Case for Other Cases*

As we move from the borderline case to more capable processes, the danger of rejecting by mistake decreases. For instance, if the process has a capability index of 1.33, only 0.0002 will be rejected by mistake even if σ_E is as high as $0.5\sigma_X$. The ratio of column 5, however, would *increase,* (more than twice as much in this case). This is because practically no items *have* to be rejected, so 0.0002 is relatively excessive. What this shows is that when the process capability increases, the cost of unjustified rejection is not high even when the measurement is rather crude. In such cases, mind, it is highly questionable whether measurement should be pursued at all. It might be needed to monitor the process occasionally, to make sure it is still centered and nothing happened to increase its variation, but as long as these measurements do not show evidence of that kind we should probably leave the process alone.

But as we move from the borderline case to *less capable* processes, the additional confusion caused by σ_E makes a bad situation much worse. For instance, if the capability index drops to 2/3, we'll have to reject 4.56% for exceeding the limits even if σ_E is ZERO. When $\sigma_E = \sigma_X/5$ (which we said above is "usually good"), we now have to reject 5%, out of which 0.44% should not have been rejected. This difference, though less than 10% relatively, is larger than the fraction of bad product we had to reject with the full capability. Furthermore, now we have to fear more for type II errors. And when $\sigma_E = \sigma_X/3$ (which we said was "often acceptable"), the probability of rejecting good product goes up from 0.44% to 1.22%, again accompanied by an increased danger of type II error.

We conclude, then, that accurate measurement is especially important with less capable processes. Unfortunately, the reality is that plants with less capable processes also tend to have less accurate measurements! Therefore, improving the measurements is often a reasonable first step on the road to better quality.

S2.2. Application-Dependent Measurement Errors

Interaction between measurements and the item measured is not uncommon. For instance, the items may be awkward and difficult to measure, which translates to measurement errors. If we really want to get reliable data *in a given application* we must experiment with actual measurements. To do this we repeat a measurement several times and obtain data to calculate σ_E. Note that one of the factors that cause variation is the fact that different persons may have different biases. Therefore, we might want to include measurements by different people in the set. We should also consider measuring in different days, so that variations due to temperature and humidity will be reflected -- they are usually part and parcel of the measurement errors.

As discussed in AT&T (1958), control charts may be used to verify whether a given measurement instrument is adequate for a particular job. The main idea there is that multiple measurements of the same item are used as subgroups, and if the measurement instrument is adequate, many points in the $\bar{x}$ chart should fall *outside* the control limits. In other words, we expect the variation between parts to be large relative to the range of multiple measurements of the same part.

AT&T's criterion is a bit fuzzy, but the methodology can be extended to obtain explicit results. The specific technical details are provided here. Background technical details are given in Box 6.1 (using the $\bar{s}$ statistic) and in Box 6.4 (using the $\bar{R}$ statistic).

σ_E can be estimated quite simply by taking n measurements from each item, and treating them as subgroups. Using s, this implies

$$\hat{\sigma}_E = \frac{\bar{s}}{c_4}$$

and, similarly, using R (which is recommended specifically if $n=2$),

$$\hat{\sigma}_E = \frac{\bar{R}}{d_3}$$

But before we can trust these estimates, as with regular control charts, we should devise an s (R) chart to determine whether the dispersion is in control. If not, we should check the measurement procedure, including the recording of data. When the dispersion chart is in control, we can proceed.

When our objective is to find the ratio between the tolerance range and σ_E, we have all we need now. When we want to estimate σ_X/σ_E, we need $\hat{\sigma}_X$ as well. Since we already have calculations for $\bar{x}_j$, it's convenient to use the formula

$$\sigma_X = \sqrt{\frac{n}{m-1}\sum_{j=1}^{m}(\bar{x}_j - \bar{\bar{x}})^2 - \frac{(\bar{s}/c_4)^2}{n}} \sim \sqrt{\frac{n}{m-1}\sum_{j=1}^{m}(\bar{x}_j - \bar{\bar{x}})^2}$$

The subtraction of $(\bar{s}/c_4)^2/n$ is because our *recorded* x's are really measurements each of which has variance $(\sigma_X^2 + \sigma_E^2)/n$, so if we estimate the variance of these values from data we must deduct σ_E/n to obtain an estimate of σ_X^2. Also note the multiplication by n of the sum of squares. Without it the first element in the root estimates $\sigma_{\bar{x}}$. The approximation is valid in our range of interest. Far from our range of interest, the argument of the first root is not even guaranteed to be positive (in the mathematical sense), but if a negative result occurs we know all we need to know: the measurement error is dominant, and far too high. It's possible to estimate both σ_X and σ_E by *ANOVA* analysis which guarantees non-negativity for both, but the results are less robust in our range of interest. Also, the version presented here is more similar to regular control chart analysis, and thus easier in our context.

Regardless of the exact estimation method we use, when we estimate a ratio between independent variances the underlying distribution is F. We really want to test the hypothesis that the ratio exceeds some thresholds (3, 5, and 7). If we cast this question as such a test, we find that to obtain powerful results with little risk we must sample many items, but the number necessary is a function of the true ratio (the higher the ratio, the less items we need to prove it's above a relatively low threshold). Generic recommendations according to which sampling 30 items is (always) enough should be taken with a grain of salt. See also Chapter 8, where we discuss a related problem and show that control chart analysis often requires larger samples than most authors claim.

A *measurement precision chart* that can replace this analysis, *Isoplot*[SM], was developed by Dorian Shainin.[1] We take two measurements of each item, x_1 and x_2, independently, and plot the results against each other. Figure S2.1 shows a simulated example with $\sigma_X/\sigma_E = 3$. Similarly, Figures S2.2 and S2.3 depict examples with $\sigma_X/\sigma_E = 5$

---

[1] *Isoplot*[SM] is a service mark of Shainin Consultants, Inc. Its details are proprietary, and I don't even know them exactly. The following coverage of measurement precision charts should not be construed as a claim that they are identical to Shainin's original.

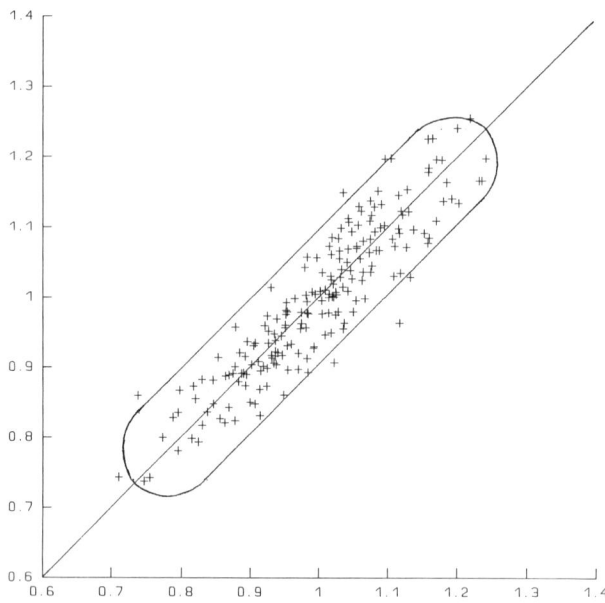

Fig. S2.1. Measurement precision chart for $\sigma_X/\sigma_E=3$ (200 items; 400 measurements).

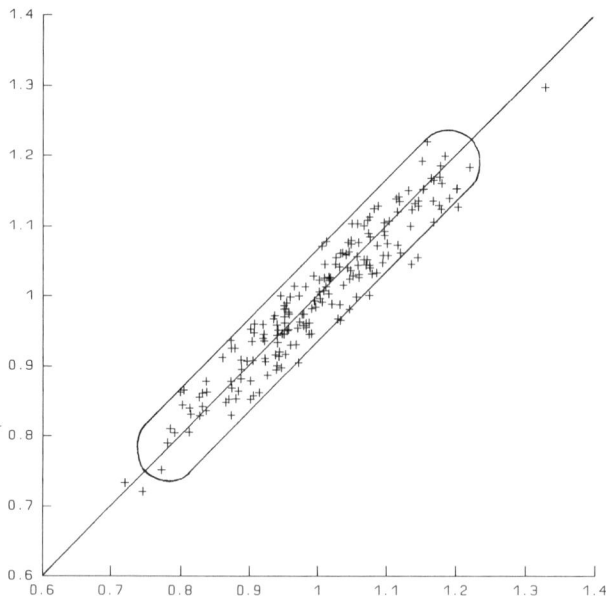

Fig. S2.2. Measurement precision chart for $\sigma_X/\sigma_E=5$.

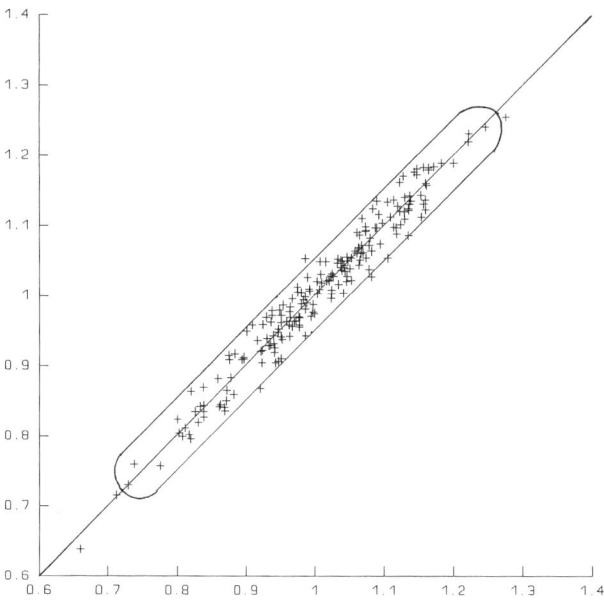

Fig. S2.3. Measurement precision chart for $\sigma_X/\sigma_E = 7$.

and $\sigma_X/\sigma_E = 7$. In all cases 200 pairs of measurements were used. Most points are scattered within a round-ended band on the 45° axis, drawn to include about 95% of the points approximately. In practice we may have to do with as few as 30 pairs of measurements, so it might be more difficult to fit a band well, but great accuracy is not required. Also, since 95% of 30 is 28.5, we should include practically all points within the band, but allow one or two out if necessary. It is safer to leave out points that are far out on the diagonal such that the length will be conservative (short).

Cursory analysis might suggest, for each band, that σ_X/σ_E is approximately the ratio between the length minus the width (i.e., the length of the rectangle between the rounded ends) and the width. This analysis is based on viewing each band as a union of confidence circles, with centers on the diagonal, such that if a real dimension is in the center of the circle, 95% of the realizations will fall within. This would suggest that the ratio between the total length of a band to its width would be $\sigma_X/\sigma_E + 1$ (i.e., 4, 6, and 8 for our set). When we study the issue in more depth, however, we discover that points outside the bands are exceptional in two ways -- not just one. First, indeed, they must be far from the real dimension (which is somewhere on the diagonal). Second, they are far *in a direction that is approximately perpendicular to the diagonal*. Thus, the round-ended band is *not* a union of circles with centers on the diagonal and such that each of them is likely to hold 95% of the realizations. Instead, each such circle has a lower probability of holding the realizations stemming from its center. Since this reduces the width more so than the length, the ratios observable in the figures are larger than 4, 6, and 8. To compensate for this we require ratios of (roughly) 5, 7, and 10. Instead, visual comparison to the round-ended bands in Figures S2.1–S2.3 may be sufficient. Kaiser & Trietsch (1997) showed that if X is normal then the distribution of the points is binormal. This suggests that we should use ellipses instead of the shapes depicted. But this would be more difficult to apply. They also provided the distribution of the points when the process is uniform across the tolerance range.

To complete the picture, Figure S2.4 depicts a case in which σ_E is so large relative to σ_X that the points plot in a circular cloud, indicating that the measurements are almost useless. But we can still check whether the average of a great many of them is at the desired location. In other words, they can only verify the accuracy of our adjustment (inefficiently). By taking many pairs of measurements of *the same item*, we should get a similar figure that can help compare two instruments or the performance of two workers. If the two measurements have a different bias, the diagonal through the center of the circle is not at 45°. If they have a different variance, we get an ellipse instead of a circle. If such results

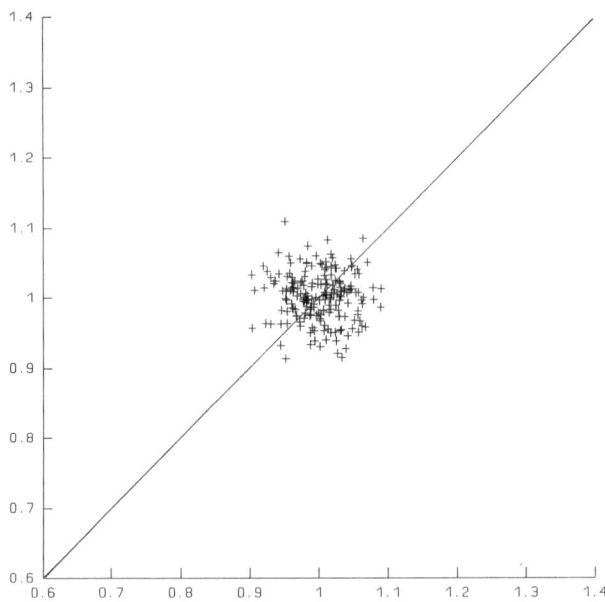

Fig. S2.4. Measurement precision chart for $\sigma_X/\sigma_E=0$.

are obtained by two persons with the same instrument and at about the same time, it suggests that at least one of them is not trained well, or there is no operational definition how to measure.

S2.3. Deriving the Shewhart/Tippett Formula

As we've seen in Chapter 2, the total cost of a sampling plan of N items, each measured n times is

$$TOTAL\ COST = N \cdot a_1 + N \cdot n \cdot a_2 = N(a_1 + n \cdot a_2)$$

where a_1 is the cost to select and fetch each item, and a_2 is the cost of each reading of the measurement. Since we measure each item n times, the standard deviation of the result, σ_Y, is

$$\sigma_Y = \sqrt{\sigma_X^2 + \frac{\sigma_E^2}{n}}$$

If we pick N items, each with this standard deviation, the standard deviation of their average is obtained by dividing the standard deviation of each by $\sqrt{N}$, i.e.,

$$\sigma_{\bar{x}} = \sqrt{\frac{\sigma_X^2 + \dfrac{\sigma_E^2}{n}}{N}}$$

This should be made to fit z times (where by Shewhart's convention $z=3$) into ε. That is,

$$z \sqrt{\frac{\sigma_X^2 + \dfrac{\sigma_E^2}{n}}{N}} \leq \varepsilon$$

Squaring and rearranging we can solve this for N to obtain

$$N \geq \frac{z^2 \left(\sigma_X^2 + \dfrac{\sigma_E^2}{n} \right)}{\varepsilon^2}$$

Substituting this expression for N in the total cost equation we obtain

$$TOTAL\ COST \geq \frac{z^2\left(\sigma_X^2 + \dfrac{\sigma_E^2}{n}\right)}{\varepsilon^2}(a_1 + n \cdot a_2)$$

which can be rearranged to get

$$TOTAL\ COST \geq \frac{z^2}{\varepsilon^2}\left(a_1\sigma_X^2 + a_1\frac{\sigma_E^2}{n} + n \cdot a_2 \cdot \sigma_X^2 + a_2 \cdot \sigma_E^2\right)$$

By taking the derivative of this expression with respect to n, and setting it to zero, the formula

$$n^* = \frac{\sigma_E}{\sigma_X}\sqrt{\frac{a_1}{a_2}}$$

is finally obtained.

Chapter 3

Partial Measurement of Quality by Loss Functions and Production Costs

Central to our theme, loss functions have been used by statisticians and operations researchers for several decades now. But in the quality field it was Taguchi who popularized them to better measure the cost of nonconformance. Taguchi intended such loss functions to be used together with other costs, specifically production costs (*PC*) and (implicitly) inspection costs (which can be considered part of *PC*). Together, these are akin to the cost of poor quality (*COPQ*), which includes cost of failure (internal and external), detection, and prevention. In this chapter we discuss various aspects of the use of loss functions, mainly concentrating on the most popular one: the quadratic loss function (*QLF*), which is now so strongly associated with Taguchi that it's often called the "Taguchi" loss function.

We must differentiate between two main types of defects that stem from two distinct types of problems. First, defects can be caused by human errors (e.g., drilling a hole in the wrong place), broken tools, or other special causes. We then get *irregular* items. Second, common variation and/or lack of adjustment can produce *out-of-tolerance* items. In this chapter we concentrate on tolerance. Shingo (1986) suggested error-proofing and source inspection techniques that can eliminate irregular defects and reject out-of-tolerance parts automatically. See also Chapter 9, where we discuss both irregular and out-of-tolerance defects.

3.1. Loss Functions

Assume 100% effective inspection, such that out-of-tolerance items are not released. Let c_0 denote the cost of replacing a defective item by a good one, or the cost of rework when applicable. Let T be the design target of some critical quality dimension, and let the allowed tolerance range be [*LSL, USL*], where $LSL = T - \Delta_0$ is the lower specification limit, and $USL = T + \Delta_0$ is the upper one. Figure 3.1 is a basic, somewhat naive, depiction of *COPQ* with respect to this dimension. In the figure, the loss associated with any value within the tolerance range is zero, while anywhere outside the limits the loss is c_0. This loss function was the implicit basis of the ZD (zero defects) movement. The idea was that if we manage

to produce to specifications, within tolerance, the products will satisfy the customers and
have zero *COPQ*.

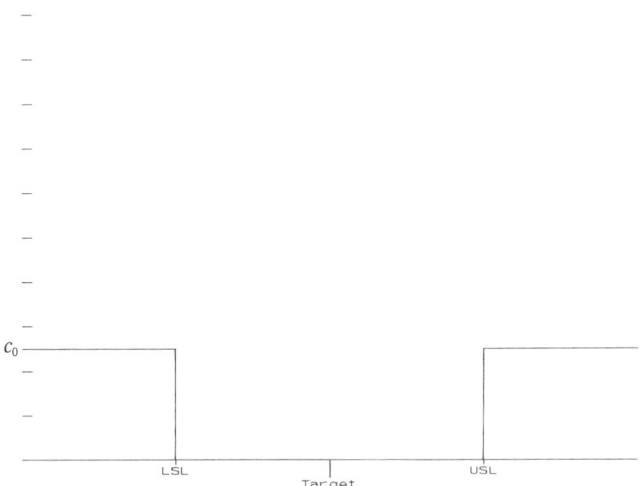

Fig. 3.1. A step loss function.

There are good theoretical and empirical reasons, however, to question the validity
of this loss function. Even if the design is really good, and the tolerance limits are
determined correctly, it is unreasonable to assume that products far from center are as good
as right on target. It is legitimate to set a limit for acceptable items, and reject beyond these
limits, but it is not reasonable to claim that items just within the limits are sizably better than
ones just outside. At best, we can say that the former are [barely] acceptable and the latter
are [just] bad enough to be rejectable. For example, stock car racers have always known that
it is better to hit the ideal design "on the nose" than to have an item that merely meets
specifications. Therefore, stock car racers often "blueprint" their critical subsystems. They
may race a stock car, but it is not taken off the dealer's floor: they take engines and power
transmissions apart and rebuild them with parts that are as close as they can get to the ideal
design, as per the blueprint. Hence the name "blueprinting." Do stock car racers like to
waste their good money exchanging one part that was within tolerance for another, without
any benefit? Or do they know something others ignore? Answer: they know something others
choose to ignore.

Indeed, when the key quality measurements of well-designed products are near target,
field failures are less likely and customer satisfaction is more likely. One well-publicized
example demonstrating this in practice was the color adjustment of Sony TV sets made in

the US, in contrast to those made in Japan. The ideal setting was 10, and the tolerance limits were 7 to 13. Practically all the US sets conformed to this tolerance, while a small fraction of Japanese sets were actually out of tolerance. But more customer complaints were registered for the American sets. It turned out that the American sets' adjustment was distributed with a higher variance than that of the Japanese sets. Thus, a larger fraction of American sets were near the specification limits, so a larger fraction of customers were unsatisfied. Sony's response was to set tighter tolerances for their American plant (and likewise for their UK plant), after which there were no further problems with this issue (Morita, 1987, p. 300).

The same message was brought home to Ford in the Eighties. Ford's Batavia, Ohio plant and a Mazda plant in Japan supplied transmissions for the Ford 1983 ATX cars. Both plants produced to the same Ford blueprint. When Ford found that their own transmissions generated much higher warranty costs than Mazda's, they decided to investigate. Ten Batavia transmissions and ten Mazda transmissions were taken apart and measured carefully. All ten Batavia transmissions met the critical specifications without fail. The Mazda transmissions, however, gave the technician a surprise: there was not *any* variation in the critical dimensions. Since the technician knew that there is no such thing as "no variation," he suspected the measurement instrument. But there was no problem with it -- except that the variation was smaller than its discrimination power. John Betti, Ford's Vice President of Powertrain and Chassis Operations at the time then said,

> While we've been making great progress in meeting my original objective of building to print, our not-so-friendly competition was making great strides in building uniform parts -- every part just like the part ahead of it, and just like the part following, with very little variation. While we were arguing about how good the parts had to be, they were working hard on making them all the same. *We* worried about specifications; *they* worried about uniformity. While *we* were satisfied and proud if we were to print, and then worried about keeping it to print, *they* started with the part to print, and worked on continuous improvement in the uniformity of the parts. Control, uniformity, continuous improvement. (Neave, 1990, p. 161.)

So, just meeting specifications is not as good as hitting the target without variation. Variation, even within tolerance, causes less than ideal fits. Some transmissions are too tight, and generate excessive friction (waste of energy), heat up too much, and may even cause seizures in extreme cases. Others have loose connections, causing vibrations, noise, and loss of oil.

Transmissions with critical dimensions on target -- especially if designed well to begin with -- will minimize the sum of the losses due to friction, vibration and oil loss. They will provide smooth, silent and reliable service for extended periods. They will create customer satisfaction, and enhance customer loyalty. Furthermore, transmissions whose critical dimensions are slightly off target will be better than those with far off ones. But this implies that the loss function of Figure 3.1 does not reflect reality. We need a loss function that satisfies the following:

♦   Being right on target is best -- it causes zero loss (or zero loss relative to the minimal possible loss under the design)

♦   Being slightly off target causes a very small loss

♦   Being far off target causes a large loss.

The *QLF*, a parabola with its minimum on target, is a simple function that meets these conditions. It is only an approximation for the true *COPQ*, but -- following Taguchi's leadership -- a convention is developed according to which the *QLF* is the default loss function to be used unless we know a better alternative. In this book we'll follow this convention.

The loss function is the cornerstone of Taguchi's teachings. To him, "Quality is the loss a product causes to society after being shipped, other than any losses caused by its intrinsic functions" (Taguchi, 1986, p. 1). This definition is not limited to quadratic loss, and Taguchi listed different loss functions for different cases; nonetheless his name is associated specifically with the *QLF* -- often called the *Taguchi loss function*. Disregarding losses due to intrinsic functions distinguishes conformance problems (e.g., foul taste of an alcoholic beverage) from *intentional* product functions, even if some would consider them harmful (e.g., alcohol's intoxicating effects). Thus, for the purpose of defining quality, Taguchi limits the loss to that caused by variability of function or by harmful [undesired] side effects (e.g., hangovers after consuming alcohol, vibrations and noise caused by machinery). Loss functions simply quantify this loss with respect to conformance. Unfortunately, the fact that Taguchi chose to define quality based on the loss function alone caused confusion among his followers, some of whom failed to notice that he considered production costs to be equally important. He considered them so with good reason: they represent loss to society *before* shipping, which is as important as loss to society *after* shipping.

Be that as it may, loss functions in general, and the *QLF* in particular, have been used by statisticians and operations researchers long before Taguchi. For instance, statisticians consider μ and σ^2 as the most important statistics of any distribution. But the former is the central location statistic that minimizes the squared loss due to errors in estimation, and the latter estimates this same loss. When our loss due to estimation errors is proportional to the absolute value of the error, the median is a better statistic for central location, and the range, or the distance between quartiles, will provide a more meaningful measure of the expected loss, but these statistics are much less popular than μ and σ^2. Likewise, regression analysis is practically always based on minimizing the sum of squared deviations, i.e., it is based on quadratic loss.

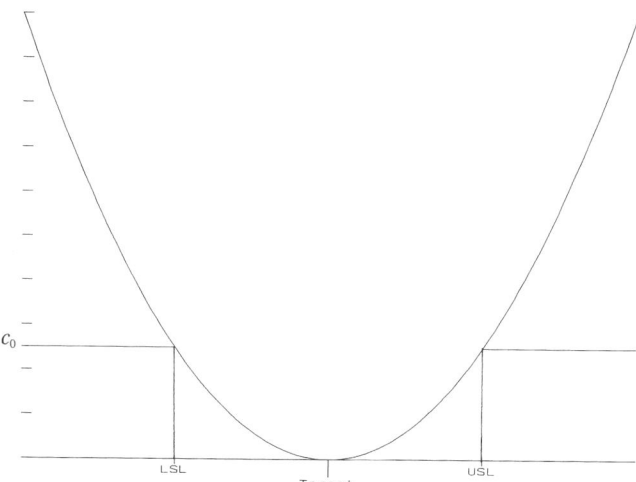

Fig. 3.2. A quadratic loss function compared to a step function.

Figure 3.2 illustrates the relationship between the quadratic loss function and the traditional one. Note that the quadratic loss function is higher everywhere, except at the tolerance limits and right on target, where the two coincide. If we inspect all items without failure, weeding out all the nonconforming items, the quadratic loss function would only apply within the tolerance range (and the loss outside will be a constant, as in Figure 3.1). But if there is no inspection and defective parts are released, it is appropriate to penalize them more if they are farther from the allowed range. In general, the probability an item outside the tolerance range will be accepted by error decreases with the distance from the limit, but the potential damage increases, sometimes very steeply. When such items are rare, we may choose to accept this steeper loss, to cut the inspection cost. For example, Sony did not inspect Japanese sets, which is why a small fraction of them were outside the tolerance range, and yet their overall quality was better than that obtained in the US after a 100% inspection. We elaborate on this issue in the next section.

3.1.1. *Calculating the Expected Quadratic Loss (EQL)*

Let T be the target, and let x be the actual dimension of an item, then the *QLF* for this item is given by

$$L(x) = K(x - T)^2$$

where $K > 0$ is a coefficient that has to be determined for each important quality dimension. This loss is zero when $x = T$, which means we ignore any profit or loss that are invariant with x. Of course, an item with several critical quality dimensions has equally many loss functions, but it's possible to treat them separately. To continue, suppose our process distribution has mean μ_X and variance σ_X^2 (but we may omit the indices where there's no risk of confusion), and let $B = \mu - T$ be the bias of the process. A classical mathematical result, proved in the following technical note, is that

$$EQL = E(L(x)) = K(\sigma^2 + B^2) = K(\sigma^2 + (\mu - T)^2)$$

=-

Technical Note:

The expected value is a linear operator, so we obtain

$$\begin{aligned}
E(L(x)) &= K\,E((x-T)^2) = K\,E((x - \mu + \mu - T)^2) \\
&= K\,(E((x-\mu)^2) + 2\,E((x - \mu)(\mu - T)) + E((\mu - T)^2)) \\
&= K\,(\sigma^2 + 2(\mu - T)E(x - \mu) + (\mu - T)^2) = K(\sigma^2 + B^2)
\end{aligned}$$

where K is outside the parentheses because it is a constant, and we substitute $(x - \mu) + (\mu - T)$ for $x - T$. Note that $E(x - \mu) = 0$ and $E((x - \mu)^2) = \sigma^2$, by definition. Q.E.D.

=-

Return now to the Sony example, and suppose that the Japanese factory has a centered process with normal distribution and $\sigma^2 = 1$, while the American factory has a uniform distribution between 7 and 13, i.e., $\sigma^2 = 6^2/12 = 3$.[1] There are no defective parts under the uniform distribution, and the bias in both cases is zero. In units of c_0 the Japanese *EQL* is 1, while the American *EQL* is 3, even *after* taking into account that about 0.27% of the Japanese sets should have been rejected, but were marketed to save the inspection costs!

As a less extreme example, suppose that the American factory also has a normal distribution, but with $\sigma^2 = 9/4$ (corresponding to $\sigma = 1.5$), and such that 100% inspection is used to weed out nonconforming sets. Rejects are reworked at a cost of c_0, by replacing a capacitor in the circuit, after which they are likely to be very close to target. Even if we ignore the cost of the inspection itself, the loss associated with the American sets will still be higher than that of the Japanese sets. To show this, we first introduce a formula for the quadratic loss associated with a centered but truncated normal distribution, which is the case here. If we have a truncated normal distribution with a given σ, such that the truncation is at $z_1\sigma$ (which is often negative) and $z_2\sigma$, and with $\mu = T$, the *EQL* of the acceptable items is given by

$$EQL = \frac{K}{\Phi(z_1,z_2)\sigma\sqrt{2\pi}} \int_{\mu+z_1\sigma}^{\mu+z_2\sigma} (x-\mu)^2 \mathrm{Exp}\left(\frac{-(x-\mu)^2}{2\sigma^2}\right) dx$$

$$= \frac{K\sigma^2}{\Phi(z_1,z_2)\sqrt{2\pi}} \int_{z_1}^{z_2} u^2 \mathrm{Exp}\left(\frac{-u^2}{2}\right) du = K\sigma^2\left(1 - \frac{z_2 e^{-z_2^2/2} - z_1 e^{-z_1^2/2}}{\Phi(z_1,z_2)\sqrt{2\pi}}\right)$$

where $\Phi(z_1,z_2)$ is the area under the standard normal curve between z_1 and z_2. We may also use $\Phi(z_1)$ to denote the area under the curve to the left of z_1: $\Phi(z_1,z_2)$ is a short form of $\Phi(z_2) - \Phi(z_1)$. Dividing by it makes the area under the truncated distribution equal to unity. The first step is by substituting $u = (x - \mu)/\sigma$. The second step is the result of integration by parts. In the symmetric case, letting $-z_1 = z_2 = z > 0$, this yields

$$EQL = K\sigma^2\left(1 - \frac{2ze^{-z^2/2}}{\Phi(-z,z)\sqrt{2\pi}}\right) < K\sigma^2 \tag{3.1}$$

In our example, $\Phi(-2,2) \approx 0.954$, and (3.1) yields $EQL = 1.74K$. This applies for items that are accepted right away. Reworked rejects cost $c_0 = 9K$ (since $\Delta_0 = 3$). The expected *COPQ* for all items, then, is $(0.954 \times 1.74 + 0.046 \times 9)K = 2.07K$, as compared to K for the $\sigma^2 = 1$ case. This result is less than $2.25K$ (due to the beneficial truncation), but it may

---

[1] For a uniform distribution between limits a and b, U$[a,b]$, $\mu = (a+b)/2$ and $\sigma^2 = (b-a)^2/12$.

be higher if we include the inspection costs. Thus, inspection is warranted only if it costs less than $(2.25-2.07)K$ per set. In Chapter 9 we present Deming's kp rule, but we show that it only applies to irregular defects. A calculation such as the one here should replace the kp rule for out-of-tolerance items.

In reality, processes are adjusted by a sample of $n \geq 1$ items, so they are never centered perfectly -- contrary to our assumption. Nonetheless, over the long run, for a normal process and quadratic loss, the same calculation applies, with the variance increased by a factor of $1+1/n$ (Trietsch, 1997–98). But if our process is far from normal, or the loss function is not quadratic, our model should be revised (even if the process is centered).

3.1.2. Loss Functions for "smaller-is-better" and "larger-is-better"

When the quality characteristic is of the "smaller-is-better" type, Kx^2 is a good quadratic loss function. Similarly, when the characteristic is of the "larger-is-better" type, we can use K/x^2. In the latter case, the result will no longer be a regular quadratic parabola, but it may still prove useful in practice.

The formula for the expected loss holds for the "smaller-is-better" case where B is the average value of the process output. That is, if the process has a mean μ and variance σ^2, then the expected quadratic loss will be $K(\mu^2+\sigma^2)$. But we don't have a similar result for the "larger-is-better" case, because the mean of $1/x$ is not $1/\mu$, and its variance is not $1/\sigma^2$. This difficulty can be circumvented, however, by estimating the expected value and variance of $1/x$ instead of doing it for x. The expected loss will then be $K(\mu_{1/x}^2+\sigma_{1/x}^2)$. Of course, the latter expected loss is in terms of the transformed loss function K/x^2.

3.1.3. Process Capability Indices

Process Capability Indices are meant to provide a measurement of the fit between a process and the demands placed on it. They attempt to measure, indirectly, the probability that the process will be able to meet the design tolerances. Tolerances are specified because no process can hit the ideal target without fail.

Process capability is measured relative to the width of the tolerance limits. When a process has a normal distribution $N(\mu, \sigma^2)$, in the long run 99.73% of its output should fall between $\mu-3\sigma$ and $\mu+3\sigma$. Therefore, if the tolerance range is 6σ, the process is considered "capable" of meeting the requirements. This implies that we are ready to accept a defect rate of 0.27%. And unless the process is centered perfectly, the defect rate will be larger. The basic process capability index, C_p, is defined in such a way that $C_p=1$ when the process is capable, as follows:

$$C_p = \frac{tolerance\ range}{6\sigma} = \frac{USL - LSL}{6\sigma}$$

σ_X is usually not known, so it may be replaced with s_X (or simply s), its data-based estimate

$$s_x = \sqrt{\frac{\sum\limits_{i=1}^{n} (x_i - \bar{x})^2}{n-1}}$$

where x_i is the ith realization, and $\bar{x}$ is the overall average of x_i for $i=1,2,...,n$. If s is estimated based on a large n, this substitution will not cause any problem. But if the sample is small, the error in the estimate of s may diminish the utility of the index, as discussed in the next technical note.

=-

Technical Note:

The error by using s instead of σ has two facets: (i) sampling error: the variance of s causes differences between samples; (ii) the estimator is biased. Thus, we have neither precision nor perfect accuracy.

If the process distribution is normal, the effect of using s instead of σ is to change the observed distribution to Student's t. Since the tails of the t distribution are thicker than those of the normal, it implies, *on average,* a higher proportion of items falling outside the $3s$ limits than would out of the 3σ limits. In reality sometimes s will be too small, which would entail too optimistic estimates, and sometimes it will be too large, leading to an opposite result. But in the former case the number of defects will tend to exceed the estimate by more than it would fall short in the latter. Hence, on average, using s is similar to understating σ.

As for the bias, it can be corrected. In Chapter 6 we discuss s charts which are also based on estimating σ by s, and there we use a coefficient, c_4 (<1), by which s is to be divided before being adopted as an estimate of σ. This division removes the bias. Similarly, in our connection here, dividing s by c_4 would be helpful too. c_4 values for samples of up to 25 are given in Table 6.1. For samples above 25, $c_4 \approx 4(n-1)/(4n-3)$, so s should be inflated by about $1/(4n-4)$, which is 1% or less for $n>25$. Since it is assumed that we use $n>25$, most authors do not bother with c_4 in this connection.

Finally, note that the t distribution is defined without c_4, so if we do use c_4 the critical values of the t distribution should be multiplied by c_4 to compensate. When we look at the critical values of the t distribution, and note that they are wider than those that apply to the normal distribution, we now see that part of the difference is due to the bias correction. But it's a small part: for example, the 0.005 critical value of t with four degrees of freedom is 4.604, as compared with the normal at 2.575. When we use a sample of $n=5$ to estimate $\overline{x}$ and s, we remain with four degrees of freedom. c_4 for samples of five is 0.9400 (the approximation yields 0.9411, although 5 is far from 25). So, if we divide s by 0.94, to remove its bias, the corrected critical value will be $4.604 \times 0.94 = 4.328$. The remaining difference is due to the [dominant] effect of variability. Similar but smaller differences may be observed for critical values associated with slightly larger probabilities.

=-

In the Sony example, if we set $\sigma=1$ we obtain $C_p=1$, and with $\sigma^2=9/4$, $C_p=2/3$. If $C_p<1$, the process is not fully capable. If $C_p>1$, the process is even better than merely "capable." Following the lead of Motorola, some companies are pursuing a "Six Sigma" quality objective. This is an objective that concentrates on achieving excellent conformance rather than good centering or good design (and as such it leaves a lot to be desired). The "Six Sigma" objective is to have processes with σ_X small enough to fit inside the tolerance range at least *twelve* times (six to either side of the center), which equates to $C_p=2$. For a normal distribution, or one that is approximately normal, this translates to practically zero defects when the process is fully centered. If the process is allowed to drift up to 1.5σ from center (as is the practice at Motorola), the fraction defective rises to 3.4 parts per million (PPM), as compared with 2700 PPM for a perfectly centered process with $C_p=1$.

On the one hand, larger drifts or lack of normality usually increase this fraction. On the other hand, shifts of less than $1.5\sigma_X$ are reputed to be undetectable by control charts, and hence it is considered necessary to tolerate them. This last statement should not be taken at face value: control charts can be devised to flag shifts that are as small as we may desire (see Section 6.6 and Supplement 6.3), but it may cost too much to do so. Also, there are advanced control charts (e.g., *CUSUM* and *EWMA* charts) that are more efficient in detecting small deviations (but slower to detect large deviations). Finally, automated control charting equipment (including electronic gauges and computerization) may make the task easier, but the use of such equipment is usually unjustified economically (at the time of this writing). Furthermore, such automated equipment often includes automatic adjustments that, depending on the algorithm used, can cause tampering (Scherkenbach, 1990). Chapter 4 recommends algorithms that do not cause such tampering.

The *QLF* suggests that it is important to keep the process adequately centered even when it is highly capable. In Chapter 4 we will see that with highly capable processes it is easy to do so, and therefore it is unacceptable to abuse high capability by neglecting this need. Using the step loss function instead of the quadratic one, however, often leads to measuring the quality of a process by counting defective items. When this is the criterion for quality, the important measure is how many standard deviations we are from the *nearest* specification limit. This gives rise to the following "improved" process capability index, C_{pk}

$$C_{pk} = \min \left\{ \frac{USL - \mu}{3\sigma}, \frac{\mu - LSL}{3\sigma} \right\}$$

where min{set} is the smallest element in the set between the curled brackets. Here μ too may have to be estimated by the data if we do not know exactly how to adjust the process to any mean we need. ($\bar{x}$, the sample average, is the traditional estimate of μ_X.) Incidentally, we now see that since Motorola allows a bias of up to 1.5σ, what they really aim for is not $C_p = 2$ but $C_{pk} = 1.5$.

Deming had this to say about the use of "an index of dispersion,"

> The fallacy of an index of dispersion, widely touted by beginners taught by hacks, is now obvious. An index of dispersion has no meaning, because the loss entailed depends far more on the position of the centre of the distribution of production than on its standard deviation. (1993, p. 224.)

For instance, we've seen that if we use a quadratic loss function, the bias is as important as the standard deviation, and with highly capable processes one may be tempted to use a high bias, since it is not likely to lead to exceeding the tolerance limits. Box 3.1 discusses such a case.

=-

Box 3.1

A Japanese manufacturer of vinyl sheets had a tolerance range of 0.8mm to 1.2mm for the width of the material,[2] and a process that was fully capable of meeting these specifications. Process improvement efforts reduced the standard deviation to a quarter of its former value, so the manufacturer decided to change the upper specification limit to 0.9mm, leaving the lower specification limit at 0.8mm. The improved process was capable of meeting these new requirements, and significant savings in materials were realized.

---

[2]The numbers used in this example are for illustration purposes, but to the best of my knowledge they are similar in magnitude to the actual case. My source, however, is second-hand.

Nonetheless, the number of customer complaints soared: the sheets were sensitive and tore easily. How could that be? A process improvement leading to reduced quality! The explanation: Before the "improvement" some sheets were close to the low tolerance but the majority were thicker (and stronger), so most customers were happy. After, the majority of sheets were close to the low tolerance, and it turned out that the customers were not well served there.

In terms of expected loss, assume that 1mm is indeed the best target in this case, so they started with a standard deviation of 0.4/6, and a centered process. The (quadratic) loss then was proportional to $(0.4/6)^2 = 1/225$. After the improvement, had they not changed the average, the loss would be reduced by a factor of 16 and become proportional to $1/3600$. Instead, they chose to introduce a bias of 0.15, and their resultant loss was proportional to $0.15^2 + 1/3600 \approx 1/44$ -- an increase of more than five-fold -- where the bias contributed most of the quadratic loss.

=-=

In contrast to C_{pk}, however, using C_p to measure the potential fit of a process to the needs does not imply negligence in centering the process, so Deming's criticism should not negate the value of C_p (Neave, 1990). For instance, in Box 3.1 the problem was that the manufacturer chose to adjust the process to meet (arbitrary) specifications economically, rather than use the process improvement to serve the customers better. As we discuss later, economical manufacturing is as important as reduced loss, but what this manufacturer did was to ignore the customer loss almost entirely.

Be that as it may, given the way C_{pk} is used by "beginners taught by hacks," most of them seem to believe that achieving high C_{pk} is sufficient. In fact, there is often a demand by customers to achieve C_{pk} of 1.33 (or more) as a condition of doing business. Centering is a practical first step towards achieving high C_{pk}, and sometimes all it takes is fixing a defective gauge or calibrating an adjustment knob. Still, the temptation not to center, once C_{pk} is high enough, exists. This is a good reason to discourage the use of C_{pk}. Indeed, after illustrating that by shifting the center the loss involved with the same distribution can greatly increase (as we've done in Box 3.1), Deming chose to conclude his (alas, last) book with further clarification of this issue,

> Moral: A measure of dispersion is by itself not an indication of achievement. Its centre is much more important. Certainly we should strive for narrow dispersion in the production of nearly everything, but this is only a first step. The next step -- essential -- is to centre it on the target value.

This simple illustration should put to rest forever use of measures of dispersion like C_{pk}, as it has no meaning in terms of loss. Moreover, it can be decreased to any value merely by widening the specifications.

Conformance to specifications, Zero Defects, Six Sigma Quality, and other nostrums, all miss the point (so stated by Donald J. Wheeler, 1992). (Deming, 1993, p. 228.)

Note now that widening the specification limits can also be used to manipulate C_p. Such manipulation is an issue only in a Management by Objectives environment, where the pursuit of numerical values (such as $C_p=2$) replaces the pursuit of real quality (maximization of net utility). Here, we'll take a positive approach and assume that specification limits are determined economically (as we discuss later), and therefore they will not be changed for the sole purpose of manipulating a number. With that caveat in place, C_p remains a valid and useful measurement. As Deming suggested, it is important to center the process as well, and we'll discuss this particular point in more detail in Chapter 4.

3.2. Production Costs as Part of Measuring Quality

If quality implies maximization of societal net utility, we should not limit ourselves to *COPQ* as experienced by customers after shipping the product. Waste during production is as pernicious as waste afterwards. Thus, for a given fitness-for-use, high quality implies low production costs (*PC*). Indeed, Taguchi never intended the loss function to be considered without regard to production costs. Instead, he explicitly recommended considering them together, and striving to reduce their sum (e.g., see Taguchi 1986, p. 27). Along this line, when comparing two processes with different variances and different production costs Taguchi recommends selecting the one for which $K\sigma^2+PC$ is minimized, even if this implies a higher variance (i.e., higher loss to customers downstream). An example is provided in Section 3.3.2.

Many quality proponents may find this difficult to accept, since so many of us predicate quality on customer needs alone. But the issue becomes really simple once we consider that customers, practically always, *pay* for production costs, and they may choose to give up a little fitness-for-use if they can get a sizable price break in return. Nor was Taguchi alone in his inclusive approach to managing quality. Deming's definition of quality implicitly included cost: "What is quality? A product or a service possesses quality if it helps somebody and enjoys a good and sustainable market. Trade depends on Quality." (Deming, 1993, p. 2.) See also Deming (1986), where his economic interpretation of quality is traced back to his mentor, Walter Shewhart (pp. 168–169). In this connection, the title of Shewhart's 1931 landmark book, *Economic Control of Quality of Manufactured Product,* speaks volumes (and likewise, Deming's last title). The Japanese quality luminary Kaoru Ishikawa was even more explicit: "There can be no quality control which ignores price, profit, and cost control" (Ishikawa, 1985, p. 45). Juran's stance against perfectionism addresses the same issue (Juran, 1988, pp. 3.27–3.29).

Thus the real objective is to minimize the combined production costs and the loss to society afterwards together. Simply put, minimizing the loss function alone is suboptimization. The loss function represents the loss to society *after* shipping, while the production cost represents loss to society *before* shipping: *our aim should be to minimize loss to society in total, both before and after shipping.* Even after doing that, our measurement will be partial, since it ignores other aspects of quality. For example, it ignores the quality of the design, the utility the product provides to the customers, etc.

Often, all that is required to minimize the sum of *COPQ* and *PC* is to compare the available options. Nonetheless, sometimes optimization is required, at least theoretically. For example, let us revisit the vinyl manufacturer case. Recall that the loss function was minimized at 1mm. Let's assume that the cost of material is 30% of the production cost, and the question is should we perhaps adjust the process slightly below 1mm after all. In this case, as the following technical note shows, a minute adjustment is indeed theoretically justified. Arguably, if this is done, however, the cost reduction should be passed on to the customer, directly or indirectly.

=-

Technical Note:

Considering that the original limits were at 0.8 and 1.2, we obtain $\Delta_0 = 0.2$, leading to $K = c_0/0.2^2 = 25c_0$. Thus the *QLF* is given by $25c_0(x-1)^2$. We also know that the cost of materials at 1mm is $0.3c_0$, and therefore the cost of material contributes $0.3c_0x$ to the production cost. Since we want to minimize the sum of the quadratic loss and the production cost we should minimize $25c_0x^2 - 49.7c_0x + 25c_0$, which implies setting the process to a mean of $49.7/50 = 0.994$. Thus, theoretically we should indeed reduce the average thickness a bit, but the optimum is much closer to 1 than the factory's choice (0.85). Even if the cost of materials would account for the whole production cost we'd still reduce the mean only to 0.98. In practice, of course, the difference here is so small that we should simply adjust the process to 1.

=-

3.3. Taguchi's Method to Estimate the QLF and Set Optimal Tolerance Limits

Our coverage is based on Trietsch (1997–98). It is limited to a single measure. As an example, we use the inner diameter of flanges, X. The nominal target value, $T=300$mm, is considered best in terms of minimizing the loss function. If X is too small, it will be difficult to fit the flange on the pipe. If X is too large, it will be difficult to weld the flange securely, leading to waste of welding material and time, and to potential welding defects. The problem is to determine the specification limits that minimize the expected total loss. These specification limits will be expressed as $T \pm \Delta_0$. (Asymmetric tolerances are beyond our scope, but they yield to similar analysis. See also Supplement 3.) A loss function for a single measure includes implicit consideration of tolerance stack problems and other interactions with other dimensions (in our example, variations in the diameter of the pipe), so looking at one measure at a time is permissible in our context. Statistical experimental design methods -- including different versions promoted by Taguchi himself (1986), Box et al. (1988), and Dorian Shainin (see Bhote, 1991) -- can be applied to set tolerances of several interacting measurements together, but this is beyond our scope.

To optimize Δ_0, we need to know the loss function, the process capability as a function of Δ_0, and the cost, c_0, to rework or scrap a part that does not meet the specifications. Let Δ_1 be a value such that a product whose absolute bias from target is Δ_1 is liable to fail in the field. This will cause high expected loss to society (in our example, loss to the users of the flanges), denoted by c_1. When estimating c_0 and c_1 we assume the loss at T is zero; this may require adjustment by subtracting the minimal loss from all loss figures (such a minimal loss is not subject to improvement by anything we do here, so it's immaterial for us). Taguchi recommends picking for Δ_1 the value at which 50% of the products fail in the field, and c_1 should reflect half the loss incurred at this point by an average unit that fails. But this recommendation is quite arbitrary, and can be replaced by other estimates. For instance, we might want to look at a point where 5% fail and take 1/20 of the damage as c_1, or 10% with 1/10, and so on. More generally, we could pick the combination of deviation and probability of failure that maximizes K (as per the calculation shown below). This is really an area where large estimation errors cannot be avoided, but we can sustain relatively large errors here since the loss function is relatively flat near the target. Following Taguchi's version, Δ_1 may be selected such that a flange with an inner diameter of $300 - \Delta_1$ cannot be fitted to pipes whose outer diameter is nominal or more (recall that the outer diameter of the pipe is random, at least within its own tolerance), while a flange with an inner diameter of $300 + \Delta_1$ cannot be welded securely to pipes whose outer diameter is nominal or less. Suppose the customer estimates that $\Delta_1 = 1.5$mm and that the cost of a field failure is 90. $c_1 = 45$, then, reflecting the expected field failure cost at $T + \Delta_1$ or $T - \Delta_1$.

By assumption, our loss function, L, is quadratic with $x - T$. Given Δ_1 and c_1 we obtain

$$K = \frac{c_1}{\Delta_1^2}$$

Considering that c_1 can be very large relative to c_0, the question is how much tighter to set the tolerance limits to avoid field failures. Taguchi sets the tolerances in such a manner that the loss at the limits will be c_0: if the product is outside these tolerance limits, the loss associated with shipping it exceeds the cost of fixing or replacing it, c_0. Conversely, if the product is within these limits, the cost of improving it (bringing it to the target, T) exceeds the loss incurred by shipping it as is. Since our objective is to minimize the total cost, this simple criterion is approximately correct. This shows that Taguchi considers production cost and subsequent loss as equally important: he compares them directly and sets the limits to minimize their sum.

The criterion can be applied to any loss function, but we continue with the quadratic one. Assuming that the process is capable, we get

$$\Delta_0 = \Delta_1 \sqrt{\frac{c_0}{c_1}} = \sqrt{\frac{c_0}{K}} \qquad (3.2)$$

Trietsch (1997–98) gives a more accurate version, but also states that the refinement is not worth the extra effort. In our example, with $c_1 = 45$ and $\Delta_1 = 1.5$mm, $K = 45/1.5^2 = 20$ (money units per mm^2). c_0 is a function of the production process, since by scrapping an item we also discard the marginal value of the processing invested in it. For example, suppose that by using a cheap cutting process we obtain $c_0 = 1.8$ (mainly, the cost of materials), leading to $\Delta_0 = 1.5\sqrt{1.8 / 45} = 0.3$mm. Alternatively, using a busy machine that is capable of holding tighter tolerances, we get $c_0 = 3.2$ (because this machine costs much more per time unit). Repeating the calculation for this process we obtain $\Delta_0 = 0.4$mm, i.e., the better process leads to *wider* tolerances. Nonetheless, given the use of a more expensive process, scrapping would indeed lead to higher losses, and thus higher tolerance limits are justified.

As a result of the wider tolerance coupled with the more capable process, the process may become highly capable indeed. This may lead some to recommend setting tighter tolerance limits after all, to "delight" the customer. The question is: do we really have to set tight tolerances merely because the process can hold them? *If workers recognize the need to produce close to target, and not merely within the limits, there is no need whatsoever to change the limits upon process improvements.* Being within specifications should not be confused with being "good." It merely means that it is less wasteful to use the product than to discard or rework it. Therefore, if our process capability is high we should use it to make excellent parts that are clustered near the ideal target. But unless our process improvements are such that the cost of scrapping or reworking an item is now lower, we should not suddenly start to reject items that we accepted before. The rule is still to minimize loss to the whole system by shipping those items that cause less loss by shipping than by scrapping.

One exception to this rule, a case we discuss in the next section, is when the process was not capable when the tolerances were set, and has now been improved. Another *apparent* exception is when customer needs become more demanding and they generate higher service and field failure costs than before, thus increasing c_1, decreasing Δ_1, or both. But this implies that the loss function should be changed regardless of our process capability, so we'll need tighter tolerances not because we can meet them but because (existing or new) customers need them.

True, as in Sony's case, if production people do not appreciate the need to center the process appropriately, tighter tolerances can be specified to achieve reasonable results. Still, the real need is to reduce the variation of the items we ship regardless of the specifications. As Deming put it, "the distributions of the chief quality-characteristics of parts, material, and service become so narrow that specifications are lost beyond the horizon" (1986, p. 49). Customers get products that are ever closer to target, but producers do not scrap occasional items that are far from center unless they are far enough to make such scrapping more economical to society as a whole. Narrowing the specification limits arbitrarily, even when done under the banner of "continuous improvement," is tantamount to scrapping more items needlessly. It is also likely to necessitate 100% inspection in cases that could have been weaned otherwise. This is simple waste -- the antithesis of quality.

3.3.1. *A Special Case: Processes that are Not Capable*

Tolerance limits may be a function of the yield if the process is not capable. In such a case, c_0 should reflect the cost of producing an *acceptable* item. For example, if bad items are scrapped, and there is a probability q of satisfying the limits, we need to produce, on average, $1/q$ items for each acceptable one. So we should use c_0/q instead of c_0 in (3.2), i.e.,

$$\Delta_0 = \Delta_1 \sqrt{\frac{c_0}{q\,c_1}} = \sqrt{\frac{c_0}{q\,K}}$$

Since q is a function of the tolerance limits, this calls for an iterative application. Thus, as we bring such a process towards $C_p=1$, q approaches 1, and the tolerance limits should be tightened by a ratio of $\sqrt{q}$. But the tolerance tightening procedure stops when $C_p > 1$ because $1/q$ is practically 1 therefrom. Taguchi recommends treating any $q \geq 0.8$ as 1 for the purpose of tolerance setting.

In our example, using the cheap cutting process with $\Delta_0=0.3$mm, suppose that the standard deviation of the process, σ, is 0.4mm. This leads to $C_p=(USL-LSL)/(6\sigma)=2\times0.3/(6\times0.4)=0.25$. Assuming a normal distribution, $q=\Phi(-0.75,0.75)\approx0.55$. Multiplying Δ_0 by $\sqrt{1/0.55}$, we see that we have to widen the tolerance limits by a ratio of 1.35, leading to $z=1.01$ and $q\approx0.69$; this calls for tightening the limits a bit back to $z=\pm0.9$, yielding $q=0.63$, etc. The widening ratio converges at about 1.24. As a result, scrap goes down from 45% to 35%. Taguchi recommends stopping after three iterations or so, without insisting on full convergence. He also recommends urgent process improvement whenever the process is not capable of producing at least 80% acceptable products, but until this is done the limits have to be adjusted.

C_p[in]:	0.05	0.10	0.15	0.20	0.25	0.30	0.35	0.40	0.45	0.50
C_p[out]:	0.102	0.163	0.216	0.264	0.310	0.355	0.399	0.443	0.486	0.530
Ratio:	2.04	1.63	1.44	1.32	1.24	1.18	1.14	1.11	1.08	1.06

C_p[in]:	0.55	0.60	0.65	0.70	0.75	0.80	0.85	0.90	0.95	1.00
C_p[out]:	0.575	0.620	0.665	0.712	0.759	0.806	0.854	0.903	0.952	1.001
Ratio:	1.05	1.04	1.02	1.02	1.01	1.01	1.01	1.00	1.00	1.00

Table 3.1. Tolerance widening ratios for incapable normal processes.

Finally, the preceding analysis requires no data about the loss function except that it is quadratic, and no data about Δ_0 except that it is the result of an optimization. Of course this means that we have to express our results in units of the original Δ_0 value. In our example we would increase the tolerance limits by 24% from ±0.3mm to ±0.37mm (which happens to be still tighter than the tolerances of the expensive process). Table 3.1 shows by how much tolerance limits should be widened to compensate for lack of process capability as a function of the initial process capability. The table only applies for normally distributed processes. For completeness, it extends beyond the range for which Taguchi recommends any adjustment (for a normal process, if $C_p>0.43$, then $q>0.8$).

Sometimes, nonconforming items can be reworked. For example, in the Sony case, the color could always be adjusted successfully by replacing a capacitor. When rework is economical, c_0 should reflect the cost of rework and no division by q is necessary. In our flange example, as is often the case, rework is plausible when the diameter is too small, but not otherwise. In such a case our tolerance range should not be symmetric. We may then optimize the two limits separately, using the cost of replacement on one side (with an appropriate q value reflecting the probability of not having to scrap the new item as well) and the cost of rework on the other. But we omit the details.

3.3.2. Selecting a Process

The criterion for selecting a process is minimization of production costs and expected quadratic loss, $PC+EQL$. Looking at our current example, suppose σ for the expensive process is 0.1, then $EQL=20\times0.1^2=0.2$; $PC=c_0=3.2$, so our total is 3.4. This process has $C_p=1.33$, and therefore, beyond maintaining the process in control, inspection is highly unlikely to pay for the minute savings by truncation. Looking at the cheap process, here $C_p=0.31$ (after widening the tolerance limits), and using (3.1) with $z=0.37/0.4=0.925$ and $q\approx0.65$ we obtain

$$EQL = 20 \times 0.4^2\left(1 - \frac{2\times0.925\,Exp(-0.925^2/2)}{0.65\,\sqrt{2\pi}}\right) = 0.81$$

PC in this case is $1.8/0.65=2.77$, so our total is 3.58. But this can only be achieved by truncation, i.e., inspection of 100% of items is assumed. Without it, the cost will be $1.8+20\times0.4^2=5$ (we assume that shipping an out-of-tolerance item causes a damage that *includes* the cost of replacement, so there is no need to divide by q). Even ignoring the likely difference in inspection cost, however, the cheap process is inferior in this case.

But lest it be said that precision should always be the main consideration, readers can verify that the picture changes when $\sigma_X\approx0.35$, and for lower values the cheap process becomes competitive. Even without inspection, if $\sigma_X\leq0.28$ the cheaper process should be selected, but note that $C_p\approx0.4$ at this limit (considering that the widening of the tolerances should be to 0.34 instead of 0.37), so the cheap process becomes economical long before it becomes capable. Let alone before it reaches $C_p=2$, which would be required under Six-Sigma.

3.4. The Lack of Validity of Signal-to-Noise Ratios

Taguchi's contribution to the field of quality was spectacular. Specifically, he popularized the use of the (quadratic) loss function, showed how to determine economic tolerances, and pioneered the use of statistical experimental design techniques to achieve off-line quality by improving process settings and even making the product more manufacturable. This includes robust design where the objective is to achieve high quality output with inexpensive inputs. A chief way to do that is to look for settings that do not translate high variability of inputs to high variability of outputs.

Nonetheless, several of Taguchi's techniques are questionable from a theoretical point of view. One of those is his use of external arrays, which could be part of the regular experimental design. But our focus does not include experimental design issues. More pertinent is his recommendation to use signal-to-noise (*S/N*) ratios to achieve robust designs. Robust design implies the use of good mean settings such that the product will be robust against variation. That is, we are concerned both with means and variances. Taguchi, however, claims that *S/N* ratios can transform data in such a way that both mean and variance can be optimized together. In other words, he rarely addresses *EQL* directly -- as we do in this book. *S/N* ratios are defined for three main cases:

◆   *smaller is better*: In this case, the squared response is the magnitude we wish to minimize. This can be done by minimizing the following transformation instead,

$$S/N = -10 \log_{10}\left[\frac{1}{n}\sum_{i=1}^{n} x_i^2\right]$$

◆   *nominal is best*: Here, Taguchi looks at the statistic

$$S/N = 10 \log_{10}\frac{mean\ squared\ response}{variance} = 10 \log_{10}\left[\frac{\overline{x}^2}{s^2}\right]$$

◆   *larger is better*: In this case we may select $1/x_i$ as the response that we should minimize, leading to

$$S/N = -10 \log_{10}\left[\frac{1}{n}\sum_{i=1}^{n} \frac{1}{x_i^2}\right]$$

The main idea here is to select settings with high signal to noise ratio, i.e., relatively strong signal, and use other factors to adjust the mean to the desired value. If these other factors do not influence the variation, it follows that we'll obtain any desired value with the minimal possible variation.

The efficacy of using signal-to-noise ratios is subject to debate. Some researchers agree that S/N ratios are effective for the first and last cases. Box (1988) does not accept even this: he shows alternatives, and recommends graphic analysis of experimental results. As for the nominal-is-best case, S/N ratios are usually invalid: there is only one special case where they work as advertised, and that's when the mean and the standard deviation are proportional to each other (see Leon et al. 1987). This is, reportedly, true in some electrical plating or chemical deposition cases, where the more we plate the larger the standard deviation. Likewise, in coating silicon wafers a similar phenomenon occurs. Trietsch (1992) shows, however, that once we take the production costs into account explicitly, using S/N ratios preempts optimization in this case too. On the one hand, this is a theoretical issue and the difference may be minute. On the other hand, it is not *necessary* to use S/N ratios. There is neither theoretical justification nor practical necessity for them.

3.5. Variance Reduction and the Pareto Principle

Simply put, the Pareto principle states that some factors account for more than their share. A popular way to state it is by the "20/80" rule of thumb: "the top twenty percent of causes account for eighty percent of the effect." It is especially important in the context of variance reduction projects. In general if X is the sum of n independent causes, and the variance of Cause i is σ_i then

$$\sigma_X = \sqrt{\sigma_1^2 + \sigma_2^2 + \ldots + \sigma_n^2}$$

Without loss of generality, let us assume that the individual causes are arranged in decreasing order of magnitude, as per the Pareto principle. Then the effect of a reduction of one unit in σ_1 will be larger than that of a similar reduction in any other cause. To see this, take the partial derivative of the variance, and the result reveals that the effect of a small reduction in σ_i is proportional to σ_i/σ_X. This, in turn, is proportional to the size of σ_i. Since we use the Pareto order, the effect is largest for σ_1. But this analysis understates the potential benefit of the Pareto principle application here. In reality improvements are likely to either remove a cause completely or reduce it by a fraction of its size which is similar across the causes. Thus, to reduce σ_i by, say, one third, should be roughly as difficult as reducing any other component, σ_j, by a third. This means that if we concentrate on the largest component, σ_1, we'll get the largest improvement per unit reduction *and* we'll get the largest reduction. Together this implies that the benefit is proportional to σ_1^2.

A numerical example should clarify this further. Let $\sigma_1=6$, $\sigma_2=5$, $\sigma_3=4$, $\sigma_4=3$, $\sigma_5=2$, and $\sigma_6=1$ represent the standard deviations of six statistically independent causes whose sum is our random variable. Thus,

$$\sigma_x = \sqrt{6^2 + 5^2 + \ldots + 1^2} = \sqrt{91} = 9.54$$

Suppose now that we can reduce σ_1 by one third, to 4, and σ_2 by one fifth, also to 4. This will reduce σ_x to 7.87. If, instead of going for these two relatively small improvements, we'd choose to eliminate the last four causes altogether (assuming it's possible to do so), we'd get $\sigma_x=7.81$. In other words, in our example shaving a bit off the top of the first two causes is roughly equivalent to a total elimination of the last four causes. But if we look at the numbers, it seems that we merely reduced the sum of standard deviations by 3 (6 − 4 + 5 − 4), as compared with 1 + 2 + 3 + 4 = 10.

The applicability of the Pareto principle to variance reduction efforts has a bright side and a dark side. The bright side is that it's enough to work on the vital few. The dark side is that it is futile to work on the trivial many. Note, however, that after a vigorous reduction of the top causes they may tend to become more equal to each other, and more difficult to reduce further. The more reduction we need, the more causes we must tackle concurrently, so the improvement process becomes progressively expensive. In conclusion, one should not be surprised that variation cannot be reduced all the way to zero, but one should not give up on the large improvements that *are* typically possible at the first stages of the improvement process.

The need to concentrate on the top implies that we must find a way to identify the vital few causes. This is often done by various experimental design approaches such as those promoted by Taguchi (1986), and Box et al. (1988). To various degrees, however, these methods are relatively sophisticated, and too difficult for beginners. Dorian Shainin, who compiled and developed several experimental designs into a competitive system of improvement tools, suggests a much simpler approach: Seder's multi-vari chart (Seder, 1950a; 1950b). It requires relatively little effort, and it is also easy to understand. It can often do the job, especially at the first stages where the major opportunities are easy to identify. It is, essentially, a graphic way to perform analysis of variance (ANOVA), but it does not require the same level of mathematical sophistication. Bhote (1991) discussed additional DOE methods that belong to Dorian Shainin's collection of improvement methods, some of which may also apply here. But Box 1.1 describes a case study where variation was reduced considerably using only Shewhart control charts and process knowledge. This, however, was done by removing "out-of-control" causes, which are typically large causes of variation. The methods above, in contrast, also apply to processes that are already in control.

Supplement 3
Asymmetrical Loss Functions

Using the quadratic loss function ubiquitously for the "nominal is best" case, as a default, is a recommended choice that is almost always better than using the former default -- the step loss function. It is also convenient mathematically because it induces a loss that is proportional to the squared bias plus the variance of the process distribution. Nonetheless, there are circumstances when the regular quadratic loss function is patently inappropriate. One such case occurs when the expected cost of exceeding the tolerance limits is not equal to the right and to the left of the target. Missing by cutting too much, for instance, may imply scrap, while cutting too little only causes rework. When this is the case one possible response is fitting a loss function that is not symmetric, and not necessarily quadratic.

One useful non-quadratic loss function has constant slopes to the two sides of the target.

$$L(x) = \begin{cases} K_1(T-x); & x \leq T \quad (K_1 > 0) \\ K_2(x-T); & x \geq T \quad (K_2 > 0) \end{cases}$$

where K_1 is the coefficient to the left of the target, T, and K_2 is the coefficient to the right. For example, JIT calls for deliveries that are exactly on time. If we deliver too soon it may involve a penalty of K_1 for each time unit (because we may be delayed until the receivers are ready), but when we deliver too late there is (usually) a much larger penalty per time unit, K_2 (Ronen and Trietsch, 1993). Another example is when an airline plans the necessary safety time for aircraft at hub airports (Trietsch, 1993). This has to be done with one of the following objectives, or a combination: (i) such that the expected value of the total hub time of aircraft and people will be minimized, assuming that aircraft wait for connecting passengers that are delayed; or (ii) such that the total waiting time costs and missed connections penalties are minimized, assuming that aircraft that can leave do so without waiting for delayed passengers. The first case is associated with the loss function we just introduced. Thus, conceptually, scheduling purchases and setting a schedule for hubs are process adjustment problems. In the latter case, setting an intelligent schedule has a strong reducing effect on the variance, because much of the variation of aircraft on-time performance is due to the very schedule that is supposed to prevent it. A better known model that uses the same loss function is the classic newsboy model, where we have to determine how much merchandise to stock in a one time purchase. Here K_1 is the loss involved with overstocking, and K_2 represents lost sales.

This loss function is asymmetric, and its slope has a discontinuity at the minimal loss point. As the next technical note proves, if we assume a continuous distribution, the process should be adjusted in such a way that

$$K_1 \Pr\{x < T\} = K_2 \Pr\{x > T\} \tag{S3.1}$$

=-

Technical Note:

To prove (S3.1), let f(x) and F(x) be the density function and the *CDF* of the process distribution *after* the adjustment we may select. The expected loss, L, is given by

$$L = K_1 \int_{-\infty}^{T} (T-x)f(x)dx + K_2 \int_{T}^{\infty} (x-T)f(x)dx$$

Refer to Figure S3.1, depicting the *CDF*, and look at the horizontal band between $F(x_1)$ and $F(x_1 + \Delta x)$. The length of the band is approximately $T - x_1$, and its width is approximately $f(x_1)\Delta x$. If we look at the limit when Δx approaches 0^+, these approximations become exact, and therefore the area below the CDF to the left of T is the first part of our expected loss, i.e.,

$$K_1 \int_{-\infty}^{T} (T-x)f(x)dx = K_1 \int_{-\infty}^{T} F(x)dx$$

x_2 has a similar band *above* the CDF, and therefore

$$K_2 \int_{T}^{\infty} (x-T)f(x)dx = K_2 \int_{T}^{\infty} (1-F(x))dx$$

So our expected loss can be rewritten

$$L = K_1 \int_{-\infty}^{T} F(x)dx + K_2 \int_{T}^{\infty} (1-F(x))dx$$

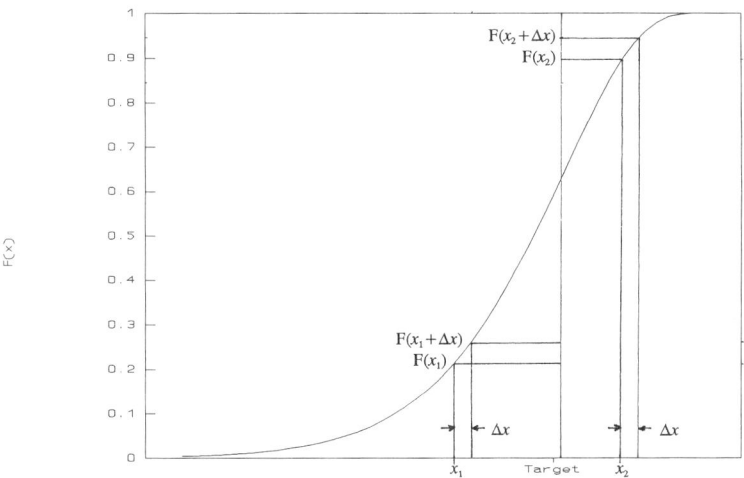

Fig. S3.1. Integrating loss for a piecewise linear loss function.

(Incidentally, similar analysis is often used for the computation of the expected value.) Taking the derivative, L' (which can be done under the integral, since the integration limits are constant), we obtain

$$L' = K_1 \int\limits_{-\infty}^{T} f(x)dx - K_2 \int\limits_{T}^{\infty} f(x)dx$$

Setting this derivative to zero, and noting that the first integral is the probability of falling to the left of T and the second one is the probability of falling to its right, our result now follows.

=-

Generalizing to discrete distributions calls for setting the process to satisfy two constraints,

$$Pr(x<T) \le \frac{K_2}{K_1 + K_2}; \quad Pr(x>T) \le \frac{K_1}{K_1 + K_2}$$

These two constraints can be satisfied simultaneously by adjusting the process to the largest possible value for which the first inequality will still be satisfied. This implies that T can, and usually should, be one of the possible realizations such that the sum of probabilities below it satisfies the first inequality and the sum above satisfies the second one. For a continuous distribution the two inequalities merge into one equality that satisfies (S3.1). For the continuous case, and usually for the discrete case as well, unless the penalties are equal this solution calls for a planned bias -- i.e., μ and T are not identical -- and the planned bias increases with the process variance.

Deming (1993) discussed a similar loss function associated with catching a train under the assumption that the train will leave exactly on time. There, on one side there is a constant slope and on the other side (being late) there is a step function. Trietsch (1993) used the same loss function for the case when aircraft do not wait for late connections. The mathematical analysis is less elegant here, requiring a numerical solution. The end result is that we should accept a very small probability of being late. A heuristic solution is to aim to arrive $3\sigma_T$ time units before the departure, where σ_T is the standard deviation of the arrival time. Again, if we can reduce σ_T, which is our process standard deviation here, we sustain a lower expected loss.

The last example of an asymmetric loss function we discuss is quadratic to either side of the target, but with different coefficients:

$$L(x) = \begin{cases} K_1(x-T)^2; & x \leq T \quad (K_1 > 0) \\ K_2(x-T)^2; & x \geq T \quad (K_2 > 0) \end{cases}$$

where K_1 (K_2) is the coefficient to the left (right) of the target, T. We are also given tolerance limits at $T - \Delta_{0,1}$ and $T + \Delta_{0,2}$ respectively (such that the loss at the limits equals the respective costs of exceeding them). A special case that is easier to deal with is when $K_1 = K_2$ but $\Delta_{0,1} \neq \Delta_{0,2}$; e.g., when the penalties at the two tolerance limits are different, but the engineers set the target off-center, this loss function may result. For the latter case the ratio between $\Delta_{0,1}$ and $\Delta_{0,2}$ should satisfy

$$\frac{\Delta_{0,1}}{\Delta_{0,2}} = \sqrt{\frac{c_{0,1}}{c_{0,2}}} \tag{S3.2}$$

where $c_{0,1}$ ($c_{0,2}$) is the loss at the lower (upper) specification limit.

For $K_1 \neq K_2$, our former result, $L = K(\sigma^2 + bias^2)$, is not valid for this loss function (or the ones discussed in this supplement before). To calculate the expected loss we need to know the distribution, which, in turn, is a function of the bias. Mathematically,

$$E(L) = \int_{-\infty}^{\infty} f(x)\,L(x)\,dx$$

$$= K_1 \int_{-\infty}^{T} x^2 f(x)\,dx + K_2 \int_{T}^{\infty} x^2 f(x)\,dx$$

In the special case where the distribution is symmetric and there is no bias, this expression becomes $(K_1 + K_2)\sigma_X^2/2$. In general, however, it may be difficult to compute, depending on the distribution. We now present two similar heuristics how to adjust a process with a given distribution under such a loss function. We aim to approximate the optimal bias to minimize the expected loss. (Assuming $K_1 \neq K_2$, the optimal solution includes a planned bias that becomes smaller when we reduce σ_X by process improvements.)

Our first proposed heuristic is the simpler one. If $\Delta_{0,1} + \Delta_{0,2} < 6\sigma_X$, i.e., $C_p < 1$, adjust the process by (S3.2). As a result we obtain an implicit symmetric quadratic loss function that reflects the losses at the specification limits correctly. Since for such processes the need for 100% inspection is highly likely, we should not care whether the approximation is good outside the limits. And since conformance is often dominant for processes with low capability we should not be too concerned whether the loss function is appropriate within the limits. For higher C_p, if $\min\{\Delta_{0,1}, \Delta_{0,2}\} \geq 3\sigma_X$, adjust the process to the target, T. Here conformance is satisfactory and we want to avoid a too large bias. If we fall between these two cases, i.e., when the tolerance range is wider than $6\sigma_X$ but the distance from target to the nearest tolerance limit is less than $3\sigma_X$, we adjust the process to fall $3\sigma_X$ from the tolerance limit that is nearer to the target (i.e., set $C_{pk}=1$).

Our second heuristic is based on the same objectives, but it goes one step further by minimizing the costs associated with rejection when $C_p < 1$. It requires knowledge of the process distribution density function, $f(x)$, for any possible adjustment. Here we adjust so that

$$f(x = LSL)\,c_{0,1} = f(x = USL)\,c_{0,2}$$

Again, once we reach $C_{pk}=1$ we start reducing the bias until it reaches zero.

If we use either of these heuristics, and we also continuously improve the process, we will move progressively towards the minimal loss point, i.e., the target. Once we start adjusting to target, the same adjustment remains the choice following further process improvements.

Chapter 4

Adjusting Processes Without Tampering

Typically, processes need to be adjusted when being set up, or when they are known or suspected, to be out of adjustment. Our study of loss functions, and specifically the quadratic loss function (*QLF*), demonstrated the value of centering a process. In terms of expected quadratic loss (*EQL*), we saw, reducing the squared bias is comparable to reducing the variance. Without doubt, upon strong evidence that a process moved out of adjustment, it should be readjusted. Control charts may supply such strong evidence. Some authorities imply that *only* control charts can do that. Nonetheless, *prudent* adjustment is often justified even with much weaker evidence. And one certainly need not use a control chart as a precondition to prudent adjustment. This is a contentious point, however: some ardent followers of Deming object vehemently to any adjustment without control chart evidence. Their reason? Most of us over-adjust, i.e., we often adjust a process that does not require it merely because some items it produced were off-center, perhaps due to common cause variation. This is tampering, and before we learn how to adjust we should learn how to avoid tampering. Indeed, the key word above is "prudent," which tampering is not. Once this lesson is clear, there is much more we need to know to adjust a process properly. This is especially true if we wish to balance the following objectives: (i) to adjust based on a large sample (so the final adjustment error will be small); (ii) to minimize quadratic loss *during* the sampling; and (iii) to do it economically.

But before we get into the statistical issues, we should mention that setup adjustments may be eliminated by appropriate engineering breakthrough techniques. SMED (Single Minute Exchange of Die) is a modern industrial engineering approach that aims to streamline setups; it often removes the need for adjustments altogether (Shingo, 1985). Typically, SMED involves (i) standardizing the outside dimensions of setup parts, so they can be interchanged without adjustment (modularity); (ii) providing stops and notches such that setup parts can be pushed to place without adjustment; or (iii) marking the exact position of machine settings by colors, so that they can be located quickly and correctly. Notches and stops can also be used to set the correct position *exactly*, with a click. The use of modular design dimensions helps further by eliminating or reducing the need for fine adjustments: instead, the machines are marked for the modular settings, and they don't require adjustment for these cases. The use of modular fixtures and jigs is also conducive to eliminating the need for adjustment, and helps implement SMED in non-repetitive job shops (Trietsch, 1992b). Such methods will not reduce the adjustment error all the way to zero of course -- this is, to the best of our knowledge, impossible -- but they may very well reduce it to a small fraction of the total process variation, in which case our objective will be satisfied.

In general, measurement errors during the setup may be responsible for adjustment errors. Without SMED this source of error is in action every time we repeat a setup. Even with SMED it applies during the preparation of the setup parts, jigs, etc. (It follows that the preparation of setup materials justifies tight tolerances, the use of excellent measurement instruments, and the use of numerous repeat measurements to reduce the error.) One of the first treatments to reduce setup adjustment errors may be by improving the measurements of settings (as opposed to measuring products).

The adjustment knobs we use and the scales attached to them (dials) have to be up to the discrimination power we need. In one case Shingo removed an error cause by attaching a large round plate to an adjustment knob, thus creating a much larger dial. A scale on the perimeter of the enlarged knob provided the necessary information for adjustment. Shingo's use of a very large dial was, in essence, equivalent to the addition of a fine-tuning knob where one was missing. When a fine-tuning knob exists, it will be the candidate to receive a larger dial if necessary. But it is important not to imply more accuracy than the instrument is capable of delivering, so the calibration should not be too fine.

Adjustment knobs always have some wobble (hopefully, imperceptible). For example, wobbly shower faucets. Once missed, we should go back by more than the amount of the miss and readjust. Part of the training of workers should include a clear articulation of the need to approach the desired setting from the same direction always, so the reading on the dial will be consistent with the adjustment itself. It is also a good idea to mark equipment to that effect, so workers who do not operate it often will know which way to go. Or set a general rule, e.g., "always adjust from the outside in," and mark exceptions clearly.

Excessive wobble (relative to the wobble that can't be reduced economically) is one indication that the equipment needs to be repaired, or it will not be able to hold tight tolerances. When we seek to reduce variation of any type, a good preventive maintenance program is necessary.

4.1. Ways and Means to Tamper

Tampering is the direct result of not understanding variation. When people do not know how much variation a process should exhibit, they often try to counteract natural variation by adjustment. So the first rule is to study the variation of the system. Control charts are very handy for that purpose. It may be their most important function. And for systems whose variation had not been measured yet, we should assume that it is larger than we think. That is, we should be hesitant before declaring results "special," and thus requiring strong adjustment. In this connection, when we say "adjustment," we include any corrective action. For example, increasing the penalties for murder adjusts the penal system, and likewise adding police officers and building ever-larger prisons. Similarly, increasing interest rates, adding a requirement for two more signatures before expenditures are authorized, increasing salaries, changing immigration quotas, and laying off workers are adjustments. While most of our discussion will be in terms of (continuous) machine adjustments, tampering should be avoided in any adjustment.

4.1.1. *The Nelson Funnel Rules*

To demonstrate tampering, Deming used the Nelson Funnel Experiment (suggested to him by Lloyd Nelson). The equipment for the experiment consists of a kitchen funnel, a marble that can pass through the funnel with little interference, a table covered with a table cloth, and a movable stand to hold the funnel. A target is marked on the table cloth.

The experiment starts by placing the funnel directly above the target, and dropping the marble through the funnel. Usually, the marble rolls a bit before it stops. But we want it to stop on target exactly. To achieve this, we may decide that we need to move the funnel (adjust). After many drops, if we mark the marble's final position each time, adjusting between drops by some method (rule), we obtain a pattern. Deming analyzed the potential results for four of the following five rules:

Funnel Rule 1: After aiming the funnel at the target the first time, *do not move it.*

Funnel Rule 2: Adjust the funnel to counteract the last error, relative to the current position (e.g., if the marble stopped 3 inches to the north of the target, *move the funnel 3 inches due south from its current position*).

Funnel Rule 2a [NOT considered by Deming]: If the last error exceeds a preestablished tolerance limit, adjust the funnel to counteract it, relative to the current position (e.g., suppose our tolerance is 2.5 inches, then if the marble stopped 3 inches to the north of the target *move the funnel 3 inches due south from its current position*; but if the marble stopped 2 inches away from target, do not move the funnel).

Funnel Rule 3: Adjust the funnel to counteract the last error, relative to the target (e.g., if the marble stopped 3 inches to the north of the target, *the new adjustment is 3 inches south from the target*).

Funnel Rule 4: Adjust the funnel directly over the last hit.

The first adjustment under Rules 2 and 3 is identical, but subsequent ones diverge. In contrast to these two rules, Rule 4 is not intended to hit the target, but rather to achieve some consistency; in this, we shall see, it fails. The former two are not too good either. To show this, Dov Trietsch and I simulated the results of 300 drops with Deming's four rules, by a computer program that he coded. (Deming 1993 used a similar simulation by Boardman and Iyer.) First, we experimented with a particular combination of funnel, marble, cloth, and surface. With the results we devised an empirical distribution for the distance and direction the marble rolls. The application simulates this distribution. Figure 4.1[a] shows the results of Rule 1, where most rolls landed within a small circle around the target. Figure 4.1[b], for Rule 2, shows a visibly wider distribution, but still a statistically predictable one. Figure 4.1[c] shows the results of Rule 3, and Figure 4.1[d] represents Rule 4. The results of Rules 3 and 4 are patently unpredictable. Rule 4 causes a drift away from the target, while Rule 3 is even worse: its pattern includes a drift comparable to that of Rule 4, but

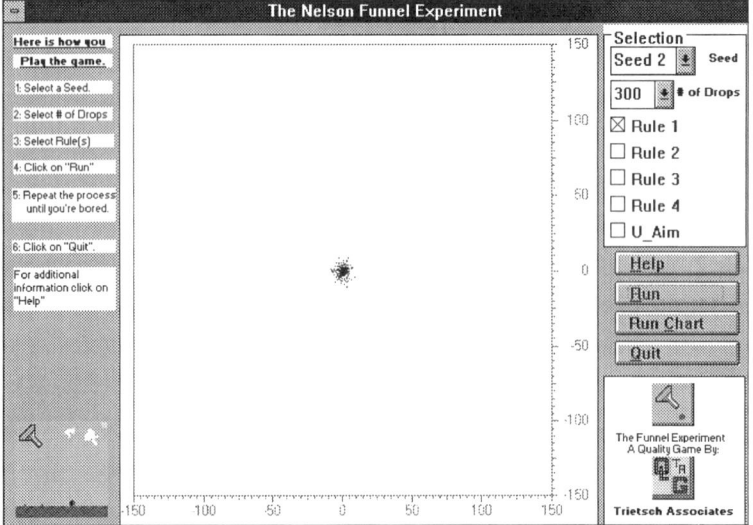

Fig. 4.1[a]

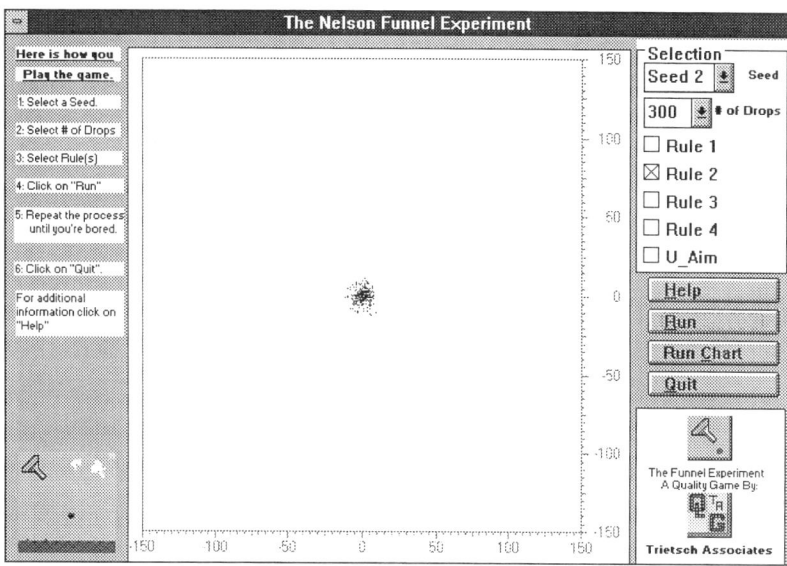

Fig. 4.1[b]

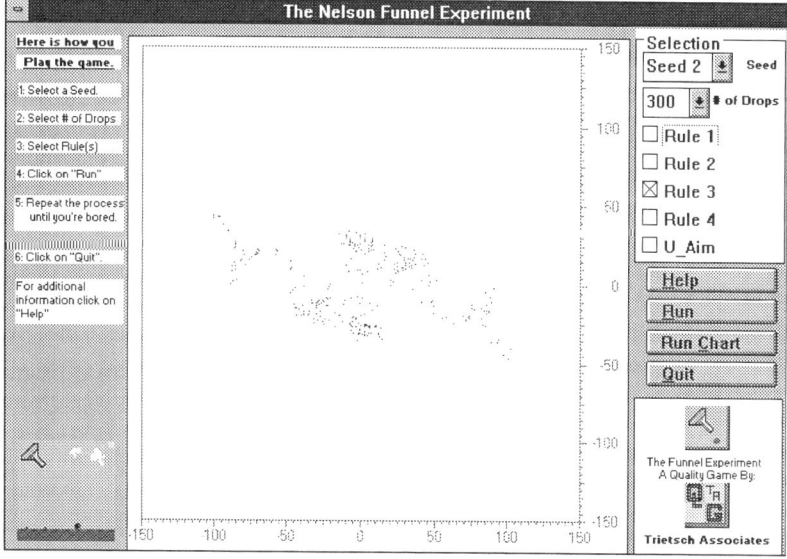

Fig. 4.1[c]

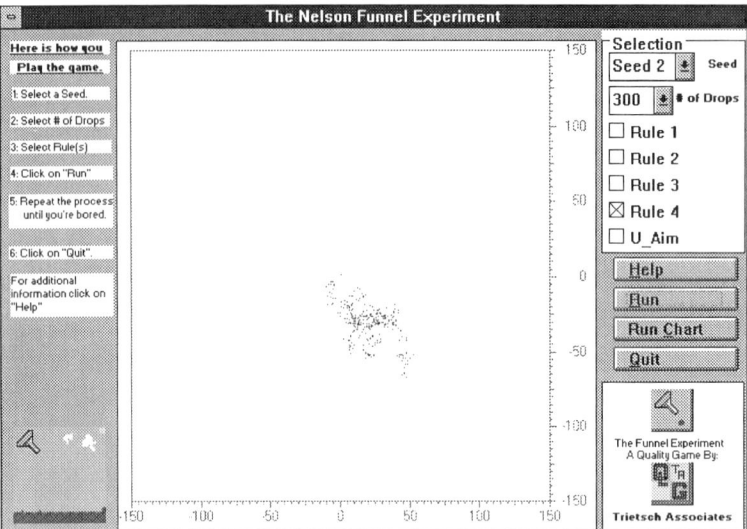

Fig. 4.1[d]

it also includes wild fluctuations across the target. To be sure, Rule 1 gives disappointing results, but when compared to the others it is superior.

In more detail, with Rule 1, although the marble tends to fall within a certain radius from the target, it practically always misses. But then again, very rarely will the marble stop at a very great distance from the target.

Rule 2 increases the radius of the circle within which the marble will usually stop by about 41%, doubling the variance. It is an example of wasteful tampering: our return for bothering with adjustments all the time is doubling the *EQL*. Rule 2a reduces the number of adjustments, but is more likely to over-adjust than Rule 2, so in terms of *EQL* it is slightly worse. Following one of these rules is "doing something," so together they are more prevalent than Rule 1. Examples of Rule 2 include (i) adjusting a process based on producing one trial unit; (ii) adjusting the sights of a gun based on shooting one bullet every day (standard in the US Navy, at least until the late eighties). Literally, these examples are equivalent to Rule 2 only in terms of the average process variance they induce. Actually engaging in ongoing strong adjustments following each and every unit, as the formal rule suggests, is less prevalent. But Rule 2a does not involve so much interaction, and for this reason it is probably the most prevalent of them all. Examples include (i) investigating every defect ever made; (ii) studying harder after receiving a low grade in a quiz, and then studying less after a good one; (iii) some automatic adjustment gadgets that adjust strongly whenever the process output approaches a tolerance limit; (iv) continuously adjusting the heating thermostat.[1]

Rule 2 is wasteful, but the system is still statistically predictable, and it usually *seems* under statistical control. (It may be identified by a pattern test, however, especially if the adjustments coincide with the control chart's subgroups.) Rule 3 does not even provide apparent control. Instead, large deviations from target are reversed each turn like a pendulum, and they tend to grow in magnitude slowly (occasionally they may also shrink). Examples of Rule 3 in action include: (i) a driver trying to get his car back on the road only to shoot over to the other side (overcompensation); (ii) voters who switch their loyalty from party to party every election, because they are always disappointed (not realizing that the system owes much of its foibles to voters like themselves). Depending on who drives the system, some of the examples given above for Rule 2 and Rule 2a may also apply to Rule 3. The difference is that the former two correct unwisely, while Rule 3 *over*corrects recklessly. (Nonetheless, in the next section we'll see that with feedback delays it's possible to do even worse: the pendulum's swings can grow quickly instead of slowly! Actually, the driver example above may really be due to this effect.)

Rule 4 is also likely to diverge slowly from the target, but it avoids the pendulum behavior. Therefore, one is quite likely to follow Rule 4 without realizing it. Examples are: (i) xerox copies of xerox copies of xerox copies of xerox copies -- enough already! -- producing grey amorphous images; (ii) worker training worker (nobody knows their job, and therefore nobody *has* a job);[2] (iii) the use of judicial precedent to slowly change the interpretation of the law (sometimes beyond recognition of the legislators' original intent); (iv) instructions going down the chain of command, and changing slightly at every stage until they are unrecognizable when they reach the workers who carry them out; (v) copycatting

---

[1]Some of the examples listed here as Rule 2a were presented by Deming and others as examples of Rule 2.

[2]According to Deming, if one doesn't know what one is doing, one doesn't have a job. This does not mean one is unemployed; rather it implies that the work done is either useless or, at least, badly flawed (in terms of promoting the purpose of the organization).

In a talk on 17 November 1993, Bruce W. Woolpert, co-CEO and President of Granite Rock, confirmed this message. He said that the company had traditionally relied on the "worker-training-worker" method. But when they tested the basic knowledge of workers in areas vital to their jobs, e.g., the knowledge of a concrete-mixer driver about concrete, it was often *the opposite of the truth.* Since such employees represent the company, Woolpert felt that this caused a major degradation of the quality of services the company was providing. This motivated him to provide an exemplary training program open to all employees on a voluntary basis (but on company time). The program played a role in the company's winning the 1992 Malcolm Baldrige National Quality Award.

a new technique (e.g., JIT) without profound knowledge, through a chain of teachers and other implementors (result: companies concentrating on superficial elements such as kanban or trying to achieve zero inventories, instead of concentrating on reducing cycle times -- Trietsch, 1992c; 1994); (vi) oral history; (vii) the Tower of Babel (diversification of languages). Last, but not least, many users of control charts use Rule 4 inadvertently when they update control limits periodically. This practice is endorsed even by respectable SQC books.

Clearly, Rule 1 is by far the best among the lot. Presently, we'll discuss one potential improvement: to allow adjusting the process prudently to avoid allowing a bias to prevail indefinitely. But in our simulation there was no bias, so Rule 1 could not have been improved. The lesson: in the short-term, variation should be expected and accepted. In the long-term we should look for ways to improve the system and reduce its variation, but unwise or reckless adjustment is not the answer. A sound approach may be to experiment with changing the height of the drop, the texture of the table cloth, the diameter and material of the marble, the funnel, etc. Don't tamper with the system, redesign it.

In conclusion, when in charge of processes that can be adjusted, Rule 1 is rarely used. Instead, people tend to use Rule 2a, Rule 4, Rule 2 and sometimes even Rule 3, the most reckless of them all. Thus, they treat any variation as special, requiring a strong response. By this they harm the system much more than the original variation would. This is tampering. Unless we understand variation and know how to adjust prudently, we're better off doing nothing. This is where Deming's Second Theorem kicks in: "We're ruined by best efforts." most of us are loath to do nothing, so we opt to tamper instead. But tampering is a waste-causing waste, and provides an excellent opportunity for improvement. All that's necessary is profound knowledge. In contrast, with statistical monitoring we can learn to remove special causes, and then we can proceed to address the common causes. This, again, can only be achieved by changing the system. Finally, allowing one of the inferior rules into the system constitutes a removable special cause. The removal is by re-centering and reverting to Rule 1. Comparing Figure 1.1 with Figure 1.2, where Rule 2a was removed, illustrates how substantial such improvements can be.

4.1.2. *Discriminating and Correcting Based on Common Variation*

In Chapter 5 we discuss another of Deming's demonstrations, the *Red Beads Experiment*. It demonstrates that sometimes workers are punished or rewarded for results that they cannot control. To punish or reward workers based on measurable results *without* evidence that they control the differences is an especially pernicious type of tampering. When we deal with such issues, which are fraught with emotional complexities, the quadratic loss function is *not* appropriate. Vicious cycles can amplify even small deviations out of proportion. These problems are much too unknowable to allow a mechanistic application of a default loss function. There may be NO prudent way to adjust the behavior of workers. Perhaps we should give them the freedom to do the right thing without "adjustment." Most of them desire to do the right thing. In this connection, according to Deming, promotions should be based on long-term achievements, which are less likely to be spurious. Bonuses should be allocated to *everybody*.[3]

4.1.3. *Regression to the Mean*

Peter Scholtes recounts an instructive story from the Israeli Air Force. Pilot trainees complained that their instructors were harsh with them when they made mistakes, and never praised them when they did well. A psychologist, firmly believing that nurturing and support would achieve more, investigated. The instructors explained that their behavior was based on experience (knowledge): "After praising, the trainees' performance typically deteriorates, and after admonishing, it typically improves." Hence, admonishing is beneficial and praising is counterproductive.

But the truth was different. Because the instructors did not understand variation, their experience-based knowledge was invalid. There is natural day-to-day variation in performance (and the trainees themselves cause only part of it). Thus, it is to be expected that occasionally a trainee will do very well or very poorly relatively. In either case, it is unlikely that he'll perform more extremely the next day. For example, if performance today is in the top 5 percentile, it's 95% certain that tomorrow's will deteriorate. But when does a trainee get praised? When he does very well, and it's already in the cards that he's likely to do worse tomorrow. Symmetrically, when he gets admonished, it's already in the cards that he's probably going to do better tomorrow. So, praising does not harm and admonishing does not help. And even hard data can be misleading in the absence of valid theory (Deming, 1993).

In this case, the necessary theory had been developed long ago. Loosely speaking, it states that extreme results are likely to be followed by more average results. This is known by statisticians as *regression to the mean*. (Unfortunately, it is less known among other professionals.) Regression to the mean occurs when the process produces results that are statistically independent or negatively correlated. With strong negative serial correlation,

---

[3]My source for the statement about bonuses is Deming's answer to a question I asked during one of his last 2-days seminars in 1993.

extremes are likely to be reversed each time (which would reinforce the instructors' error). In contrast, with strong positive dependence, extreme results are quite likely to be clustered together.

Of course, the impacts discussed here are short-term: from one day to the next. The psychologist's contention that support is beneficial concerns a long-term effect. It could only be proved by persistently encouraging trainees very often (and not only when they do exceptionally well), and doing so for a long time.

4.2. Efficient Adjustment Methods

There are two different scenarios for adjustments. One -- our main focus in this section -- is during the initial process setup or upon out-of-control signals. The other is when we suspect the process is not entirely stable, and therefore it is prudent to adjust it periodically. A recommended way to do this without tampering is by *fractional adjustment* -- a method closely related to exponential smoothing -- as we discuss in Subsection 4.2.1. Again, many consider this taboo, claiming that processes should only be adjusted when they are demonstrably out of control. Nonetheless, if we wish to reduce *EQL*, using fractional adjustment periodically, but not too frequently, is prudential. Since we do not wait for out-of-control signals to correct the adjustment this way, we should suspect that most remaining out-of-control signals are *not* due to adjustment. This implies that we must check the setup, and once we do that we have to readjust as in a setup. This is why we treat these two as one: in Subsections 4.2.2 through 4.2.6 we concentrate only on setup adjustments, but the assumption is that they also apply as part of the activities after out-of-control signals.

Our main objective in adjusting a process is to minimize the expected quadratic loss (*EQL*). Although this aim is associated with Taguchi, it's been pursued long before he became famous. Barnard (1959) devised a method to estimate by how much to adjust to minimize *EQL*. Box and Jenkins (1976) specified optimal control of adjustment with the same loss function. Grubbs (1954) proposed a simple and yet very efficient adjustment scheme -- to which we refer here as *the harmonic rule* -- with the same implicit objective. We discuss the harmonic rule in detail in Subsections 4.2.2 through 4.2.4, including some new results that are related to it. In Subsection 4.2.5 we discuss the *five/ten rule* (Trietsch, 1997–98), which is a simple adjustment method that constrains the *EQL* to a low value of $c_0/100$ (where c_0, as introduced in Chapter 3, is the production cost of the item or its rework cost, whichever is less). Finally, Subsection 4.2.6 shows how to adjust a process when the loss function is highly asymmetric and it is desired to make sure that the adjustment will not err to the wrong side. This is applicable when on one side we have cheap rework and on the other expensive scrapping. Supplement 3 provides one approach to this issue, but here we assume that it is not followed. Kelton et al. (1990) address this problem; although their method is not recommended here, readers who'd like to research the literature on adjustment will find many further references there.

4.2.1. *Adjusting an In-Control Process and Tampering are NOT Equivalent*

Deming's implication in teaching the Nelson Funnel Rules was that no adjustment should take place unless the process is out of control. Ardent followers of Deming often argue likewise. Nonetheless, when adjusting a machine, or the threshold rate of internal return for project evaluation, etc. -- but not when adjusting the behavior of workers -- this conclusion is too strong and may easily cause excessive *EQL*. We should recommend periodic adjustment, e.g., following each subgroup (if a control chart is maintained), by a fraction of the deviation from the target, *T*. If we denote the fraction by λ and we use subgroups, the suggestion is to adjust by $-\lambda(\overline{x}_j - T)$, but with a small λ. Alternatively, when we do not have a control chart, and therefore we do not take subgroups already, we may make do with measuring individual items, but this necessitates using even smaller λ. Rule 2 is similar to our recommendation, but it uses $\lambda=1$, which is why it is unwise. Rule 2a also uses $\lambda=1$, but in addition it selects conditional data for the adjustments, so it tends to create a bias (Kelton et al., pp. 389–390). In contrast, Rule 2 induces no bias.

Brown (1959, pp. 57–58) presented a basic relationship between λ and the equivalent sample size, k_λ,

$$k_\lambda = \frac{2-\lambda}{\lambda} \leftrightarrow \lambda = \frac{2}{k_\lambda + 1}$$

His result applies to exponential smoothing, but we'll show that it also applies in our context. One interpretation of this is that if we use fractional adjustment for a long time, the variance of our adjustment will be equal to that obtained by sampling k_λ items and adjusting by their average. Nonetheless, k_λ need not be an integer. If we use fractional adjustment for some time, but not a "long" time, the variance of the adjustment converges to this, from below, at a rate that increases with λ. To quantify the last statements, let D_0 be some unknown initial deviation, and let D_j be the remaining deviation after sampling and adjusting for *j* items. Let the process error of the *j*th item be ε_j, then $e_j = x_j - T$, the *j*th deviation, is given by $D_{j-1} + \varepsilon_j$. The subsequent adjustment, A_j, is $-\lambda e_j = -\lambda(D_{j-1} + \varepsilon_j)$, and $D_j = D_{j-1} + A_j = D_{j-1} - \lambda(D_{j-1} + \varepsilon_j)$. Starting with D_0, complete mathematical induction yields

$$D_j = D_0(1-\lambda)^j - \lambda \sum_{i=1}^{j} \varepsilon_i (1-\lambda)^{j-i} \tag{4.1}$$

Since $1-\lambda=(k_\lambda-1)/(k_\lambda+1)$, (4.1) can be rewritten in terms of k_λ

$$D_j = D_0\left(\frac{k_\lambda-1}{k_\lambda+1}\right)^j - \frac{2}{k_\lambda+1}\sum_{i=1}^{j}\varepsilon_i\left(\frac{k_\lambda-1}{k_\lambda+1}\right)^{j-i}$$

Setting aside the error term, for a while, after j adjustments $((k_\lambda-1)/(k_\lambda+1))^j$ of the initial deviation will remain. This expression can be approximated as follows,

$$\left(\frac{k_\lambda-1}{k_\lambda+1}\right)^j \approx e^{-2j/k_\lambda}$$

For example, if $j=k_\lambda$, about 13.5% of the initial deviation will remain ($1/e^2 \approx 0.135$, where e is the natural logarithm base). Similarly, if $j \approx k_\lambda/2$, about 37%, or $1/e$, of the initial deviation will remain. These approximations are correct for large k_λ but they are very good -- although slightly conservative -- for small k_λ. For example, with $k_\lambda=4$ (leading to $\lambda=2/5$), after 2 adjustments, only 36% of the initial deviation remains, and after 4 adjustments only 13% remain. Suppose now that we'd like to know the number of necessary adjustments to reduce the initial error to a fraction f, j_f, then

$$j_f \geq \frac{\ln f}{\ln(k-1)-\ln(k+1)} = \frac{\ln f}{\ln((k-1)/(k+1))} \approx \frac{-k\ln f}{2}$$

For example, for $f=5\%$ we obtain $j_{0.05} \approx 3k_\lambda/2$.

Look now at the stochastic error due to the error terms ε_1 through ε_j. If $Var(\varepsilon_i)=\sigma^2$ for all i (where measurement errors are included in the process error, but we assume exact adjustments), then to obtain the variance of the error term we need to square the coefficients $\lambda(1-\lambda)^{j-i}$, add them, and multiply by σ^2. The squared coefficients form a decreasing geometric series which leads to

$$Var = \frac{\sigma^2\lambda}{2-\lambda}(1-(1-\lambda)^{2j}) = \frac{\sigma^2}{k_\lambda}\left(1-\left(\frac{k-1}{k_\lambda+1}\right)^{2j}\right)$$

where if j goes to infinity we remain with $\sigma^2\lambda/(2-\lambda)=\sigma^2/k_\lambda$, and the variance increases with j towards this limit. This, by the way, is an algebraic proof of Brown's result $k_\lambda=(2-\lambda)/\lambda$ (he chose to use transformations instead). Due to the central limit theorem, for large j and small λ the error term has an approximately normal distribution. As a rule, this applies in our context. But, at least theoretically, with large λ, and if the distribution of ε is far from normal, the exponentially smoothed error term may not be approximately normal. This is because ε_j (the last term) can be dominant. For this reason we *cannot* say that the distribution of the exponentially smoothed adjustment is identical to that of the average of the last k_λ items. The latter is better approximated by the normal. Be that as it may, our *EQL* calculations do not require normality.

Thus, even if we set $\lambda = 1/3$, and the process is essentially stable, the additional *EQL* because of this adjustment will be minute: for a basic Shewhart chart with $n=5$, *at worst* it's equivalent to using samples of 25 to adjust (for low j our error variance is smaller); applying the results of Section 4.2.5, we can show that this adds less than 0.4% to the production cost relative to perfect adjustment (much less if the process is highly capable). For $C_p \geq 1.5$, even with individual items, the same high $\lambda = 1/3$ will only cause an average loss of 1% of the production cost, or less. A similar result applies for lower C_p if we specify $\lambda = 1/6$, which limits the average loss to 1% or less for $C_p \geq 1$. These claims are substantiated in Subsection 4.2.5, where we show that the results of fractional adjustment with these λ values are similar to the results of the five/ten rule.

Using λ between 0.04 and 0.1 may suit a very stable process, or one where the adjustment is automatic and very frequent. Nonetheless, we should avoid adjustments that are too small relative to the adjustment error (Subsection 4.2.3.3). As a rule of thumb, useful adjustments should exceed $2\sigma_C$, where σ_C is the adjustment error. So we cannot decrease λ below 0.04 unless our adjustment error is negligible (even 0.04 may be too small).

The advantage of fractional adjustment is that in return for a small and bounded increase in *EQL* (relative to a perfectly centered and stable process) we get protection against possible drifts. Any small drift will be counteracted on an ongoing basis. The correction will not be full, but it will limit the damage. The next technical note shows that if the mean drift between adjustments is d, there will be a consistent average adjustment bias of $d(2-\lambda)/(2\lambda) = k_\lambda d/2$.

=-

Technical Note:

Ignoring error terms (which have no bearing here, since fractional adjustment is additive), let's examine the deviation in the process following the last adjustment in a long series. Looking backwards, many previous periods contributed a deviation of d each. These deviations were counteracted partly over time, so if we look i periods back the remaining deviation from that period is $d(1-\lambda)^{i+1}$. The sum of all these is a geometric series that converges to $d/\lambda - d$. With this bias we produce some items until the next adjustment. By the next adjustment the bias will have grown by d, to d/λ. Therefore, the average bias over any period is $d/\lambda - d/2 = d(2-\lambda)/(2\lambda) = k_\lambda d/2$.

A way to check the result is to assume *some* consistent bias after adjustment: x. The bias before adjustment, then, must be $x+d$. This leads to the equation $(x+d)(1-\lambda)=x$, and the solution is $x=d/\lambda - d$, as before.

=-

To reduce this bias, we can adjust more frequently (decrease d), or use a higher λ (decrease k_λ), or both. But if we simply want to hedge against possible small drifts, the cost in terms of *EQL* is small. In short, we should treat this as a prudent safety measure. While purists may still call this "tampering," the result is a relatively centered process that will show statistical control on Shewhart charts as long as there is no special cause of a different nature. As we discuss later, however, it is important not to adjust more frequently than the natural process feedback delay; i.e., after an adjustment, we must let the process stabilize before we adjust again.

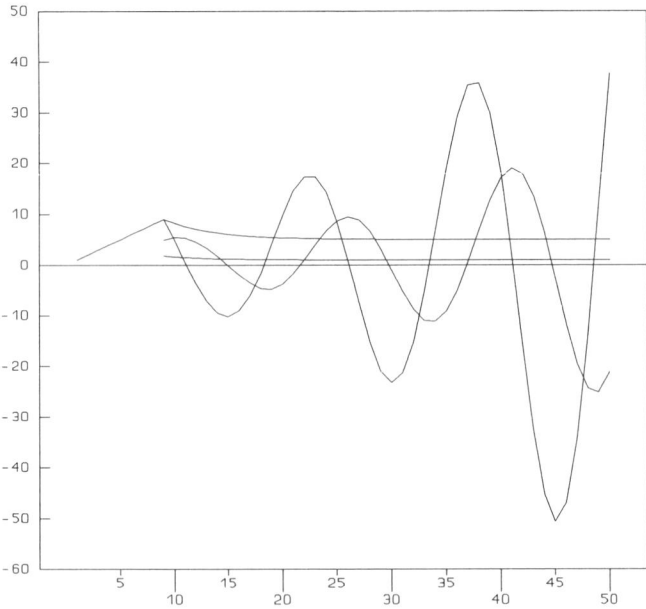

Fig. 4.2. Fractional adjustment corrects for drift, but adjusting by moving averages creates explosive fluctuations instead.

In forecasting -- where most exponential smoothing applications occur -- an identical result holds when we use the moving average of the last k_λ items (assuming k_λ is integer). Thus, every period, our forecast is the average of the last k_λ periods. To update a moving average forecast we add $(1/k)^{th}$ of the current result and subtract $(1/k)^{th}$ of the one taken $k+1$ periods ago. This equivalency of bias in the presence of a drift -- the *lagging* -- constitutes another equivalence between exponential smoothing and using a sample of k_λ items. Figures 6.19 through 6.22 provide visual evidence how similar the results can be. But for adjustment, a simplistic application of moving averages yields surprising results. Figure 4.2 demonstrates: A process with a drift of 1 unit per period is allowed to run for nine periods, at which time we initiate fractional adjustment with $\lambda = 0.2$ ($k_\lambda = 9$). The line closest to the x axis portrays the adjustments, and the line above it shows the result (before each adjustment). The process converges with a constant average bias of 4.5 (4 after each adjustment and 5 before the next one), as asserted. In contrast, the wavy line that starts at the tenth period is the adjustment by moving averages, and the even more volatile line shows the process results. The deviations grow in an explosive rate. The reason for this is that our corrections are much larger, analogous to $\lambda > 1$. With $\lambda < 1$ we obtain a calming exponential decay of errors, but with $\lambda > 1$ we obtain an explosive exponential growth of errors. This is much worse than Rule 3, where the pendulum motion grows slowly, and it may reverse completely after a long time (and start again); here, the growth is strong and consistent.

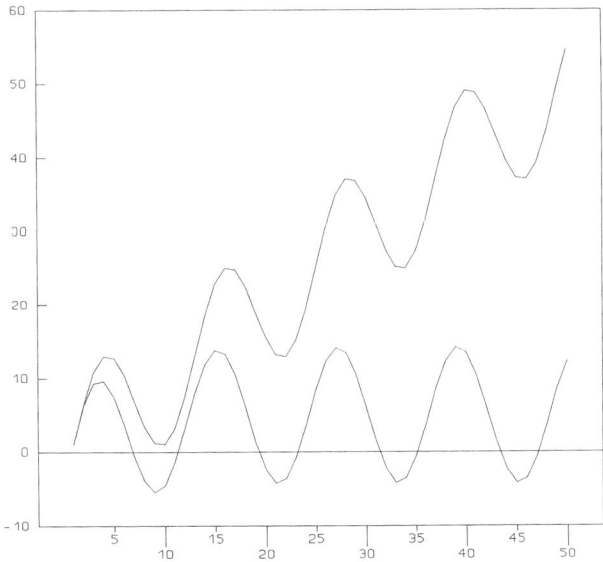

Fig. 4.3. Fractional adjustment may amplify high-frequency fluctuations slightly.

There are differences between using exponential smoothing for forecasting and using fractional adjustment. In the former the result is always a smoother sequence than the data. In contrast, Figure 4.3 shows the results of fractional adjustment on a highly fluctuating process with a drift. The adjustment takes care of the drift (with a bias, as discussed above), but it actually amplifies the fluctuations (although only slightly). These fluctuations are very frequent relative to k_λ, so there is not enough sampling to correct the adjustment. As for the amplification, it cannot be large: it happens because the adjustment corrections lag the data, so they may act exactly when *not* necessary. But, for the same reason, the correction is a fraction of the process fluctuation, so the effect cannot be large. To avoid the problem, each cycle of the fluctuation must be sampled many times. Figure 4.4 shows the same process, with the same λ, but now we adjust 10 times more often. Here, only a fraction of the fluctuations remains. By increasing the sampling we can reduce it further.

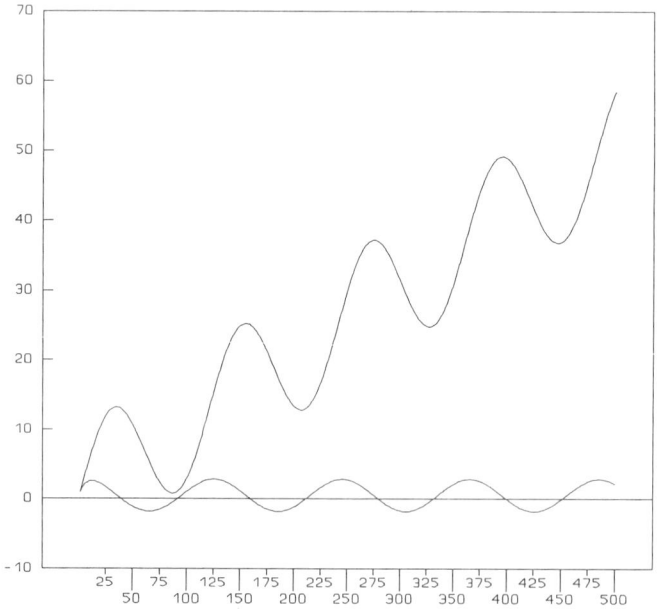

Fig. 4.4. Fractional adjustment dampens low-frequency fluctuations.

Nonetheless, frequent adjustments are not a panacea. Forrester (1961) demonstrated that feedback delays can cause strong fluctuations. This applies to fractional adjustment as well, and if we adjust more frequently we may even exacerbate the problem. Fractional adjustment, to be effective, assumes that we measure the full influence of previous adjustments before making the next correction. This implies that if there is a delay between the adjustment and the measurement, we should not adjust again during the delay. For example, if there is a delay of 3 seconds between the time we adjust the shower tap and the time the water reaches the nozzle, we should not readjust more frequently than every three seconds. Figure 4.5 demonstrates the same process as that of Figure 4.4, except now there is a delay. There are eight adjustments during the delay, all based on old influences. As the figure shows, the adjustment is highly volatile. Decreasing the delay is the best remedy: measure as close to the source as possible. Postponing adjustments is a must when the delay cannot be designed away. If necessary, it's safer to increase λ than to increase the frequency. If we ignore this, then adjustment of a process in control *is* tampering, reckless tampering.

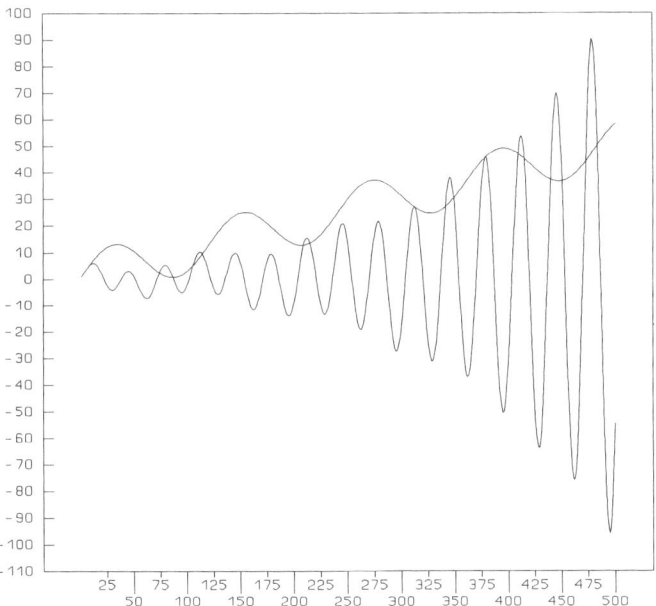

Fig. 4.5. Fractional adjustment during feedback delays may cause explosive fluctuations.

In Figure 4.5 we can also see that for a while the process behaves in a disorderly way. Figure 4.6 depicts a case where there are seven adjustments during the delay period (instead of eight). Here, the disorderly behavior continues throughout.

Finally, on the one hand, if we know by experience that the process is completely stable, ongoing adjustment is not necessary. A fully stable process is the exception and not the rule, however. On the other hand, when the drift is known and large, Section 4.3

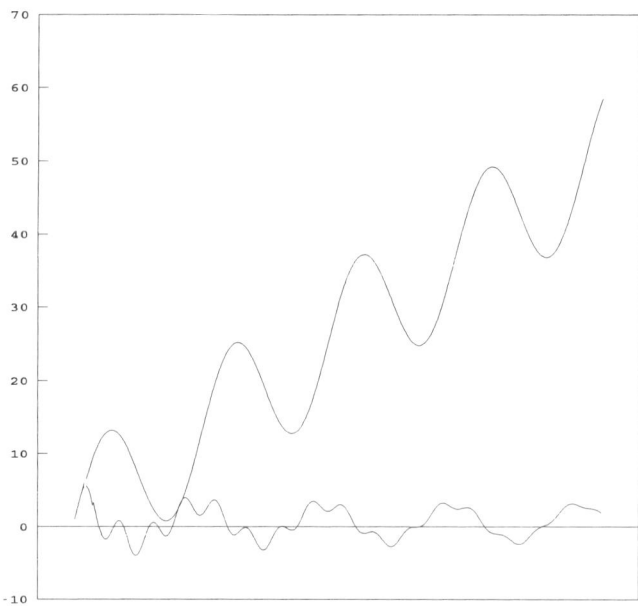

Fig. 4.6. Disorderly behavior with fractional adjustment.

suggests better ways to deal with it. True, exponential smoothing models with trend correction can compensate for a large drift. These models typically include one series to estimate the drift and another to estimate the mean.[4] Using them for adjustment is not recommended, because it is next to impossible to tell apart adjustment errors from changes in the drift. Also, they are not as simple and attractive to workers, but this would not be a problem in a computerized environment.

4.2.2. The Harmonic Adjustment Rule

Introduced by Frank Grubbs in 1954, the harmonic adjustment rule is so named here after the harmonic sequence $\{1, 1/2, 1/3, ..., 1/m, ...\}$. Its basic version states that when we adjust a process based on a sample of items, we should adjust after the first item to offset its full deviation from the target; after the second item we counteract one half of its deviation; in general, after the mth item, given the deviation $e_m = x_m - T$, we adjust by $-e_m/m$. It is also possible to use sample means instead of individual results

---

[4]Gardner (1985) is perhaps the safest source for trend-correction methods. Gardner (1984) demonstrates that not all other sources are sound: authors of dozens of books, articles and software packages copied from each other an EQL-increasing error.

while applying the rule; e.g., if we use subgroups, then after the mth subgroup we adjust by $-(\overline{x}_m-T)/m$, where $\overline{x}_m$ is the mean of the mth subgroup. The adjustment is considered adequate upon one of the following: (i) a few (say three) consecutive items are so close to target that the process cannot be adjusted (e.g., if a machine can be adjusted in steps of 1 mm, and the thirteenth through fifteenth items have deviations of 5, 4, and 6mm, we need to adjust by $-5/13$, $-4/14$, and $-6/15$, all of which are too small); (ii) a preestablished number of items, n (say 5, 10, or 25), have been sampled and adjusted for.

The rule applies to machine adjustments, firing at targets, calibrating instruments, etc. The setup variance may be unknown, and we assume that the first adjustment will likely be an improvement in spite of its relatively large error potential. Removing this assumption Grubbs obtained a model we call the *extended harmonic rule*. Let $S = \sigma_X^2/\sigma_A^2$, where σ_X^2 is the process variance and σ_A^2 is the variance of the setup, then the optimal adjustment sequence now becomes $\{1/(1+S), 1/(2+S), 1/(3+S), ..., 1/(m+S), ...\}$. If we use samples of j items each, S should be divided by j. A useful way to think about the effect of S is to imagine that we enter the former adjustment process in midstream, after S adjustments have been carried out already. Using a *new* count, the basic harmonic rule suggests that after the mth item we should adjust by $1/(m+S)$. Although S need not be integer, the extended rule really describes the same procedure.

The final result of the (extended) rule is identical to a single adjustment by the average deviation (the sum of the deviations divided by $m+S$). But the rule also minimizes *EQL during* the sampling process. Furthermore, Subsection 4.2.3 shows that using the rule is more robust than using a single adjustment, unless we specify a too large n.

Grubbs did not say how to determine n, but if we know the coefficient of the quadratic loss function, K; the process variance, σ_X^2; the cost to measure an item and adjust the process, M; and the batch size, N, then the optimal n is given by

$$n = \left[\frac{M/(K\sigma_X^2) - 1 + \sqrt{(M/(K\sigma_X^2)-1)^2 + 4(N+S)M/(K\sigma_X^2)}}{2M/(K\sigma_X^2)} - S \right] \qquad (4.2)$$

To derive (4.2) consider that the nth item reduces the expected quadratic bias loss for the remainder of the batch from $K\sigma_X^2(N-n)/(n+S-1)$ to $K\sigma_X^2(N-n)/(n+S)$. To justify sampling the nth item, this reduction must exceed the marginal cost, M. This yields a quadratic inequality. (4.2) gives the largest n that satisfies it. But we assume that adjustments are exact. Otherwise, n should be smaller (Subsection 4.2.3.1). By setting $S=0$, (4.2) applies to the basic harmonic rule.

4.2.2.1. Numerical example

Table 4.1 provides the details for a particular numerical example using the basic rule ($S=0$). The process has an initial deviation, D_0, of 12 units. In addition, variation causes individual relative deviations, ϵ_i, listed in the second column. The third column shows the anticipated results without adjustments; e.g., the first result is 9, which includes an initial deviation of 12 and an error of $\epsilon_1=-3$, and unless we adjust first, the second result would be $12+2=14$. The fourth column shows the cumulated deviations of Column 2. The fifth column shows $e_i=x_i-T$, the deviation from target of each item when the rule *is* applied. The sixth column shows the adjustment according to the rule. The seventh column shows the deviation remaining in the process *after* the adjustment, D_i. The eighth column shows the cumulated individual relative deviations, and the ninth column shows the cumulated error divided by the number of items. The seventh and the ninth columns have the same magnitude, but opposite signs. This demonstrates that after m steps the adjustment is as if we'd used a sample of m. The tenth and eleventh columns are discussed in Subsection 4.2.4.

i	ϵ_i	$D_0+\epsilon_i$	Σ	e_i	$-e_i/i$	D_i	$\Sigma\epsilon_i$	$\Sigma\epsilon_i/i$	$D_3+\epsilon_i$	$\Sigma(D_3+\epsilon_i)$
1	-3	9	9	9	-9	3	-3	-3		
2	2	14	23	5	-2.5	0.5	-1	-0.5		
3	7	19	42	7.5	-2.5	-2	6	2		
4	-4	8	50	-6	1.5	-0.5	2	0.5	-6	-6
5	3	15	65	2.5	-0.5	-1	5	1	1	-5
6	1	13	78	0	0	-1	6	1	-1	-6
7	-1	11	89	-2	2/7	-5/7	5	5/7	-3	-9

Cumulated Adj.:   -89/7

Table 4.1

The final deviation, after the seventh adjustment, is shown at the bottom of the seventh column: $-5/7$. The cumulated adjustment, shown below the sixth column, is $-89/7$. Suppose now that we decide to only adjust the process after the seven items were produced. The sum of the deviations would be 89, as per the last entry in the fourth column, and we'd adjust by $-89/7$. Thus, at the end, our situation would be identical to the outcome of the harmonic rule.

To see the advantage of applying the rule here, compare the fifth and the third columns (with and without the rule, respectively). The sum of squares for the fifth column is 208.5 (and almost 40% of that is contributed by the first item, whose deviation cannot be reduced); for the third column, without the rule, the sum of squares is almost six times larger: 1217.

4.2.3. *The Robustness of the Harmonic Rule*

In this subsection we summarize results of Trietsch (1997), where proofs and further details are given. Our aim is to examine the results of the rule when adjustments are not exact. This can manifest in two major ways. First, the adjustment itself always has an inherent variance, or imprecision. When this variance is sizable relative to the last adjustments, continuing the procedure may become worse than useless. Second, the machine may be calibrated inaccurately, and when we think we adjust by, say, 2mm, we actually adjust by 2.4 or 1.6mm (a relative bias of $B=0.2$ or $B=-0.2$). Such a bias may change frequently, so it may not always be preventable. Finally, inaccuracy and imprecision can be analyzed together (but in this summary we omit the details).

4.2.3.1. *Imprecise adjustment*

Suppose that when we intend to adjust by y units, the real adjustment is $y+\epsilon_C$, where $E(\epsilon_C) = 0$, and $Var(\epsilon_C) = \sigma_C^2 > 0$ (so adjustments are accurate but imprecise). If we employ the extended harmonic rule for this case, then the expected quadratic bias after sampling n items will be

$$\frac{\sigma_x^2}{n+S} + \frac{n^3/3+n^2/2+n/6+n(n+1)S+nS^2}{(n+S)^2}\sigma_C^2$$

where if we set $S=0$, the result applies to the basic harmonic rule. While the first element decreases with n, the second increases. Thus, there is a limit to how much we can adjust with the harmonic rule! Specifically, by taking the derivative we can see that if

$$\frac{2n^3 - n + 6Sn^2 + 6S^2n + 6S^3 + 6S^2 + S}{6(n+S)} \sigma^2_C \geq \sigma^2_x \qquad (4.3)$$

and there always exist n large enough to satisfy this inequality, then using the nth item will *increase* the *EQL*. To understand this, consider that as we increase n the expected size of the last adjustment decreases, approaching zero asymptotically. But the adjustment error applies in full force. Thus, for large n, the effect of the last adjustments is similar to adding the sum of several random variables, with zero expectation, but non-zero variance (creating a random walk, similar to the results of Funnel Rule 4). The limit presented in (4.3) shows when the variance reduction of the harmonic rule is smaller than the marginal additional variance due to the cumulative effect of the σ_C^2 elements. Add to this the cost of sampling and adjusting, and it is clear that n should be even smaller. Specifically, n as per (4.2) is too large because it ignores the detrimental effect of σ_C^2.

Nonetheless, because the problem is associated with adjustments rather than with measurements, we can ameliorate it by skipping small adjustments, and perhaps even postponing larger adjustments. Subsection 4.2.4 shows how to do this.

4.2.3.2. Inaccurate adjustment

When the adjustment is precise, but inaccurate (biased), we investigate two scenarios. Under the first, the setup variance is known and compensated for -- using the extended rule. Under the second, the basic rule is used instead. Figure 4.7 shows the *EQL* after using the extended harmonic rule based on $n=5$ items with $\sigma_x^2=1$ and a loss coefficient of 1. B in the figure is the adjustment bias, and its range is between -0.5 (adjusting by half the intended amount) and 1 (adjusting by twice the intended amount). The range of S is 0.25 to 4. As long as $|B|$ is not larger than about 0.2 the relative increase in expected loss is not large. Almost everywhere in the range of the figure the expected loss is less than twice the nominal loss without bias.

To study the extended rule, it is more pertinent to compare its *EQL* to that of a single adjustment with the same bias. Figure 4.8 shows this ratio. Note the ridge of 1 at $B=0$: without bias a single adjustment is equivalent to the harmonic rule (except for losses incurred during the sampling itself). Elsewhere, the extended harmonic rule is consistently superior, especially for small S.

Nonetheless, it is not reasonable to expect most workers to use the extended harmonic rule in practice. It involves estimating S for every single process and it is slightly

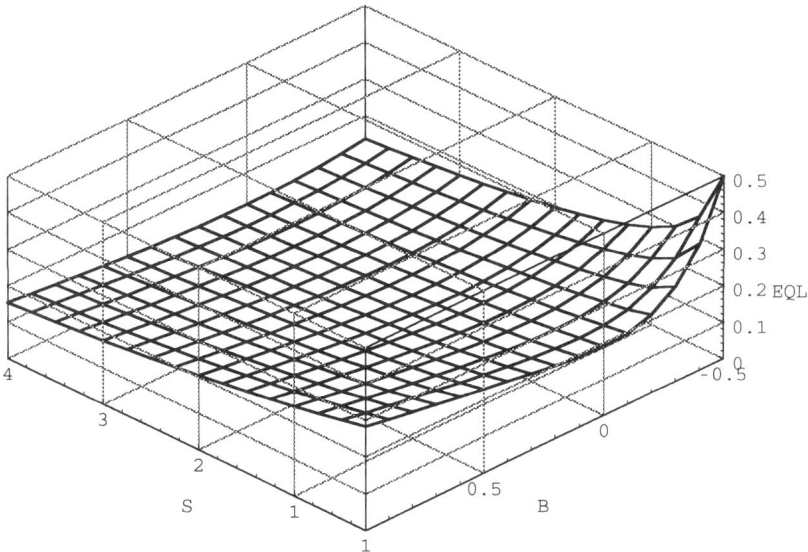

Fig. 4.7. EQL after following the extended harmonic rule ($n=5$).

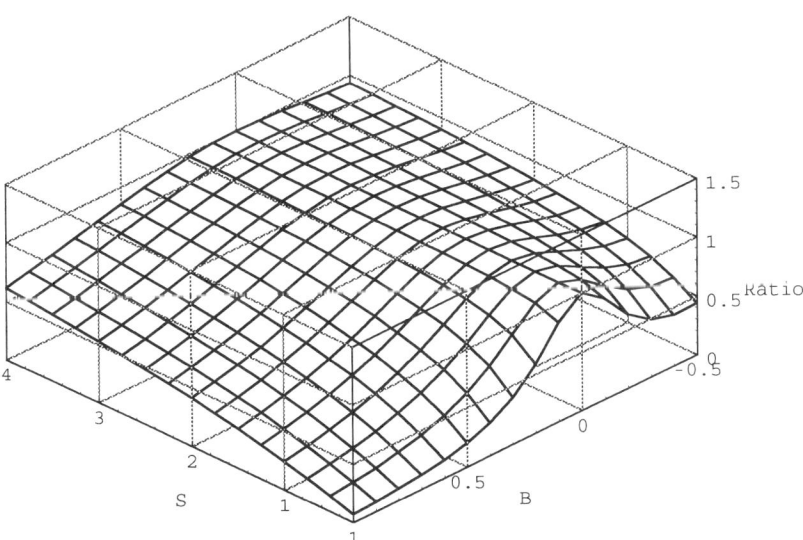

Fig. 4.8. The ratio between the EQL with the extended harmonic rule and a single adjustment ($n=5$).

more difficult to apply. Therefore we should investigate the results of the (basic) harmonic rule with an adjustment bias. Figures 4.9 and 4.10 are analogous to Figures 4.7 and 4.8, except that we do not correct the adjustments for S.

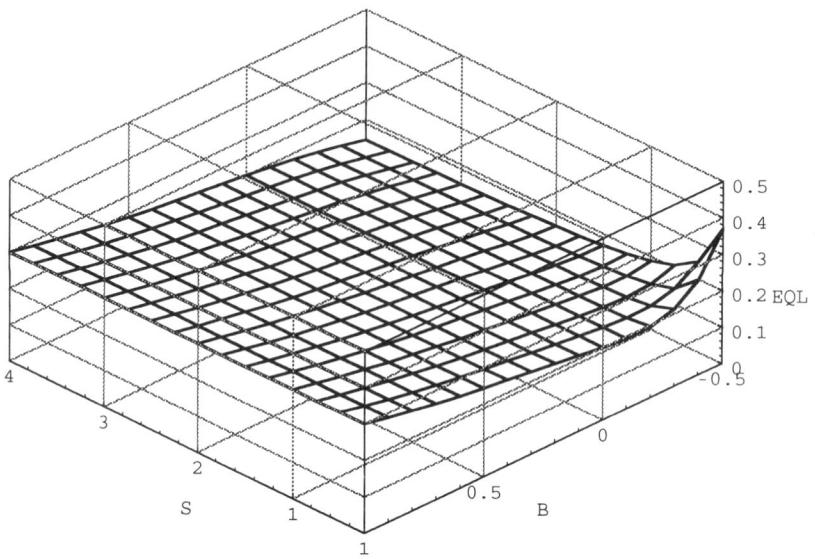

Fig. 4.9. EQL following the basic harmonic rule ($n=5$).

In studying Figure 4.9 we see that for $B=0$ we get a constant, 0.2. This should be expected because without bias the rule is equivalent to using a sample average (here, of 5 units). For $B=1$ the loss is also constant, 0.3, and the figure shows that for every positive bias the loss is practically constant for all S. This is not the case for negative biases, however. In Figure 4.10 we again see a constant value of 1 for $B=0$, as should be expected, but now we also see that for large S and small negative B there is an advantage to a single adjustment (i.e., the ratio shown in the figure exceeds 1). Returning to Figure 4.9, however, we see that this occurs where the loss under the harmonic rule is especially low, and therefore it should not concern us that it may be inflated a bit (in the range of the figure the inflation is always below 50%). The explanation is that with large S we *should* adjust by less, and the negative bias yields an effectively smaller adjustment. Finally, both Figures 4.8 and 4.10 show that for low S the harmonic rule is especially beneficial relative to a single adjustment. The figures are quite similar to each other there because with low S the rules do not differ much. Similar results for $n=10$ are even better in two ways: (i) the expected

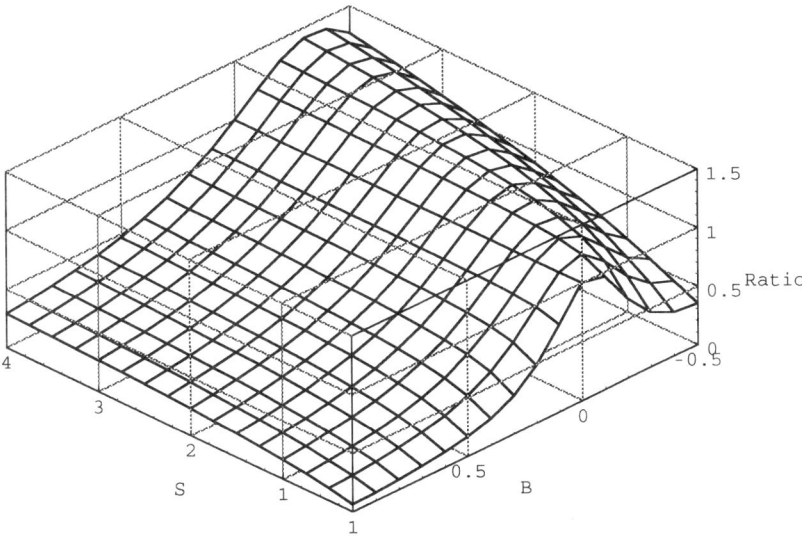

1.5

1

0.5 Ratio

0

-0.5

4

3

2

S

1

0.5

B

0

1

Fig. 4.10. The ratio between the EQL with the basic harmonic rule and a single adjustment ($n=5$).

remaining loss is roughly halved; (ii) the relative advantage of using the harmonic rule is more pronounced.

4.2.3.3. *A comparison with fractional adjustment*

In principle, fractional adjustment may also suffer from problems of imprecision and inaccuracy. To prevent the former, we should avoid specifying λ too low. However, if λ is not too small, fractional adjustment is robust against both types of problems. Biased adjustments effectively change λ to $(1+B)\lambda$, but they do not lead to any bias in the final result. If $1+B>1/\lambda$, however, we get an effective $\lambda>1$, which causes wild fluctuations (as in Figure 4.2); one more reason why λ should not be too large. Imprecisions influence future deviations, and hence they will be counteracted eventually. With the harmonic rule, as n increases, the adjustments become minute regardless of the deviations. In contrast, with fractional adjustment a relatively large deviation continues to entail a relatively large adjustment.

To achieve both small *EQL* and robustness, calls for using subgroups (to combine adjustments). For example, for a given k_λ that applies without subgroups, if we use subgroups of $j \leq k_\lambda$, we can decrease k_λ to $(1/j)^{th}$ of its former value without changing the theoretical adjustment variance. By decreasing k_λ we increase λ, and with it we increase the average adjustment.

4.2.4. *The Generalized Harmonic Rule*

Returning to the harmonic rule without bias, recall that Grubbs included a version where the sample is divided to equal subgroups, with one adjustment for each. This procedure can be considered a special case of the following skipping procedure, also introduced by Trietsch (1997). Suppose we adjust after the kth item and then skip $m-1$ adjustments, then the optimal adjustment after the $(k+m)^{th}$ item is by $-1/(m+k+S)\Sigma_{i=k+1,k+m}e_i$ (i.e., minus the sum of the last m deviations divided by $m+k+S$). The extended harmonic rule is a special case where $m=1$ (for $k=0$, 1, 2, ..., $n-1$). The basic harmonic rule is a special case with $m=1$ (for $k=0$, 1, 2, ..., $n-1$) and $S=0$. If we set $k=0$ we obtain the correct single adjustment for a sample of m items.

This makes possible skipping small adjustments without loss of information. To demonstrate, return to Table 4.1, and suppose we decide to adjust only after the third and seventh items ($k=3$, $m=4$, $S=0$). After the first three items we'd have a cumulated error of 42 units, so we'd adjust by $-42/3=-14$. The next four items, listed in the tenth column, would now include a deviation of $D_3=-2$, as per the third value in the seventh column. The cumulated deviations of the last four items would be -9, as shown in the eleventh column listing the cumulated deviations following the adjustment. Dividing by 7 (*not* by 4), and reversing the sign we obtain the necessary remaining correction of 9/7. The final total adjustment is the same: $-14+9/7=-89/7$.

As another example of skipping adjustments without losing information take the sequence mentioned above where the thirteenth through fifteenth deviations are 5, 4, and 6mm. Even though each of these alone does not justify an adjustment, we can adjust by $-(5+4+6)/15=-1$mm. Grubbs' original recommendation was to stop the adjustment process upon such a sequence. The change recommended here is to consider a final adjustment before moving on to regular production. It's also possible to continue sampling for a while, especially if the optimal n is much larger than 15.

The skipping procedure is especially important when we consider that in reality adjustments are at least somewhat imprecise. We saw that when adjustments are accurate but imprecise there exists a value n such that increasing the sample beyond it increases *EQL* instead of decreasing it. To avoid this we can simply skip small adjustments. The skipping procedure serves to avoid losing information.

Ignoring the beneficial robustness of the harmonic rule, for a while, using too many small adjustments has a detrimental effect, and since each adjustment may also have an economic cost beyond the measurement cost, we should look for ways to skip adjustments as a rule, and not just when they are patently too small. This is equivalent to measuring subgroups of items for each adjustment. But the subgroups need not be equal: Trietsch (1995d) optimized their sizes by a shortest-route network model. He then showed that they tend to grow at a geometrical rate, which leads to the following near-optimal algorithm: Let M_1 denote the cost of measuring an item, and let M_2 denote the cost of the actual adjustment (our former M is M_1+M_2).[5] Assume we make m adjustments, and our complete batch has N items. Let $n_0:=S$, $n_{m+1}:=S+N$, and define n_k ($k=1, 2,\ldots, m$) as S plus the number of the item on which we make the kth adjustment. (Thus, the variables n_k are analogous to our former $k+S$ which we used for division.) Let $\overline{n}$ denote an upper bound on n_m. The algorithm proceeds in iterative stages. At each stage we determine one decision variable, e.g., at stage k we determine a good integer value for $n_k-S=n_k-n_0$ (based on n_{k-1}). This involves (i) updating the recommended number of remaining adjustments, m_k (*not* by simply subtracting one); (ii) updating the value of the projected n_m (which may change slightly between stages); (iii) updating the desired ratio between successive n_j values, q_k (from n_k/n_{k-1} onwards); (iv) finding the nearest integer to $n_{k-1}q_k-n_0$ and setting n_k to this value *plus* n_0, subject to $n_k \geq n_{k-1}+1$. In more detail:

0.   (Initialization) Set $k:=1$; $n_0=\sigma_X^2/\sigma_D^2$, but if n_0 is very small we may opt to adjust by the full amount of the first deviation and set $n_0:=0$; $n_1:=1$; $k:=2$; solve numerically for $\overline{n}$ by

$$\overline{n} = \sqrt{\frac{K\sigma_X^2(N+n_0)}{M_1+\dfrac{K\sigma_X^2}{\overline{n}-1}}}$$

and solve numerically for q_A, the base ratio between successive adjustments, by

$$q_A = \arg\left\{\frac{M_2}{K\sigma_X^2}-1 = q_A(\ln(q_A)-1)\right\}$$

1.   Let m_k be the tentative number of remaining adjustments

---

[5]It is important to make sure that M_2 will only include real marginal costs that will be saved for every adjustment that we can avoid, and spent on every adjustment we may add. It is not appropriate to load general overhead onto M_2. A similar observation applies to M_1.

$$m_k = \text{ROUND}\left[\frac{\ln(\bar{n}) - \ln(n_{k-1})}{\ln(q_A)}\right]$$

2.   Let n_{last} denote the tentative value of the last adjustment

$$n_{\text{last}} = \sqrt{\frac{K\sigma_X^2(N+n_0)}{M_1 + \dfrac{K\sigma_X^2}{n_{k-1}\left(\dfrac{n_{\text{last}}}{n_{k-1}}\right)^{\frac{m_k-1}{m_k}}}}}$$

3.   Let q_k be the desired ratio between n_k and n_{k-1}

$$q_k = \left(\frac{n_{\text{last}}}{n_{k-1}}\right)^{\frac{1}{m_k}}$$

4.   Let

$$n_k = \text{Max}\{\text{ROUND}[n_{k-1}q_k - n_0] + n_0,\ n_{k-1}+1\}$$

5.   If $m_k = 1$, STOP; otherwise, set $k := k+1$ and return to Step 1.

This provides a static plan in the sense that adjustments are performed at predetermined intervals. The adjustment that follows the $(n_k\text{-}S)^{\text{th}}$ item is by minus the sum of deviations since the former adjustment (or since the start, if this is the first adjustment), divided by n_k. Small adjustments should be skipped, thus providing a dynamic flavor to the rule (as in the original harmonic rule, but here we do not lose the information). Dividing the sum of the deviations since the last adjustment by n_k satisfies the skipping procedure.

4.2.4.1. Numerical example

Let $N = 10000$, $M_1 = 0.5K\sigma_X^2$, $M_2 = 0.25K\sigma_X^2$, $S = 1$ (which often occurs when the setup includes producing a trial unit and adjusting to compensate for its deviation). At the initialization step we set $n_0 = 1$, $k = 1$ and we obtain $\bar{n} = 140.42$ and $q_A = 1.786275$. To wit,

$$140.42 \approx \sqrt{\frac{10000 + 1}{0.5 + \dfrac{1}{140.42 - 1}}}$$

$$0.25 - 1 \approx 1.786275 \, (\ln 1.786275 - 1)$$

At Step 1 we obtain

$$m_1 = \text{ROUND}\left[\frac{\ln 140.42 - \ln 1}{\ln 1.786275}\right] = \text{ROUND}[8.52] = 9$$

At Step 2 we obtain $n_{\text{last}} = 139.71$. This leads, in Step 3, to $q_k = 1.7312$. Multiplying by n_0 and rounding, in Step 4, we obtain $n_1 = 2$ (i.e., adjusting after the first item by half its deviation). Setting $k = 2$ we return to Step 1 for a second iteration.

Starting the second iteration,

$$m_2 = ROUND\left[\frac{\ln 140.42 - \ln 2}{\ln 1.786275}\right] = ROUND\,[7.134] = 7$$

Remarkably, m_2 is not equal to $m_1 - 1$. Although this is rare, it is why we update m at each iteration. To continue, n_{last} is now 139.61 leading to $q_2 = 1.8341$. Multiplying by $n_1 = 2$ and rounding we obtain $n_2 = 4$, and so on. Table 4.2 summarizes the results of the procedure in this case. The last column in the table provides the global optimal solution. The variable part of the objective function is 0.000054 higher under the heuristic solution, i.e., it is practically unchanged. (In all the other examples in Trietsch [1995] the heuristic yields the globally optimal solution.)

Based on this, and similar results, it's permissible to omit Step 2 after the first time (and use 139.71 throughout). Even replacing n_{last} by $\overline{n}$ is possible here, but it can lead to small errors if M_2 is very large. The sum of the measurement and adjustment costs, and the *EQL* due to adjustment bias (which, together, constitute the variable part of the objective function), is 148.79. In this case, had we utilized the harmonic rule (with optimal n and assuming exact adjustments), the comparable value would be 176.78. The difference is quite small because we specified a low M_2 value in this example. But the example shows that even with low M_2, we actually use very few adjustments per measurement (about 1/18 here). This is typically the case: the number of adjustments tends to be low. In addition, the geometric progression assures that adjustments will not tend to be very small. Thus, it's highly likely

Stage	m_k	n_{last}	q_k	n_i	n_i^*
1	9	139.71	1.7312	2	2
2	7	139.61	1.8341	4	4
3	6	139.63	1.8078	7	7
4	5	139.62	1.8196	13	13
5	4	139.63	1.8103	24	24
6	3	139.64	1.7986	43	43
7	2	139.64	1.8021	77	78
8	1	139.63	1.8133	140	140

Table 4.2

that this algorithm will not involve a sizable deterioration due to σ_C^2. Furthermore, had we forced the solution to include 9 adjustments the variable part of the objective function would grow to 148.81, with n_i values of 2, 3, 5, 9, 16, 28, 48, 82, 140. Based on this example and similar ones, especially where the initial estimate of m has a fractional part close to 0.5, it would not make much of a difference if we chose to stick with the first value. So, near the optimum the solution is not sensitive to the number of adjustments. But when M_2 is larger the savings relative to the harmonic rule are much more substantial, and this in addition to ameliorating the problem of imprecise adjustments.

Finally, to a large extent this solution retains the robustness property that we showed in Section 4.2.3. Such robustness is associated with the number of adjustments: with more adjustments we are more sensitive to imprecision but less sensitive to inaccuracy. Stipulating 5 or 10 adjustments, to balance these two evils, may be a recommended approach. The only change in the algorithm for this purpose is that we don't need Step 1 to determine m_k; instead, we stipulate it for $k=0$ and reduce it by one in each iteration. In addition, skipping small adjustments adds robustness. When the adjustments required are small even after the pre-planned skipping, it is not likely that the former adjustments were biased; hence, with five to ten pre-planned adjustments *and* dynamic skipping, the procedure is especially robust against both bias and imprecision.

4.2.5. *The Five/Ten Rule*

As we've seen, given costs of measurement and of adjustment, it is possible to optimize the adjustment process. This may be appropriate when the adjustment is performed automatically, or if the number of items subsequently produced without further adjustment is very large. But it necessarily adds complexity, and complexity can be expensive. Here, following Trietsch (1997–98), we suggest a simple rule that bypasses the need to optimize n. Instead, we allow a small constrained loss, and minimize n subject to it.

Recall that expected quadratic loss of any distribution with a given variance and a given bias relative to target is

$$EQL = E(L) = K(\sigma^2 + bias^2)$$

where the loss due to bias and the loss due to variance are independent. Bias reduction and variance reduction are equally beneficial in reducing expected quadratic loss, and this remains true regardless of the process distribution. Nonetheless, reducing bias calls for adjustment, and such adjustment *must* be based on a sample. Therefore, variance reduction promotes bias reduction. Specifically, after adjusting by the average deviation of a sample of n, the expected loss per unit due to bias will be $K\sigma^2/n = c_0/(9nC_p^2)$.

Suppose now we are willing to tolerate an average loss due to adjustment of $K \cdot bias^2 = f \cdot c_0$ (say $f = 0.01$). So n should satisfy $f > 1/(9nC_p^2)$, i.e., $n > 1/(9fC_p^2)$. In particular, for $f = 0.01$ and $C_p > 1.054$ (or for $f = 0.0111$ and $C_p > 1$), $n = 10$ is adequate; for $f = 0.01$ and $C_p > 1.5$, $n = 5$ is adequate. But, by definition, c_0 is less or equal to the cost of production (with the equality holding when defective items are scrapped, and the inequality when we can rework them). Therefore, our results induce an expected loss that is bounded by about 1% of the cost of production or the cost of rework, whichever is less (or $100f\%$ in general).

Unless our process setup is really excellent -- which is usually true only for setups that do not require *any* adjustment -- we may wish to inspect at least five items just to see that the results are reasonable, so we should not decrease n further when C_p increases beyond 1.5. Instead, we'll get an expected loss of less than $0.01 \cdot c_0$. The same applies when the process capability is between 1.055 and 1.5. Thus the five/ten rule states that for capable processes with $C_p < 1.5$ we should sample ten units and adjust by their average deviation, while with $C_p \geq 1.5$, five will be sufficient.

During the sampling we can apply the harmonic rule. This will provide robustness against bias. Furthermore, since at most we adjust 10 times, imprecision is not likely to cause a sizable problem. For $n=10$ we can choose to skip the sixth through ninth adjustments, and this will provide us with a subgroup of 5 (items 6 through 10) that can be used to check that the dispersion is in control. Likewise, we can do the same with a sample of 5 if desired. Perhaps the only disadvantage of using the harmonic rule here for the full sample (of 5 or 10) is that it makes checking the dispersion prohibitively complex. See Trietsch (1997-98) for a discussion of various dispersion control options.

Finally, the results we obtained here for process setup also have implications for ongoing process adjustment. For example, if we use fractional adjustment with $\lambda = 1/3$, this is equivalent to using subgroups of $k_\lambda = (2 - 1/3)/(1/3) = 5$ units for each adjustment, so even using such a high λ does not cause large additional EQL if $C_p > 1.5$. Likewise, for lower C_p, $\lambda = 1/6$ is good for any reasonably capable process. This is equivalent to specifying subgroups of $(2 - 1/6)/(1/6) = 11$, which fits $C_p \geq 1$ (for $C_p = 1$ the average loss is $c_0/99$). If we use such λ on subgroup results, where each subgroup includes j items, we obtain an equivalent size of $k_\lambda j$. For example, if $j = 5$ the values of λ given are equivalent to using 25 or 50 items for adjustment. Since EQL is directly proportional to $1/(k_\lambda j)$ (with subgroups of j, or set $j = 1$ otherwise), we see that this recommendation is not expensive in terms of EQL. For example, using $\lambda = 1/3$ with subgroups of $j = 5$ and $C_p > 1.5$ implies an average loss of 0.2% or less. With $C_p = 1$, it is 0.4%.

4.2.6. Adjusting Processes with Highly Asymmetrical Loss Functions

Some workers and supervisors, when faced with tolerances that imply rework on one end and scrapping on the other, insist on "conservative" adjustments that tend to err on the "safe" side (more rework than scrapping). If we use one of the heuristics suggested in Supplement 3, it will be much better if they will learn to adjust to the recommended target without a preferred additional bias: these heuristics include a bias when necessary. But if there is not enough data to implement them, we may need other methods. Kelton et al. (1990) suggest such a method, but we do not recommend it. Instead, we show how to adapt fractional adjustment to this task.

Workers are loath to approach the target from the steep side, lest too many items will be scrapped. They are rarely concerned with reducing loss, but rather with falling within the tolerance limits. For that reason they are comfortable with results that are close to the tolerance limit from the "rework" side. Neave (1990) observed that this causes high variation in the output: some items are just within the limits, and they are accepted; others are just outside, and they are reworked -- usually in such a manner that they fall far from the same tolerance limit (since it is difficult to cut very small amounts). Thus, the end result is bimodal and has a high EQL.

Barring the use of the heuristic approach of Supplement 3, we need a "conservative" adjustment method that will tend to approach whichever target we select from the "safe" side, without remaining too near to the tolerance limit. Kelton et al. developed a single-adjustment method based on three keys: (i) adjustment is only performed after an "out of control" signal; (ii) upon such a signal a sample of k items is taken to provide information for the adjustment (the last point on the control chart is not used because it is statistically biased: we know the process showed out of control; all previous information is discarded as well); (iii) the adjustment is based on a confidence interval such that the probability of crossing the target to the undesired side is 5%. A critical assumption for this purpose is that the process is so highly capable that it can be continued without adjustment during the additional sampling without exceeding the tolerance limits. One may question whether we need so much caution with such a highly capable process that creates no defects even when out of control. Next, because they don't use the loss function concept, they are only concerned with conformance, which is why the loss during the additional sampling is ignored as long as, by assumption, no out-of-tolerance defects will occur. Finally, it is not certain at all that operators will accept this method, although one of its major motivations was to satisfy typical workers.

Interestingly enough, Kelton et al. noted specifically that workers are fond of fractional adjustment, and yet they did not choose to utilize it. With relatively stable processes (in contrast to the one depicted in Figure 4.3, for example), using fractional adjustment with low λ creates a narrow confidence interval for the adjustment, and this may be enough protection against over-adjustment. Thus, our ongoing adjustment scheme could replace their method. Furthermore, we could adjust after each and every item of the k items they recommend sampling for this purpose (although it would leave 13.5% of the deviation in place). If we do this, then $\lambda = 2/(k+1)$ is a reasonable choice. And because our λ should be small, using the out of control signal itself for the first adjustment should not be too risky, and can be recommended. Nonetheless, if we simply use fractional adjustment, in the long run, unless there is a consistent drift towards the "safe" direction, the process will be adjusted to both sides of the target equally often. If we really want to reduce the probability of over-adjustment, we should also include an "aim-off" factor away from the target in the "safe" direction, A. If we adopt the recommendation to allow crossing over in 5% of the cases, A should be

$$A = 1.645 \hat{\sigma} \sqrt{\frac{\lambda}{j(2-\lambda)}} \qquad (4.4)$$

where $\hat{\sigma}$ may be calculated when the control chart is prepared. This implies that when the deviation is in the "safe" direction we adjust by less than we would without the aim-off factor, and if it is in the "steep" direction we adjust by more. In both cases we're likely to adjust by less than the absolute value of the deviation. The formula assumes either a normal process or a small λ/j (which makes the exponentially smoothed deviation approximately normal for any process distribution). Specifying a relatively high λ implies a relatively large aim-off factor, but quicker correction of large adjustment errors. So there's a tradeoff here. A sound rule of thumb, when we don't use subgroups, is to select $\lambda = 1/12$. This is smaller than 1/6 as might be suggested by the five/ten rule because here the aim-off factor increases the *EQL* substantially. With $\lambda = 1/12$ our loss due to bias should rarely exceed $c_0/10$. With subgroups of $j = 5$, even $\lambda = 1/3$ is actually quite conservative, being similar to using a sample of 25 for adjustment. Compare to 5 or 10 which we recommended in the five/ten rule.

4.3. Setting Economical Tolerances for Processes with Drift

Here we discuss the question how to adjust a process with a constant drift under the assumption that our loss function is quadratic. Processes with drift are quite numerous. For instance, in machining, tool wear causes dimensions to drift between adjustments; in chemical processes the strength of reagents may change slowly, and impurities may accumulate. Sometimes it is economical to prevent the cause of the drift, but sometimes it should be addressed by periodic adjustment. For example, with today's technology, haircuts belong to the latter group: essentially they involve adjusting the length of hair so that over a period of time it will be acceptable.

The prevalent practice for processes with a drift is to adjust the process as near as possible to one specification limit without exceeding it, and then let it drift towards the other limit until just before excessive defects will be created there (AT&T, 1958). Using C_{pk}, this policy can be stated as starting with $C_{pk} = 1$ and allowing the process to drift as long as $C_{pk} \geq 1$ (C_{pk} will increase as the process drifts towards center and then it will decrease). Note that $C_p > 1$ is a necessary condition to make this scheme possible. With $C_p = 1$ we'll have to readjust for each and every item to avoid C_{pk} from falling below 1. Motorola, as another example, expects C_p values of 2 and allows C_{pk} to drop to 1.5. This implies that the process is allowed to drift up to 1.5 standard deviations from center. Without drift this implies that Motorola allows biases of up to 1.5 standard deviations.

Neave (1990) stated that once we accept the quadratic loss function as a more realistic alternative to the traditional one, the policy described above yields undesired and (for many) counterintuitive results. Table 4.3 summarizes Neave's observation:

C_p:	1.00	1.33	1.67	2.00	3.00	5.00
EQL:	1.00	0.75	0.84	1.00	1.44	1.96

Table 4.3

The first result, for $C_p=1$, is provided as a benchmark. (As discussed above, it is only possible without drift. The explanation for the strange phenomenon, that once past $C_p=1.33$ increasing the process capability only increases the loss, is simple: by our rule, as we increase C_p, we can start and end the process between adjustments much closer to the specification limits, where the loss is large. This points to a major fault in the procedure of maximizing the drift tolerance subject to capability.

Neave notes that the table does not include the costs of adjustment (e.g., haircut expenditures), and suggests that management should make the decision how often to adjust. Here we'll show exactly how management should do that. In fact, with our method, this decision can and should be made by engineers, technicians, supervisors, or technically literate workers. We also discuss the connection between this issue and product tolerance setting.

4.3.1. Setting Optimal Adjustment Tolerances

Our average loss per item, as captured by the QLF, includes loss because of bias due to drift and loss due to process variation (these losses are the ones reflected by Table 4.3). To these we should add the cost of adjustment, which is not captured by the loss function. Let D be the absolute deviation from ideal right before or after an optimal adjustment, i.e., D is analogous to Δ_0 (Chapter 3); let d be the average drift per unit;[6] and (as before) let M_2 be the cost of adjustment.

For simplicity, assume that the process is capable, and will remain capable even after

---

[6]There are two recommended ways to estimate the drift, which are really two variations of the same theme. One is to run a linear regression on the results of several, say 30 or more, items produced in sequence. If the drift is small, we may want to sample each jth unit, and in that case the regression will estimate $j \cdot d$. The same regression analysis will also provide an estimate for σ^2, which we'll require later. The other way is by $\bar{x}$ and s (or R) control charts, where we estimate d by observing the trend between adjustments. An estimate of σ_x is always available with such charts.

we choose D (i.e., assume D will not be large enough to necessitate using the iterative method of updating the specification limits).[7] Under this assumption, the expected loss due to variation is independent of the expected loss due to bias, and therefore it should have no influence on the optimization of the process adjustment. First, let's look at the three components of the cost/loss per average unit separately. Then, we'll be able to optimize their sum. Starting with the drift-induced loss, it is given approximately by

$$\frac{K}{2D}\int_{-D}^{D}x^2\mathrm{d}x = \frac{KD^2}{3}$$

For discrete production, an exact computation involves summation over individual items. The integral is an excellent approximation under the assumption that the number of items produced between adjustments is large. It is exact for continuous processes. The division by $2D$ -- the range of the integral -- is necessary to obtain the average loss during a full drift cycle. Moving on to the average adjustment cost per unit, a range of $2D$ holds $2D/d$ units, therefore the average cost of adjustment per unit is $M_2d/(2D)$. Finally, the loss due to variation that is not associated with drift-induced bias is $K\sigma_X^2$. Therefore, the total average cost/loss per unit is

$$Average\ Cost = \frac{KD^2}{3} + \frac{M_2d}{2D} + K\sigma_X^2$$

Here D is our decision variable. Taking the derivative of the average cost with respect to D, we obtain the following expression for D^*, the optimal D value (note that σ_X^2 is not involved, since it is constant),

$$D^* = \sqrt[3]{\frac{3M_2d}{4K}}$$

By plugging D^* back into the average cost formula we obtain the minimum average cost,

---

[7]Removing this assumption is beyond our scope. It can be done, but it would render the model too complex for non-computerized solution. Be that as it may, using Taguchi's recommendation not to bother with iterations if $p \geq 0.8$, and assuming the process is at least capable when centered, then as long as D does not take us closer than $0.85\sigma_X$ to the nearest tolerance limit our assumption is acceptable. Accordingly, we can improve our solution by constraining D not to exceed $2.15\sigma_X$ or even $2\sigma_X$. The constraint will rarely be activated, however, unless the adjustment cost is very high relatively to the other production and material costs.

$$Average \ Cost = \left(\sqrt[3]{\frac{1}{48}} + \sqrt[3]{\frac{1}{6}} \right) \sqrt[3]{KM_2^2 d^2} + K\sigma^2 = \sqrt[3]{\frac{9}{16} KM_2^2 d^2} + K\sigma^2$$

Excluding $K\sigma_X^2$, which is not dependent on D, the contribution of the bias D^* induces is one half the average cost of adjustment $M_2 d/(2D^*)$, so it contributes one third of the total drift cost and loss. To wit, the third root of $1/48$ is one half that of $1/6$. Here, societal utility is maximized by asking the customer to bear one third of the drift waste through the loss function. He will also pay for the other two thirds through the price of the product.

As an example, let $c_0 = 100$, $c_1 = 10{,}000$, and $\Delta_1 = 0.5$mm, then using the results given in Chapter 3, $\Delta_0 = 0.5\sqrt{100/10000} = 0.05$mm. K, then, is 40000. Suppose now that there is drift in the process, with $d = 0.00025$mm per unit, and an adjustment cost $M_2 = 250$. Using our formula we obtain

$$D^* = \sqrt[3]{\frac{0.75 \times 250 \times 0.00025}{40000}} = 0.01055 \approx 0.01$$

Thus, the drift we'll allow here will use about 20% of the tolerance range, and will lead to a total drift related cost/loss of

$$Average \ Cost = \sqrt[3]{0.5625 \times 40000 \times 250^2 \times 0.00025^2} = 4.446$$

4.3.2. The Impact of Drift on Product Tolerance Setting

Now let $M_2 = \$6{,}250$ and $d = 0.00125$mm. Since $M_2 d$ is 125 times larger, D^* grows five-fold to ± 0.05275mm. But hold on, this exceeds the tolerance range (± 0.05mm). How can that be?

To answer this question, let us calculate the average cost per unit due to drift, including drift loss and adjustment cost. It is $111.15: twenty-five times larger than before. The tolerance limit was set at ± 0.05mm reflecting a cost, c_0, of $100 to scrap or rework an item. But now, if we do so, we'll lose $100 + $111.15. This leads to $\Delta_0 = 0.0725$mm, and now the drift is limited to 72% of the tolerance range. Theoretically, we should have corrected the tolerance limit for the former case too, but it would make much less of a difference there -- from ± 0.05mm to ± 0.051mm. In extreme cases where drift is the only significant cost, the drift-related loss/cost determines the tolerance limits by itself. D^* becomes the tolerance limit (subject to corrections due to lack of capability, an issue which is beyond our scope). Haircuts provide such an example.

4.3.3. *How to Adjust*

Our results so far imply that we should let the process drift between $-D^*$ and D^* (or D^* and $-D^*$, as the case may be, but we assume the former for simplicity of presentation). We should expect to have to adjust after every $2D/d$ items, more or less. But we can rarely trust the drift to behave exactly as expected (variation!). Therefore, we should not adjust *by* $2D$, but rather *to* $-D^*$. This can be done by the five/ten rule (possibly combined with the harmonic rule). When M_2/M_1 is very high, we should sample the process several times between the expected adjustments, to pinpoint better the time an adjustment is really required. This often applies where we must stop the process to adjust, but we can measure while it's still running (compensating for measurement delays as necessary).

When the drift is known and strong, we do NOT recommend fractional adjustment. This is because, as we saw, fractional adjustment involves a consistent bias (which is strong when the drift is strong). Adjusting to $-D^*$, as suggested above, involves no bias (on average). Mathematically, we can remove the bias of fractional smoothing by providing an aim-off of $-k_\lambda D^*$, but this only works if (i) we adjust exactly when the process reaches D^*, and (ii) we then use a single adjustment. If we add an additional adjustment right away, or too soon, the adjustment will be too large; if we adjust too late, the adjustment will not suffice. In contrast to the aim-off factor given by (4.4), which was recommended as a permanent replacement for the original target, here the true target remains $-D^*$, and the aim-off is merely a mathematical ploy. Typical workers may not react favorably to a scheme where they are given one target for the first adjustment and another for (potentially required) subsequent adjustments.

Chapter 5

Shewhart Control Charts for Attributes

Attributes are characteristics that can be described as occurring or not, e.g., a bead is either red or not. An item is either defective or not. Attribute variables are either integer non-negative counts, e.g., the number of typos in a manuscript, or rational fractions. Attribute charts monitor such variables. Their dominant application is to monitor the number or fraction of defects a process produces, but other examples exist. For instance, a supermarket manager may be interested in the fraction of shoppers who use the express lane, or an airline may monitor the fraction of passengers who prefer beef to chicken.

We begin this chapter by discussing attribute charts that count the incidence of items that possess a particular attribute in subgroups of items that we sample. This is accomplished either by *np* charts or by *p* charts. Later we'll discuss charts that count the number of occurrences in an area of opportunity, e.g., the number of typos in a manuscript. This is done either by *c* charts or by *u* charts. We also discuss demerit charts. They are quite popular but suffer from technical problems of such severity that they should be retired.

5.1. *np* Control Charts for a Single Attribute

These are the simplest control charts available. Usually they are used to control the number of defects a process creates, but they can also be used for other attributes. An interesting use of *np* charts would be to monitor consecutive results of public opinion polls to find out if the real underlying public mood is really changing (when comparing polls based on different numbers of respondents this use would call for a *p* chart application, but the principle is the same). For presentation purposes, however, unless stated otherwise, we'll assume that we are monitoring defective items. Items may be defective due to a multitude of problems, so a single attribute does not necessarily imply a single characteristic. Another example of the same sort might be in counting the percentage of minority workers, where several distinct minorities may be pooled together.

The method of monitoring used here is by taking subgroups of fixed size. We refer to the combination of all these subgroups as the *sample*. Ideally, all items created by the process should have an equal probability of being selected in the sample, but that is not usually feasible. Furthermore, in control charting it is important to monitor the behavior of processes over time, so it makes sense to take subgroups of items that were produced close together to represent the behavior of the process at that time, and repeat this periodically to observe any changes between subgroups. Thus, what we do is to take subgroups of, say, 100 or 200 items, periodically and count the number of defects.[1] Statistically, it would still be preferable to collect the subgroups at random times, but this too is rarely practicable.

Assume now that the process is in statistical control. This implies that the probability the next item will be defective is (i) the same as that of any other item; and (ii) information whether a particular item is defective or not has no direct bearing on any other item (statistical independence). Let the probability of a defect be p, and let the size of each subgroup be n. The distribution that counts the number of occurrences out of n trials, where the trials are independent and each has a probability p, is the binomial B(n, p). The mean is np, and the variance is npq (where $q = 1\text{-}p$). Therefore, we may treat the number of defects in each subgroup as a binomial random variable. There's only one problem: we don't know p. We can never know p. Nature is not in the habit of letting us know such data. In response, people sometimes stipulate p, and develop *control charts with standard given* under this stipulation. In this case the control chart is really an inspection plan to detect whether the real percent defective is sizably different from the stipulated p. When that's the case we might be better served by performing a test of the hypothesis that the percent defective equals p versus the alternative that it isn't. Another useful alternative hypothesis might be that the percent defective is higher than p (when we don't care if it's lower).

In general, however, since we don't know p, the preferred way to proceed is to estimate p from data (a case also referred to as *standards not given*). This is recommended because control charts are supposed to tell us how a process is behaving, and not whether it meets an arbitrary stipulation on the percent defective. Furthermore, with enough data we can also tell whether the process beats any given threshold, so we are not giving up anything. We estimate p from data under the hypothesis that the process is in control. It turns out that a (minimal) sufficient statistic for this purpose is the total number of defects

---

[1]To determine intelligently how large each subgroup should be is a relatively complex question. The methods discussed in Chapter 9 to devise (n, c) single-sampling plans provide some insight into this issue. In general, however, one can say that n should increase considerably as p decreases. As a rule of thumb, $np > 3$ is recommended, and the higher the better, but this may be difficult when p is very small. Therefore, np charts, and other attribute charts, are less useful when conformance is improved. This is another reason why variable charts are preferred wherever they are applicable.

as a fraction of the total number of items inspected. That is, it contains all the pertinent information from the sample. It is sufficient, however, only if the distribution is indeed binomial.

Subgroup#	Result	Subgroup#	Result	Subgroup#	Result
1	3	11	8	21	1
2	1	12	2	22	5
3	2	13	3	23	2
4	3	14	2	24	2
5	3	15	2	25	5
6	0	16	3	26	1
7	5	17	5	27	2
8	3	18	2	28	5
9	3	19	2	29	4
10	2	20	6	30	4

Sum Total: 91

Sum of first 20 subgroups: 60

Table 5.1

Suppose we've taken 30 subgroups of 100 units each, as reported in Table 5.1, and we plot the number of defects in each subgroup on a run chart (as incorporated in Figure 5.1). From Table 5.1 we see that the total number of defects was 91. The total number of items inspected was $100 \times 30 = 3000$, so we can estimate p by $\bar{p} = 91/3000 = 3.033\%$. We proceed to use $\bar{p}$ instead of p in the formulae of the binomial distribution. Thus, our hypothesis is that each subgroup represents a binomial random variable with mean $n\bar{p} = 100 \times 0.03033 = 3.033$ and $\hat{\sigma}^2 = n\bar{p}(1-\bar{p}) = 100 \times 0.03033(1-0.03033) = 2.941$, leading to $\hat{\sigma} = 1.715$ (where $\hat{\sigma}$ is our estimate of σ).

At this stage we can ask whether the hypothesis that the process is indeed in control, i.e., that each subgroup is a realization of the same binomial distribution, is indeed credible. For instance, we might be leery of this hypothesis if we find that most of the total count of defects come from just one or two subgroups, while the rest show almost no defects at all. We should be equally suspicious if it turned out that all subgroups contribute exactly the same number of defects -- a highly unlikely event under statistical control. One exception is when we monitor a process that is not likely to create defects at all. We may choose to do that, perhaps on a random basis, just to make sure that no serious deteriorations developed. In this case a long stream of zeroes is not suspicious. Shewhart's method for

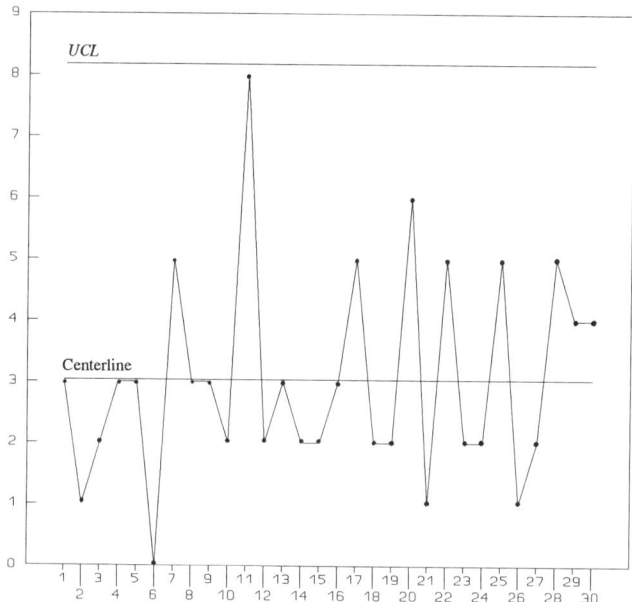

Fig. 5.1. A basic *np* chart.

deciding this question was the use of control limits such that data that fall within them is considered "in control." These control limits should be based on the data, and *not* on specification limits of any kind. As we said before, "in control" is not necessarily a synonym of "good." We can deduce from this, again, that control charts with standards given are not really Shewhart charts. This idea is key to Shewhart control charts, and it justifies repetition:

> *Shewhart recommended that control limits be based on data. This implies that they should NOT be based on specification limits. Thus, it is the PROCESS that determines the limits, NOT the needs.*

How exactly can we specify the control limits, then? Even when a process is under control, it should show some variation. When there's no variation whatsoever we should check our measuring instruments (they may not be capable of measuring with enough discrimination), and if the instruments are up to the job we should investigate the process. It may be, for instance, that there are 12 streams of output, one of which is malfunctioning so every 12th item is defective. In such a case we'll see a proportion defective that is consistently very close to 8.3%. Another possible problem may be the integrity of the data. In one case which Deming recounted the percent defective was consistent at 10%. It turned out that there was a rumor that the plant manager threatened to close the plant if the fraction defective will ever exceed 10%, so the inspector cheated (to protect the jobs of 300 people).

An important question is how much variation to accept before pronouncing that it is not *all* due to the reasonable variation that one should expect among subgroups drawn from the binomial distribution. A very convenient way to do that is to set the control limits at a distance of, say, t standard deviations above and below the sample mean. The rule is that any data that falls strictly more than t standard deviation units away from the mean is suspect, or "out of control"; data within t standard deviations (including data that falls *exactly* t standard deviations away) is pronounced "in control." But how large should t be? If we make it too small, we'll be declaring good processes "out of control"; if we make it too large we'll never correct bad processes when we should.

Although we do not use terminology such as α-risk here, our problem is essentially an instance of hypothesis testing. Our null hypothesis, H_0, is that the data represents *i.i.d.* specimen from a stable distribution associated with the process when it runs as designed. Our alternative hypothesis, H_1, is that this is not the case. Thus, under H_1, at least some data do not come from the same distribution, or the distribution is not the one we associate with the process when it runs as it is designed to run. If we cannot reject the null hypothesis, we declare this by the utterance: "The process is *in control*"; in contrast, when we reject the null hypothesis we say "the process is *out of control.*" (Deming, however, vehemently opposed treating control charts as instances of hypothesis testing; e.g., see Deming (1975) or *The New Economics*, pp. 103–104, 156, and 181. Supplement 5 argues that it may be permissible after all to treat control charts as a form of hypothesis testing, but without specifying the significance probability α. To a large extent, however, this is an issue of semantics: what I call "hypothesis testing" may differ from what Deming called "hypothesis testing.")

Based on simulation studies and extensive industrial experience, Shewhart suggested the use of $t = 3$. That is, control limits are usually set at a distance of $\pm 3\sigma$ from the mean, where both the mean and σ are estimated from data collected while the process is running.[2] If a process is well-documented, we can use the control limits from the past to judge its performance in the future. Assuming no changes were introduced intentionally, this may reveal unintentional changes that have to be investigated. Using this convention, Box 5.1 summarizes the necessary technical steps for the calculation of the centerline and control limits for *np* charts.

---

[2]The mean of variable charts should sometimes be set by design (Chapter 6). This is appropriate if and only if we can actually adjust the process mean at will, so there is no reason *not* to set it to the target of our choice.

=-

Box 5.1: Constructing np Control Charts

Let n be the subgroup size and m be the number of subgroups taken in the whole sample. Let x_i denote the attribute count (e.g., defective items) in the ith subgroup $(i=1,\ldots,m)$. Then $\overline{p}$ is defined by

$$\overline{p} = \frac{\sum_{i=1}^{m} x_i}{nm}$$

For convenience, we also define $\overline{q} = 1 - \overline{p}$. The centerline of the control chart is at $n\overline{p}$, and the control limits are

$$Centerline = n\overline{p} = \frac{\sum_{i=1}^{m} x_i}{m}$$

$$LCL = n\overline{p} - 3\sqrt{n\overline{p}(1 - \overline{p})} = n\overline{p} - 3\sqrt{n\overline{p}\,\overline{q}}$$

$$UCL = n\overline{p} + 3\sqrt{n\overline{p}(1 - \overline{p})} = n\overline{p} + 3\sqrt{n\overline{p}\,\overline{q}}$$

But if LCL (lower control limit), from this calculation, is negative, we use $LCL=0$. Similarly (but less often), if UCL (upper control limit) exceeds n we use $UCL=n$. (Points on the control limit are considered "in control," so such cases imply that the control limit in question cannot detect special causes. For instance, if $LCL=0$, the chart cannot detect a reduction in the percent defective.) If x_i is outside the control limits for one or more i, the likely special cause may also apply to other subgroups.

=-

In our example, the estimate we got for np was 3.033, and the standard deviation was 1.715. Calculating LCL and UCL we get

$$Centerline = n\overline{p} = 3.033$$

$$LCL = n\overline{p} - 3\sigma = 3.033 - 3 \times 1.715 = -2.11(i.e.,\ 0)$$

$$UCL = n\overline{p} + 3\sigma = 3.033 + 3 \times 1.715 = 8.18$$

The interpretation of the negative number is zero, because it is not possible to have a negative attribute count. Since a point on the control limit is "in control," $LCL = 0$ implies that zero defects in a subgroup is not unusual. (Certainly it is good, but not necessarily exceptional. Had it been exceptional we might want to investigate why, and use the results to improve the process if possible.) The upper control limit, 8.18, is indistinguishable from any value between 8 (inclusive) and 9⁻ (that is, up to but not including 9). Some prefer to express such a control limit as 8.5, because there is less room for confusion: 8 is "in," 9 is "out." Figure 5.1 shows the *np* chart for the data of Table 5.1. Although the eleventh point is close to the upper limit, *all* points are in control.

Looking at Table 5.1 again we see that the minimal value encountered is 0 (Subgroup 6), and the maximum is 8 (Subgroup 11). Both are within control, and the same applies to all the other values of course. As a matter of fact, the data in Table 5.1 were generated by a computer simulation of a process that has a probability of 3% to create a defect. Furthermore, they are the result of the very *first* such simulation performed for this purpose.[3] Had any points shown "out of control" it would cause an error in our diagnosis. (Such errors, also known as Type I errors, may happen, of course. The only way to avoid them is never to declare a point "out of control." So much for "Zero Defects" in control charting applications.)

According to a prevailing (but much too liberal) rule of thumb, at least 20 subgroups are considered necessary to create viable control limits. In the case reported in Table 5.1 we'd obtain virtually identical limits had we only used the first 20 subgroups for that purpose The next 10 would then show "in control," as they should. But what would happen if we'd only use the first 10 subgroups? They would lead us to estimate p as 2.5%, and this would indicate an upper control limit of 7.18, which implies that Subgroup 11 (the very next one) would register "out of control" falsely. This, by the luck of the draw, is in accordance with the rule of thumb. To see that it's a question of luck, assume we'd use the *next* 10 units, and this would lead to a p estimate of 3.5%, and to an upper control limit of 9.01 (the lower control limit would still be 0). To be reasonably safe here, it is likely that even 100 subgroups is too small a number. Nonetheless, we sometimes need to use a smaller number, such as 20, while we collect data. Chapter 8 covers this issue in detail.

The case we deal with, with p = 0.03 and n = 100, is one where the Poisson approximation for the binomial is excellent. Using this approximation, then, let us calculate the probability *under the null hypothesis* that a subgroup will show in control (with a control limit of, say, 8.5). For that purpose we can use a Poisson table, with $\lambda = np = 3$. We find that the probability of obtaining 8 or less is 0.996, so we may expect false alarms at a rate

---

[3]Simulation is a type of sampling. Often, it is possible to continue sampling until one gets the result one wants to report. This, of course, is fraudulent.

of about 4/1000. Depending on how often the process is really out of control, this may be too little or too much. Shewhart's recommendation was not to bother with this detail, and the simplicity that this offers is valuable. Had we used an upper limit of 9, the probability of a false alarm would drop to about 1/1000. The probability of obtaining more than 10, when p is really 3%, is negligible.

5.1.1. *Recalculating the Control Limits*

When we prepare control limits based on data we should also check that the data itself is in control. For this reason the chart is called a *trial* chart. Suppose now that we decide that a particular point is out of control. Once we do that we should investigate the cause. If we find such a cause, and it does not apply to the other points, we may now want to recalculate the control limits without the offending point.[4] Take the data in Table 5.2 (which is identical to that of Table 5.1, except that in two periods the number of defects is increased by 7 (see bold entries). Thus, instead of a total of 91 defective items we now see

Subgroup#	Result	Subgroup#	Result	Subgroup#	Result
1	3	11	8	21	1
2	1	12	2	22	5
3	2	13	3	23	2
4	3	14	2	24	2
5	3	15	2	25	5
6	0	16	3	26	1
7	5	17	**12**	27	2
8	3	18	2	28	5
9	3	19	2	29	4
10	**9**	20	6	30	4

Sum Total: 91

Sum of first 20 subgroups: 60

Table 5.2

---

[4]Deming dismissed the need to do this, and, indeed, in many cases the difference will not be large; i.e., the complexity involved in recalculating the limits may not be justified. Formally, however, this is a necessary step that should not be omitted without care. A similar observation holds for all types of control charts.

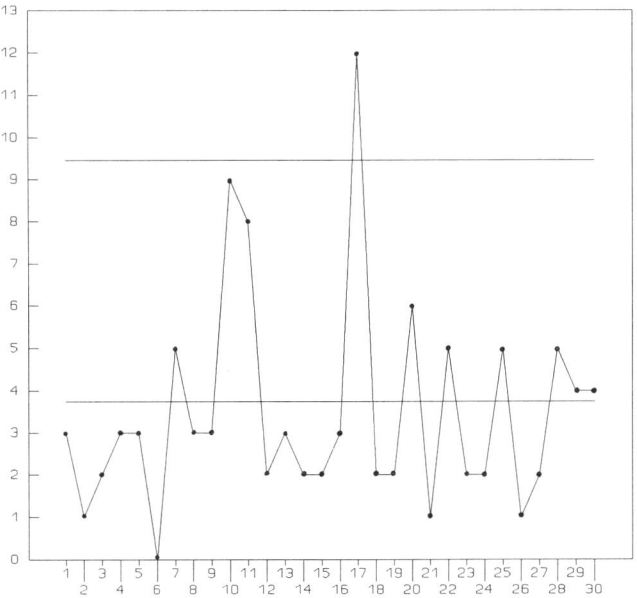

Fig. 5.2. Two points do not belong, one shows.

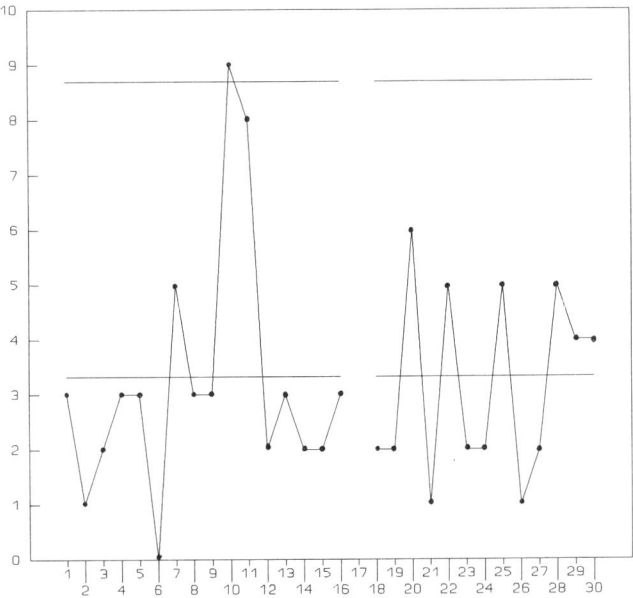

Fig. 5.3. Interim result after removing the first point.

105, leading to a new p estimate of 3.5%, and an upper control limit of 9.01 (or, equivalently, 9.5). Subgroup 17 now shows out of control (as it should), but Subgroup 10 is in control (Figure 5.2).

Suppose now that we eliminate Subgroup 17, and recalculate the limits. Our total count of defective items is now 96, which we divide by 29, and we obtain 3.31%, leading to an upper control limit of 8.678. This implies that now Subgroup 10 will also show out of control, again, as it should (Figure 5.3).

If we eliminate the new "out of control" point too, we are left with 28 observations and 84 defective items, leading to an estimate of p = 3%, and control limits of 0 and 8.118. In this case the final result agrees with the real underlying process after removing the only two points that did not really belong (Figure 5.4). But one should not expect control charts to be always that effective.

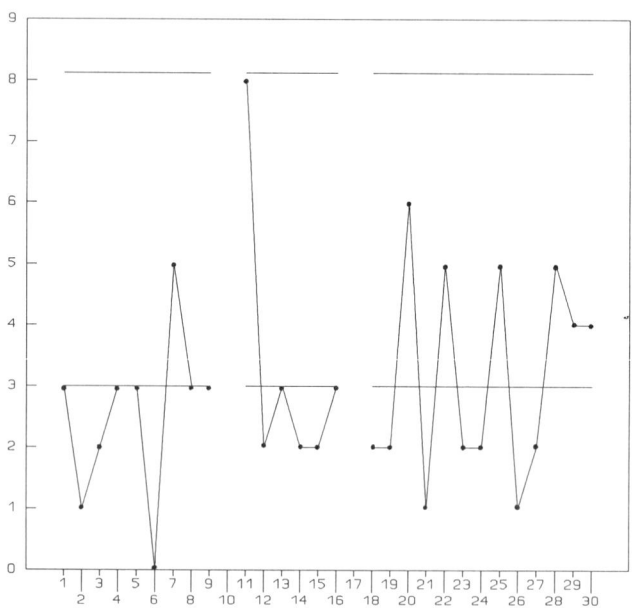

Fig. 5.4. The results after removing both points.

Once reasonable control limits are set, we should run additional data and chart it on an ongoing basis *without* recalculating the limits (it is no longer a trial chart). When the control limits are intended for such future use, however, it is strongly recommended to use at least 100 subgroups to determine them (Chapter 8 argues that even 100 may not be enough). While 20 or 30 may suffice to support process improvement projects, it would be unwise to predicate the results of ongoing charting on such a small number of subgroups. But once the limits are calculated well, based on a large enough sample, there is no further need to update them until the process is changed. Then again, if the process shows "out of control" too often without an identifiable cause, we may need to verify that the control limits were not set too tightly, based on a set of unusually good initial runs. Usually, when the chart is reliable, we should find that something changed, such as raw materials supply, the condition of the equipment, new workers who are not well trained, etc.

5.1.2. *An Example: Deming's Red Beads Experiment*

During his Four Days Seminars, Deming performed an on stage demonstration: The Red Beads Experiment. In the experiment, participants (playing as "willing workers") are asked to scoop 50 beads from a well mixed container with 3200 white beads and 800 red beads. Although they are not allowed to prevent the scooping of red beads the workers are told that it is their responsibility to only collect white beads: red beads are counted against them. Deming sternly admonished workers who collected the most red beads and encouraged those who collected less. The results of a particular session (at San Jose in November 1990), at which I was present, are reproduced in Table 5.3.

	Qt. 1	Qt. 2	Qt. 3	Qt. 4	Sum
Linda	10	9	11	14	44
Wayne	9	7	10	10	36
Don	7	8	11	14	40
Fernando	9	8	9	15	41
Mud	7	10	5	11	33
Judy	10	9	14	7	40
All six	52	51	60	71	234

Table 5.3

The table sorts the red beads by worker and by quarter, and provides sums for each worker across all periods and for each period across all workers. In general, such tables may be used to answer two questions: (i) is there a difference between workers; (ii) is there a difference between periods. Statisticians have developed extensive methods to do that, including *analysis of variance (ANOVA)*. Control charting, when done intelligently, can give the same type of answer as these more sophisticated methods, sometimes at a glance. In fact, control charts are very similar to ANOVA if they are based on *rational subgrouping*, that is, when data from different sources (e.g., different workers or different periods) are collected separately. And well-designed control charts are always based on rational subgrouping with respect to all suspected sources of variation.

The null hypothesis here is that all workers at all periods exhibit the same distribution. The alternative is that the null is wrong. Under the alternative, workers are not the same, periods are not the same, or both. It is easy to calculate $\bar{p}$ under the null $(234/(24 \times 50) = 0.195)$. This leads to control limits of 9.75 ± 8.405, i.e., 1.35 and 18.15. Thus, any integer value between 2 and 18 (inclusive) is deemed "in control," which implies the null should not be rejected. In our case all 24 results indeed fall between these control limits. Figure 5.5 shows such a control chart, where the sequence is by workers (i.e., the data in the table is charted row by row).

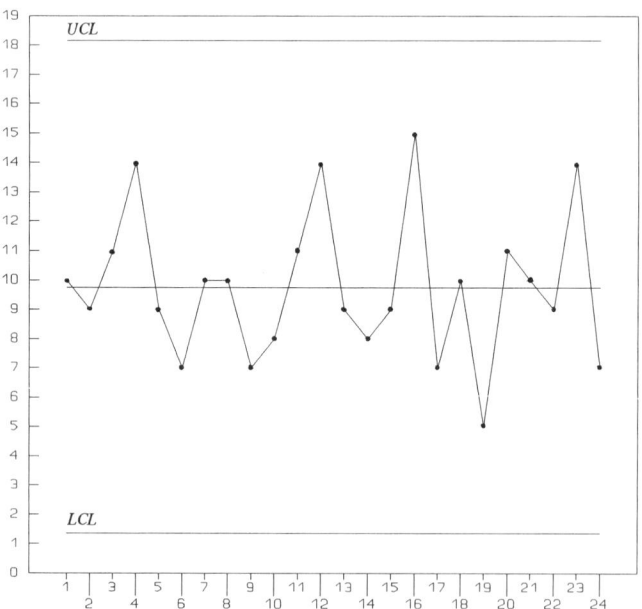

Fig. 5.5. The red beads experiment results (by workers).

The control chart suggests, correctly in this case, that there are no differences among the workers. Without it (or equivalent statistical analysis) we might be tempted to draw some conclusions from the uncontestable fact that while Mud only made 33 defects during the year, Linda made 44. Similarly, there is a negative trend during the last quarter that might be considered important without the correct analysis. Or one might want to draw conclusions from the fact that in spite of the negative trend of the group as a whole Judy has improved considerably during the same quarter. In fact, she was at the bottom or next to the bottom for the first three quarters, but her vast improvement in the fourth quarter put her annual performance in the middle of the group. Should she continue that way, one might argue, she could potentially become our best worker. In contrast, Mud, although his results over the whole year were the best, showed a relatively strong negative trend: he can become a liability soon!

In this case there was little or no difference between workers and between periods. Deming, acting as a stern supervisor, made sure of that. But in general, to check all possibilities, we might want to arrange the control chart based on periods and based on workers and see if any suspicious pattern emerges. In Figure 5.5 the sequence is by workers. In Figure 5.6 the sequence is by quarters. By observing the results of Figure 5.5, we see no obvious pattern by workers, and therefore we cannot reject the null hypothesis. People can often see pattern where none exists, and vice versa, but basically Figure 5.5 is a textbook example of how control charts should look like in the absence of any special cause; but, as we'll see in Chapter 7, Figure 5.6 shows [probably false] signs of special causes (in the form of special patterns).

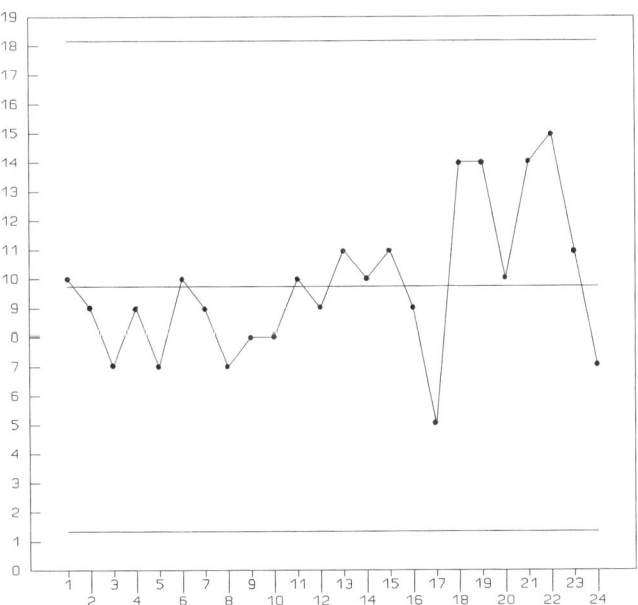

Fig. 5.6. The red beads experiment results arranged by quarters.

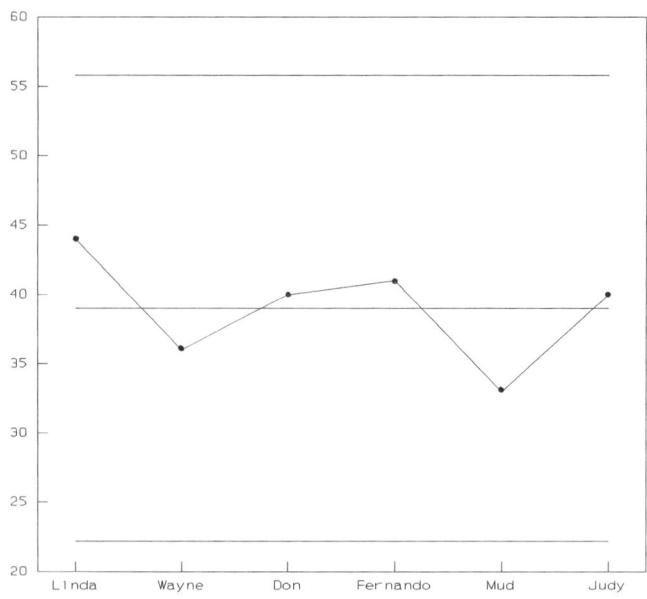

Fig. 5.7. The annual results by workers.

To emulate a basic ANOVA analysis here, we do not trust our judgement whether there is a pattern or not. As discussed, such judgements are quite likely to lead to error. ANOVA too, when conducted with technical prowess but no profound knowledge, often leads to spurious results. Nonetheless, to provide a flavor of how ANOVA analysis is conducted, we'll use this example to perform an ANOVA-like analysis. The procedure is simple: in spite of the fact that we only have 4 quarters and 6 workers, our data for each quarter and for each worker is based on relatively large subgroups (300 and 200 respectively, combined with a large p). So, what we can do is prepare a control chart by quarters (showing the total quarterly production), and another by workers (showing the total production per worker through the year). The control chart for the total production of each worker is based on subgroups of 200, has a mean of 39, and control limits at $39 \pm 3 \times 5.603$ (i.e., $LCL = 22.19$ and $UCL = 55.809$). All the data are well within the control limits, so we cannot reject the null hypothesis that the workers belong to the same system of causes. The control chart for the total quarterly production are calculated with $n = 300$, and the relevant calculations yield $58.5 \pm 3 \times 6.862$, leading to $LCL = 37.9$ and $UCL = 79.087$. Again, all the results are well within these control limits, so there is no discernible influence by quarters either. Figures 5.7 and 5.8 show these two control charts. There is an apparent trend in Figure 5.8, but (i) it is well within the control limits, and (ii) a trend of less than six periods (i.e., less than five consecutive increases or decreases) is not conclusive: it is highly likely to happen by chance (as was the case here). It is not even a run of 4 out of 4, since the second period is lower than the first.

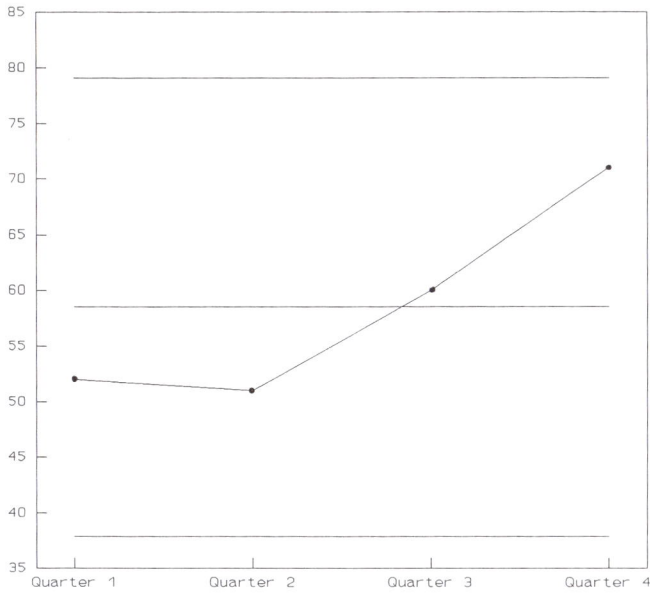

Fig. 5.8. The results by quarters.

Did Deming actually prove that there was no difference between workers here? No. Nor did he set out to do so in the first place. At least not with the data. Deming convinced the audience that the process was such that the workers had no chance to make a real personal difference. He then showed that the observed differences were, indeed, fully explainable by system variation alone. Thus, *he showed that the hypothesis that there was no difference could not be rejected.* So there is no evidence to justify discriminating between workers. To be sure, there are instances when it is the duty of management to act without sufficient statistical evidence. As Deming said, the unknowable should also be managed. For example, rational physicians did not wait for statistical proof that smoking is harmful before recommending against it. In effect, they were saying that the null hypothesis in this case should be that smoking *is* harmful, in spite of the tobacco industry's great achievement in making the alternative into the null (which they succeeded to do because smoking was already well-established). Nonetheless, in this instance, discriminating among workers without statistical evidence is actually harmful. Deming asserted that in 94% of the cases defects were due to the system and not the responsibility of individual workers. Juran cites 85%. But if a worker was badly trained, and is therefore creating defects that can be assigned to her personally, Deming would still count these defects against the system, since the system is responsible for the defective training.

But workers can and do make a difference in a minority of the cases, or on the margin. Suppose that similar proportions between the performance of individual workers were observed over 60 periods (instead of 5, and it may make more sense to think about a period now as a day, or we'd be lucky to have the same workers with us, doing the same job, for so long). That is, instead of totals ranging between 33 to 44 we'd have 495 to 660. When we devise control limits in our ANOVA-like analysis the subgroup size for each worker now is 3000 (instead of 200), so our control limits would be 585 ± 65.1, i.e., $LCL = 519.9$ and $UCL = 650.1$. This would place both Mud and Linda outside the control limits. Mud would provide an opportunity to learn how the process can be changed, if what he would be doing right could be identified and disseminated. Linda might require special attention. (In reality, of course, if we repeat the experiment for 60 periods the proportions between best and worst worker would be much closer to 1, so we'd still be likely to have statistical control.)

Under this scenario, would we have evidence that Linda is an inferior worker and Mud a superior one? Maybe, and maybe not. Such results would just prove that it makes sense to investigate the personal performance of these two individuals and see what's the special cause that probably exists there. Suppose, for instance, that Mud found a way to stash his defective output. This is a more common practice than one would like to believe in companies that evaluate individuals by results of this sort. Actually, one of the workers in the experiment did dump a pallet when he saw that it contained too many red beads. Deming either did not notice or chose not to pursue the issue. People in the audience, however, reacted by laughter, and that was the last time this tactic was observed. Quality goals are an invitation to do some more hiding of the truth. Maybe Linda was the only worker who did *not* cheat. But, arguably, *cheating is caused by the system* (although a particular business may not be the responsible party, as it may start at early childhood).

The difference might also be found to be due to the ergonomic design of the system. For instance, the rules of basketball are such that seven feet tall players may have a real advantage, but it is very rare that a 5'4" player will be hired under such circumstances. In general one expects a good system design to accommodate the ergonomic needs of as wide a range of human beings as possible. Then, it's the responsibility of management to hire workers to jobs that they can perform. And they should receive competent training to do so.

One may say that waiting 60 periods to be able to detect a difference of the magnitude involved here is too long. Depending on the circumstances it may indeed be possible to obtain significant results in a shorter time period by measuring more intelligently or more often. But ultimately, it will always be true that if we want to discern small differences with some degree of reliability it may become excessively expensive or downright impossible to do so. Understanding this unpleasant fact of life goes a long way towards understanding variation and understanding the need to live with and to manage the unknowable. In a nutshell, we can only discern differences that are large relative to the natural variation, and in order to make such differences large enough we may need to collect data over a long period of time, collecting, if you will, enough difference to show through the "fog" which variation creates.

Of course, data may provide evidence sooner, especially if the differences are larger. For instance, suppose Mud would be the best of the lot during four quarters out of four. Under the null hypothesis the probability this would happen is $1/6^4 = 1/1296$, and we might be justified in assuming that a special cause was present. Even three times in a row might convince many. And similarly for Linda to be the worst worker three or four times in a row. The probability, under the null, that both will occupy these two positions respectively is ridiculously low: out of 6! arrangements of 6 workers, 4! are such that Mud is first and Linda is last. Thus, the probability this will happen once by chance is $4!/6! = 1/30$. For the same phenomenon to repeat 3 times in a row the probability under the null hypothesis is $1/27000$, and four times can only happen with a probability of $1/810000$. Even a run of eight or nine consecutive times a worker is above or below average might provide convincing evidence for a special cause (as we discuss in Chapter 7). But none of these things occurred in the actual experiment. A likely special cause in such cases may be the "success to the successful" system archetype discussed by Senge (1990).

Deming was once asked, in a seminar, how to select workers for layoffs without ranking and rating them. He responded: "Roll the dice."[5] And he probably meant not only that choosing by lottery is better than by rating and ranking, but also that the workers should know it. This way, the laid-off workers will not have to deal with rejection issues on top of their other problems.

5.1.3. *Mixtures*

One of the important uses of control charts is to detect unwanted effects of mixtures. The null hypothesis is that all items come from the same process and each has the same

---

[5] *Quality Progress,* March 1994, p. 32.

probability of a defect, p. Suppose that in reality there are several sources (e.g., six workers), and suppose each of them has the same p. In this case, inasmuch as the results are concerned, the workers are considered part of the same process: we cannot tell their output apart. But what if, indeed, some of the sources had a different rate of defects? Our ANOVA-like analysis was designed to find such differences. To that end we utilized rational subgroups, i.e., we took care *not* to mix the output of the workers before the inspection. What would happen if the sources would be mixed? Could we still tell that there might have been differences at the source?

Theoretically, if we mix binomial sources *before* sampling, the result will no longer possess a binomial distribution. Unfortunately, for small p values the result will be *approximately* binomial (see technical note below). Our charts, however, are designed to detect only strong deviations from the binomial distribution. Thus, if we mix sources before charting, we'll likely not be able to find it later, and the information will be lost.

=-=-=-=-=-=-=-=-=-=-=-=-=-==-

Technical Note:

The sum of several independent binomials, $B(n_i, p)$, is also a binomial, $B(\Sigma n_i, p)$. But the sum of binomials with a different p is not binomial. In contrast, the sum of several independent Poisson random variables, $P(\lambda_i)$, is Poisson, $P(\Sigma\lambda_i)$.

For small p/n, however, a binomial can be approximated by a Poisson, so the sum of several such binomials, as the sum of Poissons, is approximately Poisson. That Poisson, in turn, is approximately binomial. Thus, the sum of binomials with small p_i/n_i ratios is approximately binomial: it can hardly be distinguished from the binomial $B(\Sigma n_i, \Sigma(p_i n_i)/\Sigma n_i)$.

=-=-=-=-=-=-=-=-=-=-=-=-=-==-

The situation is much better if we do not mix sources before sampling. In such cases, the overall fraction defective we use to estimate p will be an average of more than one rate, but the data will not behave as a binomial random variable. Instead, many data will be close to the control limits, and some of them may actually show out of control. Therefore, a control chart based on the null hypothesis that the number of defects is binomial will show out of control more often than is explainable by chance alone. While investigating such points that are out of control we may find that the various sources are different: actually, it's the first thing we should check for. Table 5.4 summarizes simulated data about a process that is really a 50-50 mixture of two processes. One process induces 1% defects, on average, while the other has 5%. Together, they show about 3%, as did the data in Table 5.1. But out of a hundred subgroups taken, three show out of control in the trial control chart, which

Subgroup#	Result	Subgroup#	Result	Subgroup#	Result
1	2	11	1	21	2
2	12	12	5	22	5
3	0	13	1	23	0
4	8	14	4	24	8
5	0	15	0	25	0
6	8	16	6	26	0
7	0	17	1	27	1
8	3	18	7	28	6
9	1	19	1	29	3
10	8	20	4	30	3

Sum Total (100 subgroups): 305

Sum of last 30 subgroups (listed here): 100

Table 5.4

is exceptionally high for a binomial under control. The table, for conciseness, only shows the last 30 points (which happened to contain the largest of the three deviations (the other two being both 9, at subgroups 2 and 62). For comparison, another run of 100 subgroups was run without mixing (with $p = 0.03$), and this time, in spite of the fact that the trial control limits happened to be tighter, there was not a single point out of control (although it could well happen that at least one would show out of control by error).[6] Figure 5.9 shows the control chart of these 30 results. When compared to Figure 5.1 there are two striking traits: (i) the points tend to be away from the center; (ii) since the subgroups were (intentionally) taken from the two sources on an alternating basis there is a see-saw pattern, and the data rarely stays on the same side of the average more than once (on average it should stay on the same side twice, as per the geometric distribution with $p=0.5$, but this is a volatile random variable).

In conclusion, with np charts we must make sure not to mix sources before sampling. As we'll see later, with variable control charts it is sometimes possible to find

---

[6]Again, as in Table 5.1, the results of the first simulation trial were used in Tables 5.4 and 5.5, without any attempt to get a "convincing" outcome. But running this experiment with only 30 subgroups failed to provide convincing results on the first trial. In fact, it failed roughly as often as it succeeded. This is not unusual: one should not expect Shewhart charts to signal small problems very quickly.

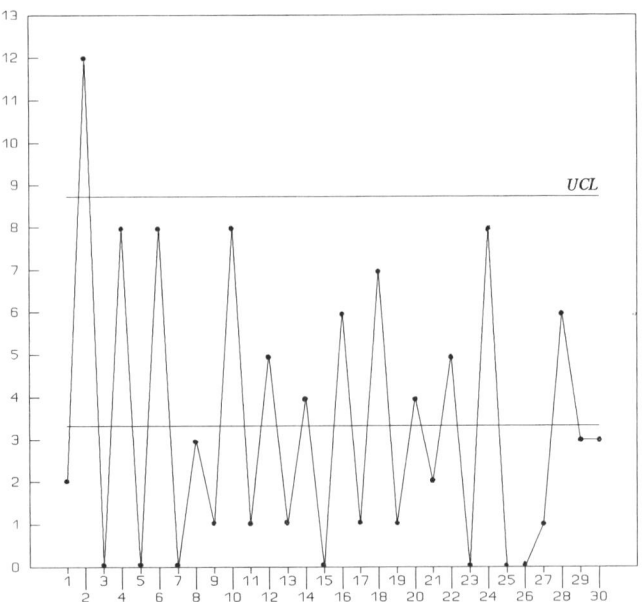

Fig. 5.9. A mixture from two alternating sources.

evidence for mixtures even when they occur before sampling, but there too mixing should be avoided.

Incidentally, if we would only use the results of the first 70 subgroups to calculate the control limits the upper control limit would be just below 8. This would cause nine points to show out of control, five of which happen to cluster in the last 30 that are reported. Such relatively large differences as a result of chance causes are to be expected as part of the deal. This is in line with our recommendation not to base control charts on 20 or 30 subgroups when we can afford a 100 or more.

To conclude our discussion of *np* charts, Box 5.2 discusses an example of their use for teaching.

=-

Box 5.2: **An Application of *np* Charts to Teaching**

While control charts are often associated with manufacturing applications, it is possible to use the same techniques in services and in the social sciences as well. This often involves the analysis of questionnaire results. (But see Chapter 2 for important reservations about using questionnaires.) Here we discuss a particular example where I used the control charts methodology to find out what my customers, students in this case, thought about their reading assignments, and to what extent they actually read them with enough attention to remember that they did. Formally speaking, the example does not involve an ongoing process. It really demonstrates using trial control charts as a substitute for classic analysis of variance. Similarly, workers trained in the use of control charts can perform such analyses without further training.

To promote honest responses as much as possible, I distributed an anonymous questionnaire. In spite of the fact that individuals should be less afraid to be honest with this anonymity, I also wanted to prevent spurious responses by those who did not read the assignments carefully. Therefore, I intentionally included an article that was not disseminated in the list of reading assignments, and I told the students that "at least one" such article was included. I asked them to refrain from expressing opinions on any article they do not remember, so I expected most of them not to comment on the "red herring." Altogether there were 22 legitimate articles in the list. For each article, students could respond on a scale from 0 to 5, according to the following legend:

> 5: Outstanding: Remarkably relevant and useful
>
> 4: Good: Relevant and useful
>
> 3: Indifferent: I was not really impressed by this article
>
> 2: Bad: Reading this article was a chore, and I doubt it's useful
>
> 1: Disaster: Totally useless, and/or badly written
>
> 0: Sorry, I do not recall reading this article

After omitting the responses of two students who expressed an opinion about the article they never read, the results for 19 students and 22 articles are given in Table 5.5 (where 2.5, or 3.5, stand for a mark that covered both 2 and 3, or 3 and 4). Here, we'll only analyze the number of articles not read. (For further analysis of the responses see Box 6.3.) In the table, dashes are used to denote articles not read. The last column counts the number of dashes per row (i.e., per article), and the last row counts the number of dashes per column (i.e., per student).

The data can be depicted in two different *np* charts. We can investigate whether any article was exceptional in terms of the number of students who failed to read it, and we can investigate whether any students were exceptional in terms of the number of articles they read. We'll follow both these approaches, starting with the articles. The necessary data to plot the points are provided in the last column. To compute the control limits consider that each article could be read by 19 students. Our formulae for the centerline and the control limits yield,

4	4	2.5	3	3	3	—	3	4	4	5	5	4	—	5	4	—	5	5	4	—	1
4	4	2.5	3	3	3	—	2	4	4	5	5	4	—	4	4	—	4	5	4	—	1
4	—	2.5	—	3	4	—	—	4	4	—	4	4	—	4	—	—	4	4	4	—	8
5	5	2.5	3	4	3	—	3	4	4	5	5	4	—	4	4	—	4	4	4	—	5
4	4	2.5	3	3	3	—	3	5	5	5	4	4	—	4	4	—	4	4	4	—	4
4	—	2.5	—	3	—	—	3	5	5	4	4	4	—	4	4	—	4	4	4	—	10
5	5	5	5	5	5	5	4	5	5	5	5	5	5	5	5	4	4	4	4	5	0
5	4	5	4	5	5	4	3	4	4	4	4	4	4	4	4	4	5	5	5	4	2
5	5	4	4	5	5	5	4	3	3	3	4	4	4	3	4	3	5	5	4	5	0
—	4	4	—	3	—	4	5	4	4	3	4	4	4	4	3	4	4	3	3	4	3
5	4	4	4	4	5	3	4	4	3	3	4	4	4	—	2.5	3	5	5	5	4	4
4	3	4	3	4	3	4	3	3	3	3	4	4	—	3	3	3	4	3	3	3	6
3	4	4	—	3	4	5	5	5	3	5	4	4	—	3	4	—	5	5	5	4	5
4	4	4	4	4	5	4	4	3	5	4	4	—	—	3	4	—	5	5	5	4	4
4	—	4	—	5	4	4	3	5	5	3	4	—	—	—	4	—	5	5	3	4	6
5	3	4	4	4	4	4	3	4	3	4	5	5	—	—	4	—	5	5	5	3	5
5	4	3	3	5	3	5	4	3	5	4	4	—	—	3	4	—	4	4	3	4	5
4	2.5	—	4	4	4	4	5	4	4	5	4	3	4	5	5	—	5	5	5	5	7
5	3	—	5	5	5	4	4	5	4	3.5	—	—	—	4	3	—	5	4	4	—	5
5	5	4	4	5	3	4	4	5	4	—	4	—	—	5	5	—	4	4	—	—	7
5	3	4	4	4	4	4	4	4	4	—	—	4	—	3	5	—	4	5	—	—	5
5	4	4	—	4	4	4	—	4	4	3	4	—	—	3	3	—	3	5	—	—	5
5	5	3	3	5	5	4	4	4	4	5	—	4	—	3	5	3	—	5	—	—	10
5	5	5	5	4	4	4	3.5	4	4	3.5	—	3.5	—	4	4	3	—	3	3	3	8
—	4	4	—	4	4	4	4	4	4	4	4	4	—	4	4	4	—	5	4	4	5
3	3	0	10	5	8	0	0	7	8	13	13	2	10	4	1	0	12	104			

Table 5.5. Students' opinions about reading assignments.

Each row represents an article; each column represents a student. The last entry in each column is the number of articles not read by each student. Similarly, the last column gives the number of students that did not read the article. 104=total not read (out of 22×19=418 possible).

$$Centerline = \overline{np} = 19\frac{104}{418} = 4.73$$

$$LCL = \overline{np} - 3\sqrt{\overline{np}(1-\overline{p})} = 4.73 - 3\sqrt{4.73\left(1 - \frac{104}{418}\right)} = 4.73 - 5.64 \ (i.e., \ 0)$$

$$UCL = 4.73 + 5.64 = 10.37 \approx 10.5$$

Therefore, any article that was not read 11 times or more should be considered special. Two articles (the sixth and twentieth) are close, with 10, but all are formally within control.

Repeating the same procedure for students, each across 22 articles, we obtain,

$$Centerline = \overline{np} = 22\frac{104}{418} = 5.47$$

$$LCL = = 5.47 - 3\sqrt{5.47\left(1 - \frac{104}{418}\right)} = 5.47 - 6.08 \ (i.e., \ 0)$$

$$UCL = 5.47 + 6.08 = 11.55 \approx 11.5$$

Thus, any student who failed to read 12 articles or more should be considered special. Three students (#12, 13, 22) do indeed show out of control based on this criterion. Formally speaking, we should now examine the data again with the data from these three students removed (an exercise left for the interested readers).

Even without analyzing the data further, we can reach a few conclusions based on the data provided. First, although most students and articles are "in control," a very large proportion of the assignments were not done (about 25% before removing the two special cases, and 18% after removing special cases iteratively). This indicates that the reading load was too high for most students, or that they did not consider it important to read all the assignments. It was not possible to investigate the special causes associated with the students that were above the control limit, since the questionnaire was anonymous. Similarly, the two students who expressed opinions about an unknown article were special cases too. Nonetheless, since the results were discussed in class, some students got a signal that their performance was below par. Incidentally, this example also demonstrates, in principle, that it is possible to base grading decisions on similar statistical analysis.

=-

5.2. *p* Control Charts for a Single Attribute with Varying Subgroup Size

Instead of devising a control chart for *np*, we could divide the center line, the control limits, and all the entries by n, and nothing would change in terms of accepting or rejecting. The new control chart would show the *fraction defective,* instead of the *number* of defective items. Its centerline would be at $\overline{p}$. The standard deviation would be calculated by $\sqrt{p\,q\,/\,n}$ instead of $\sqrt{n\,p\,q}$.[7] When n is constant across all subgroups we get an equivalent result. But when the subgroups are not equal the p chart alternative becomes superior. What we can then do is to determine p based on many subgroups, but calculate the control limits separately for each subgroup. The control limits are tighter for larger subgroups. This reflects the fact that larger subgroups are more likely to exhibit an average that is close to the expected value. Box 5.3 gives the necessary technical steps for the calculation of the centerline and control limits for p charts.

=·=-

Box 5.3: Constructing p Control Charts

Let n_i be the size of the ith subgroup, where $i=1,\ldots,m$, and let x_i be the associated attribute count (e.g., defective items). $\overline{p}$ is defined by

$$\overline{p} = \frac{\displaystyle\sum_{i=1}^{m} x_i}{\displaystyle\sum_{i=1}^{m} n_i}$$

and $\overline{q}=1-\overline{p}$. The centerline of the control chart is at $\overline{p}$, and the control limits for x_i/n_i are

$$LCL_i = \overline{p} - 3\sqrt{\frac{\overline{p}(1-\overline{p})}{n_i}} = \overline{p} - 3\sqrt{\frac{\overline{p}\,\overline{q}}{n_i}}$$

$$UCL_i = \overline{p} + 3\sqrt{\frac{\overline{p}(1-\overline{p})}{n_i}} = \overline{p} - 3\sqrt{\frac{\overline{p}\,\overline{q}}{n_i}}$$

where we need the index i because the limits vary with n_i. If LCL_i, from this calculation, is negative, we use $LCL_i=0$. Similarly (but less often), if UCL_i exceeds 1, we use $UCL_i=1$. (Points *on* the control limit are considered "in control," so such cases imply that the control

---

[7]To verify this consider that the variance of the sum of independent variables is the sum of their variances. Also, for any constant, say α, $\text{Var}(\alpha X)=\alpha^2\text{Var}(X)$. In particular, the average is the sum of n *i.i.d.* random variables each of which has a variance of pq, and each of which is multiplied by $\alpha=1/n$. The variance of each component, then, is pq/n^2, and since we have n of them we obtain pq/n.

limit in question cannot detect special causes.) If x_i/n_i is outside the control limits for one or more i, the likely special cause may also apply to other subgroups.

=-

Since the ratio between the sizes of the control limit is inversely proportional to the square root of n_i, only large differences count; if the difference between the largest and smallest subgroup size is less than, say, 25%, we may set the control limits as per the average subgroup size. Table 5.6 shows the results of 30 subgroups from a stable process with sizes ranging between 100 and 200 units. Figure 5.10 shows the trial p chart for these data.

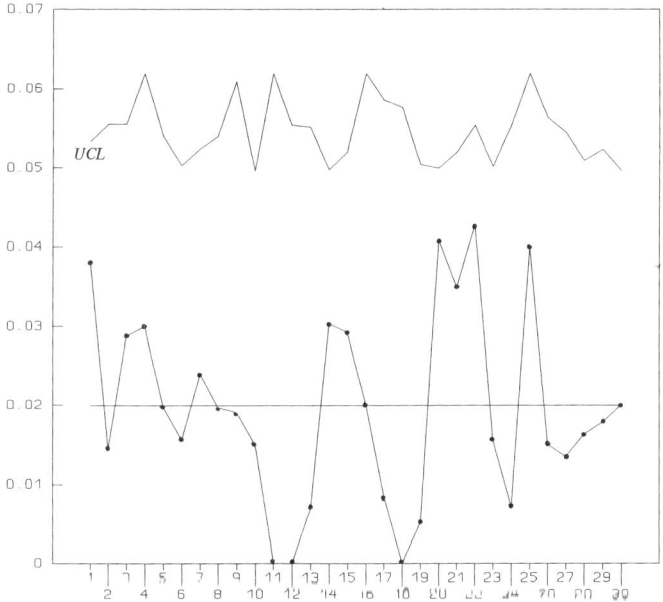

Fig. 5.10. A p chart with variable upper control limit ($LCL = 0$ throughout).

As it happens, all the points in Figure 5.10 fall within the control limits of the largest subgroup (i.e., the tightest limits). This leads to a shortcut: We mark control limits based on the largest and smallest subgroup sizes that exist in the group (in our case, $\sqrt{pq/200}$ and $\sqrt{pq/100}$). Every point that's within the tighter limits is certainly in control. Likewise, any point that's outside the looser limits is certainly out of control. For these cases there is no need to compute the exact limit. Only points that fall between the inner and outer control limits require an individual calculation. In more detail, let n_{max} and

#	n_i	x_i	x_i/n_i	UCL_i
1	158	6	0.037974	0.053325
2	139	2	0.014388	0.055533
3	139	4	0.028776	0.055533
4	100	3	0.030000	0.061902
5	152	3	0.019736	0.053977
6	192	3	0.015625	0.050226
7	167	4	0.023952	0.052413
8	152	3	0.019736	0.053977
9	105	2	0.019047	0.060891
10	200	3	0.015000	0.049615
11	100	0	0	0.061902
12	140	0	0	0.055406
13	142	1	0.007042	0.055155
14	198	6	0.030303	0.049764
15	171	5	0.029239	0.052032
16	100	2	0.020000	0.061902
17	118	1	0.008474	0.058570
18	124	0	0	0.057624
19	190	1	0.005263	0.050385
20	196	8	0.040816	0.049916
21	172	6	0.034883	0.051938
22	140	6	0.042857	0.055406
23	193	3	0.015544	0.050148
24	140	1	0.007142	0.055406
25	100	4	0.040000	0.061902
26	133	2	0.015037	0.056327
27	148	2	0.013513	0.054434
28	184	3	0.016304	0.050877
29	168	3	0.017857	0.052317
30	200	4	0.020000	0.049615

$\Sigma n_i = 4561$

$\Sigma x_i = 91$

$\overline{p} = 91/4561 = 0.019951$

Note: LCL = 0 for all subgroups.

Table 5.6

n_{min} denote the largest and smallest subgroups respectively, then LCL_{tight}, UCL_{tight}, LCL_{loose}, and UCL_{loose} are

$$LCL_{tight} = \bar{p} - 3\sqrt{\frac{\bar{p}\bar{q}}{n_{max}}} \; ; \quad UCL_{tight} = \bar{p} + 3\sqrt{\frac{\bar{p}\bar{q}}{n_{max}}}$$

$$LCL_{loose} = \bar{p} - 3\sqrt{\frac{\bar{p}\bar{q}}{n_{min}}} \; ; \quad UCL_{loose} = \bar{p} + 3\sqrt{\frac{\bar{p}\bar{q}}{n_{min}}}$$

If $LCL_{tight} = 0$, then $LCL_i = 0$ for all i. All the subgroup results such that x_i/n_i falls between the tight control limits are "in control," all the subgroups such that x_i/n_i falls outside the loose control limits are "out of control," and all other points need to be checked individually by the exact limits LCL_i and UCL_i.

Attribute control charts may apply in services, and they need not necessarily be limited to tracking defective manufactured items. For instance, we mentioned a potential use where an airline monitors the number of passengers who prefer a particular diet. Since the number of passengers on each flight varies, this requires the use of a p chart (rather than an np chart). Box 5.4 speaks to another non-manufacturing application of p charts.

=-

Box 5.4

A Canadian politician claimed that a tough anti drink-and-drive bill had been instrumental in reducing the incidence of alcohol-related accidents in the province of Manitoba. He compared the number of alcohol-related accidents during one period of half a year following the introduction of the bill to the number during same period in the previous year. Such claims by politicians, citing similar evidence, are not rare.

Spiring (1994) used basic p chart analysis to show that the real variation was well within the natural variation the accident process exhibited over a long period. The proportion he investigated was the ratio between alcohol-related accidents to the total number of accidents in each period. Since the total number of accidents varies between periods, the use of a p chart (as opposed to an np chart) is indicated. By using the *proportion*, Spiring effectively neutralized the effects of causes that are common to all types of accidents. As it happened, there were unusually few accidents (of *all* types) during the period in question, but this did not contaminate Spiring's analysis. His conclusion was that the politician's claims were totally without statistical confirmation.

As is usually the case in statistical analysis, Spiring did not set out to prove that the bill did *not* have an effect: just that such an effect could not yet be discerned based on the data. The actual change in this case was really minute, however.

=-

5.2.1. *Mixtures*

Mixtures can be a problem with *p* charts as with *np* charts. If we *find* that a mixture is involved, everything is fine. Otherwise, however, false out-of-control signals may cause tampering. Box 5.5 provides an example.

=-

Box 5.5

At Mare Island Naval Shipyard the personnel of a machine shop monitored the cost of poor quality on an ongoing basis, and maintained a *p* chart for the fraction defective products that they were producing each week. They were taught to do these things by a representative of America's largest quality training organization.

One glance at the *p* charts revealed that the proportion was out of control about once per month. Under the null, the time between signals should be measured in years! To my question how they dealt with the apparent problems, as well as the *COPQ* data, the foreman responded that they met every week to discuss the defects and find ways to improve the processes. I asked whether they've seen any improvement following these meetings, and he said no. Nor did the control charts show any discernible improvement.

I then observed that since the product mix was changing constantly, and because some products were much more liable to be defective than others, the percentage they were monitoring reflected a mixture. As a result, most out-of-control signals were false. The team spent much time chasing phantom special causes that did not exist. (The use of individuals charts [Section 6.5], although not theoretically sound in this case, would still be much better: it would not underestimate the true variation in the data.)

The sad part of this story is not only the waste that was caused while the wrong chart was used, but that this experience soured the team against control charts so much that I was not able to convince them to try doing it right neither then nor later. Nor did they wish to try any other statistical method. The bright side was that they could devote more time to breakthrough projects, in which they achieved remarkable results (Trietsch, 1992a; 1992b).

=-

5.3. *c* Control Charts for the Number of Occurrences in a
Constant Area of Opportunity

Sometimes there may be more than one defect per item, and we need to control the total number of defects. For instance, we may want to monitor the number of spelling errors in a newspaper, or the number of punctuation errors per page. Other examples might be the total number of defects in a roll of carpet, the total number of blemishes on a roll of paper, the total number of fires per annum in a particular region, the number of accidents per month, or the number of equipment failures per 100 hours of operation. In such instances we can regard each unit on which we count the attributes (such as each edition of the newspaper, each page, each roll, each year, each month, or each block of 100 hours of operation) as representing an equal *area of opportunity*.

When a single defect is enough to disqualify a whole unit, we are often more interested whether the unit is completely free from defects (acceptable), or not (rejectable). In such a case, we may choose to use an *np* chart. But sometimes defects are not very critical when taken separately (e.g., if you reject a whole book because of a typo, or even three issues on which you don't agree with the author, you will soon be left with nothing to read). In such cases we may want to control the total count of defects.

If the probability of an occurrence on a small area segment is constant and the probability of two or more occurrences generated very close to each other is negligible, the "arrival" of occurrences follows a Poisson process. The total number of occurrences, then, has a Poisson distribution. If we monitor the number in question for many such areas of opportunity, we can estimate the parameter of the Poisson distribution and devise a control chart for the count, to see if the process is in control.

Most often, the Poisson distribution is presented with a parameter λ (where $\mu = \sigma^2 = \lambda$), but for control charts it is customary to use the letter *c* (for "count") instead. The resulting chart is called a *c chart*.

Because the Poisson distribution is an approximation of the binomial distribution with large *n* and small *p*, and because *np* charts are often based on large values of *n* and small values of *p*, *there is no way to tell a c chart apart from an np chart just by looking at the sequence of values (i.e., the run chart part)*. The control limits associated with the *c* chart are slightly wider than those of the *np* chart, but this difference is negligible for small *p*. In short, a *c* chart looks and behaves like an *np* chart. The only difference is that instead of reporting the number of defective items in a subgroup of *n*, it reports the number of defects in a constant area of opportunity. Box 5.6 provides the technical details necessary to construct *c* charts.

=-=

Box 5.6: Constructing c Control Charts

Let m be the number of units checked. Let x_i denote the pertinent count (e.g., the number of defects) in the ith unit ($i=1,...,m$). $\bar{c}$ is defined by

$$\bar{c} = \frac{1}{m} \sum_{i=1}^{m} x_i$$

The centerline of the control chart is at $\bar{c}$, and the control limits are

$$LCL = \bar{c} - 3\sqrt{\bar{c}} \; ; \quad UCL = \bar{c} + 3\sqrt{\bar{c}}$$

But if LCL, from this calculation, is negative, we use $LCL=0$. (Points *on* the control limit are considered "in control," so $LCL=0$ implies that the lower control limit cannot detect special causes.) If x_i is outside the control limits for one or more i, the likely special cause may also apply to other units.

=-=

To illustrate the use of a c chart, and at the same time to demonstrate how similar it is to an np chart if n is large and p is small, we'll use an example with data generated by a simulated Poisson process with $\lambda = 3$. Recall that Figure 5.1 was based on a binomial process with $n = 100$ and $p = 0.03$, yielding $np = 3$. So, we may expect the results of our

Subgroup#	Result	Subgroup#	Result	Subgroup#	Result
1	4	11	5	21	1
2	4	12	1	22	5
3	3	13	2	23	6
4	4	14	3	24	3
5	5	15	3	25	3
6	2	16	4	26	2
7	4	17	2	27	0
8	1	18	3	28	6
9	1	19	0	29	3
10	2	20	2	30	0

Sum Total: 84, $\bar{c}$ = 84/30 = 2.8, LCL = 0, UCL = $2.8 + 3\sqrt{2.8}$ = 7.82

Table 5.7

new (independent) simulation to behave similarly, and we may expect the trial control chart to look similar to the trial *np* chart in Figure 5.1. Table 5.7 gives the numerical results, and Figure 5.11 is the appropriate trial *c* chart.

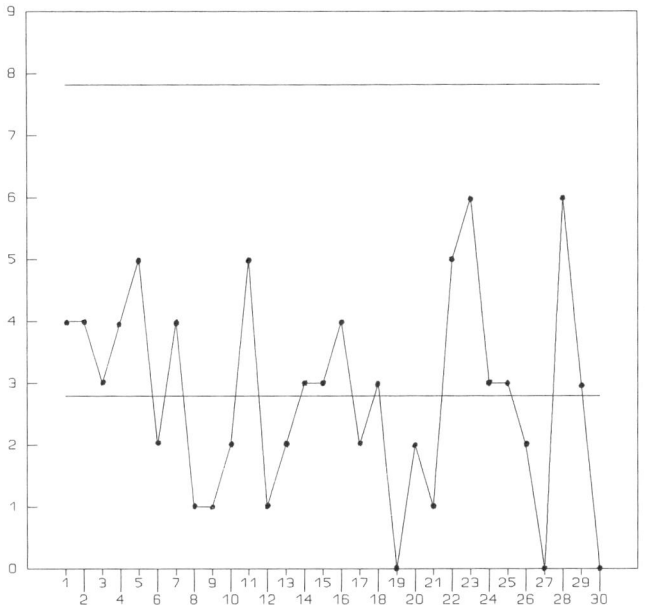

Fig. 5.11. A *c* chart.

5.3.1. *Demerit Control Charts*

Not all defects are equal. Sometimes it is desired to sort defects according to their seriousness. For instance, the highly influential Bell System classification plan sorts defects to four classes (Juran with Gryna, 1988, pp. 18.41-18.44).

♦ **Class A -- Very Serious Defects:** Class A defects are such that the unit is expected to fail in the field if shipped. Fixing the trouble after shipping is expected to be very expensive, and they may even cause personal injury or property damage.

♦ **Class B -- Serious Defects:** Defects that are likely (but not certain) to cause failure in the field that is difficult to correct, or are certain to cause a failure in the field that is easy to fix. Units that are certain to operate at a substandard fashion, or that are certain to cost more to operate and have shorter service life are also considered serious. Finally, extreme defects in finish (which the customer will almost surely object to), or defects that require the customer to invest significant extra efforts in installation fall into this category too.

♦ **Class C -- Moderately Serious Defects:** Units that may possibly fail in the field (but not likely to do so often), or units that are likely to cause trouble that is less serious than an operating failure, such as substandard operation, or require minor extra effort during installation, or display major (but less than extreme) finish problems, such as scratches.

♦ **Class D -- Not Serious Defects:** Defects that are not likely to cause any trouble in the field, or minor defects of appearance.

One should treat the plan as a template only, and sort defects based on the particular needs that are specific to each firm, especially considering that this classification plan is of pre-WW II vintage. Our main interest here, however, is how to control the number of defects when they are indeed deemed different. Essentially, there are two ways to do that. One is to chart the incidence of each class separately. This, we'll see, is the recommended approach. AT&T (1958), the formal quality control source that AT&T applies to its own operations, also recommends it. Nonetheless, there is another, quite popular, possibility: to assign *demerits* to each class, and chart the total demerits an area of opportunity presents. The result is a control chart for demerits. We now discuss this chart.

It is customary (but not necessary) to assign 100 demerits to Class A defects, 50 demerits to Class B, 10 to Class C, and 1 to Class D. Once we do that, even if defects of each class arrive as per a Poisson process, the random variable created by the total demerits per unit is *not* a Poisson random variable. Had all the weights been equal to 1, and assuming defects of each class appear as per independent Poisson processes, then their sum *would* be a Poisson random variable: the sum of individual Poisson random variables is Poisson. However, assigning equal weights to all classes defeats the purpose of the classification. And with *different* weights the demerit collection process violates the Poisson process condition that the count can only increase by one at a time. Therefore, the weighted sum we deal with does not have a Poisson distribution. Nonetheless, if each class separately has a Poisson distribution we can calculate the mean and the variance of our random variable based on information about the individual Poisson processes. So we can devise a control chart after all.

Denote the number of demerits per unit by P, then $P = \Sigma w_i c_i$ where w_i is the weight (in demerits) of Class i, and c_i is the average number of defects of Class i per unit. Specifically, for the four-class system we presented we obtain

$$P = w_A c_A + w_B c_B + w_C c_C + w_D c_D = 100 c_A + 50 c_B + 10 c_C + c_D$$

P is a weighted sum of independent random variables. In general, the expected value of such a sum is the equivalently weighted sum of the individual expected values, and the variance is also a weighted sum of the individual variances, but this time the original weights are squared. Using, these relationships we obtain the following parameters for our proposed control chart

$$LCL = \Sigma w_i \bar{c}_i - 3\sqrt{\Sigma w_i^2 \bar{c}_i}; \quad UCL = \Sigma w_i \bar{c}_i + 3\sqrt{\Sigma w_i^2 \bar{c}_i}$$

5.3.2. The COPQ Chart -- A Special Case of the Demerit Control Chart

The demerit system has its roots in the early days of statistical quality control. A refinement that has its roots in the Fifties concentrates on the monetary damage associated with each type of defect. Each defect is investigated individually, and assigned a monetary penalty according to the estimated damage it causes. Thus, we are really monitoring the cost of poor quality (*COPQ*). For instance, a defect that warrants scrapping a $5000 part is assessed at $5000. A defect that has a probability of 10% to cause a damage of $5000 is assessed at $500 (unless it's cheaper to scrap the unit, in which case we should do so, and assess the cost accordingly). The cumulated monetary penalties are collected for each area of opportunity -- say each day or each week of production -- and a control chart is devised for all to see.

Because it is difficult to devise control limits to what is, essentially, a demerit system with an unbounded number of classes, sometimes, the control limits are omitted, and we obtain a mere run chart. Or we may devise an individuals control chart for the data. In the former case the run chart, which is quite likely to *seem* quite erratic, is as likely to cause tampering and damage as it is to do good. In the latter case, there is a theoretical problem in that the control limits in individuals charts are based on the standard assumptions that the variables are normal, and *COPQ* data is often *far* from normally distributed. For a random variable to have a normal distribution it should be a sum of many small causes, none of which dominates. With *COPQ* data, the occasional big damage that is always around the corner, *and does not necessarily indicate a special cause,* is likely to dominate when it appears, and give a false signal. Note that it is important to deal with large causes, but it is also important to do so based on sound information whether we should look for a common cause or for a special cause. An "out of control" signal indicates that we should look for a special cause where none may exist, leading to tampering. Nonetheless, control charts that are based on the normality assumption are often remarkably effective even when this assumption is not justified.[8] A more serious problem that the *COPQ* chart shares with other demerit control charts is our next subject.

5.3.3. *Critique of Demerit and of COPQ Control Charts*

Monitoring demerits only makes sense when we want to assign different weights to different classes. Therefore, from the outset we should know that by using this method we take a risk of allowing one type of defects that might be easy to correct be hidden by another type of defect that may be difficult to correct: the incidence of defects in some classes, when observed individually, may be out of control, but when commingled with the other types, and assigned a low weight, they often seem in control.

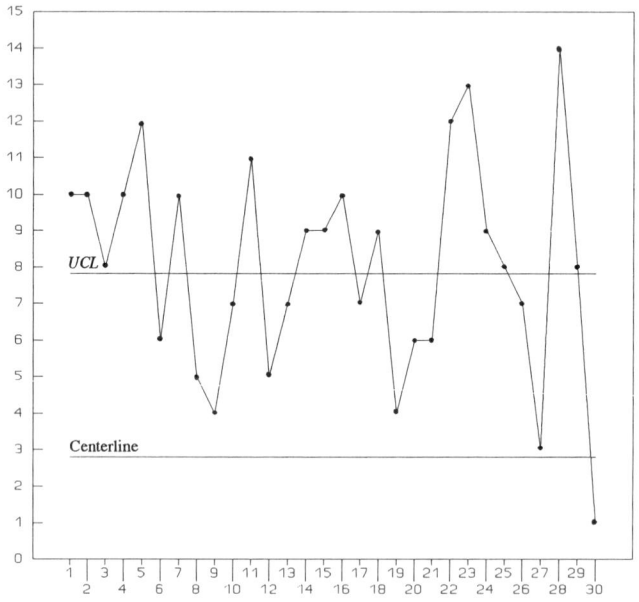

Fig. 5.12. A *c* chart for Class D defects without commingling (*LCL*=0).

---

[8]We should also mention that it is sometimes possible to use transformations that make a non-normal distribution behave approximately as normal. In such cases the use of an individuals chart *following* such a transformation is theoretically sound, and the transformation should not even be "perfect" to be useful (since control charts are robust to slight deviations from normality). For *COPQ* we might try transformations that reduce the tail to the right, such as the square root transformation. Nonetheless, doing this is tantamount to assigning a more equal weight to all problems, which is definitely *not* the intention in *COPQ* or demerits charts.

An example serves to illustrate this possibility. For simplicity, we only consider two classes: Class A (with 100 demerits) and Class D (with 1 demerit). Assume that the incidence of the two classes is the same, with a mean of 3. However, the defects that belong to Class D are out of control, and their arrival rate in reality is 9. Figure 5.12 is a separate c chart for Class D defects, and roughly half the points show that the process is indeed badly out of control. Figure 5.13 is a demerit chart with the Class A demerits totally masking the Class D problem. The data for the two charts is summarized in Table 5.8.

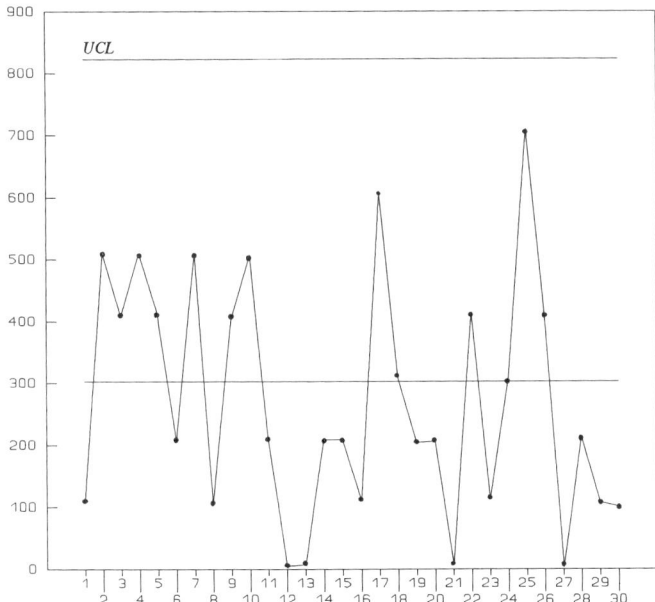

Fig. 5.13. A demerit chart with the data of Fig. 5.12 commingled with the Class A defects. The chart is falsely in control.

An identical observation holds for *COPQ* charts, where big problems mask small problems. In conclusion, if small problems are important, monitor them separately. Lumping them together with large problems is likely to hide them. An idea that is useful in some environments is to assign the responsibility of monitoring smaller problems to more junior workers. This provides them with useful training and allows the more senior personnel to monitor the more important issues.

#	D	A	Demerits	
1	10	1	110	*
2	10	5	510	*
3	8	4	408	*
4	10	5	510	*
5	12	4	412	*
6	6	2	206	
7	10	5	510	*
8	5	1	105	
9	4	4	404	
10	7	5	507	
11	11	2	211	*
12	5	0	5	
13	7	0	7	
14	9	2	209	*
15	9	2	209	*
16	10	1	110	*
17	7	6	607	
18	9	3	309	*
19	4	2	204	
20	6	2	206	
21	6	0	6	
22	12	4	412	*
23	13	1	113	*
24	9	3	309	*
25	8	7	708	*
26	7	4	407	
27	3	0	3	
28	14	2	214	*
29	8	1	108	*
30	1	1	101	

* Class D defects count is out of control when treated separately

$LCL = 0$, $UCL = 822.6$, Centerline $= 303$

Table 5.8

5.4. u Control Charts for the Number of Occurrences in a Variable Area of Opportunity

As we've seen, c charts are Poisson-based and similar to np charts. Likewise, u *charts* are Poisson-based and similar to p charts. They are used when the "arrival" of defects behaves as a Poisson process but the area of opportunity varies. For instance, if we want to compare the numbers of forest fires in several regions with different areas; or if we want to compare the number of typos in several books of different length.

As in p charts, the control limits here vary for each area of opportunity i. Box 5.7 provides the necessary technical details.

=-

Box 5.7: Constructing u Control Charts

Let m be the number of units checked. Let x_i denote the pertinent count (e.g., the number of defects) in the ith unit ($i=1,\ldots,m$), and let a_i be its area of opportunity. $\overline{u}$ is defined by

$$\overline{u} = \frac{\sum\limits_{i=1}^{m} x_i}{\sum\limits_{i=1}^{m} a_i}$$

The centerline of the control chart is at $\overline{u}$, and the control limits for x_i/a_i are

$$LCL_i = \overline{u} - 3\sqrt{\frac{\overline{u}}{a_i}}; \quad UCL_i = \overline{u} + 3\sqrt{\frac{\overline{u}}{a_i}}$$

But if LCL_i, from this calculation, is negative, we use $LCL_i=0$. (Points *on* the control limit are considered "in control," so $LCL=0$ implies that the lower control limit cannot detect special causes.)

Let a_{max} and a_{min} denote the largest and smallest opportunity areas among the units respectively, then LCL_{tight}, UCL_{tight}, LCL_{loose}, and UCL_{loose} are

$$LCL_{tight} = \overline{u} - 3\sqrt{\frac{\overline{u}}{a_{max}}}; \quad UCL_{tight} = \overline{u} + 3\sqrt{\frac{\overline{u}}{a_{max}}}$$

$$LCL_{loose} = \overline{u} - 3\sqrt{\frac{\overline{u}}{a_{min}}}; \quad UCL_{loose} = \overline{u} + 3\sqrt{\frac{\overline{u}}{a_{min}}}$$

All the units whose x_i/a_i falls between the tight limits are "in control," and those whose x_i/n_i falls outside the loose control limits are "out of control"; other points need to be checked individually by the exact limits LCL_i and UCL_i. If $LCL_{tight} = 0$, then $LCL_i = 0$ for all i. If x_i is outside the control limits for one or more i, the likely special cause may also apply to other units.

=-

To demonstrate the similarities between u charts and p charts, we again simulate a similar example. This time we use areas of opportunity that are equal to the subgroup sizes reported in Table 5.5, with $u = 0.02$. The results are summarized in Table 5.9. The trial u chart depicted in Figure 5.14 should be compared to Figure 5.10: The control limits are almost identical. The run charts, of course, are different, since the processes are independent.

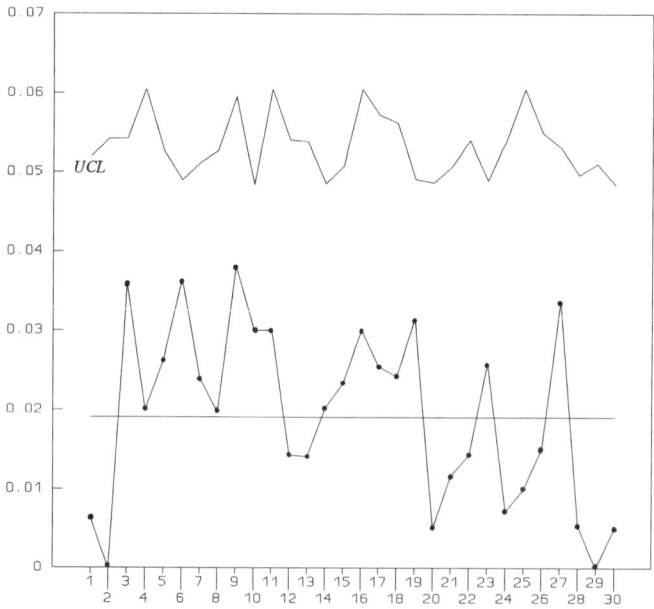

Fig. 5.14. A u chart.

5.4.1. Demerit Control Charts with Unequal Areas of Opportunity

Demerit control charts can be extended for unequal areas of opportunity as well. The control limits for the ith unit are

#	a_i	x_i	x_i/a_i	UCL_i
1	158	1	0.006329	0.052037
2	139	0	0	0.054218
3	139	5	0.035971	0.054218
4	100	2	0.02	0.060508
5	152	4	0.026315	0.052681
6	192	7	0.036458	0.048976
7	167	4	0.023952	0.051136
8	152	3	0.019736	0.052681
9	105	4	0.038095	0.059509
10	200	6	0.03	0.048372
11	100	3	0.03	0.060508
12	140	2	0.014285	0.054092
13	142	2	0.014084	0.053844
14	198	4	0.020202	0.048520
15	171	4	0.023391	0.050759
16	100	3	0.03	0.060508
17	118	3	0.025423	0.057217
18	124	3	0.024193	0.056283
19	190	6	0.031578	0.049133
20	196	1	0.005102	0.048670
21	172	2	0.011627	0.050667
22	140	2	0.014285	0.054092
23	193	5	0.025906	0.048899
24	140	1	0.007142	0.054092
25	100	1	0.01	0.060508
26	133	2	0.015037	0.055002
27	148	5	0.033783	0.053132
28	184	1	0.005434	0.049619
29	168	0	0	0.051041

$\Sigma a_i = 4561$

$\Sigma x_i = 87$

$\overline{u} = 87/4561 = 0.019074$

Note: $LCL_i = 0$ for all subgroups.

Table 5.9

$$LCL_i = \Sigma w_j \bar{u}_j - 3\sqrt{\frac{\Sigma w_j^2 \bar{u}_j}{a_i}}; \quad UCL_i = \Sigma w_j \bar{u}_j + 3\sqrt{\frac{\Sigma w_j^2 \bar{u}_j}{a_i}}$$

where $\bar{u}_j$ is obtained for each class j by dividing the total number of defects that belong to Class j by the total area of opportunity covered by all the subgroups, Σa_i.

Unfortunately, the critique that we cited against the use of demerit control charts with constant area of opportunity is still valid. So, our recommendation is to run a separate u chart for each class that is deemed important enough to warrant the effort.

5.5. Common Errors to Avoid

♦ Recalculating limits without evidence that the process changed in an acceptable way. This is tantamount to defining "in control" as "what happened recently," which is an instance of using Funnel Rule 4.

♦ Using data that is not the result of a single process: for instance, using a p chart in an environment with unstable mixture of products and processes.

♦ Similarly, combining several sources of variation in one chart (as in demerit charts or $COPQ$ charts), which leads to hiding potential problems if they are relatively small. (If they are not important enough to know about, it is wasteful to monitor them in the first place; otherwise, they should be monitored separately.)

♦ Using subgroups for attributes that are too small to reveal problems (e.g., when using subgroups of 200 for a defect rate of 0.0005, about 90% of the subgroups will not even have one defect; thus they are next to useless unless we plan to monitor the frequency of non-zero results as our control variable).

Supplement 5

The Relationship Between Control Charts and Hypothesis Testing

One of Deming's major crusades was an almost Quixotic fight against the use of computed probabilities of risk in *analytic studies*. Deming held that such probabilities apply only to *enumerative studies*. In an enumerative, or *descriptive*, study -- and the quintessential example is a census, a subject on which Deming was a leading technical expert -- we sample units from a statistical frame to estimate parameters about the whole.[1] In descriptive studies it is conceptually possible to simply investigate the whole frame instead of sampling. The reason we may prefer sampling for such purposes is economical: it is often excessively expensive, or even impossible, to measure all the frame. Sometimes the measurement is destructive, e.g., when we want to know how many matches fail to ignite in a given batch of *existing* matches, unless we use sampling we'll remain with matches that will all fail to ignite now. Be that as it may, the results of an enumerative study are estimates of the parameters of the frame. The way we use these estimates is usually direct, e.g., we use the Congressional representation census to decide how many representatives to allocate to various regions. Or, based on our estimate of the number of defective items in a lot we decide whether to accept it or not, and, perhaps, how much to pay for it.

Why the italics on the word "existing" in the former paragraph? Because if we try to draw conclusions about the fraction of matches in other batches that will be manufactured in the future or that were manufactured under conditions that may have been different from the batch we studied, we just crossed into the realm of analytic, or *comparative, studies*. Analytic studies are concerned with action. We wish to know whether we should select one process over another, change our process or leave it unmolested, etc. This requires *prediction,* rather than simple *estimation.* Note that the future matches do not exist yet. We should be very cautious in making the assumption that the future population of matches will be indistinguishable from the existing population we sample now. The process might change (e.g., a new supervisor, or new workers), the wood may be different (e.g., drier), the chemicals may be different, and so on. Based on a sample one can state that the probability

---

[1] The frame is often referred to as the "population." This usage did not meet with Deming's approval either.

that more than 1 % of the matches in the present population will fail to ignite is less than 5 %. What is often done, however, is to extend this information and make statements such as: "When you buy our matches we can assure you, based on extensive testing, that the risk you take that more than 1 % of them will fail to ignite is less than 5 %." This statement can only be true if the probability that something will be different in the future is *zero*. No statistical tools have been invented yet that can prove that the future will be like the present. Furthermore, the conditions under which the study is performed cannot be said to represent all the myriad of realistic scenarios.[2] There is an honest solution to this problem, however. We can simply predicate statements about the future by an explicit condition such as: "If this process will behave in the future as it behaved in the past, then ...." In fact, every prediction should be predicated with a similar statement, and even if it is not, the customer is well-advised to assume that such a caveat is indeed attached.

But there is an additional problem which would still remain unresolved. This has to do with the fact that even in enumerative studies statisticians often use assumptions about distributions that are, at best, only approximations of reality. For instance, the assumption that all items a process produces are independent of each other is practically never absolutely true. So, any probability calculation that is based on such an assumption should be suspected. Such calculations, in my opinion, can and should be used as approximations, however, and it is possible to measure the deviations from the assumptions and get an idea how reliable the probabilities in question are.

A related question is whether control charts are in essence associated with enumerative or analytic studies. The answer is quite fuzzy. Deming preferred to view control charts as tools for action, and thus associated with analytic studies. This is certainly true in the context of an engineering study, such as the process improvement study described in Box 1.1. But when a control chart is used to monitor a process, one can also argue that it is used to verify whether the population of items being produced are similar enough to the items that were used to create the control chart. This, in spite of Deming's vehement objections, is

---

[2]Using professional judgement, it is a good idea to perform analytic studies under conditions that are intentionally extreme. For instance, if we can show that our output is robust to extreme temperatures we may be more confident that it will perform well in the range of temperatures that we'll encounter in practice. To decide which conditions are important, and what "extreme" means in their context, takes professional knowledge that statisticians cannot provide (at least not while wearing the "statistician" hat). Be that as it may, DOE (design of experiments) usually includes testing at such extremes. In the same context, Taguchi's *external array* is supposed to represent a variety of possible realistic conditions for this purpose (but there is no mathematical or practical need to use external arrays; the same conditions can be incorporated into the main design, i.e., the internal array).

essentially a question of choosing between hypotheses. That is, control charts *can* be used to make decisions that are identical to the decisions involved in hypotheses testing.

Be that as it may, for these reasons, Deming deemed practically all statements of probability as unacceptable. His solution was to use similar predictions, but without stating pseudo-exact probabilities of error. At best, he said, you can state that under the conditions stated the probability of error is *small*. One might say that he was content to treat such probabilities as unknowable. Deming (1975) explains this issue further. Also, the following quote from *The New Economics,* p. 181, is apt

> It is a mistake to suppose that the control chart furnishes a test of significance -- that a point beyond a control limit is "significant." This supposition is a barricade to understanding. *Use of a control chart is a process for achievement of a stable state, the state of statistical control.* (italics added)

Opponents, however, contend that approximate results may be better than no results at all. (Note that Deming did not oppose the use of approximations in general. It is almost always necessary.)

Because hypothesis testing is associated with statistical tests, which, in turn, are associated with probabilities of error, ardent followers of Deming abhor the treatment of control charts as an instance of hypothesis testing. The following excerpt from *Out of the Crisis,* p. 369, applies to the readers of this text, at least formally. According to Deming they should look elsewhere for study materials about control charts (Deming's recommended sources may be found there too).

> Most of the books nevertheless contain bear traps, such as [...] modified control limits, areas under the normal curve, acceptance sampling. [....] Some books teach that use of a control chart is test of hypothesis: the process is in control, or it is not. Such errors may derail self-study.
>
> The reader should also avoid passages in books that treat confidence intervals and tests of significance, as such calculations have no application in analytic problems in science and industry....

In p. 351, Deming quoted another source, C.I. Lewis, *Mind and the World-Order* (Sribner's, 1929; Dover, 1956; p. 283).

Incidentally, the risk of being wrong in a prediction cannot be stated in terms of probability, contrary to some textbooks and teaching. Empirical evidence is never complete.

Deming provided me personally with a great amount of inspiration, much beyond any other teacher, and I tend to agree with his opinions even when they are outrageous by conventional standards. In this case, however, I still think that even without explicitly specifying an α-risk -- i.e., a rate of false signals (*RFS*) -- what we're doing in control charting can and should be described as hypothesis testing. I also think that stating approximate risk probabilities subject to explicit assumptions is not necessarily more wasteful than throwing away the information they provide. Usually one can say that the risk is *at least* as much as the theory says, and this is useful information too. For instance, if I know the risk is at least 5% we will expect false signals at least that often, and our situation is better than it would be without this information. As for the use of confidence intervals, here, in my opinion, Deming himself laid a bear trap: the ubiquitous use of the mean alone, when only a confidence interval can come near to describing reality, is likely to follow (Tukey, 1991). In my opinion, control charts *are* a form of confidence intervals. (In Chapter 8 we devise confidence intervals for control charts that are very useful in measuring the effects of variation.)

To recap, the arguments why control charting is an example of hypothesis testing are as follows: first, control charting is not necessarily an analytic study concerned only with prediction of the future. It is also a method to determine if a process has been well-behaved during the period in which the charting took place. As such, it meets some tests of an enumerative study for which even Deming accepted the validity of the statistical methods in question. Second, in practice *the behavior* of people who use control charts is identical to the behavior of people who are testing hypotheses, with one exception: the decision limits are not based explicitly on predetermined *RFS*. I don't think that exception is enough to set this behavior so apart from hypothesis testing that one should not be allowed to use that terminology any more. Furthermore, by not stating the risks numerically we do not necessarily increase our profound knowledge, which Deming treasured.

Be that as it may, although Shewhart, Deming's mentor, decided not to work directly with the *RFS*, he did get pretty close to using it explicitly. The following excerpts from *Economic Control of Quality of Manufactured Product,* pp. 276-277, shed some light on Shewhart's approach to this issue. This is the place where Shewhart finally recommends the use of $\pm 3\sigma$ (after studiously avoiding doing so for 275 pages). Here **P** is the probability that a well-behaved process will show "in control" as it should, i.e., **P** is the complement of the *RFS*.

How then shall we establish allowable limits on the variability of samples? Obviously, the basis for such limits must be, in the last analysis, empirical. Under such conditions it seems reasonable to choose limits [...] such that the associated probability **P** is *economic* in the sense now to be explained. If more than one statistic is used, then the limits on all the statistics should be chosen so that the probability of looking for trouble when any one of the chosen statistics falls outside its own limits is economic.

Even when no trouble exists, we shall look for trouble (1-**P**)*N* times on the average after inspecting *N* samples of size *n*. On the other hand, the smaller the probability **P** the more often in the long run may we expect to catch trouble if it exists. We must try to strike a balance between the advantages to be gained by increasing the value **P** through reduction in the cost of looking for trouble when it does not exist and the disadvantages occasioned by overlooking troubles that do exist. [....] Furthermore, it is obviously necessary to adopt some value which will be acceptable for practically all quality characteristics, although the economic value **P** for one quality may not be the same as that for another. [....]

For these reasons we usually choose a symmetrical range characterized by limits

$$\overline{\Theta} \pm t\,\sigma_\Theta \tag{86}$$

symmetrically spaced in reference to $\overline{\Theta}$. Tchebycheff's theorem tells us that the probability **P** that an observed value of Θ will lie within these limits as long as the quality standard is maintained satisfies the inequality

$$P > 1 - \frac{1}{t^2}.$$

We are still faced with the choice of t. Experience indicates that $t = 3$ seems to be an acceptable economic value.

One can safely say that instead of using an arbitrary *RFS* (or its complement, **P**), Shewhart chose to use simple "catch all" control limits (while allowing **P** to vary for different distributions). However smart that decision was, there is no valid reason to go overboard in condemning people who prefer to use arbitrary figures in a different manner. But using the *RFS* explicitly is, at worst, such an equivalently arbitrary usage of figures; at best it may be used to strike a more economical balance in specific cases.

As an example of an arbitrary choice of **P**, we may decide to set it as close to 99% as possible, and claim that this is the most economical value on average. Many authors use **P** = 0.9973. The immediate result of this approach is that the computation of control limits becomes much more complex, and for that reason it may not be appropriate for manual application. But this is a minor technical issue. The crux of the matter is that choosing **P** arbitrarily is theoretically not less valid than choosing t arbitrarily. Both approaches can be pursued with Shewhart's objective of reaching an economical result, and both can be based on empirical evidence.

Nonetheless, the particular choice **P**=0.9973 is often a result of the lack of knowledge Deming referred to. It is based on an erroneous claim that it is the value associated with Shewhart charts. With mean $(\overline{x})$ and dispersion charts, if the chart is based on a very large sample, it is indeed the (approximate) probability the $\overline{x}$ chart *alone* will show "in control" when the process is indeed in control. But the dispersion chart also contributes erroneous "out of control" signals, and typically does so with a higher rate than the $\overline{x}$ chart. With p, np, c and u charts there is no dispersion chart, but still the *RFS* is usually far from 0.0027. It only provides a good approximation when p (or u) is large enough to make it behave approximately as a normal variate. One necessary but not sufficient test for that is that *LCL* should be > 0. Furthermore, as discussed in Chapter 8, all these probabilities are stated under unrealistic assumptions (that the sample is very large and includes no "out-of-control" points). Typical sampling errors may inflate or decrease these *RFS* several folds. They also tend to increase the average *RFS*.

Be that as it may, in my opinion, and perhaps the opinion of many who persist in using such probabilities explicitly, the use of approximations is not enough to discredit hypothesis testing. As stated, this is a question of opinion, but Deming was not tolerant to different opinions in this area (among others), and therefore some of his followers are not tolerant to them either. In conclusion, my personal recommendation to the interested readers is that they delve into the issue and judge for themselves. Another source for that purpose is Woodall and Faltin (1996), who provided extensive references, discussed some of the points to a much greater depth, and delineated several alternative control charts that are beyond our scope.

Chapter 6
Control Charts for Continuous Variables

Attribute control charts are appropriate when they are concerned with pure attributes (e.g., red vs. white, male vs. female), and when the theoretical distributions fit the models, at least approximately. But when the attribute is conformance, it is often based on a measurement of a continuous variable; e.g., when the diameter of a shaft falls outside the tolerance limits, the attribute is "defective." The main problem with this practice is that we lose a lot of information during the transformation of continuous measurements to attributes. Figure 6.1 demonstrates this point: the defect rate is roughly equal in the three process distributions depicted. Therefore, attribute charts will fail to differentiate between them. All three processes might even show statistical control on attribute control charts (although in Figure 6.1[c] this is less likely).

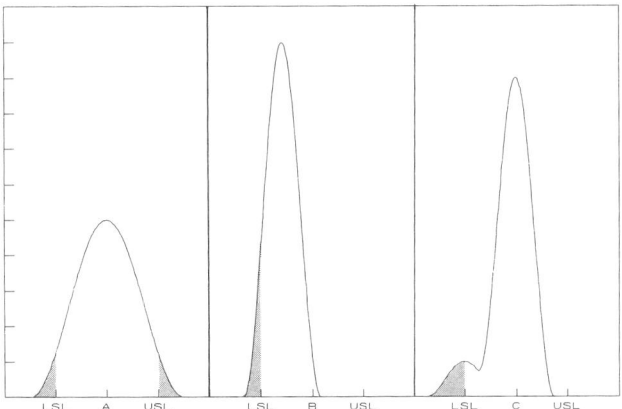

Fig. 6.1. Three different processes with a similar conformance.

But there are important differences between the three distributions. Figure 6.1[a] represents a process that is in statistical control, but is not capable of meeting the specifications consistently. We can say this because all parts seem to come from the same distribution (control), but the tails are outside the specification limits. The distribution in Figure 6.1[b], in contrast, represents a potentially capable process that is out of adjustment,

159

so it creates defects (and excessive quadratic loss). Finally, the process behind Figure 6.1[c] is capable, and adjusted reasonably well, but it is out of control a fraction of the time (perhaps due to two types of raw materials that require adjustment when changed over), and creates defects then. In conclusion, three cases that may look the same when reduced to attributes provide a wealth of additional information when we look at the original data.

The three cases depicted in the figure call for three different improvement approaches. In Figure 6.1[a], we need to improve the process by reducing its variability. This can be done by investigating the sources of variation and addressing the largest ones. In Figure 6.1[b] the first improvement we should consider is to center the process. Once we do that the process is likely to produce good items consistently. Such centering may or may not be easy. Sometimes the problem is simply a defective gauge, or a biased measurement instrument. The use of Funnel Rule 4 (in the past) may also be the culprit, when we adjust the process based on recent output that may reflect previous deterioration. In other instances it is not always trivial to adjust a process -- it may not be just a question of moving a dial 1mm to move the center by 1mm -- but it is often possible to manipulate the process inputs to achieve a better adjustment. To that end, statistical experimental design methods can provide information on how to adjust a process, and to what extent it is possible and economical to do so. Incidentally, Taguchi showed that when using these methods we can often reduce the variation concurrently (which is why they also apply to the former case). Finally, in Figure 6.1[c] the best immediate response is probably to find out what causes the exceptional results. This is the case control charts are designed to show: the process is out of control, and if we can bring it to control, it will become fully satisfactory (Box 1.1 provides an example).

What would be the results of responding differently? Suppose, for instance, that we respond to the first case by looking for special causes. The problem is that we're not likely to find any special causes there, and we'll just get ourselves frustrated and demotivated. This would be tampering. A less prevalent problem is addressing the third case by trying to reduce the variation. As a result, the out of control situation would not be designed away from the process, and we'd still have a high defect rate. Furthermore, one of the problems in this case is lack of predictability, because one can't expect the frequency of special causes to be stable. The second case is least likely to lead to the wrong response, since the signal is loud and clear.

Variable control charts such as $\overline{x}$ and s, $\overline{x}$ and s^2, or $\overline{x}$ and R charts can distinguish between such cases, and thus help steer improvement efforts in the right direction. Data is collected in subgroups and the variance is estimated by statistics that measure the variation exhibited *within* the subgroups, i.e., ignoring differences *between* subgroups. In all three cases we employ a pair of charts in parallel: one for dispersion (s, s^2, or R), and one for the mean ($\overline{x}$). And in all three cases the statistics collected for the dispersion chart are used as input to devise the control limits for the mean chart. When s or s^2 charts are used, the variance of the process is estimated by the s^2 statistics of the subgroups, while the use of R involves the range between the smallest and largest measurements in each subgroup.

$\overline{x}$ and s control charts -- which should be recommended in most cases -- are covered in Section 6.2, and the others will be covered in Sections 6.3 and 6.4. Wheeler (1995, Chapter 3) discusses and compares several other possibilities (without endorsing them). He also cautions against some of the worst ways to abuse data, chief among which being the use of subgroup-to-subgroup dispersion as a basis for the calculation of control limits. The methods we cover in this chapter, in contrast, are all meritorious, depending on the circumstances. Using R wastes data, but most authors and practitioners consider this waste tolerable for small subgroups (say up to five items, and certainly no more than ten). Indeed, most variable control chart applications employ this scheme, usually with subgroups of five or four. In this text we refer to $\overline{x}$ and R charts with subgroups of five or four as *basic Shewhart control charts,* to reflect the popularity of these particular combinations. But the popularity of basic Shewhart control charts should not be construed as a recommendation to prefer them. While using R may be easiest (in the absence of computers or statistical calculators), using s^2 is most efficient in terms of the amount of data necessary, and in terms of efficiency s is in-between. The popularity of using R stems from the historical fact that control charts were developed before the advent of computers and of cheap electronic calculators. s is the next most popular method, and it also happens to be the one Shewhart recommended for small and medium subgroups. For large subgroups, Shewhart recommended the use of s^2. In Supplement 6.1 we discuss the implications of these choices in terms of efficiency (see Figure S6.1.1), and we argue that in spite of Shewhart's recommendation s charts are excellent for large subgroups. Furthermore, efficiency is not the only important consideration. Later in this chapter we'll show that s charts are based on a statistic that is more robust against outliers (i.e., against data that does not really belong to the process, and which the control chart should help us identify). Thus, for *large* subgroups we can recommend s charts without reservation, while for small subgroups the user has to weigh the advantages of efficiency (associated with using s^2) against robustness (associated with s) before making a selection. Usually, robustness is more important than efficiency, so there is a good argument in favor of using s as the dispersion statistic of choice for *all* subgroup sizes. *This distinction is only important when estimating the inherent process variance (i.e., when creating trial control charts), since it's possible to construct* *control limits for s^2 that will signal exactly together with traditional control limits for s, and vice versa.* One case in which it is clearly more convenient to use s^2, however, is when the subgroups are not equal to each other. As for R charts, they are acceptable for small subgroups and convenient for manual application. But in many modern applications there's no need for manual calculations. Nonetheless, most computerized packages feature these charts, without any theoretical or practical technical justification whatsoever (a practical marketing need may be argued, to cater to customers even when they err).

Variable control charts also exist for individual data, i.e., data that is not collected in subgroups. It is technically possible, and often advantageous, to use such charts to monitor various counts. So, in a sense, variable control charts are all we really need, since they can replace attribute charts. Nonetheless, as we'll show by example later in this chapter, individuals charts are not powerful relative to other available alternatives. Therefore, their use should be limited to cases where it is impossible or expensive to collect meaningful subgroups. Even then we should consider more powerful versions to analyze the results. We discuss these issues in Sections 6.5 through 6.7.

All the technical details necessary to construct $\bar{x}$ and $\bar{s}$-, $\bar{x}$ and s^{2}-, and $\bar{x}$ and $\bar{R}$ charts are given in Boxes 6.1, 6.2, and 6.4, respectively. Explanations, derivations, and examples are provided separately, with some of them relegated to Supplements 6.1, 6.2 and 6.3.

6.1. Principles Common to All Shewhart Variable Control Charts

Shewhart charts are designed to identify special causes. Special causes may be defined as causes that are large in their effect and either rare or change slowly. A cause that is in action all the time without change, even if large, is not special. A cause that is rare or changes slowly, but is small, is not likely to be identified, and therefore it does not meet the criteria for a special cause *as operationally defined by showing out of control in a Shewhart chart.* We can also argue that such a cause is not important economically, so it is not bad that a Shewhart chart is not likely to identify it.

The way Shewhart charts identify special causes is by (i) comparing the variation exhibited by each subgroup to an estimate of the inherent *short-term variation* that the process demonstrates; and (ii) comparing the variation between subgroups to the variation expected based on this short-term process variation. To be considered "in control," (i) the items in each individual subgroup must be *consistent enough,* and (ii) when compared to each other the subgroups have to be "consistent enough." The techniques involved in this endeavor define operationally what "consistent enough" means here.

What all this implies is that we want to monitor the process over extended periods, and compare the process output to the range we expect based on short-term variation. *So we need a measurement for dispersion that is not likely to be influenced by medium- and long-term causes.* The results are typically used to estimate σ, and we may denote the estimate by $\hat{\sigma}$. (It's important to remember that, almost surely, $\hat{\sigma} \neq \sigma$.)

The most obvious way to estimate short-term variation is by taking subgroups of few consecutive items and seeing how much variation the items in each subgroup exhibit relative to each other. This is assumed to represent the inherent short-term variation. As long as the successive units are not dependent on each other -- which is often the case unfortunately -- this assumption is reasonable. If we then compare this variation to the variation between subgroups taken far from each other, we might be able to tell the short-term variation apart from other causes of variation that may have manifested between the two subgroups. The final result is that we take periodic subgroups of few consecutive items, estimate σ based on the *internal* variation each of them exhibits, and devise control limits for the mean, $\overline{x}$, which we also derive from each subgroup, at the centerline $\pm 3\sigma_{\overline{x}}$. We'll see presently that the centerline is determined independently of the estimation of σ, but often it is also based on data, more specifically, the grand mean of the data.

So far we have implicitly assumed that the short-term variation does not change from one period to the next. In effect this assumption is equivalent to assuming that only the location of the mean is subject to change. In reality, of course, the variation may also be "out of control," so to speak. For example, in production processes loose attachments, worn fixtures, loose bearings, or fluctuations in electrical power or in hydraulic pressure may well cause increased variation that is not always combined with shifting the mean (increased variation will practically always cause shifts in the *observed* mean, but that is not equivalent to actually shifting it). Therefore, the Shewhart methodology includes checking the variation too. This is done in the dispersion portion of the chart. Essentially, if the observed dispersion in a particular period seems excessive, we declare the process "out of control." To that end, control limits are provided for the variation, based also on $\pm 3\sigma_D$, where σ_D is the standard deviation of the dispersion statistic we use to represent the variation (D is a mnemonic for dispersion, and may be replaced by R, s, or s^2 as necessary).

It is customary, and generally convenient for analysis purposes, to draw the $\overline{x}$ chart directly above the dispersion chart, on the same sheet (see Box 1.1, for example). Sometimes we may even observe informative correlations between the two. For a normal distribution in control the two charts should *not* be correlated, so if we see such a correlation we may suspect that either the distribution is not normal or the process is not in control. For instance, if the dispersion tends to be high when $\overline{x}$ is high the distribution may be skewed to the right, and if the dispersion tends to be high when $\bar{x}$ is low the distribution may be skewed in the opposite direction. When the dispersion statistic is out of control, the $\bar{x}$ measurement may be meaningless. This is why we have to check the dispersion chart first. Nevertheless, a distribution need not be normal to be considered "in control," so such correlations do not necessarily justify action. Finally, when a process is out of control even points that look in control may not be representatives of the "in control" process distribution. They can just be less influenced by the problem.

6.1.1. *Drawing the Centerline for the $\bar{x}$ Chart*

Most sources recommend only one way to determine the centerline for the $\bar{x}$ chart: use the grand mean of the data, i.e., the average of the $\bar{x}$ values, usually denoted by $\bar{\bar{x}}$. This simple method is the one Shewhart recommended originally, and it is also the best way to estimate the centerline from data to minimize the quadratic loss due to estimation error. But there is another way that should be used when appropriate: draw the centerline *where it is supposed to be based on the design of the product or process*. The test whether we should do so is simple: if we know how to adjust the process mean to the target, the centerline should be drawn there; otherwise, we should use $\bar{\bar{x}}$.

When appropriate, setting the centerline to target yields a better control chart, capable of detecting deviations from target more reliably. This is because we can and should demand that the process not only be "in control" but also be centered, which is why we draw the centerline where it is *designed* to be. When we do not know how to center the process, we limit our efforts to checking whether the process is at least consistent, i.e., in control, and such consistency is relative to the grand mean. Again, when we *can* adjust to target, signals due to the process not being adjusted correctly are justified and potentially helpful; but if we cannot adjust, we should not generate signals just because the results are far from where we'd like them to be. To do that would be ignoring the voice of the process.

Sometimes it is impossible to adjust the process to the desired design target, but we know how to adjust it to other values. In such cases the centerline should be drawn as close to the design target as we can adjust the process to. As far as process adjustment is concerned, this feasible value is our target. But under no circumstances should the centerline be drawn at some desired position we cannot adjust to, because this may lead to unwarranted out-of-control signals (and thus, tampering). That's why we use $\bar{\bar{x}}$ when we cannot adjust to target.

When we do not know how to adjust the process mean to the desired target, we have an opportunity to study the process better, and learn to adjust it. This can often be done by experimental approaches. Recall from Chapter 3 that the measurable expected quality cost includes K times the squared bias and the variance, as well as the operating costs. Concentrating on bias and variance, it is plausible that in order to reduce the quadratic loss we'll intentionally design some bias into the process. Once we do that, however, we obtain a new target which we should strive to hit accurately.

6.1.2. *Monitoring Quadratic Loss Directly -- An Option*

In a mature quality operation, many processes should be known well enough so we'll be able to draw the centerline of $\overline{x}$ charts according to our decision on how to adjust the process. But this does not mean that we assume that the process is so adjusted! One reason for the control chart is because we're not sure the process is adjusted as it should be, so when we are far enough from target to register an out-of-control signal we'll adjust it. As mentioned in Chapter 4, it's also legitimate to adjust without waiting for an out-of-control signal (e.g., adjust by a small fraction of the difference following each sample). Of course, if our process never requires adjustment and never goes out of control, it should not be charted at all. Thus, our assumption is that the process is less than perfect, and it may not be adjusted exactly as desired. Therefore, while we collect our dispersion statistic, we cannot assume that we know the process mean. This implies that we should use the statistic

$$ s^2 = \frac{\sum (x_i - \overline{x})^2}{n-1} $$

or the range statistic (which is invariant with the average). The former statistic has $n-1$ degrees of freedom; we lose one degree of freedom because we use the data to estimate $\overline{x}$. Had we known that the process is centered, however, it would be advantageous to use

$$ s^2 = \frac{\sum (x_i - T)^2}{n} $$

where T is the target, and all n degrees of freedom are retained. The additional degree of freedom implies that we have more information, and thus a more efficient statistic *if* the process is indeed adjusted. But the price is that when this statistic is too large we have to investigate further to find out if it is due to a shift of the mean or an increase in variation. For this reason this statistic is rarely, if ever, used for control charting purposes. It is certainly inappropriate for constructing control charts: it is not robust against adjustment errors, and may yield excessive variance estimates.

Nonetheless, when we have an adjustable process, a case can be made to monitor the latter statistic *only*, and thus control the quadratic loss directly. When the loss is excessive relative to the level that the process is likely to produce, we investigate to find out why (shifted mean or increased variation). Preliminary simulation results suggest that this may be a powerful method to monitor a process subject to quadratic loss: it signals relatively quickly if there is a large bias or increased variance. As might be expected, it is not sensitive to small biases, but we may not really want our control charts to be very sensitive to small biases, which contribute little quadratic loss. See also MacGregor and Harris (1993), where the same statistic is used, but with exponential smoothing. They show that it signals more effectively than regular Shewhart charts. They also consider the use of the former statistic, where the objective is to monitor variance alone, while letting the mean drift (as it sometimes does in chemical and other production processes).

6.1.3. *The Normality Assumption*

The theory behind the various calculations associated with control charts usually assumes a normal process distribution. This assumption, when applied to the $\bar{x}$ part of the chart, is not strong if the real distribution is at least roughly symmetrical. The reason for that is that $\bar{x}$ is the subgroup average, and the average, when based on a large subgroup, behaves approximately as a normal random variable. This is true even for small subgroups if the distribution is roughly symmetrical. When the distribution is skewed, the normal approximation is less appropriate for a small subgroup. The central limit theorem -- the theoretical basis for the use of the normal distribution -- is formally valid only in the limit when the subgroup size goes to infinity. The following technical note quantifies somewhat the behavior of the average for a finite subgroup, as a function of the distribution.

=-

Technical Note

When the distribution of the population has known moments, the expected value of $\bar{X}$, the average of a sample of n units, is μ and its standard deviation, $\sigma_{\bar{x}}$, is $\sigma_x/\sqrt{n}$. The expected value and variance are the first and second moments. Let us now introduce two additional statistics associated with higher moments: k measures the skewness (or lack of symmetry), and β_2 measures the flatness (or kurtosis) of a distribution. We'll follow Shewhart's notations and choice of statistics, but we should also note that there is another popular statistic for skewness in wide use -- Pearson's skewness coefficient -- that should not be confused with k. These statistics are defined as follows:

$$k = \frac{\sum_{i=1}^{n}(x_i - \bar{x})^3}{n\hat{\sigma}_x^3} ; \quad \beta_2 = \frac{\sum_{i=1}^{n}(x_i - \bar{x})^4}{n\hat{\sigma}_x^4}$$

To follow Shewhart's notation exactly, we should use

$$\hat{\sigma}_x = \sqrt{\frac{\sum_{i=1}^{n}(x_i - \bar{x})^2}{n}}$$

instead of dividing by $n-1$, as we usually do to obtain an unbiased estimator for σ_x^2. For the normal distribution $k=0$ and $\beta_2=3$. A distribution with negative k is skewed to the right, and with positive k it is skewed to the left, but while $k=0$ for symmetric distributions, $k=0$ does not imply perfect symmetry; rather it implies balance between the third moment to the right and to the left of the mean.

Distributions with small k and β_2 close to 3 are approximately normal. Our concern is whether this is the case for the sample average. In general, $k_{\bar{x}}$ and $\beta_{2\bar{x}}$, i.e., the skewness and flatness of the sample average, are connected to the respective values of the original distribution by the following functions of n

$$k_{\bar{x}} = \frac{k}{\sqrt{n}} ; \quad \beta_{2\bar{x}} = \frac{\beta_2 - 3}{n} + 3$$

Clearly these values tend to 0 and 3, respectively, when n is large. And they do so quicker when the starting values are close to 0 and 3.

For example, let's take a right-triangular distribution (which was also used by Shewhart when he developed control charts). For this quite skewed and asymmetric, distribution, k and β_2 are 0.5661 and 2.3978 respectively. Using $n=4$ leads to 0.283 and 2.849 for the sample mean, which yields a distribution that is not far from normal. Using $n=5$ yields 0.253 and 2.880. We'll return to these examples later.

=-

Nonetheless, control charts have practical value even if we don't know the distribution (let alone know it to be normal). The only thing we cannot do properly without knowledge of the distribution is to calculate the rate of false signals (RFS), but such calculations are rarely necessary in typical applications. Indeed, when Shewhart developed the theory of variable control charts he tested them by extensive simulation studies, involving both normal and non-normal process distributions. Thus, control charts were never meant to be restricted to normal processes.

To demonstrate that control charts work for non-normal distributions we'll use a non-normal example. For a distribution not known to be normal, there is no theoretical justification for that usage, even approximately. But there is empirical evidence, beginning with Shewhart's work, that it works very well for a wide range of distributions (Wheeler, 1995). With regard to $\overline{x}$ charts, we will show similar results in this chapter and in Supplement 6.2. Dispersion charts, however, are more sensitive to deviations from normality, so we should allow for the possibility of more (or less) false signals from the s chart (or any other dispersion chart, for that matter). Because s charts may be more sensitive, the best recommendation may be to use them but not allow out of control signals that do not have a clear explanation to preempt the usage of (the more reliable) $\overline{x}$ charts. The $\overline{x}$ charts will be more reliable in spite of the fact that they use data from the dispersion chart. To show this, we start by discussing $\overline{x}$ and s charts in detail.

6.2. $\overline{x}$ and s Control Charts

Box 6.1 provides the technical details necessary to construct $\overline{x}$ and s charts. Afterwards, we show examples, discuss the details and provide explanations.

=-

Box 6.1: **Constructing $\overline{x}$ and s Control Charts**

Let m be the number of subgroups taken, and let n be the subgroup size, such that the n measurements in each subgroup are taken close together, and the m subgroups are taken apart from each other. Let x_{ij} be the measurement of interest of the ith item in the jth subgroup (where $i=1,2,...,n$ and $j=1,2,...,m$).

Construction of the s chart

Let s_j be calculated for the jth subgroup by the formula

$$s_j = \sqrt{\frac{\sum_{i=1}^{n}\left(x_{ij}-\overline{x}_j\right)^2}{n-1}}$$

where $\overline{x}_j$ is the subgroup mean of the jth subgroup, i.e.,

$$\bar{x}_J = \frac{\sum_{i=1}^{n} x_{ij}}{n}$$

and define $\bar{s}$ by

$$\bar{s} = \frac{\sum_{j=1}^{m} s_j}{m}$$

Plot the s_j values in a chart with control limits at

$$LCL_s = B_3\bar{s}; \quad UCL_s = B_4\bar{s}$$

Where the factors B_3 and B_4 are given by Table 6.1 for various n values. They are based on the formulae

$$B_3 = Max\left\{0, \ 1-3\frac{\sqrt{1-c_4^2}}{c_4}\right\}: \quad B_4 = 1+3\frac{\sqrt{1-c_4^2}}{c_4}$$

c_4 is another factor given by Table 6.1; its derivation is given in Supplement 6.2. We can also draw a centerline at the $\bar{s}$ level (but this centerline does *not* coincide with the median). By substituting t for 3 in these equations we can obtain similar multipliers for use with an s chart if we choose not to use Shewhart's convention of setting $t=3$.

If and only if all the s values fall within these control limits, we may proceed to construct the $\bar{x}$ chart. Otherwise -- especially if a large percentage of points are without the limits -- we should investigate what, if anything, is special about the outliers or the process in general. If necessary, upon finding special causes, or making a decision to ignore points that are suspect (a sometimes necessary expedient, but not without its risk of ignoring what may be the most important data), the control limits may have to be recalculated based on subgroups that are considered "in control,"[1] or new data has to be collected (if the process was changed in response to the new information). Once control limits are established based on enough subgroups (e.g., at least 100 but preferably 400, although many consider 25 to be enough), there is no need to update them unless there is reason to believe that the process has changed (and we do not choose to change it back), or that the control limits were not based on enough data after all (see Chapter 8).

---

[1]This step is not worthwhile according to some experts, including Deming.

n	A_3	B_3	B_4	c_4
2	2.659	0	3.267	0.7979
3	1.954	0	2.568	0.8862
4	1.628	0	2.266	0.9213
5	1.427	0	2.089	0.9400
6	1.287	0.030	1.970	0.9515
7	1.182	0.118	1.882	0.9594
8	1.099	0.185	1.815	0.9650
9	1.032	0.239	1.761	0.9693
10	0.975	0.284	1.716	0.9727
11	0.927	0.321	1.679	0.9754
12	0.886	0.354	1.646	0.9776
13	0.850	0.382	1.618	0.9794
14	0.817	0.406	1.594	0.9810
15	0.789	0.428	1.572	0.9823
16	0.763	0.448	1.552	0.9835
17	0.739	0.466	1.534	0.9845
18	0.718	0.482	1.518	0.9854
19	0.698	0.497	1.503	0.9862
20	0.680	0.510	1.490	0.9869
21	0.663	0.523	1.477	0.9876
22	0.647	0.534	1.466	0.9882
23	0.633	0.545	1.455	0.9887
24	0.619	0.555	1.445	0.9892
25	0.606	0.565	1.435	0.9896

For $n > 25$ use $c_4 \approx 4(n-1)/(4n-3) \approx 1$, $A_3 = 3/(c_4\sqrt{n}) \approx 3/\sqrt{n}$,
$B_3 = 1 - 3/(c_4\sqrt{2(n-1)}) \approx 1 - 3/\sqrt{2n - 2.25}$,
$B_4 = 1 + 3/(c_4\sqrt{2(n-1)}) \approx 1 + 3/\sqrt{2n - 2.25}$.

Table 6.1

Construction of the $\bar{x}$ chart

If we know how to adjust the process, we can draw the centerline at the desired target. Otherwise, define the overall mean by $\bar{\bar{x}}$

$$\bar{\bar{x}} = \frac{\sum\limits_{j=1}^{m} \bar{x}_j}{m} = \frac{\sum\limits_{j=1}^{m}\sum\limits_{i=1}^{n} x_{ij}}{mn}$$

and draw a centerline for $\bar{x}$ at $\bar{\bar{x}}$. Once a centerline is drawn, one way or another, add control limits as per

$$LCL_{\bar{x}} = Centerline - A_3\bar{s}; \quad UCL_{\bar{x}} = Centerline + A_3\bar{s}$$

where $A_3 = 3/(c_4\sqrt{n})$ is given by Table 6.1. By substituting $t/(c_4\sqrt{n})$ for A_3 we can devise $\pm t\sigma_X$ control limits. Plot $\bar{x}_j$ on the chart, sequentially. The process is considered out of control if any point $\bar{x}_j$ is outside the control limits. Other tests are discussed in Chapter 7.

=-

Let's illustrate by a simple example. Table 6.2 shows the results of 125 drops of a quincunx, collected in 25 subgroups of 5 beads each.[2] Each subgroup is listed in a separate row with the five items listed in the first five columns. Thus, each row represents a subgroup of five consecutive items sampled from a process that is in control, and possesses an approximately normal distribution. The sixth column in the table is the average of each subgroup. The seventh column provides an estimate of the standard deviation, s. The eighth column is the range, or difference between the smallest and largest value (which we'll require in Section 6.4). For instance, in the first row the average is $(10+12+13+10+13)/5 = 11.6$, the s statistic is obtained by

$$\sqrt{\frac{(10-11.6)^2 + (12-11.6)^2 + (13-11.6)^2 + (10-11.6)^2 + (13-11.6)^2}{5-1}} \approx 1.52$$

---

[2]Also known as a *bead-board*, a quincunx (pronounced kwin-cux) is an instrument where beads are dropped through a grid of pins phased in such a way that at each stage beads hit a pin and must shift to the right or to the left (with a roughly equal probability). After going through several stages like that each bead falls at a horizontal distance from its origin that is a discrete random variable. The beads are collected in separate cells (columns) that form a histogram of the results. Theoretically, the random variable is a shifted binomial with $p=0.5$ and n equal to the number of stages the beads go through. In the case reported here this number was 10. Large bead-boxes are often displayed in scientific museums to illustrate the normal distribution.

j	x_{1j}	x_{2j}	x_{3j}	x_{4j}	x_{5j}	$\overline{x}$	s	R
1	10	12	13	10	13	11.6	1.52	3
2	11	12	11	12	12	11.6	0.55	1
3	13	16	10	10	12	12.2	2.49	6
4	14	11	12	11	13	12.2	1.30	3
5	13	13	13	11	12	12.4	0.89	2
6	10	12	15	13	14	12.8	1.92	5
7	11	9	15	10	9	10.8	2.49	6
8	15	14	13	17	11	14	2.24	6
9	11	12	17	16	13	13.8	2.59	6
10	17	14	10	13	13	13.4	2.51	7
11	16	14	13	12	14	13.8	1.48	4
12	12	13	16	12	13	13.2	1.64	4
13	14	14	13	12	13	13.2	0.84	2
14	16	12	14	14	10	13.2	2.28	6
15	11	16	10	10	15	12.4	2.88	6
16	14	11	12	12	9	11.6	1.82	5
17	8	13	13	11	15	12	2.65	7
18	15	10	11	14	10	12	2.35	5
19	11	11	11	15	11	11.8	1.79	4
20	13	9	10	8	13	10.6	2.30	5
21	12	14	12	14	16	13.6	1.67	4
22	15	14	15	12	15	14.2	1.30	3
23	13	13	14	16	14	14	1.22	3
24	11	13	14	14	9	12.2	2.17	5
25	11	12	12	11	14	12	1.22	3
						12.584	1.8447	4.44

Table 6.2

and the range is $13-10=3$. Incidentally, many textbooks recommend a neat shortcut formula for s,

$$s = \sqrt{\frac{\sum\limits_{i=1}^{n} x_i^2 - \frac{\left(\sum_1^n x_i\right)^2}{n}}{n-1}} = \sqrt{\frac{\sum\limits_{i=1}^{n} x_i^2 - n\bar{x}^2}{n-1}}$$

For example, in our case,

$$s = \sqrt{\frac{196+256+121+144+256-\dot{5}134.56}{4}} \approx 1.52$$

Gunter (1993) shows that this formula may lead to numerical errors when used with large samples with relatively small coefficient of variation σ/μ. Accordingly, he recommends rejecting software packages that utilize it. Still, it is convenient for manual calculations with few data.

When we take the average of the s_j values, we obtain $\bar{s}=1.8447$. One might think that this could serve as our $\hat{\sigma}_X$, but $\bar{s}$ is *not* considered to be a good estimate of σ_X. This is because while s^2 is an unbiased estimate of σ_X^2 (regardless of the distribution), s is *not* an unbiased estimate of σ_X. (Mathematically, this has to do with the fact that taking the square root induces a nonlinear transformation. The effect is most pronounced with small subgroups and becomes negligible with large subgroups.) While it is not imperative to restrict ourselves to unbiased estimators, most practitioners prefer to correct for this bias. The expected bias, generally speaking, is a function of the process distribution, so formally we cannot correct it unless we know what our distribution is. In practice, however, we resort to our regular default, and assume that the process is distributed normally. To obtain an unbiased estimate of σ_X under this assumption we divide s by the correction factor c_4 (given in Table 6.1 and discussed in more detail in Supplement 6.2), i.e.

$$E(\sigma_X) = \frac{\bar{s}}{c_4}$$

c_4 is a function of the subgroup size. For instance, for $n=5$, and for the normal distribution, $c_4 = 0.9400$, so $\bar{s}/0.9400$ is an unbiased estimate of σ_X. Therefore, in our case our estimate will be $\hat{\sigma} = 1.8447/0.9400 = 1.9624$.

Before we can use this estimate for the $\bar{x}$ chart, however, we need to check whether the variance itself is under control. This is done by the s chart. For this purpose we need σ_s, so we can create control limits for s at $\bar{s} \pm 3\sigma_s$. As we show in the following technical note, we can use a simple expression for this purpose:

$$E(\sigma_s) = \sigma_X \sqrt{1 - c_4^2}$$

=-

Technical Note

   To prove this relationship recall that S^2 is an unbiased estimator of σ_X^2, and therefore

$$\sigma_S^2 = E[S - E(S)]^2 = E(S^2) - [E(S)]^2 = \sigma_X^2 - \sigma_X^2 c_4^2 = \sigma_X^2(1 - c_4^2)$$

Our result follows by taking the square root. This relationship is valid for any distribution for which we might calculate c_4. (Our table relates to the normal distribution only, however.)

=-

   Substituting $\bar{s}/c_4$ for σ_X, we can now obtain $\pm 3\sigma_s$ control limits for the s chart. The lower control limit, LCL_s is given by

$$LCL_s = \text{Max}\left\{0, \bar{s} - 3\bar{s}\frac{\sqrt{1 - c_4^2}}{c_4}\right\} = \text{Max}\left\{0, \bar{s}\left(1 - 3\frac{\sqrt{1 - c_4^2}}{c_4}\right)\right\} = B_3\bar{s}$$

where the Max operator ensures that the result will not be negative, or we'd set $LCL_s = 0$. The upper limit, UCL_s is

$$UCL_s = \bar{s} + 3\bar{s}\frac{\sqrt{1 - c_4^2}}{c_4} = \bar{s}\left(1 + 3\frac{\sqrt{1 - c_4^2}}{c_4}\right) = B_4\bar{s}$$

   For our particular example, $\bar{s} = 1.8447$. $B_3 = 0$ (for subgroups of five), so $LCL_s = 0$, and $B_4 = 2.089$, leading to $UCL_s = 3.8536$. The trial s chart is given in the lower part of Figure 6.2 (this is a trial chart because it utilizes its own data to create the control limits). Since all points are in control, we may proceed to construct the trial $\bar{x}$ chart. This trial chart is given in the upper part of the same figure. All the points are in control. Additional points, in the future, should be added to the chart without changing the limits -- unless we decided to gather more data to obtain more reliable estimates, as discussed in Chapter 8.

   Although the factors we used above, such as c_4, B_3, B_4, and A_3 are all based on the assumption that the process is normal -- an assumption that is approximately correct in the

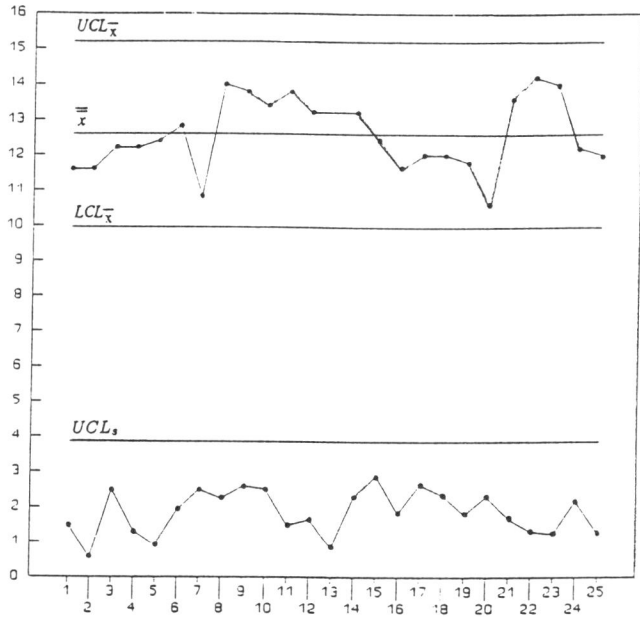

Fig. 6.2. An $\bar{x}$ and s trial chart for the quincunx results.

quincunx case -- we can and should use the same factors for other distributions as well. The only adverse effect is that the *RFS* as well as the power of the chart may not be equal to those associated with the normal distribution. This usage is especially benign for roughly symmetric distributions with central modes. To demonstrate the robustness of the methodology against deviations from normality, the most skewed distribution Shewhart used in his (manual) simulations was a right triangular distribution where X ranges between -1.3 and 2.6. Experience suggests that the right triangular distribution is indeed more skewed than most practical distributions, so if it's true that the process mean with this distribution is close enough to normal, then it is also usually true in practical applications.[3] Technically, he used 40 chips marked as -1.3, 39 marked as -1.2, and with each increment of 0.1, one less chip, leading to a single chip marked 2.6. The sampling was done at random and with returns (i.e., after sampling a chip it would be returned and all the chips would be mixed

---

[3]A notable exception is the highly skewed exponential random variable, which measures the gaps between arrivals of a Poisson process (such as false signals). Supplement 6.2 shows that the dispersion chart for this variable, if based on the normal factors, leads to $RFS \approx 5\%$, which is certainly too high for most applications.

well so that the probability the same chip would be sampled again would be as before).
Shewhart chose these numbers so that their expected value is 0, and it can be shown that the
variance is 0.91, or $\sigma_X = \sqrt{0.91} = 0.954$. Shewhart reported satisfactory results with this
distribution.

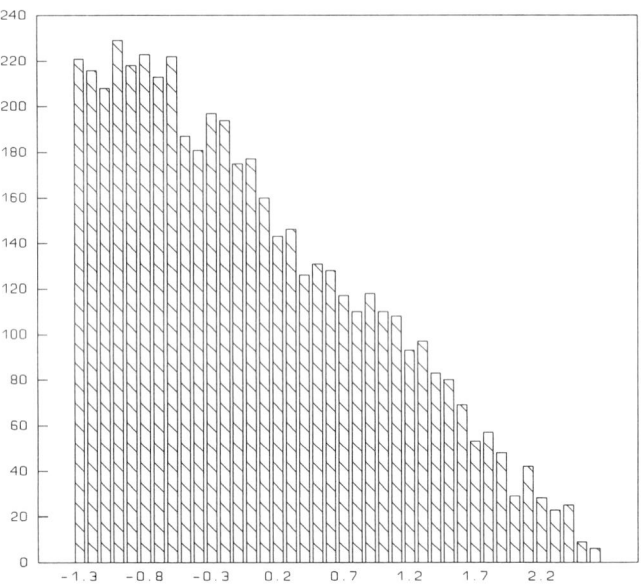

Fig. 6.3. A sample of 5000 items from Shewhart's right-triangular distribution.

Here, we'll follow in Shewhart's footsteps and use a (computer-generated) right
triangular distribution with the same parameters to simulate a process that's in control. For
the purpose of the numerical examples we'll assume that we cannot adjust the process at will
(and thus we'll compute the centerline by the data). The first step in the simulation is to
sample the right triangular distribution 5000 times to create a data base from which we can
work later. To demonstrate that the data is indeed triangular, Figure 6.3 shows a histogram
of the results. Note that the histogram is not a "perfect" right triangle, nor should we expect
it to be even with a sample of 5000. (To check the hypothesis that this is a viable result from
a triangular distribution we may employ the Chi-square test. In this case we have 40 degrees
of freedom and the result is 30.96, which is well within control. Interested readers can find
details about the chi-square test in any introductory statistics textbook.)

Table 6.3 shows the first 250 items, arranged in 50 rows, each with 5 items listed
in the first five columns. Thus, each row represents a subgroup of five consecutive items
sampled from a process that is in control, and possesses a triangular distribution. As in

x_{1j}	x_{2j}	x_{3j}	x_{4j}	x_{5j}	$\overline{x}$	s	R
-1.1	0.5	1.8	-0.2	-0.7	0.06	1.1415	2.9
0.3	0.8	0.5	2.1	-0.6	0.62	0.9783	2.7
1.2	-0.7	-1.2	-1.3	-0.4	-0.48	1.0085	2.5
0.6	-0.4	-1.3	-0.3	-0.6	-0.4	0.6819	1.9
0.9	-0.8	-0.8	0.8	-1.1	-0.2	0.9670	2.0
-1.2	0.2	-0.5	-0.7	0.2	-0.4	0.6042	1.4
-0.2	0.9	-0.7	1.6	-0.9	0.14	1.0738	2.5
-0.3	-0.6	0.6	-0.4	-0.9	-0.32	0.5630	1.5
-1.1	0.4	-0.8	-1.3	-1.3	-0.82	0.7120	1.7
1.8	-0.9	0.6	-0.5	0.2	0.24	1.0502	2.7
0.5	0	0.7	-0.6	-0.6	0	0.6042	1.3
-0.1	0.3	-1	-0.6	0.6	-0.16	0.6504	1.6
2	-1.3	0.6	1.1	-1.2	0.24	1.4502	3.3
-0.6	-0.5	1.6	-0.7	1.3	0.22	1.1300	2.3
1.9	0.4	-0.3	0.2	0.5	0.54	0.8204	2.2
1.7	-0.2	0	0	-0.3	0.24	0.8264	2.0
-0.1	-0.8	-0.4	-0.5	0.4	-0.28	0.4550	1.2
0	2.2	0.7	-0.2	1.5	0.84	1.0114	2.4
0.4	-0.7	-0.1	-1.1	-0.6	-0.42	0.5805	1.5
0.5	0.6	1.1	-1	0.3	0.3	0.7842	2.1
0.6	-0.3	-0.7	-0.5	-0.9	-0.36	0.5814	1.5
0.4	0	-1.3	-0.6	-0.3	-0.36	0.6427	1.7
-0.3	-1	-0.7	-1.2	0	-0.64	0.4930	1.2
-0.6	-0.6	-0.6	1.3	0	-0.1	0.8246	1.9
-1	-1.1	0.3	0.3	0.7	-0.16	0.8295	1.8
0.6	-0.1	0.9	-0.3	-1.3	-0.04	0.8591	2.2
0	1.1	0.9	-0.5	-0.2	0.26	0.7021	1.6

-0.4	-1.1	-0.8	-0.6	-0.7	-0.72	0.2588	0.7
-1.2	0.4	1.2	-0.4	-0.7	-0.14	0.9476	2.4
0.7	-0.9	0	0.6	0	0.08	0.6380	1.6
-0.1	0.2	-0.2	1.2	0.4	0.3	0.5568	1.4
0	-0.6	0	-0.6	-0.2	-0.28	0.3033	0.6
0.6	-0.2	-1.2	-0.3	1.3	0.04	0.9503	2.5
0.3	0.3	1.2	1.6	0.3	0.74	0.6189	1.3
-0.9	-0.9	-1	0.6	-1.2	-0.68	0.7259	1.8
-0.3	-0.6	-0.9	-0.2	-0.1	-0.42	0.3271	0.8
-1.1	0.3	-0.2	1	-0.6	-0.12	0.8106	2.1
-0.2	-1.2	0.7	-0.2	0.2	-0.14	0.6986	1.9
-1.2	-0.7	-1.1	-0.6	-0.8	-0.88	0.2588	0.6
-0.5	-0.8	-0.3	-0.9	2.4	-0.02	1.3737	3.3
0	0.2	-0.4	-0.3	-1.1	-0.32	0.4970	1.3
2.3	-1.1	-0.6	-0.3	-1.2	-0.18	1.4342	3.5
-0.7	-0.1	0.8	2.2	1.3	0.7	1.1424	2.9
0.3	-0.3	0	0.7	-0.9	-0.04	0.6066	1.6
1.7	0	-1.1	0.3	-1	-0.02	1.1389	2.8
-0.5	-1.2	-0.4	1.1	0.7	-0.06	0.9397	2.3
1.4	0.8	-0.9	-0.7	-0.4	0.04	1.0065	2.3
0.9	0.3	0.2	0.3	-0.8	0.18	0.6140	1.7
1.8	-0.8	-0.6	1	0.1	0.3	1.0954	2.6
-0.6	-0.8	0.2	-1.2	-0.3	-0.54	0.5273	1.4

Table 6.3

Table 6.2, the sixth column in the table is the average of each subgroup. The seventh column provides an estimate of the standard deviation, s, and the eighth column is the range.

Shewhart demonstrated that $\bar{x}$ for subgroups with four or five is approximately normal even with this highly asymmetrical distribution. We can show the same results based on our sample as well. Figure 6.4 shows the distribution of $\bar{x}$ for 1250 subgroups of four

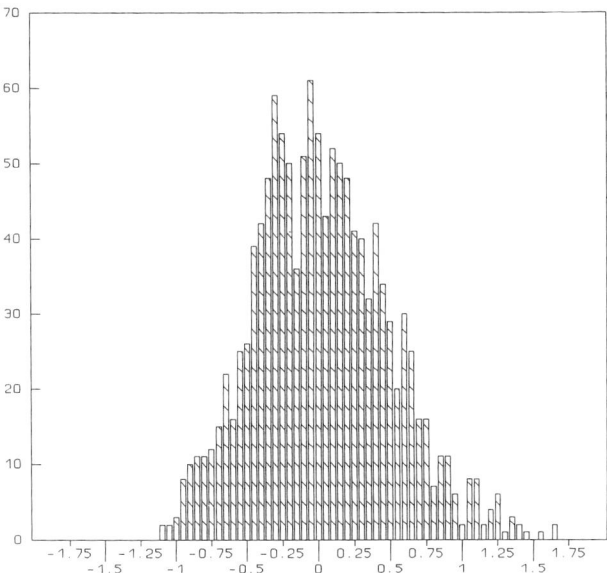

Fig. 6.4. The distribution of the average of samples of four from Shewhart's right-triangular distribution.

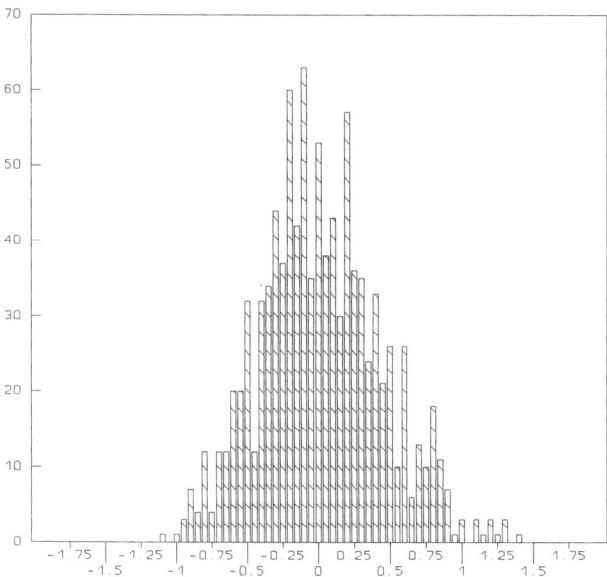

Fig. 6.5. The distribution of the average of samples of five from Shewhart's right-triangular distribution.

drawn from our 5000 triangular random variables. Figure 6.5 shows a similar picture for 1000 subgroups of five each. Note that if we should choose to select fewer groups for our histograms the picture would be even closer to normal. They are shown in this less smooth format to make a point: this is how random data looks like.

To construct an $\overline{x}$ and s chart for this process, the first step is to calculate $\overline{s}$ based on a large enough sample. Since we have 1000 subgroups we can specify a very large sample if we so choose, but this is not a cost-free decision. For example, it is certainly not justified to take the time and effort to collect 1000 subgroups before even starting the analysis of the process. Thus, we need to use a smaller sample, at least for initial analysis. The prevailing rule of thumb for this purpose is to use at least 20 subgroups, preferably 25 or 30. We discuss the sample size issue in detail in Chapter 8, but here we'll follow the rule of thumb, and use 25. One reason for doing that is to demonstrate the results. Another reason is to make it easier to trace the calculations. We'll show that using this rule of thumb leads to volatile results. This volatility is *not* due to the use of a non-normal distribution, but due to the use of a small sample. Indeed, when we use more data the results will be much better.

Accordingly, we'll use the first 25 subgroups reported in Table 6.3. Column 6 provides the data we need, s, and the average of the first 25 values is $\overline{s}$ = 0.8186. Divided by c_4 = 0.9400, our estimate will be $\hat{\sigma}$ = 0.8186/0.9400 = 0.8709. To check whether the variance itself is under control we construct the trial s chart. Using the shortcut factors, B_3 and B_4, i.e., 0 and 2.089 in our case (with $\overline{s}$ = 0.8186), we obtain LCL_s = 0, and UCL_s = 2.089x0.8186 = 1.710. The s chart for the first 50 items -- with control limits calculated by the first 25 of them -- is given in Figure 6.6.

Since all our s values fall within the control limits, we may now proceed to construct the control limits for $\overline{x}$. Our centerline is determined by the overall average of the first 25 subgroups, $\overline{\overline{x}}$ (under the implicit assumption that we do not know how to adjust the process), and we obtain −0.0664. Using the factor, A_3 (1.427 for n=5, by Table 6.1), we obtain for $LCL_{\overline{x}}$ and $UCL_{\overline{x}}$

$$LCL_{\overline{x}} = -0.0664 - 1.427 \times 0.8186 = -1.2345$$
$$UCL_{\overline{x}} = -0.0664 + 1.427 \times 0.8186 = 1.1017$$

Figure 6.7 shows the $\overline{x}$ chart. In this case, all the points are the results of a process in control. Nonetheless, using our current trial limits, 13 subgroups of five, among the 1000 subgroups that were simulated, violate the upper control limit. This means that, on average, the process would be stopped by error once every 76.92 inspections. There are

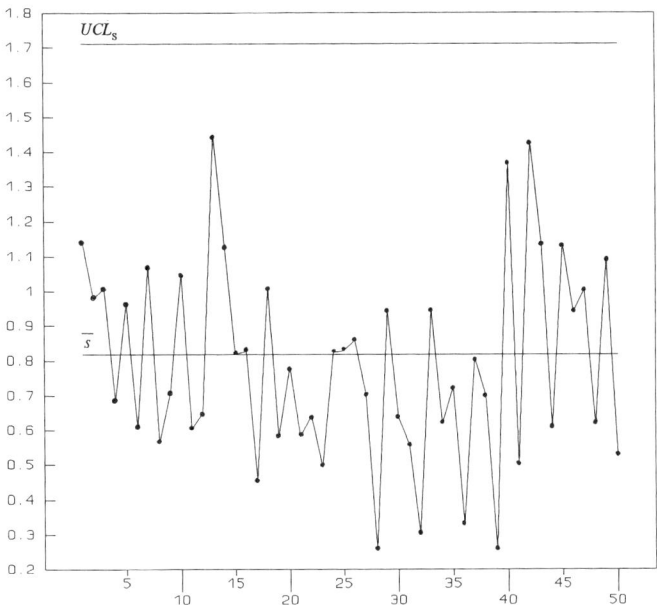

Fig. 6.6. The s chart associated with the data in Table 6.3, with UCL_s based on the first 25 samples.

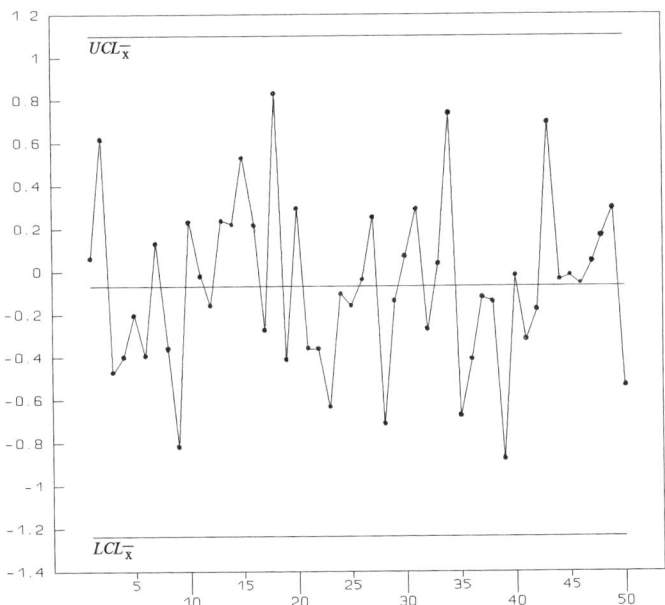

Fig. 6.7. The $\bar{x}$ control chart based on $\bar{s}$.

false out-of-control signals at Inspections 59, 92, 152, 310, 322, 331, 356, 400, 401, 712, 758, 768, and 947. (Furthermore, suppose we were looking at a hundred points starting at Inspection 305 and until Inspection 404, we would see the process go out of control 6 times, and we might conclude that it only stays in control an average of 16.67 times. This, of course, would be a large error. Therefore, our estimate that the process would continue to be out of control every 76.92 times -- although it is based on more evidence, and is thus more reliable -- is also suspect.)

Discerning readers might have noticed that our estimate of σ_X was too low. Instead of the true value of 0.954 we obtained 0.8709, which is about 9% too tight. Therefore, our control limits were too tight, and this is why so many points showed out of control. One might then suspect that this problem is due to the fact that our distribution is not really normal. But before we jump to such conclusions let's try to estimate σ_X by another set of 25 subgroups. For example, if we pick the last 25 subgroups (not listed in Table 6.3) instead of the first 25, we obtain $\bar{s}=0.9672$, leading to $\hat{\sigma}_X=1.0289$. $\bar{\bar{x}}$ for this set is -0.0272, which leads to $LCL_{\bar{x}}=-1.4073$ and $UCL_{\bar{x}}=1.3529$. With these limits, only one point would show out of control (subgroup 59). Indeed, our estimate of σ_X is excessive here: $0.9672/0.9400=1.0289\,(>0.954)$. So, one set of 25 subgroups led us to a too small estimate of variation and another led to a too large estimate. To appreciate the impact of this variation note that the ratio between the number of points that showed out of control as a result was 13 to 1!

Some reflection suggests that the variation between the two estimates is not due to the fact that c_4 was calculated for another distribution, but simply because 25 subgroups are not sufficient to provide a reliable estimate. To demonstrate this, suppose now that we'd use control limits based on the full sample of 1000 subgroups. This leads to a very different result, with $\bar{s}=0.8978$, yielding $\hat{\sigma}_X=0.955$, which compares very favorably with the true σ_X, 0.954. This is empirical proof that c_4 for the right triangular distribution with $n=5$ is not far from 0.9400, and thus the normality assumption is *not* the problem. Furthermore, in this case only Subgroups 59 and 238 appear "out of control." Stopping on two subgroups out of 1000 is within what we should expect theoretically for the $\bar{x}$ chart. The following technical note elaborates on this point.

=-

Technical Note

Since $\bar{x}$ is approximately normal, and assuming the variance estimate is good -- which happens to be the case here -- the probability of a stoppage is about 0.0027 for each subgroup. Since we have 1000 opportunities to stop, the number of stoppages is a binomial

B(1000, 0.0027). This can be approximated very well by a Poisson P(2.7). Using three standard deviations, we'd expect 2.7 ± 4.9 stoppages. So any number between 0 and 7 (inclusive) should not surprise us. However, the real practical problem is that usually the variance estimates are not reliable (it is rare to use as many subgroups as we did). For example, recall that when we used the first 25 subgroups to estimate control limits we got 13 stoppages, which is far above 7, and this happened mainly as a result of the low estimate of σ (the error in the centerline location was also a factor).

=-

In conclusion, we can say that even for a process that is as far from normal as the one we used, using the techniques that are based on the normal distribution will not lead us far astray as far as the analysis of the $\overline{x}$ chart is concerned. But using too small samples may cause problems. We can draw two conclusions: (i) it is advisable to base the control limits on larger samples if possible; (ii) the number of false signals is a quite volatile random variable. This volatility is not because the underlying distribution is not normal. Non-normality should only change the *RFS*, but it should not make it more volatile. Given a process in control with a prescribed *RFS* the arrival of false signals is approximately a Poisson process, and as such there is a sizable variability associated with it. But here we also observe that the *RFS* itself seems to vary considerably. Chapter 8 elaborates on this issue.

6.3. $\overline{x}$ and s^2 Charts

Historically, for small subgroups, Shewhart recommended the use of $\overline{s}$ to estimate σ_X. As described in Box 6.1, this involves calculating s separately for each subgroup and then averaging across all subgroups. For large subgroups, however, Shewhart recommended another method, whereby instead of averaging s_j we should average s_j^2, i.e., use $\overline{s^2}$. Some practitioners use this method for small subgroups as well, and it has two major advantages: (i) it makes the best use of data (Figure S6.1.1 shows that this is especially beneficial for small and medium-sized subgroups, in spite of Shewhart's opposite recommendation); and (ii) it is relatively easy to implement with subgroups of different sizes. The former is due to the fact that this method uses a sufficient statistic that retains all the useful sample information (at least for the normal distribution), which none of the others do. The latter may come in handy under several scenarios: for instance, if we want to change the subgroup size in mid-stream, or if some individual items are considered special (e.g., we suspect recording errors) and we still want to use the other data.

The main disadvantage of using $\overline{s^2}$ to estimate $\hat{\sigma}$ and create control limits is that it is less robust against outliers (Tukey, 1960; Huber, 1981). Even a small contamination of the sample data with points that do not belong to the basic distribution may render this statistic inferior to the s statistic. To see this let's look at a simplified example. Suppose we construct a control chart based on 10 subgroups and suppose 9 of them are true representatives of the process but one has a standard deviation that is inflated by 100%. If we identify this point as an "out of control" point, and recalculate the limits, it makes little difference whether we use $\overline{s}$ or s^2. But suppose we either do not identify the point or decide not to bother with removing it. The readers can verify that the expected inflation of $\overline{s}$ will be by 10% and of s^2 by 30%. Even after taking the square root of s^2 the expected remaining error will be inflated by about 14%, which is more than 10%. Thus, $\overline{s}$ is more robust than s^2 against outliers. In practice, since processes are rarely in control during the entire data collection process, this statistic tends to specify wider control limits than necessary. The result is a less powerful and reliable chart, in spite of the increased efficiency.

Furthermore, in Supplement 6.2 we show that the efficiency advantage of s^2 approaches zero as the subgroups increase. Therefore, in spite of Shewhart's contrary recommendation, we can say that $\overline{s}$ is definitely a better choice for large n, where the efficiency gap is small and yet $\overline{s}$ is more robust. In contrast, for small subgroups the efficiency gap is larger, and the best choice of dispersion statistic depends on the circumstances (what's more important: robustness or efficiency?). The prevailing recommendation, however, is that robustness is more important, and therefore one should only use s^2 for subgroups of varying sizes (where it is complex to use $\overline{s}$).

Be that as it may, the crucial difference between using s^2 and $\overline{s}$ is only in the way we estimate σ_X. Once we have an estimate of σ_X it is used in the $\overline{x}$ chart exactly the same way as it is done when σ_X is estimated by $\overline{s}$ (or by $\overline{R}$). Furthermore, if we should choose to do so, we may monitor the dispersion under this version in exactly the same way we do for s charts (and, similarly, even when we use $\overline{s}$ to estimate σ_X we can use the other methods discussed here to monitor dispersion). But the convention for this case *is* different: most practitioners who prefer this dispersion statistic monitor s^2 directly, and do so by specifying *probability limits*. Probability limits are designed in such a way that if the estimate of σ_X is correct (a big "if"), and if the process distribution is normal (a somewhat less important "if"), then the rate of false signals will have a prescribed value, say α. (Probability limits can also be used in other charts, including np, p, c, u, and $\overline{x}$ charts. For instance, in Britain the convention for $\overline{x}$ charts is to use control limits of $\pm 3.09\sigma$, since these provide probability limits of 0.001 on each side, or $\alpha = 0.002$ when combined. As always, these probabilities are subject to the unrealistic assumptions that the variance estimates are exact and that $\overline{\overline{x}}$ is centered.)

We will show how to devise such probability limits here, and also demonstrate other alternatives (see Box 6.2). The purpose of discussing more than one way is not only to clarify that there is no inherent reason to use probability limits with s^2 charts, but also to strengthen the point that the specification of control limits is quite arbitrary. In practice none of the methods we discuss in this chapter works exactly as advertized anyway. As Deming said, the most we can claim is that the rate of false signals is "small."

=-

Box 6.2: Constructing $\bar{x}$ and s^2 Control Charts

Let m be the number of subgroups taken, and let n_j be the size of Subgroup j (but if the subgroups do not vary we may use n for all of them), such that the n_j measurements in each subgroup are taken close together, and the m subgroups are taken apart from each other. Let x_{ij} be the measurement of interest of the ith item in the jth subgroup (where $i=1,2,\ldots,n_j$ and $j=1,2,\ldots,m$), and let $\bar{x}_j$ denote the average of all the items in Subgroup j.

Construction of the s^2 chart

Let s_j^2 be calculated for the jth subgroup by the formula

$$s_j^2 = \frac{\sum_{i=1}^{n_j}\left(x_{ij}-\bar{x}_j\right)^2}{n_j-1}$$

and define $\bar{s}^2$ by

$$\bar{s}^2 = \frac{\sum_{j=1}^{m}s_j^2(n_j-1)}{\sum_{j=1}^{m}(n_j-1)} = \frac{\sum_{j=1}^{m}s_j^2(n_j-1)}{\sum_{j=1}^{m}n_j-m} = \frac{\sum_{j=1}^{m}\sum_{i=1}^{n_j}\left(x_{ij}-\bar{x}_j\right)^2}{\sum_{j=1}^{m}n_j-m}$$

When the subgroups are equal, this simplifies to

$$\bar{s}^2 = \frac{\sum_{j=1}^{m}s_j^2}{m}$$

Plot the s_j^2 values in a chart with control limits at

n	$S2_{0.999,n}$	$S2_{0.995,n}$	$S2_{0.005,n}$	$S2_{0.001,n}$	$(B_5)^2$	$(B_6)^2$
2	0.000	0.000	7.879	10.828	0.000	6.793
3	0.001	0.005	5.299	6.908	0.000	5.180
4	0.008	0.024	4.279	5.422	0.000	4.359
5	0.023	0.052	3.715	4.617	0.000	3.856
6	0.042	0.082	3.350	4.103	0.001	3.513
7	0.064	0.113	3.091	3.743	0.013	3.261
8	0.086	0.141	2.897	3.475	0.032	3.068
9	0.107	0.168	2.744	3.266	0.054	2.913
10	0.128	0.193	2.621	3.097	0.076	2.787
11	0.148	0.216	2.519	2.959	0.098	2.681
12	0.167	0.237	2.432	2.842	0.119	2.591
13	0.185	0.256	2.358	2.742	0.140	2.513
14	0.201	0.274	2.294	2.656	0.159	2.444
15	0.217	0.291	2.237	2.580	0.177	2.384
16	0.232	0.307	2.187	2.513	0.194	2.330
17	0.246	0.321	2.142	2.453	0.210	2.282
18	0.260	0.335	2.101	2.399	0.225	2.238
19	0.273	0.348	2.064	2.351	0.240	2.198
20	0.285	0.360	2.031	2.306	0.254	2.162
21	0.296	0.372	2.000	2.266	0.267	2.128
22	0.307	0.383	1.971	2.228	0.279	2.097
23	0.317	0.393	1.945	2.194	0.291	2.069
24	0.327	0.403	1.921	2.162	0.302	2.042
25	0.337	0.412	1.898	2.132	0.312	2.017
26	0.346	0.421	1.877	2.081	0.323	1.994
27	0.355	0.429	1.857	2.079	0.332	1.972
28	0.363	0.437	1.839	2.055	0.342	1.952
29	0.371	0.445	1.821	2.032	0.351	1.933

30	0.379	0.452	1.805	2.010	0.359	1.914
35	0.413	0.485	1.734	1.919	0.397	1.836
40	0.443	0.513	1.679	1.848	0.429	1.775
45	0.468	0.536	1.634	1.790	0.456	1.725
50	0.489	0.556	1.597	1.742	0.480	1.683
55	0.509	0.574	1.565	1.701	0.500	1.647
60	0.526	0.589	1.538	1.667	0.519	1.616
70	0.555	0.616	1.493	1.610	0.550	1.566
80	0.580	0.638	1.457	1.564	0.575	1.526
90	0.600	0.656	1.428	1.528	0.597	1.493
100	0.618	0.672	1.404	1.498	0.616	1.465

Table 6.4

$$LCL_{S^2} = \frac{\overline{s^2}}{n_j-1}\chi^2_{1-\alpha/2,\,n_j-1}; \quad UCL_{S^2} = \frac{\overline{s^2}}{n_j-1}\chi^2_{\alpha/2,\,n_j-1}$$

where α is the nominal RFS we're willing to assume for each point on both sides of $\overline{s^2}$ combined, and $\chi^2_{p,k}$ is the p-critical value of a chi-square random variable with k degrees of freedom. These limits vary with n_j.[4] The critical χ^2 values can be found in statistical tables. For convenience, we may define the factors $S2_{p,n}$, where p is a given probability, as follows,

$$S2_{p,n} = \frac{\chi^2_{p,\,n-1}}{n-1}$$

Using these factors we obtain

$$LCL_{S^2} = \overline{s^2}S2_{1-\alpha/2,\,n_j}; \quad UCL_{S^2} = \overline{s^2}S2_{\alpha/2,\,n_j}$$

Table 6.4 provides $S2_{p,n}$ for $p=0.999$, 0.995, 0.005, and 0.001 (i.e., for $\alpha=0.002$ and for $\alpha=0.01$). For n values below 100 that are not reported, linear interpolation may be used

---

[4]Montgomery (1991), p. 238, recommends not to present charts with variable limits to management. One assumes he knows by experience that typical managers may get confused by them. It's up to today's students and teachers whether tomorrow's typical managers will also be statistical ignoramuses.

without any practical problems (note how little the values change as n increases by steps of 5 or 10 for $n \geq 30$ or $n \geq 60$). p-wise linear interpolation is much less exact and should not be expected to give the correct nominal *RFS* even when the variance is known and the process is indeed normal (the actual *RFS* will be lower than the interpolated value under these conditions). Nonetheless, since the reported probabilities are never achieved exactly in practice anyway, such interpolation may still be useful.

If and only if all the s^2 values fall within these control limits, we may proceed to construct the $\overline{x}$ chart. Otherwise -- especially if a large fraction of points are out of the control limits -- we should investigate what's special about the outliers. If necessary, the control limits have to be recalculated based on subgroups that are considered "in control," preferably using new data. (This is more important for this dispersion statistic than for $\overline{s}$ or $\overline{R}$, because it's less robust.)

Alternative construction of control limits for the s² chart

Instead of using χ^2 critical values, we might prefer, for simplicity and consistency, to use Shewhart's template to devise control limits; i.e., to set them at $\overline{s^2} \pm 3\hat{\sigma}_{s^2}$. To this end recall that when the process has a normal distribution the statistic $(n-1)s^2/\sigma_x^2$ is distributed χ^2 with $n-1$ degrees of freedom. Recall also that the expected value of the χ^2 with k degrees of freedom is k, and the variance is $2k$. This leads to the following control limits,

$$LCL_{s^2} = Max\left\{0, \ \overline{s^2}\left(1-3\sqrt{\frac{2}{n_j-1}}\right)\right\}; \quad UCL_{s^2} = \overline{s^2}\left(1+3\sqrt{\frac{2}{n_j-1}}\right)$$

where $\overline{s^2}$ serves as our unbiased estimator of σ_x^2. In this case $LCL > 0$ only for $n_j \geq 20$, while the former method specifies $LCL > 0$ for $n \geq 3$. After discussing the construction of the $\overline{x}$ chart we'll provide another way to construct control limits for s^2, which makes them operationally identical to those associated with s charts, so there we'll obtain $LCL > 0$ for $n \geq 6$.

Construction of the x̄ chart

If we know how to adjust the process, draw the centerline of the $\overline{x}$ chart at the desired target. Otherwise, define the overall mean, $\overline{\overline{x}}$, by

$$\overline{\overline{x}} = \frac{\sum\limits_{j=1}^{m} n_j \overline{x}_j}{\sum\limits_{j=1}^{m} n_j} = \frac{\sum\limits_{j=1}^{m}\sum\limits_{i=1}^{n_j} x_{ij}}{\sum\limits_{j=1}^{m} n_j}$$

where if the subgroups are equal this simplifies to

$$\bar{\bar{x}} = \frac{\sum\limits_{j=1}^{m} \bar{x}_j}{m} = \frac{\sum\limits_{j=1}^{m}\sum\limits_{i=1}^{n} x_{ij}}{mn}$$

(Replacing n by the average n_j, this expression can serve as an approximation, especially if the subgroups vary mildly.) Draw a centerline for $\bar{x}$ at $\bar{\bar{x}}$. Once the centerline is drawn (one way or another), add control limits at the centerline $\pm 3\hat{\sigma}/\sqrt{n_j}$, where $\hat{\sigma}$ is given by

$$\hat{\sigma} = \left[1 + \frac{1}{4\left(\sum\limits_{j=1}^{m} n_j - m - 1\right)}\right]\sqrt{\frac{\sum\limits_{j=1}^{m}(n_j-1)s_j^2}{\sum\limits_{j=1}^{m}(n_j-1)}} \approx \sqrt{\frac{\sum\limits_{j=1}^{m}(n_j-1)s_j^2}{\sum\limits_{j=1}^{m}(n_j-1)}} = \sqrt{\overline{s^2}}$$

where the expression in the brackets, which is close to one and thus may be omitted, is based on c_4 and corrects for bias. For equal subgroups this simplifies to

$$\hat{\sigma} = \left[1 + \frac{1}{4n - 4m - 1}\right]\sqrt{\frac{\sum\limits_{j=1}^{m} s_j^2}{m}} \approx \sqrt{\frac{\sum\limits_{j=1}^{m} s_j^2}{m}} = \sqrt{\overline{s^2}}$$

For instance if we use as few as 25 subgroups of 5 units each, the brackets add about 0.25% to $\hat{\sigma}$, and for larger samples the difference is even smaller. Since, as was the case with $\bar{x}$ and s charts, it is recommended to use at least 100 and preferably 400 samples, this correction is rarely important.

The control limits, both of the $\bar{x}$ and the s^2 charts, vary with n_j. As we've done with p and u charts, we can define tight control limits by using the maximal n_j value and loose ones by using the minimal n_j, and pronounce any points beyond the loose limits as "out of control" and any point within the tight limits "in control." Of course, if *some* points are out of control, the whole process may be out of control.

One more alternative construction of control limits for the s^2 chart

Suppose we'd prefer to monitor s_j instead of s_j^2, but use $\hat{\sigma}$ as defined above instead of $\bar{s}/c_4$ as our unbiased estimate of σ_X. Since $E(\bar{s}) = c_4 E(\hat{\sigma})$, instead of using dispersion control limits of $B_3\bar{s}$ and $B_4\bar{s}$ we need new factors, B_5 and B_6, such that $B_5 = c_4 B_3$ and $B_6 = c_4 B_4$, i.e.,

$$B_5 = Max\left\{0,\ c_4 - 3\sqrt{1-c_4^2}\right\}; \qquad B_6 = c_4 + 3\sqrt{1-c_4^2}$$

These factors are often tabulated for the purpose of devising control limits for s charts when σ_X is considered known (Montgomery, 1991, p. 232). Using $\hat{\sigma}$ to represent this "known" σ_X we obtain

$$LCL_s = B_5\hat{\sigma} = B_5\sqrt{\overline{s^2}}; \quad UCL_s = B_6\hat{\sigma} = B_6\sqrt{\overline{s^2}}$$

To monitor s^2 directly, we need to square these limits, i.e.,

$$LCL_{s^2} = (B_5)^2\hat{\sigma}^2 = (B_5)^2\overline{s^2}$$

$$UCL_{s^2} = (B_6)^2\hat{\sigma}^2 = (B_6)^2\overline{s^2}$$

Thus, $(B_5)^2$ may replace $S2_{1-\alpha/2,n}$ and $(B_6)^2$ may replace $S2_{\alpha/2,n}$. Table 6.4 lists these values. In terms of pronouncing a point in control or not, it makes no difference whether we monitor s^2 with limits based on these squared factors, or monitor s with limits based on $B_5\hat{\sigma}$ and $B_6\hat{\sigma}$. Furthermore, if we use many subgroups from a process that's in control, then the estimate of σ_X based on $\overline{s}/c_4$ should be the same as our $\hat{\sigma}$ (both are unbiased estimates of σ_X), so the RFS associated with these squared factors are theoretically identical to those associated with s charts.

=-

Regardless of how we perform the exact computation of the dispersion chart control limits, it may be justified to monitor s^2 directly, rather than monitor s (*after* a control chart is established). This recommendation is not based on statistical considerations: theoretically, s charts and s^2 charts can be adjusted to give identical signals for any subgroup, so statistically they are equivalent. Rather it reflects the general position that the quadratic loss function should be the default loss function. By monitoring s^2 directly we monitor one of the main ingredients of the quadratic loss function. (The other ingredient, the squared bias, may be computed by data provided by the $\overline{x}$ chart.) Sophisticated customers, if they are large enough to have a say about the quality of the materials they purchase, should actually demand to see data about s^2 as well as $\overline{\overline{x}}$ to estimate the quadratic loss that is incorporated in the materials they purchase. Today, such customers usually settle for an $\overline{x}$ chart, or even a p chart, showing statistical control. Theoretically, the necessary information *can* be derived from an $\overline{x}$ chart, but monitoring s^2 directly not only facilitates the task, but also makes the vendor pay more attention to the quadratic loss. The contract might even specify a deduction for quadratic loss, which would be the fair thing to do. In such a case, to calculate K for any critical quality measurement we can set the loss at the specification limits equal to the purchase price. Such contracts would clarify that centering is important even for subcontractors.

To conclude our discussion of $\bar{x}$ and s^2 charts, and provide an example of using varying subgroup sizes, Box 6.3 continues the analysis which we started in Box 5.2.

-=-

Box 6.3: **An Application of** $\bar{x}$ **and** s^2 **Charts to Teaching**

In Box 5.2, we analyzed the number of articles students did not read. Based on that analysis, it can be concluded that five students were special cases. Due to anonymity, it was impossible to investigate the reasons, so we'll ignore them. Nonetheless, it must be understood that this implies some self-selection, since we're going to use only the opinions of the students who read enough articles. One may suspect that one reason for not reading is that the article in question is not attractive, in which case disregarding students who did not read many articles is disregarding students who have negative opinions about many articles. Depending on the exact procedure followed, one can either declare all articles in control (which we'll do here), or state that one article is also out of control. In this case, however, investigation revealed that the article in question was simply long and its due date was relatively late, so there's no reason to doubt the opinions of the students who read it. In conclusion, we analyze for 14 students and 22 articles. We do so in terms of the grades (between 1 and 5). Table 5.5 (in Box 5.2) provides the raw data necessary for this purpose. The number of articles each student read varies, and so does the number of readers each article had. This means that if we want to devise control charts we'll need to use the formulae for varying subgroup sizes.

Before doing that, we should note that this example is not a typical control chart application: it does not represent an ongoing process. Strictly speaking we should call it an experiment. As such, we might want to verify the results by repeating the experiment, following the usual scientific manner. Furthermore, when viewed as an experiment, we should ask whether using $\pm 3\sigma$ limits is appropriate. Advanced methods, such as ANOM (analysis of means), may be used to adjust the width of the limits according to the number of subgroups (to account for the fact that with many subgroups the probability of at least one false signal increases), and in such a manner that the α-risk will be at some level chosen by the experimenter (e.g., see Wheeler [1995], Chapter 18). In practice, using ANOM amounts to fine-tuning the chart. Arguably, there is practical value in using the control chart methodology here "as is."

Control chart for students

The main purpose of the questionnaire was to investigate the articles assigned as reading material, *not* to investigate the students. Nonetheless, to be sure that the evaluators (the students) were at least roughly representative of a single population (which may then be hypothesized to represent other students), it is advisable to begin by verifying that they used similar scales in their evaluation. Otherwise, difficulties may arise due to our mixture of sources. To that end we start by devising $\bar{x}$ and s^2 charts for students, where each student will be "measured" by the evaluations he or she gave. Thus we have 14 subgroups of up to 22 measurements in each. Table 6.5 provides s_j^2, dispersion control limits, $\bar{x}_j$, $LCL_{\bar{x}}$, and $UCL_{\bar{x}}$ for each student. The dispersion control limits are based on $(B_5)^2$ and $(B_6)^2$. In this case $\bar{s}^2 = 0.4814$ and $\bar{\bar{x}} = 4.025$.

As an example of calculating control limits for the s^2 chart let's take the first student. This student read 19 articles, grading 11 of them as "outstanding" (5) and the remaining 8 as "good" (4). Thus the average grade given was $87/19 = 4.579$. With this data we can calculate s^2, as follows,

$$s^2 = \frac{11\left(5 - \frac{87}{19}\right)^2 + 8\left(4 - \frac{87}{19}\right)^2}{19 - 1} = 0.2573$$

To devise the dispersion control limits, observe in Table 6.4 that for $n = 19$ $(B_5)^2 = 0.240$ and $(B_6)^2 = 2.198$. Multiplying these by $\bar{s}^2 = 0.4814$ we obtain the limits reported in Table 6.5 -- 0.116 and 1.058. Next we calculate the control limits for the $\bar{x}$ chart,

$$LCL_{\bar{x}} = 4.025 - 3\sqrt{\frac{0.4814}{19}} = 3.547; \quad UCL_{\bar{x}} = 4.025 + 3\sqrt{\frac{0.4814}{19}} = 4.503$$

where the minute difference relative to Table 6.5 is because the figures in the table were rounded only after all the calculations were completed, while here we used rounded figures as input for interim calculations (a procedure that should be avoided, when possible, to prevent accumulating errors).

While the s^2 chart is in control (see Figure 6.8), the $\bar{x}$ chart shows two points -- the first and third students out of the remaining fourteen -- out of control (see Figure 6.9), and one more point -- the twelfth student -- in control, but close to the upper limit. It seems that the first student had a distinctly higher opinion of the reading materials than his or her peers,

Student#	s_j^2	LCL_{s^2}	UCL_{s^2}	$\bar{x}$	LCL_x	UCL_x
1	0.257	0.116	1.058	**4.579**	3.548	4.503
2	0.556	0.116	1.058	4.000	3.548	4.503
3	0.702	0.134	1.009	**3.523**	3.581	4.469
4	0.684	0.101	1.099	3.941	3.520	4.530
5	0.721	0.101	1.099	3.706	3.520	4.530
6	0.615	0.077	1.176	4.000	3.469	4.582
7	0.381	0.134	1.009	4.000	3.581	4.469
8	0.513	0.134	1.009	4.318	3.581	4.469
9	0.543	0.085	1.148	3.600	3.488	4.563
10	0.335	0.077	1.176	3.714	3.469	4.582
11	0.305	0.122	1.041	4.100	3.560	4.491
12	0.382	0.108	1.077	4.500	3.535	4.516
13	0.262	0.129	1.024	4.190	3.571	4.479
14	0.537	0.134	1.009	4.182	3.581	4.469

Bold denotes "out of control"

Table 6.5

so much so that s_j^2 was also low (there is not much room for variation when you evaluate near the top), while the third student exhibited opposite trends: lower than average opinion and, with it, a relatively high internal variation (since these opinions were at the center of the scale while the average opinions were medium high). It turns out, however, that it does not make much of a difference whether we drop these two students from our subgroup. The results of the analysis of the articles will be the same.[5] (In the following analysis we do drop them, however.)

---

[5] The students in question were all military officers part of whose job is to evaluate their subordinates. These evaluations are crucial to the careers of said subordinates. Would you prefer to serve under an officer who tends to evaluate higher than the norm, or lower? We also dispensed with the opinions of five officers who either did not read enough *not just relative to a standard, but relative to their peers*, or did not read carefully enough to remember what they read. Would you like to be evaluated by officers who do their homework and know about you or those whose attention is elsewhere? It is for such reasons, among others, that Deming opposed performance evaluations so vehemently.

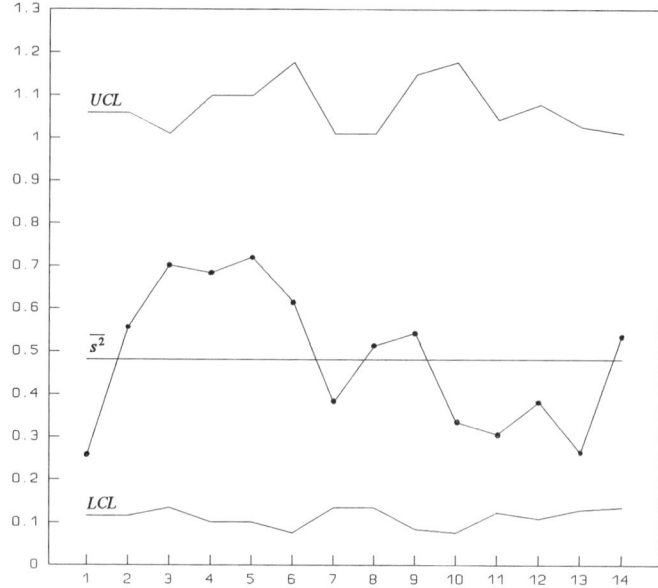

Fig. 6.8. s^2 chart of students.

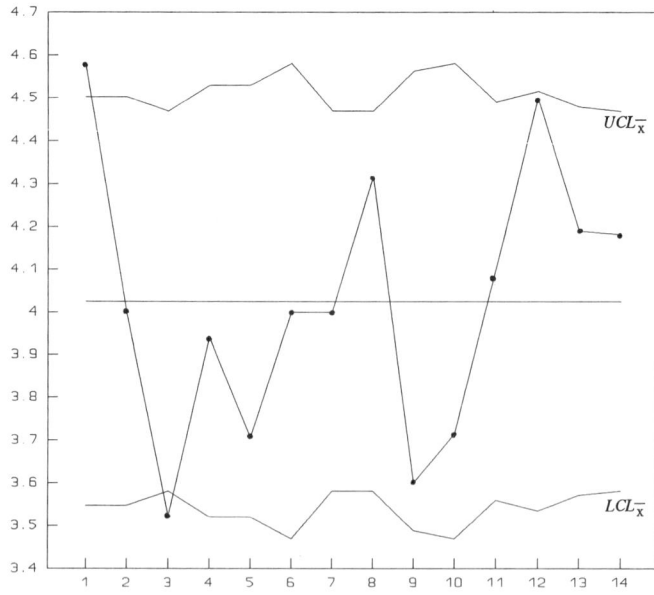

Fig. 6.9. $\bar{x}$ chart by students.

Control chart for articles

To investigate the articles we first devise $\bar{x}$ and s^2 charts for them, where each of the 22 articles will be measured by the evaluations it received from the 12 students (or 14, if we choose not to discard the two outliers discovered in the students' $\bar{x}$ chart). Thus we have 22

Article#	s_j^2	LCL_{s^2}	UCL_{s^2}	$\bar{x}$	LCL_x	UCL_x
1	0.333	0.058	1.253	3.833	3.443	4.647
2	0.697	0.058	1.253	3.833	3.443	4.647
3	0.111	0.026	1.408	4.111	3.350	4.741
4	0.194	0.026	1.408	4.222	3.350	4.741
5	0.322	0.037	1.347	4.100	3.386	4.705
6	0.400	0.000	1.698	4.000	3.194	4.897
7	0.205	0.058	1.253	**4.750**	3.443	4.647
8	0.333	0.058	1.253	4.167	3.443	4.647
9	0.545	0.058	1.253	4.000	3.443	4.647
10	1.018	0.047	1.296	3.727	3.416	4.674
11	0.618	0.047	1.296	3.727	3.416	4.674
12	0.750	0.026	1.408	4.000	3.350	4.741
13	0.489	0.037	1.347	4.400	3.386	4.705
14	0.233	0.037	1.347	3.700	3.386	4.705
15	0.500	0.026	1.408	4.000	3.350	4.741
16	0.611	0.026	1.408	4.111	3.350	4.741
17	0.558	0.037	1.347	3.850	3.386	4.705
18	0.455	0.047	1.296	4.364	3.416	4.674
19	0.855	0.047	1.296	3.636	3.416	4.674
20	0.238	0.006	1.577	4.286	3.257	4.834
21	0.778	0.026	1.408	3.944	3.350	4.741
22	0.233	0.037	1.347	4.300	3.386	4.705

Bold denotes "out of control"

Table 6.6

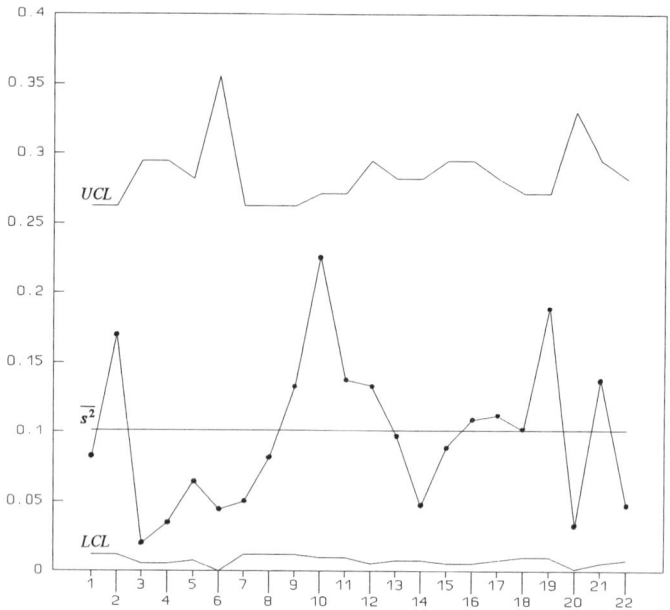

Fig. 6.10. s^2 control chart for articles.

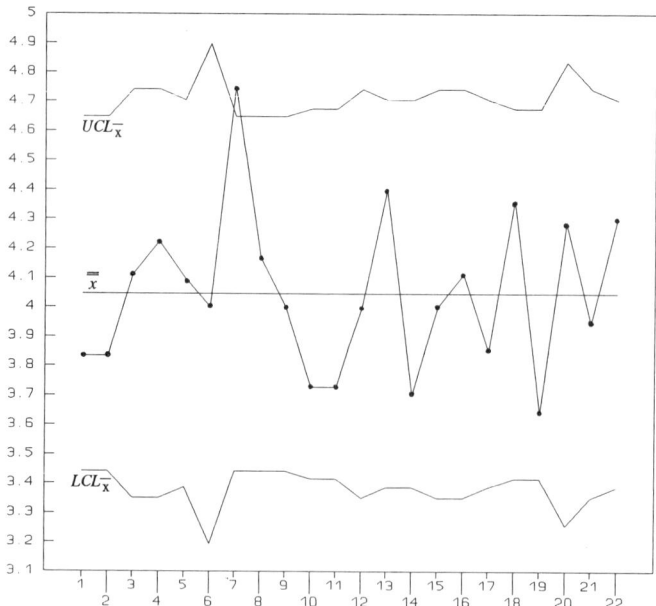

Fig. 6.11. $\bar{x}$ chart for articles.

subgroups of up to 12 (14) measurements each. Table 6.6 provides s_j^2, dispersion control limits, $\overline{x}_j$, and control limits for the mean for each article. $\overline{\overline{x}}=4.045$ and $s^2=0.4835$. As Figure 6.10 shows, the s^2 chart is in control. But Figure 6.11 shows an outlier in the $\overline{x}$ chart -- Goldratt and Cox (1992), *The Goal* -- which is above the control limits. This particular reference has been very popular with my students ever since I first assigned it, so this result was not surprising. But it provided statistical verification for anecdotal evidence.[6]

=-

6.4. $\overline{x}$ and R Control Charts

Calculating the s statistic involves relatively complex arithmetic manipulations, i.e., squaring, summing, dividing, and taking the square root. When Shewhart developed his control charts, calculations were done manually, and the calculation of S was problematic. At about the same period (i.e., the nineteen-twenties) other researchers, notably Tippett, showed that most of the information one gets from the s statistic can be discerned by simply looking at the range statistic, i.e., the distance between the smallest and largest value in each sample. This is especially true for small samples, where there are few intermediate values between the two extremes, and thus relatively little information is lost. Shewhart, who was aware of these results, investigated the use of the range for this purpose, and found it inferior. But in spite of Shewhart's contrary recommendation, the use of R became the de-facto standard. With modern computerized SQC software, the original reason for preferring R is totally irrelevant. Even for manual application, cheap electronic calculators exist that can calculate both $\overline{x}$ and s for any series of values (mine cost $10 in 1990). Nonetheless, respectable consultants and software writers continue to recommend the use of R, and for completeness we must also cover it here. Besides, in some instances charts should still be easy to construct manually even without the use of calculators. Furthermore, as mentioned already, with small subgroups the waste associated with using R is tolerable. In terms of robustness, R is comparable to s. Box 6.4 provides the necessary technical details for the construction of these charts.

=-

Box 6.4: **Constructing $\overline{x}$ and R Control Charts**

Let m be the number of subgroups taken, and let n be the subgroup size, such that the n measurements in each subgroup are taken close together, and the m subgroups are

---

[6]I have recommended *The Goal* to my operations management students for years (starting with the first edition), since I think it is highly effective and generally useful. But this does not imply that I endorse each and every point the book makes. Altogether its message is too simplistic.

taken apart from each other. Let x_{ij} be the measurement of interest of the ith item in the jth subgroup (where $i=1,2,\ldots,n$ and $j=1,\ldots,m$).

Construction of the R chart

For the jth subgroup, R_j is the range between the largest and smallest measurements. That is, if the smallest item in the subgroup is $x_{min,j}$, and the largest is $x_{max,j}$, then

$$R_j = x_{max,j} - x_{min,j}$$

When there is no danger of confusion, we may drop the index and refer simply to R. $\overline{R}$ is given by

$$\overline{R} = \frac{\sum\limits_{j=1}^{m} R_j}{m}$$

Plot the R_j values in a chart with control limits at

$$LCL_R = D_3\overline{R}; \quad UCL_R = D_4\overline{R}$$

D_3 and D_4 (which are analogous to B_3 and B_4) are given in Table 6.7 for various n values. We can also draw a centerline at the $\overline{R}$ level (but this centerline does *not* coincide with the median).

If and only if all the R values fall within these control limits, we may proceed directly to construct the $\overline{x}$ chart. Otherwise -- especially if a large percentage of points are without the limits -- an investigation is in order, to find what, if anything, is special about the outliers or the process in general. If necessary, upon finding special causes, or making a decision to ignore points that are suspected (a sometimes necessary expedient, but not without its risk of ignoring what may be the most important data), the control limits may have to be recalculated based on subgroups that are considered "in control". (Some experts, notably Deming, recommend not to bother with such recalculations, however.) Once control limits are established based on enough subgroups (e.g., at least 100 but preferably 400, although many consider 25 to be enough), there is no need to update them unless there is reason to believe that the process has changed, or that the control limits were not based on enough data.

Construction of the $\overline{x}$ chart

Define the subgroup mean, $\overline{x}_j$, by

$$\overline{x}_j = \frac{\sum\limits_{i=1}^{n} x_{ij}}{n}$$

n	A_2	D_3	D_4	d_2	d_3
2	1.880	0	3.267	1.128	0.853
3	1.023	0	2.574	1.693	0.888
4	0.729	0	2.282	2.059	0.880
5	0.577	0	2.114	2.326	0.864
6	0.483	0	2.004	2.534	0.848
7	0.419	0.076	1.924	2.704	0.833
8	0.373	0.136	1.864	2.847	0.820
9	0.337	0.184	1.816	2.970	0.808
10	0.308	0.223	1.777	3.078	0.797

Table 6.7

When there is no danger of confusion, we may drop the index and refer simply to $\overline{x}$. If we know how to adjust the process, draw the centerline of the $\overline{x}$ chart at the desired target. Otherwise, define the overall mean, $\overline{\overline{x}}$, by

$$\overline{\overline{x}} = \frac{\sum_{j=1}^{m} \overline{x}_j}{m} = \frac{\sum_{j=1}^{m} \sum_{i=1}^{n} x_{ij}}{mn}$$

and draw a centerline for $\overline{x}$ at $\overline{\overline{x}}$. Once the centerline is given (one way or another), add control limits

$$LCL_{\overline{x}} = Centerline - A_2\overline{R}; \quad UCL_{\overline{x}} = Centerline + A_2\overline{R}$$

where $A_2 = 3/(d_2\sqrt{n})$ and d_2 are given by Table 6.7. Plot $\overline{x}_j$ on the chart sequentially. (A_2 is analogous to A_3.)

Calculation of control limits of $\pm t\sigma$

The factors A_2, D_3, and D_4, are useful under Shewhart's convention of setting control limits at the centerline $\pm 3\sigma$. In general, we may want to use control limits based on $\pm t\sigma$ from the centerline, where t need not be 3. In Britain, for instance, the convention is to use $t = 3.09$, which (supposedly) yields $RFS = 0.002$ in the $\overline{x}$ chart. One may even want to use different t values below and above the centerline. To that end, the formulae for the control limits are based on two factors given by Table 6.7, d_2 and d_3, as follows

$$LCL_R = \bar{R}\min\left\{0,\ 1-t\frac{d_3}{d_2}\right\}; \quad UCL_R = \bar{R}\left(1+t\frac{d_3}{d_2}\right)$$

$$LCL_{\bar{x}} = Centerline - \bar{R}\left(\frac{t}{d_2\sqrt{n}}\right); \quad UCL_{\bar{x}} = Centerline + \bar{R}\left(\frac{t}{d_2\sqrt{n}}\right)$$

If desired, different values of t may be used in all these cases.

=-

As an example, and to explain the factors, let's return to the triangular process which we already analyzed with $\bar{x}$ and s charts. As was the case there, in spite of the fact that the control chart factors we used were devised specifically for a normal distribution, it is practically permissible to use them for unknown distributions or for non-normal distributions. The eighth column in Table 6.3 lists the range values and if we use the first 25 samples again we find that $\bar{R}$ is 1.992. Let d_2 be the ratio of $E(\bar{R})$ and σ_X (i.e., $E(\bar{R})=d_2\sigma_X$). d_2 is a distribution-dependent function of n, which we show how to derive in Supplement 6.2. Table 6.7 gives d_2 values for the normal distribution (e.g., for $n=5$, $d_2=2.326$). d_2 is used to estimate σ_X as follows,

$$\hat{\sigma}_X = \frac{\bar{R}}{d_2} = \frac{1.992}{2.326} = 0.8564$$

(Compare to 0.8709 that we obtained with the $\bar{s}$ statistic.) $\hat{\sigma}_X$ can be used directly to compute the upper and lower control limits for the $\bar{x}$ chart. Before we construct control limits for the $\bar{x}$ chart, however, it is necessary to verify that the range data comes from a process with a relatively stable variance. To that end, we have to construct the R chart. For this we need to estimate the standard deviation of R, σ_R. This is done by using a known relationship between $\bar{R}$ and σ_R (as shown in Supplement 6.2),

$$\sigma_R = d_3\sigma_X$$

where d_3 is a distribution-dependent function of n. Substituting $\hat{\sigma}=\bar{R}/d_2$ for σ_X and using Table 6.7 to find $d_3 = 0.864$ (for $n = 5$), we obtain

$$\hat{\sigma}_R = \frac{\bar{R}}{d_2}d_3 = \frac{1.992}{2.326}0.864 = 0.7399$$

Hence, we can calculate the control limits for R as $1.992 \pm 3\times0.7399$. This leads to a lower bound that is negative, and which we replaced by 0, and an upper bound of 4.212. This method can be used to calculate control limits based on any multiplication of σ_R, but since Shewhart recommended using 3 exclusively we use shortcut factors, D_3 and D_4 (analogous to B_3 and B_4 that apply to the s chart),

$$D_3 = Max\left\{0, \ 1 - 3\frac{d_3}{d_2}\right\}; \quad D_4 = 1 + 3\frac{d_3}{d_2}$$

that are multiplied by $\overline{R}$ to obtain the lower and upper control limits for R. These factors
are also listed in Box 6.7. In our case, they are 0 and 2.114. Thus, the control limits for
the R chart are $LCL_R = 0$ and $UCL_R = 2.114 \times 1.992 = 4.211$. Figure 6.12 shows the R
chart for the data of Table 6.3. (In this particular case, unless the process changes, it is
impossible for a range to be out of control, since the maximal possible range under this
distribution is 3.9.)

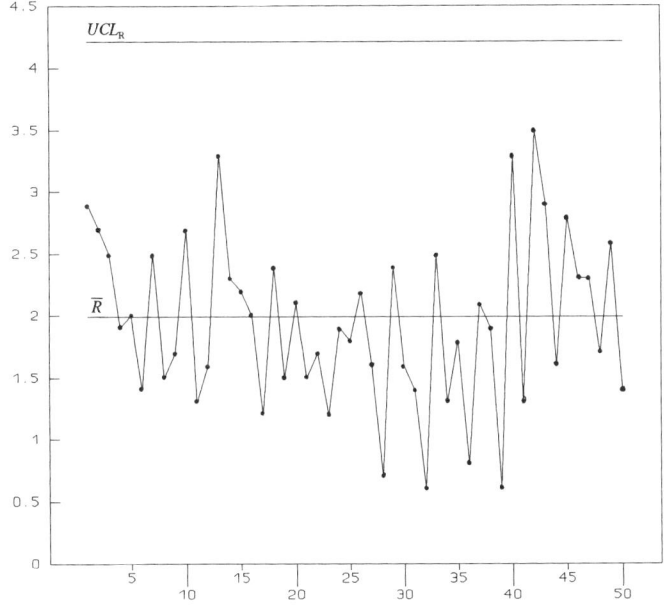

Fig. 6.12. The R portion of the $\overline{x}$ and R control chart for the first 50 samples of five (control limit
based on the first 25 samples).

Now that we've verified that the variation seems under control, we can indeed
devise the control limits for the $\overline{x}$ chart. Recall that $\hat{\sigma}_X$ is $\overline{R}/d_2$. We want to multiply this
by 3 and divide by $\sqrt{n}$, and then subtract the result from $\overline{\overline{x}}$ to obtain LCL, or add it to
$\overline{\overline{x}}$ to obtain UCL (in this example we cannot adjust the mean at will, so $\overline{\overline{x}}$ is our
centerline). To make the task more convenient, we can devise a new shortcut factor, A_2,
(analogous to A_3),

$$A_2 = \frac{3}{d_2\sqrt{n}}$$

which is also listed in Box 6.7. For $n = 5$, $A_2 = 0.577$. This leads to

$$LCL_{\overline{x}} = \overline{\overline{x}} - A_2\overline{R}; \quad UCL_{\overline{x}} = \overline{\overline{x}} + A_2\overline{R}$$

or, in our case $LCL_{\overline{x}} = -1.216$ and $UCL_{\overline{x}} = 1.083$. Figure 6.13 shows the control chart.

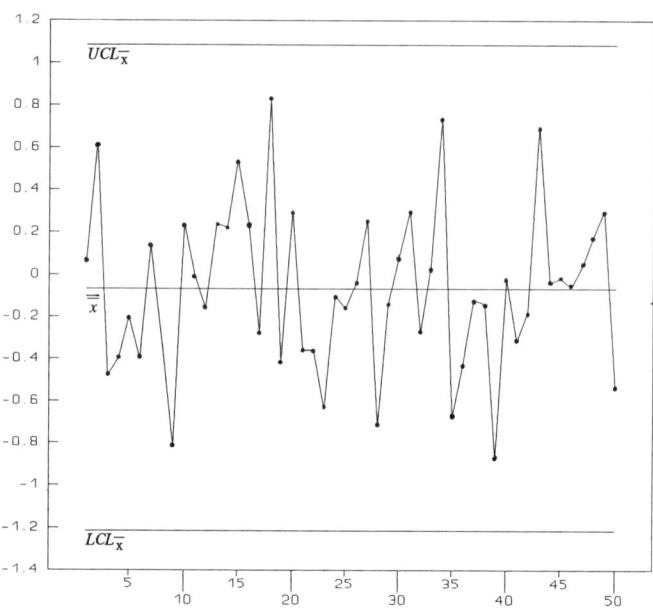

Fig. 6.13. The $\overline{x}$ portion of the $\overline{x}$ and R control chart for the first 50 samples of five (limits based on the first 25 samples).

Remarkably, although the control limits are not identical to those we obtained by using $\overline{s}$, when applied to our full set of 1000 subgroups practically the same points show out of control. The only difference is that Subgroup 190 is now also "out of control." When we compute the limits based on the last 25 subgroups we obtain $\overline{R} = 2.360$ and $\overline{\overline{x}} = -0.0272$, leading to $UCL_R = 4.989$, $LCL_{\overline{x}} = -1.389$ and $UCL_{\overline{x}} = 1.335$. In this case the process would show out of control erroneously just once out of a 1000 subgroups (at Subgroup 59), as was also the case when we used $\overline{s}$. Finally, when we estimate σ_X based on all 1000 subgroups here, the overall $\overline{R}$ computed by all 1000 subgroups is 2.1637. This would lead to a σ_X estimate of 0.9316, which is excellent considering that (i) we know it should be 0.954, and (ii) there is no reason to assume that $\overline{R}$ is related to σ_X correctly here, because the process is definitely *not* normal. Nonetheless, this result is inferior relative to the one we obtained with $\overline{s}$ (0.955). The final conclusion is that using R is not much different from using s, but s still has the advantage. For this reason R charts should only be recommended if the calculations are done manually and the subgroups are small. Indeed, even strong supporters of the use of R do not recommend it for subgroups larger than 10.

Finally, note that in the special case where $n=2$, the use of R is equivalent to the use of s -- i.e., they both capture the same information. Indeed, as Figure S6.1.1 shows, the two estimators are equally efficient for $n=2$. In this case the relative ease of calculation suggests that R is a better choice. This point is especially relevant in the next section, where we recommend the use of a moving range of 2 units when subgrouping is not used.

6.5. Control Charts for Individual Data

There are instances where it is either not economical, or not feasible, to obtain meaningful subgroups. For instance, some chemical mixtures, including alcoholic beverages, are notoriously consistent: it makes no difference if we sample material from the top of the vat, the bottom, or the middle. Each vat, at each point in time, can provide only one meaningful measurement (although multiple measurements of the same unit, aimed to reduce the measurement error, are sometimes useful). In such cases we need to estimate the short-term variation without subgroups, and devise control limits for the individual values.

To do this we can treat each pair of successive points as a subgroup of 2. If the process changes dramatically from one period to the next, we will obtain excessive estimates of the short term variation (since it will be mixed with longer term variation reflecting the time between inspections), but in relatively well-behaved cases we may obtain meaningful results. Let the range associated with Point i be $R_i = |x_i - x_{i-1}|$ ($i=2, 3,..., m$). Because the same intermediary point x_i ($i=2, 3,..., m-1$) appears in two successive range calculations, the result is a *moving* range. The set of the two charts, for x and for the moving range, is often denoted as an *xmR* chart. The centerline of the moving range is $\overline{R} = \Sigma R_i/(m-1)$; e.g., for $m=2$ it is simply the first moving range. Since each moving range is based on two points, we can use Table 6.7 (in Box 6.4), where we find that $d_2=1.128$. Therefore, $\sigma_x = \overline{R}/d_2 = \overline{R}/1.128$. $D_3=0$ (for n=2) and $D_4=3.267$, so $UCL_R = 3.267\overline{R}$. For the x chart, however, we cannot use A_2 because our subgroup size is 1 instead of 2, so we use $3/d_2 = 2.66$ instead, setting our control limits at the centerline $\pm 2.66\overline{R}$, where the centerline is set either at the target or at $\overline{x}$, the average of the m individual points. The formal assumption behind this usage is that the process is normally distributed, but recall that the use of R charts *in general* is predicated on the same assumption, so it is less specific to this

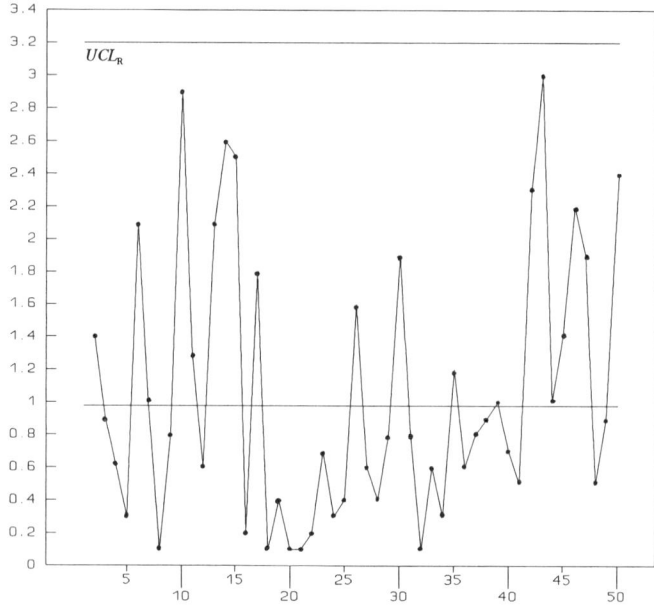

Fig. 6.14(a). An individuals chart based on a right-triangular distribution -- the moving range portion.

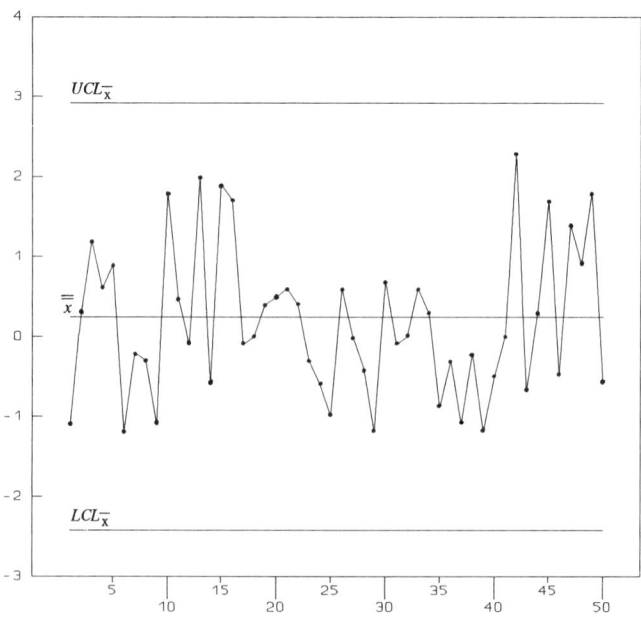

Fig. 6.14(b). An individuals chart based on a right-triangular distribution -- the x portion.

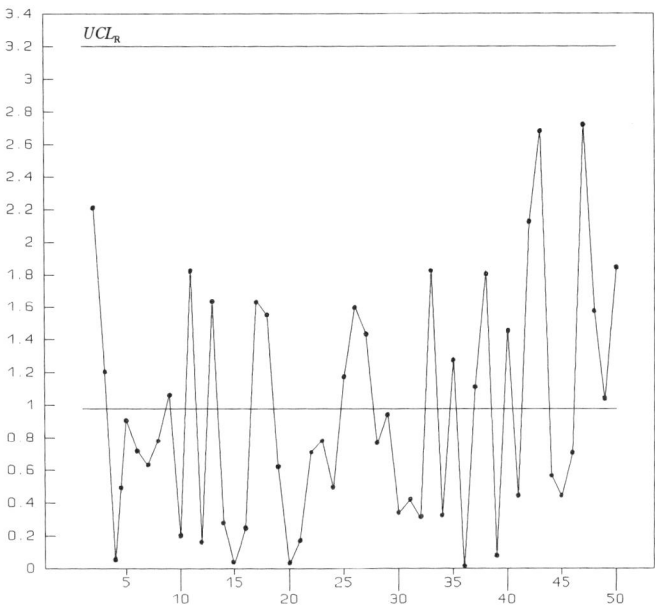

Fig. 6.15(a). An individuals chart based on a normal distribution -- the moving range portion.

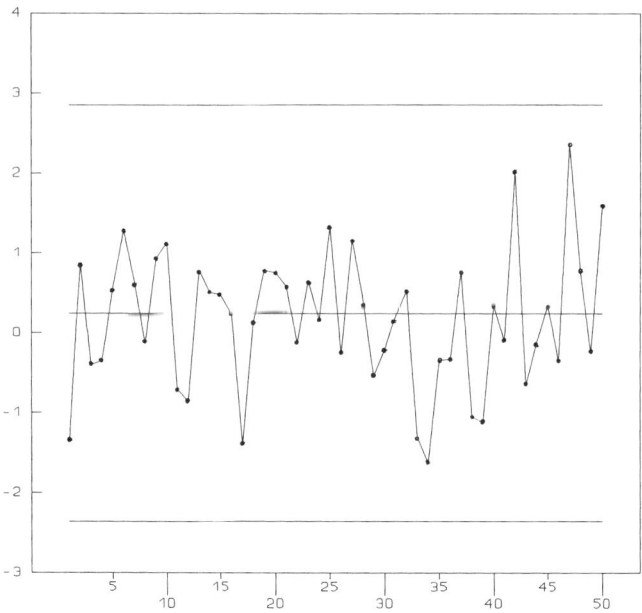

Fig. 6.15(b). An individuals chart based on a normal distribution -- the x portion.

case than one might suspect based on the literature: many authors take care to stress this point in this connection, who hardly even mention it in the regular context. Note also that since with $n=2$ all the dispersion information is captured by R, there is no theoretical advantage in this case to use the s statistic. The use of s^2 is more efficient, but suffers from lack of robustness. Therefore, xmR charts are the recommended (as well as prevailing) alternative in this case. Another possibility is to use an exponentially smoothed estimate, also based on the moving range (e.g., see Montgomery and Mastrangelo, 1991).

To illustrate this point, Figure 6.14 uses simulated data from a triangular distribution to show the control limits that result. Figure 6.15 uses normal data with the same variance and mean.

Each pair of successive points in the R chart are statistically dependent, since they share one individual x value. An unusually large or small x will tend to cause R to be large both when it happens and in the next period. Thus, there is a definite correlation between the x portion and the R portion of the chart even when the underlying distribution is normal. Furthermore, when one of the x values is especially large or small, it may well happen that only one of the R values that is associated with it will be out of control, because R depends on an additional point. Thus, an out of control R in this case may apply to the period in which it appears, or the former one. In general, one can say that the theoretical foundation of the individuals control chart is less satisfying than that of the regular control chart, but often it's the best alternative we have.

Wheeler (1995) recommended the use of xmR charts to monitor count data, i.e., as a replacement for np, p, c, and u charts. The advantage Wheeler cited for this usage is that it is not predicated on the theoretical assumptions of the binomial distribution (for np and p charts) or the Poisson distribution (for c and u charts). Technically, when the areas of opportunity are equal, this can be done directly on the count, but otherwise it should be done on normalized data, i.e., in the p or u format. In the latter case there is a problem because the data does not come from a single distribution with constant variance. Wheeler's recommendation, then, can only be endorsed fully if the areas of opportunity are (at least roughly) equal. For example, in the case cited in Box 5.5, the areas of opportunity would not be equal. Nonetheless, an individuals chart of p might still be the best solution there. At least it would not underestimate σ_X, and thus it would not cause so much tampering.

Individual time series data are often analyzed by the moving average method. This involves taking the last n measurements, averaging them, and plotting the result. In the next period, we drop one measurement from the bottom, add the new one to the top, and repeat the process. Control limits are devised by $\pm 3\hat{\sigma}/\sqrt{n}$, where $\hat{\sigma}$ is determined in the usual way by $\overline{R}/1.128$ (i.e., based on the *xmR* analysis before devising the moving averages). One advantage of this method is that it can detect small shifts of the mean more accurately (by effectively increasing the subgroup size, as we discuss later). A secondary benefit is that the chart is less sensitive to the process distribution. Similar benefits can also be achieved by using an exponentially weighted moving average (*EWMA*) chart. We discuss the technical details of such charts in the next section (among other things), but essentially it is a moving average method that gives more weight to recent data.

In addition to the benefits listed above, moving averages are useful if we want to smooth away seasonal data. For instance, suppose we take one sample each day, but we suspect that there is a difference between the days of the week, we can then monitor the moving average of the last seven days (or the last 14 days, 21 days, and so on). Such a moving average will always include the same number of measurements for each day of the week, and therefore any seasonality that may be associated with the days of the week should be smoothed out. (We may still need to study the seasonality by different means, however, because seasonality is invariably an important source of variation wherever it exists.) *EWMA* charts, however, because they involve unequal weights, are not effective to smooth away seasonality, but they are advantageous when seasonality is not evident.

Whenever we use moving averages, exponentially weighted or not, the result is a series of smoothed averages that are highly dependent on each other (since they share a lot of data). So we should not expect these results to show similar variation patterns to those associated with *i.i.d.* values. Instead, they are likely to look cyclical, or "wavy." This implies that pattern tests, which we discuss in Chapter 7, are not applicable to such smoothed data.

We'll use a real example to illustrate some of these points -- the compression strength of concrete mix after 28 days at the Spancrete plant in Yerevan, Armenia.[7] The plant manufactures pre-cast reinforced concrete slabs, and technical standards require to test the concrete compressive strength for each mix at the top and the bottom of a slab. For economic reasons (specific to the Yerevan location), only three samples were taken from each location and each mix, and they were tested destructively after three, seven, and twenty-eight days. Thus, each of these tests provides an individual data point. In other Spancrete plants, nine samples are taken instead of three, so each test is based on a subgroup of three. Thus, the use of individuals here does not imply that concrete is a homogeneous mixture: it is *not*. The data in the table relates to the twenty-eighth day test of the bottom

---

[7] I am grateful to Roy M. Stephen, P.E., for providing the data for this example, and the explanation for the signals it contains.

mix. Similar results can be shown for the top mix, although the two are not equal (the bottom mix tends to be wetter, and therefore a bit weaker on average). Figure 6.16 is a run chart of this data.

Let us create an individuals control chart for the concrete strength. We'll use the first 50 points for this purpose, and examine Points 51 through 111 based on the control limits

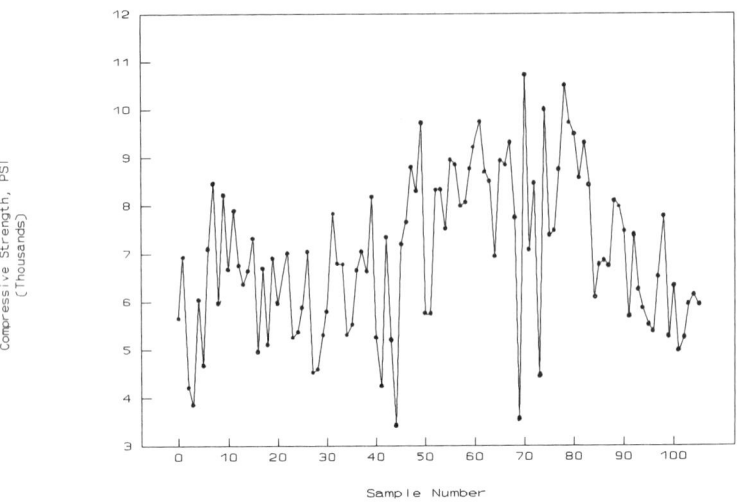

Fig. 6.16. A run chart of concrete strength results.

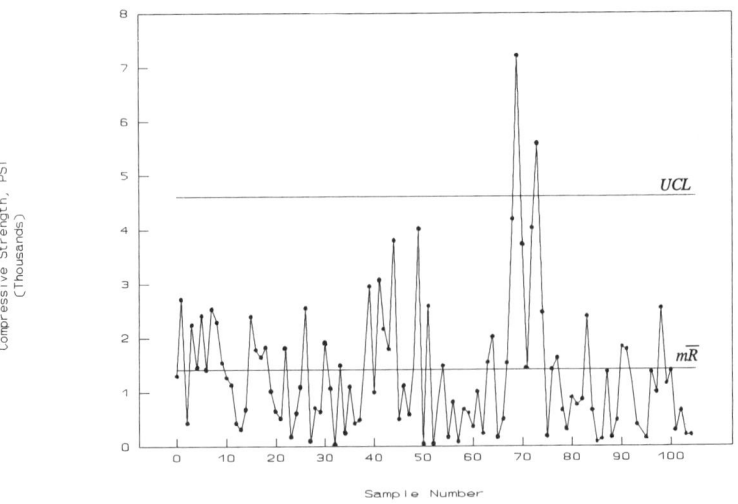

Fig. 6.17. A moving range chart for concrete strength (limits based on the first 50 points).

that we have obtained. Figure 6.17 is the moving range chart. Clearly, the first 50 points
(which belong to the trial chart) are in control. The other points also seem in control with
two exceptions. These exceptions are related to two instances of relatively low points (about
4000 psi) following relatively high points (about 10000 psi). It is plausible that these low
points represent an out of control situation (which was not analyzed originally, so it is
virtually impossible to do so now). Figure 6.18 is the x chart. It, too, is in control in the
trial chart segment, and seems in control with few exceptions thereafter. In both cases the

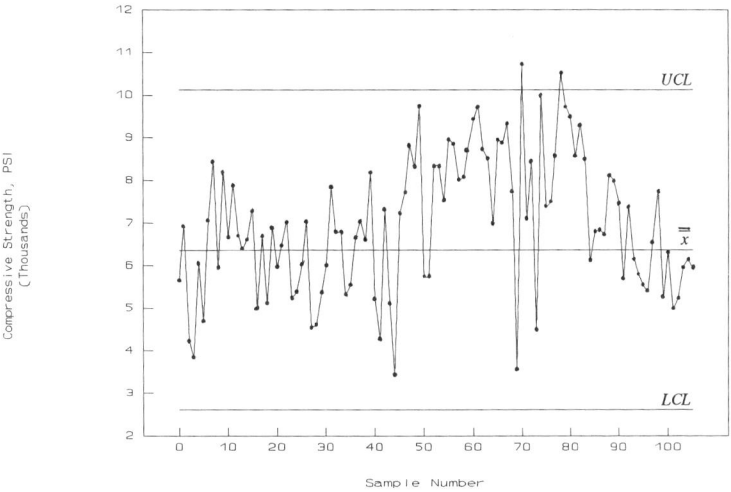

Fig. 6.18. Individuals chart for concrete strength (limits based on the first 50 points).

special points do not show until sample 70. (Some of the patterns discussed in Chapter 7,
however, appear much before that time.) Nonetheless, it is clear that the high variation
between units is so high in this case that it's difficult to tell whether the mean changed
significantly. In the next section we'll show that moving average charts, as well as *EWMA*
charts, do show that the process average changed significantly here. This change was caused
by switching from local Armenian concrete to Russian concrete which occurred for a while.
Roy Stephen identified this change originally by using a 10-point moving average chart. This
is shown in Figure 6.19, where it is obvious that Point 53 is already significantly above the
average of the first 50 points. In fact, it is plausible that the first 50 points are not all with
the same average. Incidentally, Roy Stephen did not even use control limits to make this
judgement. As this example demonstrates, the use of individuals charts may fail to detect
even clear shifts for a long time. And this is not an atypical example.

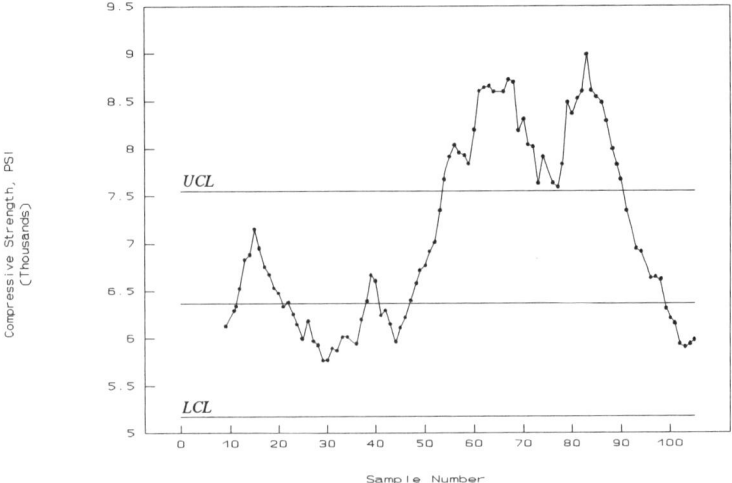

Fig. 6.19. A 10-point moving average chart for concrete strength (limits based on the first 50 points).

6.6. On the Power of Control Charts

The problem we encountered in our last example (concrete strength) is lack of power [to detect process changes]. The individuals chart we used took a long time to identify a shift in the mean that occurred during the process. Even when it did show some points out of control, it was not clear whether the mean shifted, or these points were special. This leads us to the general issue of power in control charts.

A complete investigation of the power of control charts has to take into account that there should be two control charts working together to detect two types of shifts. The dispersion chart monitors shifts of the variance, and the $\bar{x}$ chart monitors shifts of the mean. But first, we limit ourselves to the $\bar{x}$ chart, and we limit our discussion to the general effect of the subgroup size on the power of the chart to detect deviations of the mean.

Recall from Chapter 3 that with a quadratic loss function we should not really be worried about very small shifts of the mean relative to the target, but our concern should grow progressively with the size of the deviation. For example, if we adopt the five/ten rule (Chapter 4), we actually design a small average deviation into our process. For instance, when using ten units to adjust, a $\pm 3\sigma$ range for the plausible deviation is given by $\pm 3\sigma/\sqrt{10}$, leading to plausible absolute deviations of up to 0.95σ. A similar calculation for the case when we use five items yields 1.34σ. Typical cases will involve much smaller deviations, of course. Nonetheless, by adopting this rule we practically declare that we are willing to accept a deviation of about 0.3 to $0.5\sigma_X$ units on average, and we accept the possibility that the actual deviation will often be larger. True, in the latter case, when the deviation is much larger than average, we might wish that the control chart will alert us, so we can try again. But only rarely will we be interested in flagging deviations of less than $0.5\sigma_X$.

To study the details of the power of control charts we must first clarify exactly how they will be constructed and used. Our assumption is that the control limits will be determined based on a sufficient number of subgroups -- at least 100, preferably 400 -- and then the process results will be plotted and checked against these limits. In contrast, some practitioners recommend updating the control limits based on the last 25, 50, or 100 points (Montgomery, 1991, p. 210). As a result, the control limits tend to adapt themselves to the data, and the power of the chart to detect trouble is reduced, since the charts are really trial charts where out of control points tend to increase $\hat{\sigma}$ and to shift $\overline{\overline{x}}$ (Hillier, 1969; Walker et al., 1991, verified this phenomenon by simulation). Here, we'll assume that control limits are based on the true parameters of the distribution, an assumption that is acceptable when enough data is used in their construction. In reality we never know the theoretical control limits, so we should expect variation around this value. We'll investigate the case of control limits based on data in Chapter 8.

There are several common ways in which processes deviate from the ideal "in control" pattern. To be "in control," as defined operationally by Shewhart control charts, a process has to comprise a set of statistically independent random variables with the same distribution. So, in general, an ideal control chart would signal an out of control situation either if the points come from different distributions or if they are not independent statistically. Most often, points will have different distributions because the mean has shifted, or because of a freak occurrence. The latter is indicated by a single point out of control in an otherwise satisfactory chart. Some of the possible causes for shifts of the mean may be (i) a drift (e.g., due to tool wear, or due to increasing pressure to finish a quota leading to erosion in conformance); (ii) loose setting (which may also cause excessive or even erratic variation); (iii) cyclical influences, such as temperature differences during the day, coffee breaks (every time a process is restarted it may take a while to stabilize again); change in the incoming materials and parts (especially when different vendors are involved, but also when different batches from the same vendor have different properties). Loose connections, vibrations from an external source, operating at specific speeds that reinforce vibrations and other causes may also increase (or, rarely, decrease) the variation, and thus, again, change the distribution.

An ideal control chart would never show an "out of control" signal unless the process is indeed out of control. Likewise, an ideal control chart will always show an "out of control" signal when the process is indeed out of control, and it should do so immediately. Such an ideal control chart has not been invented yet; and, based on our general knowledge about the inherent limitations of measurement and the random variation of processes, we can safely speculate such a chart will never exist. So, even with theoretical limits, there is a risk of showing an "out of control" signal by error, or "type I" error, which is sometimes called the α-risk. If we use control charts on a continuous basis, it's just a question of time until we'll make such an error. To prevent confusion with the probability of stopping by error *sometime*, which is also called the α-risk by some authors (in the context of a control chart with N points where there may or may not be at least one false "out of control" signal), we'll speak here of the *RFS* (rate of false signals), which is the risk we'll stop by mistake at a given point (e.g., *now*). It is also useful to speak of the expected number of points between signals (false or otherwise). This value is known as *average run length (ARL)*. When associated with false signals, $ARL = 1/RFS$. The *RFS* is usually kept to a very low value; e.g., the theoretical *RFS* associated with the $\overline{x}$ portion of the chart is approximately 0.0027 (or $ARL = 370$).

There is another risk, the β-risk, of *not* showing an "out of control" signal when the process is indeed out of control. The probability of obtaining an "out of control" signal when the process is indeed out of control, $1 - \beta$, is the *power* of the control chart. Usually, the power increases with the severity of the deviation from control. When the deviation is a shift of the mean, it is easy to calculate the power of the $\overline{x}$ chart, because we can safely assume that its distribution is normal. Note now that if the only way in which the process is out of control is a shift of the mean, then the dispersion chart should not detect any difference: it is only supposed to react when the variation changes (but it has its own *RFS* of course, so it may provide a signal *falsely*). If we use subgroups of n to compute $\overline{x}$ and let D denote the deviation of the process from center in units of σ_X, then the power is given by

$$1 - \beta = \Phi(-3 + D\sqrt{n}) + \Phi(-3 - D\sqrt{n})$$

where $\Phi(z)$ is the area under the normal density function from $-\infty$ to z (so the equation combines the areas under the tails of the distribution). Note that this equation assumes control limits at $\pm 3\sigma$. Table 6.8 reports the power of the $\overline{x}$ chart to detect deviations from the center expressed in σ_X units. *RS*, the value reported in the second column, is the rate of signals (false or true). The first row reflects a process that is in control, so its *RS* (0.0027) is our *RFS*. The table assumes subgroups of $n = 5$.

Dev	RS	ARL
0.00	0.0027*	370.4**
0.25	0.0075	133.3
0.50	0.0302	33.1
0.75	0.0934**	10.7*
1.00	0.2236**	4.47*
1.25	0.4188**	2.39*
1.50	0.6383**	1.57*
1.75	0.8186**	1.22*
2.00	0.9292**	1.08*

*We'd like this number to be as small as possible.
**We'd like this number to be as large as possible.

Table 6.8

For instance, if the mean shifts 1 standard deviation from center, the table shows that the power to detect this is 0.2236. Accordingly, as the third column of the table reports, it takes about 4.5 times on average to detect such a deviation. A shift of 0.5σ has an *ARL* of about 33, but in most applications we should not be too concerned with such a small shift, since its associated quadratic loss is small; often, such a shift does not even justify the necessary effort to adjust correctly, let alone the effort necessary to detect it.

Note that between 1.25 and 1.5 the power becomes larger than 0.5 for the first time. With subgroups of only 4, the power at a deviation of 1.5 is just over 0.5 (0.50135 to be exact). Consequently, people often say that the Shewhart control chart does not have enough power to detect deviations of less than $1.5\sigma_X$.

As we've seen, it's simple to compute the power of Shewhart $\bar{x}$ charts against deviations from the mean. Changes in the variance, however, cause a response that is much more complex to analyze. The most obvious expected effect of an increase in the variance is an increase of the dispersion statistic, and thus the dispersion chart will detect such a change if it is large enough. But changes in the variance also impact the location of $\bar{x}$, so the result may be that an out of control signal will be generated by the $\bar{x}$ part of the chart because of an increase in the variance. In fact, there is a correlation between the probabilities of those two potential signals (when the variance is excessive). This dependence is the cause of the complexity in the analysis. Table 6.9 reports the combined power of a Shewhart $\bar{x}$ and R chart to detect excessive variance and bias at various levels. The first row corresponds

Inflator:	1	1.25	1.5	1.75	2.0	2.25	2.5
bias							
0	173.	17.9	5.68	2.96	2.02	1.60	1.38
0.25	90.5	15.1	5.25	2.86	1.99	1.58	1.37
0.5	30.4	9.56	4.30	2.59	1.89	1.54	1.35
0.75	10.3	5.53	3.31	2.28	1.75	1.48	1.32
1.0	4.42	3.34	2.49	1.93	1.60	1.40	1.28
1.25	2.37	2.18	1.92	1.66	1.46	1.33	1.23
1.5	**1.56**	1.60	1.55	1.44	1.34	1.25	1.19
1.75	**1.23**	**1.29**	1.30	1.28	1.24	1.19	1.15
2.0	**1.07**	**1.13**	**1.16**	1.17	1.16	1.13	1.11

Note: $ARL=173$ implies 865 items in 173 subgroups, etc.

Table 6.9: ARL values for Shewhart $\bar{x}$ and R chart (subgroups of 5).

to a bias of zero, and the first entry in this row corresponds to a process that is in control. The first column is similar to Table 6.8, but here there are two potential "out of control" signals, and therefore ARL is lower. The table is based on a simulation study (each entry in the table is based on 100,000 subgroups of 5 normal deviates), and the results are offered only as a rough guide. The rows are associated with the bias, ranging from 0 to 2 standard deviation units. The columns are associated with various values of the standard deviation relative to nominal. Thus, in the first column the standard deviation is nominal (multiplied by 1), in the second column it is multiplied by 1.25, and so on. Looking at the first row, and using the convention that β should be about 0.5 (i.e., $ARL \leq 2$) to be considered "powerful," we see that the Shewhart chart is not powerful against increases in variance of 300% or less (i.e., an inflator of 2 or less), unless a strong bias is also present.

Some researchers, myself included (until running this simulation), assume intuitively that the Shewhart chart is more powerful with both the multiplier of the standard deviation and the bias from center. Indeed, looking at the columns of Tables 6.9 and 6.10 (which provides similar results for subgroups of $n=4$) we see that the power increases (ARL decreases) with the bias at all levels of variation. But looking at the rows, the bold entries in the tables indicate regions where increasing the variance while holding the bias constant, actually *decreases* the power of the chart. This is one example of the correlation between the two charts that makes their analytic analysis difficult. (This phenomenon occurs because with

Inflator:	1	1.25	1.5	1.75	2.0	2.25	2.5
bias							
0	148.	19.4	6.38	3.35	2.29	1.79	1.52
0.25	96.3	16.5	5.93	3.23	2.24	1.78	1.52
0.5	37.2	11.0	4.91	2.96	2.15	1.72	1.49
0.75	14.5	6.67	3.83	2.58	1.97	1.65	1.45
1.0	6.17	4.12	2.93	2.21	1.80	1.56	1.40
1.25	3.19	2.72	2.24	1.88	1.63	1.46	1.34
1.5	2.00	1.93	1.79	1.62	1.48	1.37	1.29
1.75	**1.45**	1.50	1.49	1.43	1.35	1.29	1.23
2.0	**1.19**	**1.26**	1.29	1.28	1.26	1.22	1.18

Note: $ARL=148$ implies 592 items in 148 subgroups, etc.

Table 6.10: ARL values for Shewhart $\overline{x}$ and R chart (subgroups of 4).

large variance the wide part of the tail extends into the range that is considered in control in the $\overline{x}$ chart.)

The "common wisdom" that Shewhart charts are not powerful against shifts of less than 1.5σ only applies to basic charts with subgroups of $n=4$ or $n=5$. If we specify larger subgroups we can discern much smaller deviations powerfully. Using the convention that β should exceed 0.5, let D be a deviation that is considered "important," in units of σ_x, and suppose $n \geq n_0$

$$n_0 = \left\lceil \frac{9}{D^2} \right\rceil$$

(where $\lceil x \rceil$ is the "round-up" function), then the chart will be powerful enough to detect the deviation. To see this consider that a chart with subgroups of n_0 will have a control limit coincide with D, and therefore there is a probability of about 0.5 that the realization will be outside the limit (assuming the use of $\pm 3\sigma$ limits; for $\pm t\sigma$ limits replace "9" in the formula by "t^2"). For example, if we want to detect deviations of $D=\sigma_x$ powerfully, we need subgroups of 9 at least; and to detect deviations of $D=1.5\sigma_x$ we require subgroups of 4 or more. Charts based on subgroups of $n=5$ are powerful against shifts of $1.34\sigma_x$ or more. (Note that this analysis ignores the probability of falling outside the opposite control limit. This probability is usually minute, and it is associated with a misleading signal -- we're liable to adjust the process in the opposite direction to what's necessary upon such a signal.)

Clearly, within the basic technology of Shewhart charts (i.e., without pattern tests, which we cover in Chapter 7), if we want to increase the power we must increase the subgroup size, and this may be costly in terms of both time and money. The choice of n should strike a good balance between these objectives.[8] The prevalent use of small n reflects a belief that frequent monitoring against *large* shifts is better than infrequent monitoring against both small or large shifts.

This highlights a problem associated with individuals charts: they are the least powerful in terms of detecting small shifts of the mean. In terms of the process distribution, this is a generic problem. It is much more serious than the fact that individual data are less likely to follow a normal distribution than averages. By using a moving average, however, we can ameliorate the problem, at least with respect to deviations that persist long enough to influence most or all the elements that are included in the moving average. For example, in Figure 6.19 we used a moving average of 10 points. This means that each point on the chart is the average of the result of that period and the nine previous periods. (The first nine periods, therefore, do not have points plotted.) It can be shown that the expected time to detect a small shift with a well-chosen moving average scheme is less than without, in spite of the fact that it takes a while for the deviation to be fully incorporated (as was the case in Figure 6.19). In the next section we discuss two methods that are also based on the idea of incorporating past data into the decision statistic in order to reduce the average detection time of small deviations.

A related problem is to minimize the total number of measurements necessary to flag a shift of D standard deviations. Supplement 6.3 shows that this is achieved, approximately, by setting

$$n = \text{ROUND}\left(\frac{3.326}{D}\right)^2$$

where ROUND is the rounding function. This implies that the power of each subgroup is approximately 0.63 (assuming the use of $\pm 3\sigma$).

6.7. *CUSUM* and *EWMA* Control Charts

In addition to moving averages, other technologies exist to obtain more power in the context of process monitoring. All these methods -- similarly to moving averages --

---

[8]Montgomery (1991) is a good source for methods to optimize control chart parameters. Usually, however, these methods require so many assumptions about the ways in which a process may go out of control, and the damage associated with it, relative to the damage associated with false signals, that it is questionable whether they should be used.

incorporate data from former subgroups or individuals into the statistic used to make the decision, and thus they increase the effective subgroup size. But by doing so, they may sacrifice power to detect large shifts which were not reflected in the former subgroups yet. Two approaches exist for this purpose, and we discuss them now. Wheeler (1995) is a good source for more detailed comparisons between these methods and Shewhart charts.

The two approaches we discuss here are *CUSUM* (cumulated sum) charts and *EWMA* (exponentially weighted moving average) charts. In the former case, and sometimes the latter, the charts relate to a desired target, *T*. This is done under the implicit assumption that it is possible to adjust the process average to the target exactly. As we already discussed, the target should be the best value we can adjust to methodically -- which is different from the best value we ever recorded (the latter may have been due to luck or due to a random estimation error). This implies, necessarily, that these charts are intended for process maintenance, rather than for process improvement studies, because during such studies we may not yet know how to best adjust the process. Furthermore, during such studies we are usually more interested in patterns that the data may exhibit than during process maintenance, and Shewhart charts are more suited to the purpose of exhibiting such patterns when they exist. In contrast, the mathematical operations necessary for the construction of these alternative charts usually destroy patterns in the data.

6.7.1. *CUSUM Charts*

CUSUM charts look at the cumulated sum of deviations from the center and when that sum exceeds a particular dynamic limit (which increases as a function of the number of subgroups collected), an "out of control" signal is generated. The limits of *CUSUM* charts must be dynamic because the sum of deviations of a process that is in control is a random variable whose distribution is a function of the number of points. Sometimes, masks with the shape of a V are used to represent these dynamic limits, but it is also possible to achieve the same effect by programmable algorithms.

Theoretically, *CUSUM* charts are more powerful than Shewhart charts against small deviations; i.e., their expected average run length (*ARL*) between true out-of-control signals is lower when the bias is small (Champ and Woodall, 1987). Nonetheless, they are less powerful against sudden large shifts. Advanced versions of *CUSUM* charts, with a parabolic extension of the V mask, are more powerful than Shewhart charts both for large and small deviations (Lucas, 1973), but using such methods either increases the *RFS* or sacrifices some power against small shifts (there's no free lunch). Furthermore, Lucas (1982) recommended a combination of a Shewhart chart with a *CUSUM* to capture both large and small shifts;

arguably, this implies that the parabolic extension idea is not strongly recommended even by its originator. Of course, such a combination must either increase the *RFS* or trade power between small and large deviations. (A similar scheme, but with *EWMA* charts instead of *CUSUM*, is suggested in Supplement 6.3.)

CUSUM charts, in spite of their superior power against small shifts, are not very popular. One reason is the undisputable fact that they are considerably more complex to devise. A second reason is that the basic *CUSUM* chart does not detect *large* shifts quickly enough, and many users are more concerned with large shifts than with small ones. Finally, a very serious application problem with *CUSUM* charts is that much of the material published about them is based on erroneous risk calculations (for more details see Woodall and Adams, 1993). As a result, the actual performance of many implementations of these charts, including the performance of several software packages, is not even nearly as advertized. Typical errors in estimates of the *ARL* are by a ratio of three to five. One may speculate that these flawed applications did not do much to enhance the popularity of the method.

6.7.2. EWMA Charts

EWMA charts are simpler, and roughly equivalent in power to *CUSUM* charts. They too are not very popular yet as control charts, although the same technology is widely used for forecasting time-series. They are especially appropriate for individuals charts, where they can make up for the small subgroup size effectively (as does the *CUSUM* chart too). Let λ be a weighing factor between 0 and 1 (values between 0.1 and 0.2 are used frequently, but see Supplement 7 for a discussion of cases that require much higher values). Suppose the former moving average was A_{i-1}, then after the ith point, x_i (which may be an individual point or the average of a subgroup), the new moving average is computed as per

$$A_i = (1 - \lambda)A_{i-1} + \lambda x_i$$

When the chart is started we use $A_1 = x_1$ and the smoothing starts with the second point. Alternatively, when we have a target (T) we can adjust to, we may choose to set $A_0 = T$, so $A_1 = [1 - \lambda]T + \lambda x_1$. To calculate control limits for the moving average, we define a number, k_a as follows

$$k_a = \frac{2 - \lambda}{\lambda}$$

k_a serves as the equivalent of the subgroup size for calculating control limits (but it need not be integer). For instance, if we use $\lambda = 0.15$, and even if every x_i represents a single unit (rather than a subgroup), then $k_a = 12.33$, and this is part of the explanation why an *EWMA* chart can detect small shifts better than a basic Shewhart chart with $n=5$ or $n=4$. Setting $\lambda=1/3$ will yield $k_a=5$, and $\lambda=0.4$ leads to $k_a=4$, making the *EWMA* chart more comparable to a basic Shewhart chart. But there is another feature that makes an *EWMA* chart more powerful against recent shifts, and this is the fact that it gives a higher weight to recent data, while still enjoying the benefits of the reduced risk associated with large subgroups.

To continue with the construction of the chart, suppose σ_P is the standard deviation of x_i, then the $\pm 3\sigma$ control limits for A_i is given by

$$LCL = T - \frac{3\sigma_P}{\sqrt{k_a}}: \quad UCL = T + \frac{3\sigma_P}{\sqrt{k_a}}$$

when we have a given target, or we replace T by a previously established average otherwise. Note that if x_i is the average of a subgroup of n points, then we should use the standard deviation of the process, σ_x, divided by $\sqrt{n}$ for σ_P. Thus the equation becomes

$$LCL = T - \frac{3\sigma_x}{\sqrt{k_a n}}; \quad UCL = T + \frac{3\sigma_x}{\sqrt{k_a n}}$$

Otherwise, σ_p is identical to σ_x, and may be estimated by a moving range.

Incidentally, the connection between k_a and λ can be expressed also in the opposite direction, i.e.,

$$\lambda = \frac{2}{k_a + 1}$$

which may be useful for the purpose of choosing λ. The idea is to increase λ as much as possible (to increase the weight of recent data) while still maintaining the properties of a large k_a. Using a large k_a value is equivalent to using a large subgroup for estimation: it is more reliable, less sensitive to deviations from normality, and more capable of detecting small shifts. Conversely, it is slower to detect sudden large shifts. For example, let us return to the concrete strength example cited in the previous section. We already saw the chart associated with a 10 point moving average (with control limits and a centerline using $\overline{\overline{x}}$ and $\hat{\sigma}_x$ based on the first 50 points). The width of the control limits there is obtained by dividing $\hat{\sigma}_x$ by $\sqrt{10}$, since each point in the chart is the average of $n=10$ data points. Figure 6.20 shows an *EWMA* chart for the same points with $\lambda=2/11$. Calculating k_a for this smoothing factor we obtain $(2-2/11)/(2/11)=10$, which implies that we can use the same control limits. The data is smoothed as of the second period. Comparing the last two figures we see that they are almost identical, but the latter *almost* gave a signal a good seven points earlier. To clarify this issue further, let us show two additional renditions of the same data. Figure 6.21

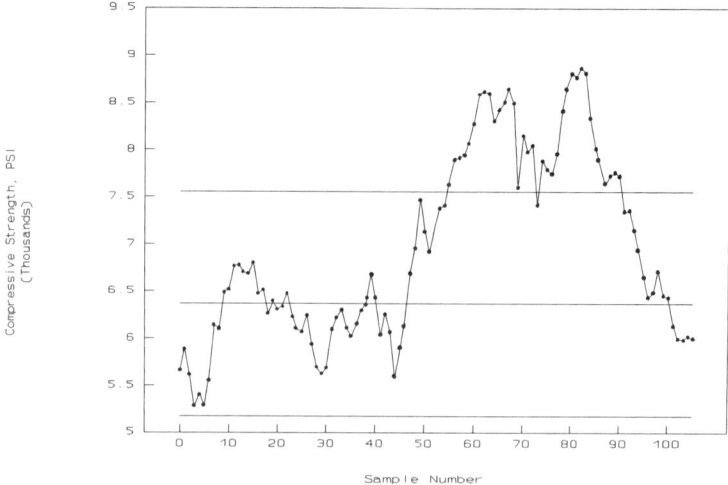

Fig. 6.20. An *EWMA* chart for concrete strength with $\lambda = 2/11$ (limits based on the first 50 points).

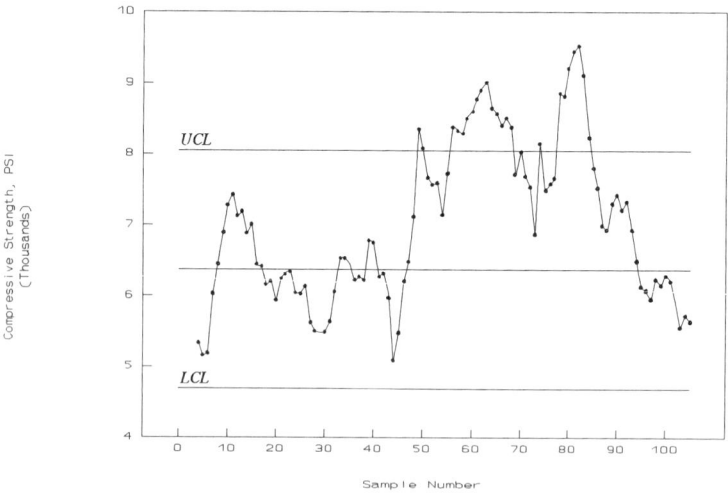

Fig. 6.21. A moving average chart with 5 points (limits based on the first 50 points).

is a 5-point moving average, and Figure 6.22 is an *EWMA* with $\lambda = 1/3$, i.e., $k_a = 5$. Again, the two charts share the same control limits and centerline based on the first 50 tests. The first out of control signal is given at the same point (55) in both cases, but the second one is one point earlier in the latter case (60 instead of 61). Thus, *EWMA* charts enjoy a minute advantage over moving average charts. More important, they are easier to update: all we need is the last A value, x_i, and λ.

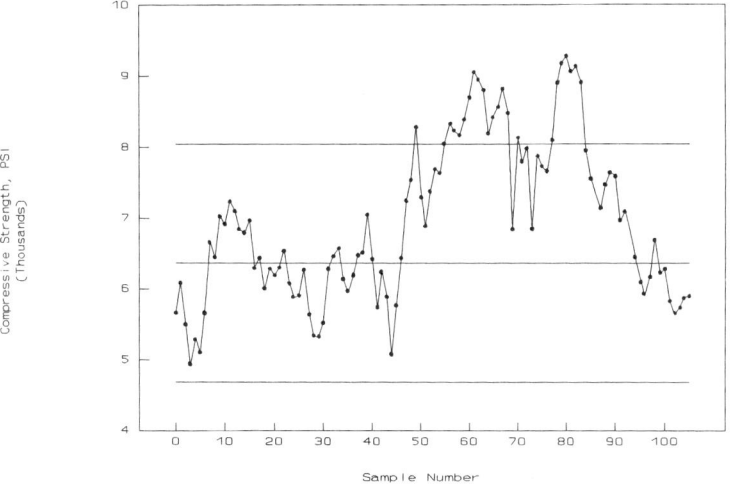

Fig. 6.22. An *EWMA* chart with $\lambda = 1/3$ ($k_a = 5$) (limits based on the first 50 points).

6.7.3. *Pattern Tests and the Power to Detect Small Shifts*

Whether we use moving averages, *EWMA*, or *CUSUM*, the resulting sequence of statistics comprises highly dependent points. For this reason, pattern tests (which we discuss in Chapter 7) -- are not applicable to any of these charts. It turns out that these pattern tests are very relevant to the power issue. Wheeler (1995, Chapter 10) shows that by using some of these pattern tests *instead* of smoothing by a moving average -- specifically Tests 1, 2, 5 and 6 by the notation of Chapter 7 -- the *xmR* chart is roughly as powerful as any smoothed version for shifts that exist in the data for a while, but it is *more* powerful against recent shifts (that may not yet be fully incorporated in the moving averages). The conclusion is that smoothing by moving averages is an inferior alternative in terms of power. But it must also be realized that specifying these tests increases the rate of false signals several folds (typically, each separate test has about the same *RFS* as an $\overline{x}$ chart). The final conclusion is that pattern tests may be commendable, but the other versions discussed here still have an advantage in terms of power for a given risk.

6.8. Median and Range Control Charts

A somewhat simplified version of Shewhart control charts is based on charting the median of a (preferably odd) subgroup instead of charting the average, $\overline{x}$. Strictly speaking, these charts have not been proposed by Shewhart (although he did investigate the efficiency of using the median, and found it wanting), and thus they should not be called "Shewhart charts." Nonetheless, their general approach is based on Shewhart's methodology, except that they aim to do away with the need to calculate the subgroup mean -- a daunting task for a small minority of workers.

While using the median instead of $\overline{x}$ is not efficient for normal data, these charts have the advantage that for odd subgroups (of 3, 5, or 7 usually) no computations are necessary once the control limits have been determined. Also, these charts have the advantage that they record the data of all the items sampled. Furthermore, the median is more robust against few outliers than the mean. For example, if there is an equal number of outliers above and below the distribution, the median will not change at all! Otherwise, if there are, say, k more outliers above the distribution than below, the median will shift approximately by $k/2$ points upwards. Thus, there is also a good theoretical reason to prefer them over regular Shewhart charts. This robustness, as usual, comes at a price of less efficient use of data.

To use the median and R control chart a worker measures the units of a subgroup, and plots the results one above the other for each subgroup. She then checks whether the median is within the control limits that were established for it, where the median is the $((n+1)/2)^{th}$ item, e.g., item 2 for subgroups of 3, item 3 for subgroups of 5, item 4 for subgroups of 7 (or the average of the $(n/2)^{th}$ and $((n/2)+1)^{th}$ items, when n is even). If the median is within control, the worker checks whether the range is also within control. This can be done by comparing the distance between the largest and smallest results to the limit established for it -- a task that can be done either by measuring the distance between the extreme points or using a mask or a gauge with markings for the maximal allowable range value. Since this procedure is slightly simpler than calculating the mean, median charts are promoted by some as a good way to ease control charting into an environment with less educated workers. Nonetheless, for employers who can afford spending $10 per worker on a statistical calculator and when the workers are capable of using it -- and if they are not, we should question their ability to measure and record data in the first place -- this argument is moot. Also, these charts are less directly applicable to quadratic loss: as we saw, quadratic loss is reduced by reducing the bias from the mean (and not the median).

The range part of the chart is identical to that of $\overline{x}$ and R charts, and the median part is established by taking the average median, $\overline{M}$, from the m subgroups, and adding or subtracting 3 standard deviations of the median from it. Technically, this is done by the following equations,

$$LCL_M = \overline{M} - A_6 \overline{R}$$

$$UCL_M = \overline{M} + A_6 \overline{R}$$

where A_6 is provided in Table 6.11.

Subgroup size:	3	5	7	9	11
A_6:	1.187	0.691	0.509	0.412	0.350

Table 6.11

Note that the median chart is more appropriate for asymmetrical distributions. Yet A_6 is based on the (ubiquitous) assumption that the process is normal (and thus symmetric). For more details on median charts see Nelson (1982) or Wheeler (1995).

6.9. Common Errors to Avoid

♦ Using attribute charts when the underlying data is continuous.

♦ Recalculating limits without evidence that the process changed. This is tantamount to defining "in control" as "what happened recently," which is an instance of using Funnel Rule 4.

♦ Confusing control limits with tolerance limits. It is important to realize that (i) control limits are determined by the *data the process generates*, while tolerance limits may or may not be influenced by the process, but ultimately they are determined exogenously (see Section 3.3); (ii) except for individuals charts, control limits are calculated for the average of several units while tolerance limits apply to each and every unit, therefore, control limits and tolerance limits are based on different scales altogether (it's not enough that $\bar{x}$ is consistently within the tolerance limits to ensure that the process is capable).

♦ Mixing the output of several process streams before collecting data for control charts.

♦ Using the variation exhibited by the full sample to devise control limits for variable charts, instead of using the average within-subgroup dispersion for this purpose (see -Wheeler, 1995).

Supplement 6.1

On the Efficiency of Various Dispersion Statistics

The main purpose of this supplement is to compare the efficiencies of the three dispersion statistics, $\overline{R}$, $\overline{s}$, and s^2. We'll do this by measuring the variance of $\hat{\sigma}$, the estimate of σ_X that is induced by each of these statistics. Recall, however, that in Chapter 6 we showed that the $\overline{s}$ statistic is more robust against undetected points whose variance is out of control, so efficiency is just one part of the picture.

Formally speaking, one cannot compare efficiencies without specifying the process distribution: different distributions may be associated with different sufficient statistics. A sufficient statistic is one that retains all the pertinent information in a sample. Using a sufficient statistic effectively, therefore, leads to maximal efficiency. For example, let us look at the efficiency of the range statistic in the case of the uniform distribution, U[a,b]. It turns out that the range is capable of providing all the necessary information for the purpose of evaluating the variance in this case, while (for $n > 2$) the s^2 statistic is less efficient. Indeed, a (minimal) sufficient statistic for the uniform distribution is the pair x_{min} and x_{max}, and only their difference is necessary to estimate the variance. The picture becomes less clear once we decide to take m subgroups instead of a single consolidated sample, but this is not important to us here.

Our analysis, then, will be based on the ubiquitous assumption that the process has a normal distribution. On the one hand, we cannot tell in advance that this will indeed be the case for any real process. On the other hand, the normal distribution is a reasonable default choice when we have no information to the contrary. Certainly we have no special reason to select a statistic that is *not* suitable for the normal distribution (such as x_{min} and x_{max}, for instance), unless we know exactly what the distribution is, and what statistic is best for it. In Supplement 6.2, for example, we show that the variance estimation that we get for several non-normal distributions is quite accurate even when we assume such normality, so it makes sense to study the relative efficiency of the various statistics under the normality assumption. In conclusion, it is exactly *because* we don't know the distribution that the use of the normal default makes sense.

In the case of the normal distribution, subject to our generic decision *not* to assume the process is well adjusted while we collect our sample, $\overline{x}$ and s^2, together, are a minimal sufficient statistic for each subgroup, and Σs^2 is a sufficient dispersion statistic for the whole sample. (Because s^2 is the minimal sufficient statistic for a subgroup, the same applies to s, which retains all the information in s^2. When looking at the whole sample, s^2 is a one-to-one function of the sufficient statistic, so it retains the sufficient information. $\overline{s}$, however, does not retain all this information, because we take the square root *before* averaging.) While s^2 is most efficient, the use of R is more convenient and both R and s are more robust. But if we select R, or even s, we should know the price we're paying in terms of efficiency -- our subject here.

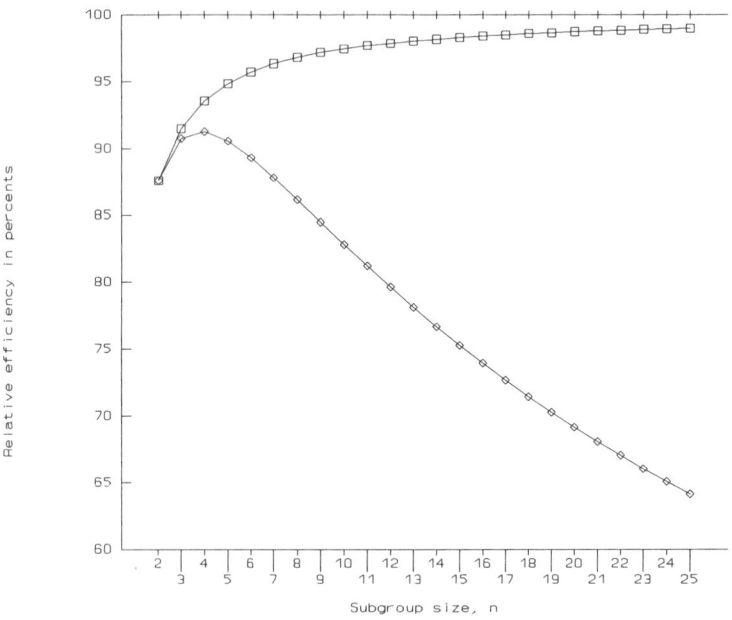

Fig. S6.1.1. Comparing the efficiencies of the three dispersion statistics (top to bottom: $\overline{s^2}$=100%, $\overline{s}$, $\overline{R}$).

Figure S6.1.1 provides the answer graphically. Using the efficiency associated with $\overline{s^2}$ as our basis, with the value 1, the figure shows the efficiency associated with the use of s and of R, in that order from top to bottom. It shows clearly that for small n the efficiency of s^2 is much higher than that of both $\overline{R}$ and $\overline{s}$, while for large n the difference between $\overline{s}$ and s^2 decreases, as the relative efficiency of s approaches 1 asymptotically. The relative efficiency of $\overline{R}$, in contrast, approaches 0 asymptotically. As a practical consequence, suppose we use subgroups of $n=5$, then if we use $\overline{R}$ we are effectively throwing away about 9.4% of the information, and if we use $\overline{s}$ we still waste about 5.1%. Thus, to obtain comparable results to s^2 with $\overline{R}$ we would have to increase the sample by a factor of $1/0.906$, or about 10% additional subgroups; and if we use $\overline{s}$ we'd have to increase the sample by a factor of 5.4%. Nonetheless, for large n the $\overline{s}$ statistic is definitely the best choice because it is almost as efficient as s^2, *and* it is more robust. For small n we have to trade efficiency for robustness, and no generic recommendations can be made. In the remainder of this supplement we discuss in detail how the data for this figure was obtained.

Our approach will be to first compare the efficiency of $\overline{R}$ to that of $\overline{s}$, and later to compare the efficiency of $\overline{s}$ to that of s^2. But we start with a discussion of the efficiency of using $\overline{R}$ as a function of n.

S6.1.1. The Efficiency of $\overline{R}$ as a Function of n

Regardless of the statistic we may select to compute $\hat{\sigma}$, recall that we always obtain an unbiased estimate for σ_X. The three statistics are equivalent in this respect. The remaining key to the efficiency of a statistic, where the three do differ, is the variance it induces onto $\hat{\sigma}$. The most efficient statistic is the one that induces the lowest variance. One way to quantify the value of such reduced variance is to compare the total sample size necessary to obtain a particular variance. A more efficient statistic requires a smaller sample.

But efficiency is not only a function of the selection of the statistic, e.g., R, s, or s^2. It is also a function of n. Let's investigate this function for the case of using $\overline{R}$ to estimate σ_X. Suppose we have m subgroups of n each, and we use $\overline{R}$ to estimate $\hat{\sigma}$. Let $d_2(n)$ and $d_3(n)$ be the control chart factors we introduced in Chapter 6, expressed as explicit functions of n. Under these conditions the variance of $\hat{\sigma}$ is given by

$$\sigma_{\hat{\sigma}}^2 = \left(\sigma_x \frac{d_3(n)}{d_2(n)\sqrt{m}} \right)^2 = \sigma_x^2 \frac{d_3(n)^2}{d_2(n)^2 m} \qquad \text{(S6.1.1)}$$

To see this consider that $\overline{R}$ is the average of m random variables, the expectation of each of which is $\sigma_X d_2(n)$, and the standard deviation is $\sigma_X d_2(n)$. The fraction in the brackets, therefore, is the coefficient of variation of $\hat{\sigma}$, and when multiplied by the expected value of $\hat{\sigma}$, σ_X, we obtain the standard deviation of $\hat{\sigma}$.

This expression is a function of both m and n. Suppose now we have a sample of N normal deviates, and we wish to divide them into subgroups of n, find the range for each subgroup, R, and estimate σ_X by the relationship $\hat{\sigma} = \overline{R} d_2(n)$. What is the optimal n if we

n	$d_3\sqrt{n}/d_2$	n	$d_3\sqrt{n}/d_2$	n	$d_3\sqrt{n}/d_2$
2	1.068	10	0.819	18	0.861
3	0.909	11	0.823	19	0.867
4	0.855	12	0.828	20	0.873
5	0.831	13	0.833	21	0.878
6	0.820	14	0.838	22	0.884
7	0.815	15	0.844	23	0.890
8	0.814	16	0.849	24	0.896
9	0.816	17	0.855	25	0.901

Table S6.1.1

wish to minimize the variance of our estimate? A mathematical model of the same question is to minimize the following expression,

$$\sigma_x \frac{d_3(n)}{d_2(n)\sqrt{\dfrac{N}{n}}} = \frac{\sigma_x}{\sqrt{N}} \frac{d_3(n)\sqrt{n}}{d_2(n)}$$

Since $\sigma_x/\sqrt{N}$ is a constant, we simply need to find n to minimize $d_3(n)\sqrt{n}/d_2(n)$. Straightforward comparison shows that the optimal n for this purpose is 8, and 7 is almost equally efficient. Table S6.1.1 lists $d_3(n)\sqrt{n}/d_2(n)$ values for n between 2 and 25, and Figure S6.1.2 shows them graphically. Using larger n is wasteful of data in the sense that we can do better with the same total number of measurements. The same applies to smaller n, but at least there we have the advantage of more frequent sampling, allowing us to capture really large shifts earlier.

This, incidentally, is a good reason to recommend against using the R dispersion statistic with subgroups of more than 10. Furthermore, if we have subgroups of 12 or more, it is a good idea to split each of them to two or more sub-subgroups as close to 8 or 7 as possible. But as Figure S6.1.1 suggests, using s^2 or s instead is much better. This is because, in terms of variance reduction, both these statistics consistently improve as we increase n (although the improvement potential is decreasing with n); at the same time $\overline{R}$ becomes progressively less efficient in absolute terms, and even more so relatively.

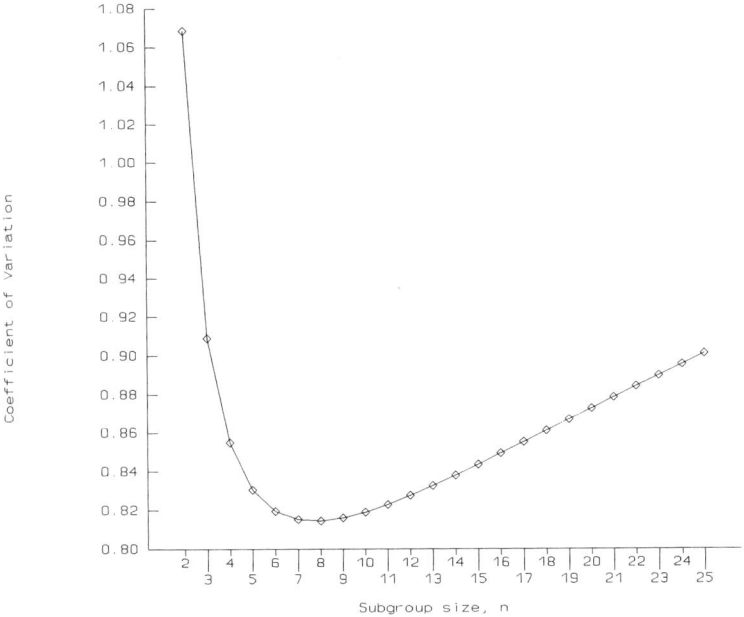

Fig. S6.1.2. $d_3(n)/(d_2(n)\sqrt{n})$ as a function of n.

S6.1.2. The Efficiency of $\overline{R}$ Relative to $\overline{s}$

When we want to investigate the efficiency of using $\overline{s}$, instead of (S6.1.1) we should now look at the expression

$$\sigma_{\hat{\sigma}}^2 = \left(\sigma_x \frac{\sqrt{1-c_4(n)^2}}{c_4(n)\sqrt{m}} \right)^2 = \sigma_x^2 \frac{1-c_4(n)^2}{c_4(n)^2 m} \qquad (S6.1.2)$$

By looking at the ratio between (S6.1.1) and (S6.1.2) we can find the relative improvement we obtain by using $\overline{s}$ instead of $\overline{R}$ as a function of n. Suppose that we use m_R subgroups with $\overline{R}$ estimation, and we want to find a number m_s such that if we use m_s subgroups with $\overline{s}$ we'll obtain the same variance for $\hat{\sigma}$. If m_s is consistently smaller than m_R for all n, we know that we have a more efficient statistic. Table S6.1.2 shows the ratio m_s/m_R for n between 2 and 25. The table shows that for $n=2$ the two statistics are equivalent (which they should be, because they contain the exact same information), but for larger n the $\overline{s}$ statistic is progressively superior (as Figure S6.1.1 suggests as well). Since the efficiency drops faster for larger n values, it becomes obvious that R should not be utilized beyond $n=10$.

n	m_s/m_R	n	m_s/m_R	n	m_s/m_R
2	1.000	10	0.850	18	0.725
3	0.992	11	0.831	19	0.712
4	0.975	12	0.814	20	0.700
5	0.955	13	0.797	21	0.689
6	0.933	14	0.781	22	0.678
7	0.911	15	0.766	23	0.668
8	0.890	16	0.751	24	0.657
9	0.869	17	0.738	25	0.648

Table S6.1.2

Incidentally, due to rounding differences the values in the table may not agree exactly with the ones based on the values reported in Tables 6.1 and 6.4. The rounding here was performed only after the computations. For example, using the rounded data from these tables we would find a difference between m_R and m_s for $n=2$, but with exact data these two are exactly equal, as the theory suggests they should be.

S6.1.3. The Efficiency of $\overline{s}$ Relative to $\overline{s^2}$

First, recall our approximation $c_4 \approx (4n-4)/(4n-3)$. Based on this approximation, for a (large) subgroup of size k, we obtain

$$\frac{\sqrt{1-c_4(k)^2}}{c_4(k)} \sim \frac{1}{\sqrt{2k-2.25}} \sim \frac{1}{\sqrt{2(k-1)}}$$

Suppose now that we use m subgroups of n (where n is not necessarily large but mn is large), and let $k=m(n-1)$, then the variance of our estimate is given by

$$\sigma_{\hat{\sigma}}^2 \sim \sigma_x^2 \frac{1}{2m(n-1)-2.25} = \frac{\sigma_x^2}{m} \frac{1}{2(n-1)-\dfrac{2.25}{m}} \sim \frac{\sigma_x^2}{m} \frac{1}{2(n-1)} \qquad (S6.1.3)$$

For any given m and those n values for which we have tabulated c_4, we can now compute the ratio between (S6.1.3) and (S6.1.2), without necessarily neglecting the element $2.25/m$. For large m we can use the approximation by neglecting that element. Table S6.1.3 lists the results of this calculation under the assumption that m is large. The same results are depicted in Figure S6.1.1.

For larger n we can replace (S6.1.2) by a similar approximation (but for the values depicted in Figure S6.1.1 this is not necessary). Thus, for large m and large n we obtain the following ratio

$$\frac{2n-2.25}{2n-2-2.25/m} \approx \frac{2n-2.25}{2n-2} = 1 - \frac{1}{8n-8} \tag{S6.1.4}$$

which approaches 1 asymptotically with n. The data in Figure S6.1.1 were computed under the assumption that m is large, i.e., the element $2.25/m$ was neglected. Finally, Table S6.1.4, whose elements are the products of the elements of Tables S6.1.2 and S6.1.3, gives the ratio between the efficiency of using s^2 and $\overline{R}$.

We now see that Figure S6.1.1 depicts the information in Tables S6.1.3 and S6.1.4. Incidentally, by observing (S6.1.4) we may deduce that for $m<9$ $\overline{s}$ is more efficient than s^2, but this is only a result of the approximations we used. (S6.1.4) is really valid only in the limit for large m. In reality, s^2 is superior for any $m>1$, and equal for $m=1$.

As a final note, Shewhart (1931) devoted a lot of space to the discussion of various statistics. Specifically, his Figure 98 (p. 287), although applicable to a single subgroup only, is similar to our Figure S6.1.1. Strangely enough, Shewhart recommended the use of s^2 for *large* subgroups (ibid, p. 305), while we've shown that for large subgroups the difference

n	m_{s^2}/m_s	n	m_{s^2}/m_s	n	m_{s^2}/m_s
2	0.876	10	0.975	18	0.986
3	0.915	11	0.977	19	0.987
4	0.936	12	0.979	20	0.987
5	0.949	13	0.980	21	0.988
6	0.957	14	0.982	22	0.989
7	0.963	15	0.983	23	0.989
8	0.968	16	0.984	24	0.989
9	0.972	17	0.985	25	0.990

Table S6.1.3

n	m_{s^2}/m_R	n	m_{s^2}/m_R	n	m_{s^2}/m_R
2	0.876	10	0.828	18	0.714
3	0.907	11	0.812	19	0.703
4	0.913	12	0.796	20	0.691
5	0.906	13	0.781	21	0.681
6	0.893	14	0.767	22	0.670
7	0.878	15	0.753	23	0.660
8	0.862	16	0.739	24	0.651
9	0.845	17	0.727	25	0.641

Table S6.1.4

is smaller, and due to robustness considerations this is a domain where $\bar{s}$ is probably the best choice. Thus, Shewhart's recommendation should be reversed, if we decide to use s^2 at all.

Supplement 6.2

On the Computation of Control Chart Factors

As we discussed in Chapter 6, the control chart factors are based on the assumption that the process distribution is normal. But we also demonstrated that they work well for the triangular distribution, even though it is far from normal. Be that as it may, in this supplement we discuss how the factors are computed. For this purpose it is enough to show how to derive c_4, d_2 and d_3. All the other factors we introduced are based on these, as discussed in the chapter. Some of the results here require familiarity with the chi-square distribution, which in turn utilizes the gamma function. Interested readers should be able to find details about this in most probability texts or advanced calculus texts.

S6.2.1. Deriving c_4

This is a classic derivation, but missing from most SQC books (Ryan, 1989, is an exception). All the results for the S^2 statistic, or its square root, S, are associated with the χ^2 distribution. The density function of a χ^2 with $n-1$ degrees of freedom (as we have) is given by

$$f(x) = \frac{x^{\frac{n-3}{2}} e^{\frac{-x}{2}}}{2^{\frac{n-1}{2}} \Gamma\left(\frac{n-1}{2}\right)}; \quad x>0$$

To obtain c_4 we must compute the expectation of the square root of a χ^2 random variable. But when we devise the appropriate integral, we may note that the integrand is associated with the density function of a χ^2 with an additional degree of freedom, which facilitates the solution (as per the following sequence)

$$E(S) = \frac{1}{2^{\frac{n-1}{2}} \Gamma\left(\frac{n-1}{2}\right)} \int_0^\infty x^{\frac{1}{2}} x^{\frac{n-3}{2}} e^{\frac{-x}{2}} dx = \frac{1}{2^{\frac{n-1}{2}} \Gamma\left(\frac{n-1}{2}\right)} \int_0^\infty x^{\frac{n-2}{2}} e^{\frac{-x}{2}} dx$$

$$= \frac{2^{\frac{n}{2}} \Gamma\left(\frac{n}{2}\right)}{2^{\frac{n-1}{2}} \Gamma\left(\frac{n-1}{2}\right)} = \frac{\sqrt{2} \, \Gamma\left(\frac{n}{2}\right)}{\Gamma\left(\frac{n-1}{2}\right)}$$

Recalling that to obtain S from a χ^2 with $n-1$ degrees of freedom we multiply the χ^2 by σ_x^2, divide by $n-1$, and then take the square root, we can now state

$$c_4 = \frac{E(S)}{\sigma_x} = \sqrt{\frac{2}{n-1}} \frac{\Gamma\left(\frac{n}{2}\right)}{\Gamma\left(\frac{n-1}{2}\right)}$$

This solution is analytic because we can evaluate the Gamma function exactly for $k/2$ when k is any integer. This stems from the basic result

$$\Gamma(z) = \int_0^\infty e^{-t} t^{z-1} dt = (z-1)\Gamma(z-1)$$

When k is even, this yields the factorial $(k-1)!$. When k is odd we can start the chain by setting $\Gamma(0.5) = \sqrt{\pi} \approx 1.772454$, or, equivalently, $\Gamma(1.5) = \sqrt{\pi}/2 \approx 0.886227$.

To obtain the approximation for large n, $c_4 \approx 4(n-1)/(4n-3)$ we can replace the exact factorials in the result by Stirling's approximation, which states

$$\Gamma(x) \approx x^x e^{-x} \sqrt{\frac{2\pi}{x}} \left[1 + \frac{1}{12x} + \frac{1}{288x^2} - \ldots\right]$$

Only the first one or two elements in the brackets really count for large x. When this is applied to the formula of c_4, the exact result depends on the approximation one selects for the element $(n/(n-1))^{(n-1)/2}$, which is obtained during the derivation. The correct way to do this is to represent the power by multiplying $(n-1)/2$ by the natural logarithm of $n/(n-1)$. Depending on the series we can select to represent the logarithm, the results obtained based on the dominant members of the series span the range $(4n-5)/(4n-4)$ to $(4n-3)/(4n-2)$, and the approximation suggested is in the middle of this range. It is also the one that works best, starting with very low n values. For instance, for $n=2$ this approximation yields 0.8, which is quite close to 0.7979; and it only gets better for larger n. The necessary series are given in various mathematical texts.[1]

S6.2.2. Deriving d_2 and d_3

These factors are based on quite intensive numerical integration results, using the normal density function as the basis. Tippett (1925), while not the first to discuss the range, is

---

[1]For instance, *Standard Mathematical Tables*, Samuel M. Selby (ed), The Chemical Rubber Co., Cleveland, OH.

perhaps the most important paper on the subject, since it gave the impetus to the use of the range to estimate the variance. Practically exact results, along with a historical background of the range calculations, were given by Harter (1960). Essentially, the approach is to determine the density function of the range, $g(R)$, and then it is straightforward (but, without a computer, extremely laborious), to calculate the moments of the distribution by the formula

$$E(R^k) = \int_0^\infty R^k g(R) dR$$

We are interested in the first moment, yielding d_2, and the second moment, which is related to d_3 by the formula

$$E(R^2) = d_3^2 + d_2^2$$

To complete the theoretical background, let us find $g(R)$ for any continuous process, say with density function $f(x)$ and CDF $F(x)$. When substituting the density function and CDF of the standard normal distribution we'll get the parameters that we require.

Recall that $R = x_{max} - x_{min}$. We proceed to discuss the density function of x_{min} and that of x_{max} conditional on x_{min}. Denote the density function of x_{min} by $f_{min}(z)$, and the CDF by $F_{min}(z)$. Let's look at the complement of the CDF, $1 - F_{min}(z)$. This is the probability $x_{min} > z$, and this happens if and only if *all* the items in the subgroup exceed z, an event whose probability is $(1 - F(z))^n$. It follows immediately that

$$F_{min}(z) = 1 - [1 - F(z)]^n$$

By taking the derivative of this CDF we obtain the density function,

$$f_{min}(z) = n f(z) [1 - F(z)]^{n-1}$$

Similar reasoning shows that the distribution of x_{max} is given by

$$F_{max}(z) = [F(z)]^n$$
$$f_{max}(z) = n f(z) [F(z)]^{n-1}$$

Nonetheless, we should recall that x_{min} and x_{max} are not independent statistically. For instance, it is clear that x_{max} cannot be less than x_{min}, which implies that information about x_{min} changes our conditional distribution of x_{max}. Suppose $x_{min} = y$, then the conditional CDF of any of the other $n-1$ items is provided by

$$F(z|z>y) = \frac{F(z) - F(y)}{1 - F(y)}$$

By raising this to the power $n-1$ we obtain the CDF of x_{max} conditional on x_{min}

$$F_{max}(z|z>x_{min}) = \left[\frac{F(z) - F(x_{min})}{1 - F(x_{min})} \right]^{n-1}$$

The CDF of the range, $G(R)$ may be obtained by the following integral

$$G(R) = \int_{-\infty}^{\infty} f_{min}(x) F_{max}(x+R|R>0))dx$$

$$= n \int_{-\infty}^{\infty} f(x)[F(x+R) - F(x)]^{n-1}dx$$

To see this consider that *given* x_{min} the probability the range will be less than R is given by the conditional CDF of the remaining $n-1$ items with the argument $x_{min}+R$, and by integrating this expression over all the possible values of x_{min} we obtain $G(R)$. Next, by taking the derivative of $G(R)$ with respect to R (which can be done within the integral, since the integration limits are not functions of R), we obtain $g(R)$, our required density function

$$g(R) = n(n-1) \int_{-\infty}^{\infty} f(x) \int_{0}^{\infty} f(x+R)[F(x+R) - F(x)]^{n-2}dR\,dx$$

As discussed above, to find the kth moment of the range, we need to include R^k within this integral, i.e.,

$$E(R^k) = n(n-1) \int_{-\infty}^{\infty} f(x) \int_{0}^{\infty} R^k f(x+R)[F(x+R) - F(x)]^{n-2}dR\,dx$$

Harter (1960) gave this formula, cast in terms of the standard normal distribution, and he also provided extensive tables for the results up to the fourth moment, with at least nine exact digits (which is above and beyond the needs of the vast majority of users). Here, to close the cycle, so to speak, we provide the results for the triangular distribution. We'll transform Shewhart's original triangular distribution in two ways, sequentially: (i) first, for convenience, we'll shift it to the origin and invert it, i.e., the probability of a chip of 0.1 will be 1/820 and that of a chip of 4.0 will be 40/820; (ii) next, to avoid the need to translate our formula to a discrete distribution, we'll use a continuous approximation, with f as follows,

$$f(x) = \begin{cases} \dfrac{x}{8.2}; & 0.05 \le x \le 4.05 \\ \\ 0; & \text{otherwise} \end{cases}$$

Note that with this approximation the variance is 0.910305 instead of 0.91 exactly, as was the case with the original distribution. The difference is minute, indicating that the approximation is good. To solve for $E(R^k)$ here we need to solve the integral

$$E(R^k) = n(n-1) \int_{0.05}^{4.05} \frac{x}{8.2} \int_0^{4.05-x} R^k \frac{x+R}{8.2} \left[\frac{(x+R)^2 - x^2}{16.4} \right]^{n-2} dR\, dx$$

For $n=5$, the results for the first two moments are $E(R)=2.1847$ and $E(R^2)=5.2881$, leading to $\sigma_R=0.7179$. Recall however that to get results that are comparable to d_2 and d_3 these numbers have to be divided by the standard deviation of the distribution, i.e., 0.9541, yielding the final results: d_2[right triangular]=2.290 and d_3[right triangular]=0.752. Compare these to 2.326 and 0.864 which apply to the normal distribution, and we find that the estimation of σ_x is excellent, while the estimation of the variance of R, σ_R, is about 13% too low. Note now that in Chapter 6 we showed that the control limits for R were too wide to capture any outliers, but now we see that we specified them almost 15% too wide, i.e., at about $\pm 3.45\sigma$. From a practical standpoint, however, there is nothing sacred about the convention of $\pm 3\sigma$, so the results are still excellent.

It would be misleading, however, to say that the constants, and especially d_3, work well for any theoretical distribution we may come up with. Take for instance the exponential distribution, which is not only asymmetrical, but also has a relatively thick tail (to the right). Using our formula we find in this case d_2[exponential]=2.083 and d_3[exponential]=1.193 (for $n=5$). We see that the expected range is lower by about 10% relative to the normal case, but its variation is larger by about 38%. Therefore, if we construct control charts based on the regular constants for a population that is really exponential, and supposing we use a really large sample, then the range we'll obtain will be smaller than what we should expect given the process variation, and as a result the control limits of the $\bar{x}$ chart will be drawn at about $\pm 2.7\sigma_X/\sqrt{5}$, leading to RFS $\approx 1.5\%$ (instead of 0.0027).[2] Worse yet, in the case of UCL_R the ratio d_3/d_2 is understated by the normal constants so much that instead of a $3\sigma_R$ limit we'll get a $1.95\sigma_R$ limit, and using our density function, $g(R)$ we can show that this implies RFS $= 4.8\%$ (which is more than ten times the value associated with the normal random variable, 0.0046). The problems of estimation discussed in Chapter 8 add even more confusion to the picture.

Two points are in order here. First, under a restricted view of "statistical control" (which we have not adopted in this text), if a process does not possess a normal distribution something is assumed wrong with it. Indeed, sometimes when a process is not normal we can find special causes and remove them, but this is not always true. The second point speaks to a practice that exists in relatively sophisticated quality control environments, where defects are so rare that some authors recommend control charting the time between defects. But, under plausible conditions, when the process is in control, the time between defects has an exponential distribution. Specifically, this is true when the arrival of defects is as per a Poisson process. So control charting the time between defects should be done with care.

The exponential distribution has a much higher coefficient of variation than that associated with most production processes, and we've seen that even in this case the major problem occurred in the R chart. In conclusion it seems that for most cases, $\hat{\sigma}$, the estimate of σ_X, will at least be in the ball park when we use the constants that are based on the normal assumption, but the variance using the estimation σ_R is wider. We might even want to consider changing the prevailing practice in this area, and estimate σ_R directly from the data. Simulation studies suggest that similar observations hold for the case when we use s^2 or s as our dispersion statistic. Incidentally, in contrast to the calculation of d_2 and d_3, which are computationally intensive but theoretically straightforward, calculating c_4 for non-normal distributions -- when we don't usually have an analytic distribution similar to χ^2 -- is a difficult proposition. Thus the need for simulation.

---

[2]This numerical result is not based on the normal table, but rather on numerical integration based on the Erlang distribution (which is a special case of the Gamma distribution). The Erlang random variable is defined as the average of n exponential random variables, so it is appropriate for this need. The density function of this distribution is

$$f(t) = \frac{(\mu n)^n}{(n-1)!} t^{n-1} e^{-n\mu t}; \qquad t \geq 0$$

The expected value of this distribution is $1/\mu$, and its variance is $1/(n\mu^2)$. By setting $n = 0$ we obtain the exponential distribution as a special case. (Note that some authors define the exponential, and thus the Erlang, with a parameter that is equal to our $1/\mu$. Unfortunately, there is no consensus on this issue.)

Supplement 6.3
More on the Optimal Subgroup Size in Shewhart Control Charts

As we've seen, charts based on subgroups of five or four items in each subgroup are not powerful against mean deviations of less than about one and a half process standard deviation. In response other types of charts, e.g., *CUSUM* or *EWMA* charts have been proposed and are used by many. These charts are capable of detecting small shifts faster, but at the expense of taking longer time to detect large shifts. In most of the literature, however, it is not stressed that regular control charts are also adjustable in terms of the minimal deviation they have the power to detect, and that they too include a tradeoff. Clearly, the more items in a subgroup, the smaller shifts one can detect with reasonable power, but since sampling many items is not only costly but also implies no correction *during* the sampling process, it follows that if we count the items until detection of a shift the use of large subgroups to detect small shifts must have delayed the detection of large shifts--exactly as

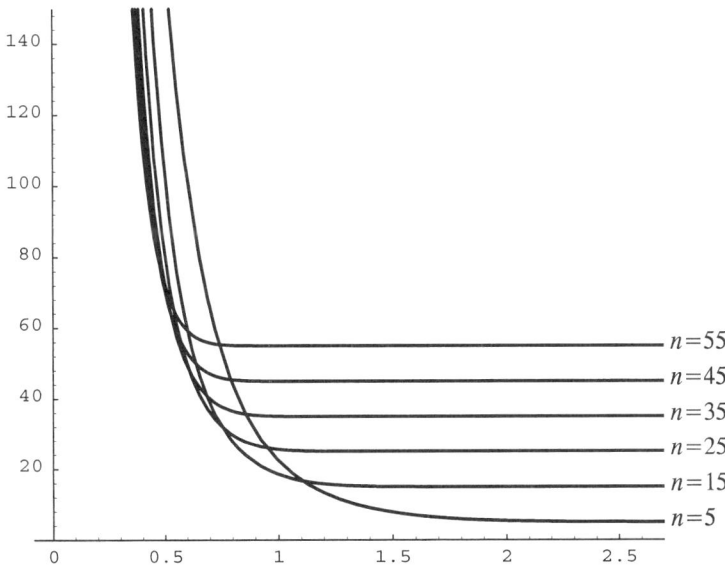

Fig. S6.3.1

is the case with *CUSUM* and *EWMA* charts. Figure S6.3.1 shows the power of $\bar{x}$ control charts with different n to detect a given deviation. The figure is presented in terms of the expected number of items (*ARL*) that have to be sampled (within subgroups of n) to detect a shift of D standard deviations. Note that as n grows the performance for small deviations improves, but the minimal number of items necessary, which must exceed n, grows too, thus making the chart relatively weak against large deviations. As a result, each n is the best for a range of D values, and thus given the D we wish to control against we can use such a figure to select n (Wadsworth et al., 1986, p. 222).

Here we provide an excellent but simple approximation to determine the necessary number of items in each subgroup as a function of the magnitude of D for which we desire fast detection. The result can also serve to determine the weight coefficient in *EWMA* charts. It is based on simple numerical experimentation and applies to the conventional use of $\pm 3\sigma_{\bar{x}}$ control limits. Similar results can be obtained for other cases.

S6.3.1. An Approximate Optimization of Subgroup Size to Detect a Shift of $D\sigma_x$

Table S6.3.1 provides information about the optimal subgroup sizes necessary to minimize the expected number of items tested to detect a shift of $D\sigma_x$ (using $\pm 3\sigma_{\bar{x}}$ control limits). This data is given in the second column, and it is based on simple numerical search. The third column gives the expected minimal ARL associated with this subgroup size and the deviation from the mean as listed in the first column. Note that for small deviations the ratio between *ARL** and n^* is practically constant: about 0.628 (177/282). That is, the probability of signal after each subgroup is approximately 0.628. Using a normal distribution table, this can be translated to the following relationship between D and the subgroup size

$$n = \text{ROUND}\left(\frac{3.326}{D}\right)^2$$

where ROUND denotes the rounding function.

The third and fourth columns in Table S6.3.1 are presented to show the quality of the approximation. The fourth column is the subgroup size according to the approximation, and the fifth column gives the associated *ARL*. The only differences between column 4 (the approximation) and column 2 (the exact optimal value) is for $D=0.25$ (176 vs. 177) and $D=2.75$ (1 vs. 2). The difference in terms of *ARL* is negligible for $D=0.25$, and about 1.3% for $D=0.25$, i.e., quite small. Note that for $D=0.25\sigma_x$ the loss due to bias is very small. On the other hand, any D beyond $3\sigma_x$ will certainly imply the optimality of $n=1$. Thus Table S6.3.1 covers the full spectrum of practical needs. It follows that the approximation is very good in the whole practical range.

D/σ_X	n^*	ARL^*	$(3.32/D)^2$	ARL
0.25	177	281.9	176	281.9
0.50	44	70.49	44	70.49
0.75	20	31.33	20	31.33
1.00	11	17.62	11	17.62
1.25	7	11.28	7	11.28
1.50	5	7.83	5	7.83
1.75	4	5.78	4	5.78
2.00	3	4.42	3	4.42
2.25	2	3.50	2	3.50
2.50	2	2.84	2	2.84
2.75	2	2.45	1	2.49
3.00	1	2.00	1	2.00

Table S6.3.1

Incidentally, the same type of approximation holds for control limits with $\pm t\sigma_X$ in general, and not just $t=3$. For example, if we select $t=3.2$ the approximation

$$n = \text{ROUND}\left(\frac{3.61}{D}\right)^2$$

provides a perfect match for the optimal n that applies. But, surprisingly, if we set $t=2$ and assume a normal process, then $n=1$ is optimal in the whole range. The only rationale for using subgroups with such narrow limits is to assure an approximate normal distribution for the mean when the process is not known to be normal. This observation should not be construed as a recommendation to use such narrow limits: as many argue, $t=2$ is not appropriate in control charting applications (in contrast to scientific experiments that are based on the premise that a signal of two standard deviations or more is important, but only in the sense that it justifies experimenting again to verify the results).

S6.3.2. Using the Approximation with *EWMA* Charts

Assuming the use of individual items in an EWMA chart with a weight coefficient λ, we've seen that the results are similar to using moving averages with

$$n = \frac{2-\lambda}{\lambda} \quad \Leftrightarrow \quad \lambda = \frac{2}{n+1}$$

Thus, we can easily translate n to λ. Since it is not necessary to use integer n in this case, we can say that if we wish to detect a deviation of D efficiently with an EWMA chart we should use

$$\lambda = \frac{2}{\left(\dfrac{3.326}{D}\right)^2 + 1}$$

If an EWMA chart is used based on small subgroups of, say, k items each, we obtain

$$\lambda = \frac{2}{\dfrac{n}{k}+1} = \frac{2}{\dfrac{3.326^2}{D^2 k}+1}$$

Here, if $k \geq n$ we should not use exponential smoothing.

S6.3.3. Charts with Power to Detect Both Small and Large Deviations

By Figure S6.3.1, there's no single chart that can provide power both against small and large deviations. Nonetheless, if we use a combination of two charts it is possible to obtain efficient results over a wide range. For example, numerical experience suggests that using both $n=5$ and $n=45$ provides a wide range of efficient detection. To facilitate the actual collection of two charts in parallel, we can collect subgroups of five (e.g., a basic Shewhart chart), and smooth their $\overline{x}$ values in a parallel *EWMA* chart with $\lambda=0.2$. Similar results are obtained with $n=4$ and $n=44$, which is doable by using a basic Shewhart chart with subgroups of 4, and a parallel *EWMA* chart of the $\overline{x}$ values with $\lambda=2/13$. Specifying slightly wider control limits for both charts in these cases can adjust *RFS* to the level of a single chart, but there is no special reason to do that: we just need to know that *RFS* will be slightly higher.

Chapter 7

Pattern Tests for Shewhart Control Charts

An advantage of control charts over other types of statistical analysis is that we can observe the behavior of the process over time to see if any special patterns occur. Any pattern, or "run," that is rare may be important, especially if we identify it and then, *later*, it repeats. A nonrecurring pattern may be meaningless. A good analogy to this is the probability that a continuous variable will assume some specific value. The probability this will happen for a *predetermined* value is zero, but the probability it will happen for *some* value is one! The probability it will then repeat is zero. Similarly, suppose we observe a pattern of three points in a row above the centerline, followed by four points below, two above and three below again. This is a rare pattern: the probability it will repeat in the next 12 points is $0.5^{12} = 0.00024$; but the probability an equally rare pattern will occur is one.

Thus, there are only two types of patterns that concern us: (i) a pattern that repeats *after* being tagged as potentially special; and (ii) one that belongs to a subset of *predetermined* patterns that we decide to use as signals. In the latter we should limit the total rate of false signals (RFS). To that end we either limit the number of patterns in the subset, or require each of them to have a very low *RFS*, or both.

There are no rules which patterns may be considered suspect so that when we see them recurring we'll decide to act. This should be part of the normal maintenance of control charts, especially since each process may have some unique pattern(s) associated with it. But there are conventions about the selection of a generic subset of predetermined patterns that are recognized as signals of special cause. These patterns are selected because generic process problems can cause them. So we need patterns that are rare when the process is under control, but likely otherwise. The 3-4-2-3 pattern mentioned is not associated with such a generic problem, but if 12 points in a row would show above the centerline most people would agree that the centerline is not likely to be near the median of the actual distribution, and thus this is a reliable signal that the process is out of control. The patterns described in this chapter belong to this group. Figure 7.1, which is similar to the one given by Nelson (1984), shows eight examples of patterns that are often specified. We discuss these eight patterns, plus one, in this chapter.

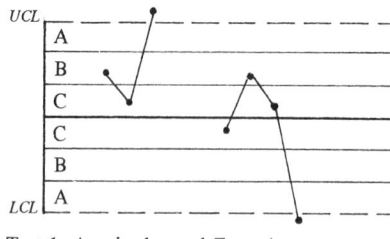

Test 1: A point beyond Zone A

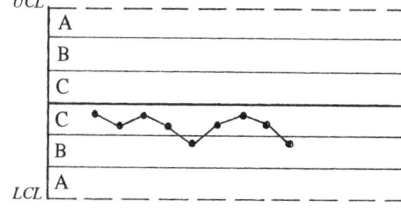

Test 2: 9 points on one side of the centerline

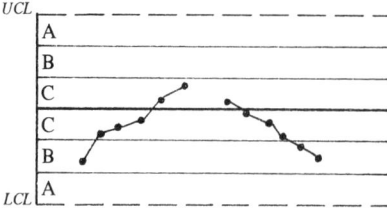

Test 3: 6 points steadily increasing or decreasing

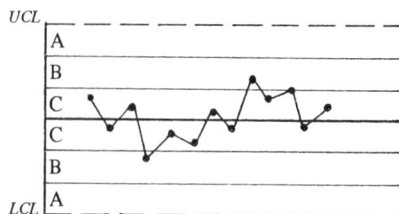

Test 4: 13 points alternating up and down

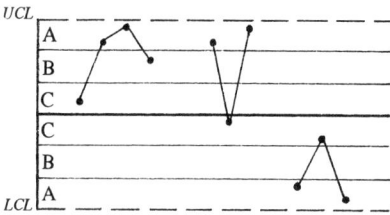

Test 5: 2 points out of 3 beyond Zone B on one
side of the centerline

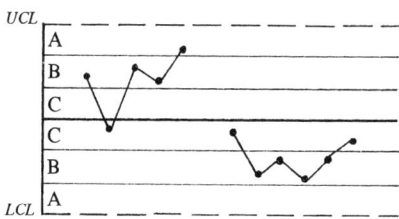

Test 6: 4 points out of 5 beyond Zone C on
one side of the centerline

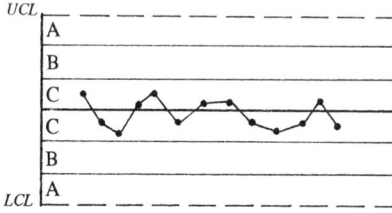

Test 7: 13 points in Zone C on both sides of
the centerline

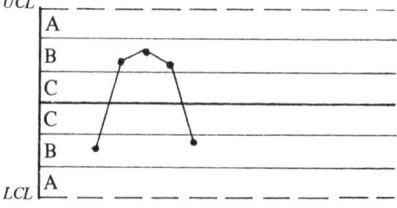

Test 8: 5 points outside Zone C on both sides
of the centerline

Fig. 7.1. Eight popular pattern tests.

By testing for such patterns we increase the power of the control chart to detect associated special causes. But we do so for a price: we also increase the *RFS*. The *RFS* of each pattern test is a function of the pattern length we specify (e.g., some sources specify Test 2 with 7 or 8 points instead of 9). A conventional way to determine the desired pattern length is to obtain *RFS* as close as possible to that of Test 1, namely 0.0027. Nonetheless, influential sources -- specifically AT&T (1958) and Nelson (1984, 1985) -- are grossly misleading in their calculation of *RFS* for various patterns, and therefore they obtain different recommendations than those reflected by Figure 7.1. Following Hwang and Trietsch (1996), we'll provide a simple way to calculate *RFS* correctly for each test. Hwang and Trietsch were not the first to note the errors in former sources; e.g., see Adams et al. (1992). Furthermore, it is possible to use many combinations of tests, and the combined *RFS* is larger than that of any single test. For practical purposes we can use a simple upper bound on the combined *RFS:* the sum of the individual rates. It is also possible to find the combined *RFS* of some tests (excluding tests 3 and 4) by a Markov chain analysis (Champ and Woodall, 1987), but this is a computationally intensive application. We'll discuss these issues in more detail after presenting the tests more fully. Finally, Supplement 7 addresses less prevalent tests, and introduces methods for controlling processes with autocorrelation.

7.1. Tests for Assignable Causes

We address nine tests for special causes, including Shewhart's basic test, eight of which are widely used for the purpose of diagnosing processes. They apply to continuous data. Some, including Shewhart's basic test, perform differently for different distributions. In these cases, the *RFS* we provide only applies for the normal distribution (e.g., for $\overline{x}$ control charts, at least approximately). Others are *nonparametric*: they work equally well for any continuous distribution. Nonparametric tests apply to dispersion charts and to individuals charts, regardless of the population distribution (as long as it's continuous), with the same *RFS*. Formally, we assume continuous distributions, so attribute charts are disqualified. Nonetheless, some tests still apply, and we'll discuss this in further detail later. Also, in Chapter 8 we show that our treatment of *RFS* here is too simplistic. See also Trietsch and Hwang (1997).

Some of the tests -- namely 5, 6, 7 and 8 -- require partitioning the area between the control limits of the chart to six zones of equal width, labelled A, B, C, C, B, A (Figure 7.1). Thus, Zone A would be the name of the two strips next to the control limits from within (including points *on* the control limits), Zone C would denote the two adjacent strips that hug the centerline, and Zone B would denote the two strips between A and C. A point that is *on* a boundary between two zones is considered to belong to the zone that is nearer to the centerline, i.e., the zone with the higher alphanumeric value. For instance, a point on the boundary between Zone B and Zone C is considered in Zone C. A point is called "beyond" a zone when it belongs to a zone with a lower alphanumeric value or when it is strictly outside the control limits. For example, to be beyond Zone C, a point may be in B, A, or outside the control limits. A point on the centerline itself is definitely not beyond Zone C. For most tests, such a point is considered in Zone C. For tests 2 and 4a it is important to distinguish between the two parts of Zone C, and we will have to ignore points on the centerline.

A normally distributed process in control will tend to have very few, if any, points beyond Zone A; *some* points in Zone A (roughly 5%), but very rarely consecutively; *more* points in Zone B, but rarely more than two or three consecutively; and roughly two thirds of the points will be in Zone C. Even if we drop the normality assumption, a process in control should not exhibit runs of many points consistently above or below its median (which coincides with the centerline for symmetrical distributions), nor should there be runs of too many points with a seesaw pattern. A long consistently increasing or decreasing set of points is even more unlikely. We should suspect special causes whenever one of these conditions is not met. The tests quantify some of the vague statements we made, define them operationally if you will. For instance, instead of saying "there should be no runs of many points consistently above or below the median," we may say: "When we observe nine consecutive points above the centerline, we should investigate."

Test 1:   Any single point falls beyond Zone A (Shewhart's basic test -- also known as "Criterion I"[1]).

Test 2:   7, 8, or 9 points on the same side of the centerline. This test is designed to identify shifts from center quicker than Test 1. It applies to *any* symmetrical distribution, the normal included. To make it fully nonparametric we should replace the centerline by the median of the distribution whenever the distribution is not symmetrical.[2] Most sources, including AT&T (1958), suggest 8 here.

---

[1]Shewhart (1931) proposed four additional criteria, II through V, which have not gained popular acceptance.

[2]For dispersion charts, this implies that we should replace the conventional centerline at $\bar{s}$ (or at $\bar{R}$) by a somewhat lower line. Conceptually, this requires the calculation of an additional factor. Or we could use the trial data, with which the chart is created, to estimate the median. When based on enough data, the result should be reliable enough for the purpose of pattern tests. Conceptually, the same idea can be used to add bands such that each A band will include about 2.5% of the points, and each B band about 15%. Again, the correct location of these bands can also be calculated analytically, as functions of $\bar{s}$ (or of $\bar{R}$) and of n. Doing this is tantamount to transforming the dispersion distribution to normal, an alternative suggested by Quesenberry (1991).

Grant and Leavenworth (1980) and Deming (1986) specified 7. Nelson suggested 9, leading to a *RFS* of 0.00195 for both sides combined (compare to 0.0027 for Test 1). Since specifying 8 almost doubles this *RFS,* our recommendation is also 9. But 8 is excellent if the test is applied to one side only, yielding practically the same *RFS* as 9 on both sides. If a point falls *on* the centerline -- which may happen after rounding -- Trietsch and Hwang (1997) recommended ignoring it; thus, on the one hand, it is not counted, but on the other hand, it does not break a pattern if the points before it and after it are to the same side of the centerline. Another approach, which is not recommended here, is to assign such points to sides in a manner that will increase the evenness of the data and increase the number of runs above and below the median (Duncan, 1974). This approach is much more complex, and there is no justification to increase the number of runs above and below the median because, as we'll see, it will also decrease the number of runs that cross the median every time. Furthermore, this approach assumes that it's legitimate to shift the centerline continually, and this constitutes tampering.

Test 3:   6, 7 or 8 points increasing or decreasing. Here, the last point of an increasing run is the first point of a decreasing run, and vice versa. If two successive points are equal, Trietsch and Hwang recommend ignoring one of them. The test is nonparametric. As for the pattern length, Nelson recommends 6, without comment, and Trietsch and Hwang concur; Deming recommends 7; most others recommend 8. But 7 or 8 are highly too conservative relative to the other tests. Davis and Woodall (1988) found, by simulation, that this test is unlikely to signal *first* upon a drift, so they recommend against it. However, it may be useful for run charts, where there are no control limits.

Test 4:   13 or 14 points in a row alternating up and down. This pattern is known as the "egg-timer effect," because the sand in egg-timers does not flow in the exact same rate in both directions. Nelson reports that his choice of 14 is based on simulation, which yielded *RFS* of about 0.004. In contrast, Hwang and Trietsch show that 13 is enough to reduce the *RFS* to 0.0026, and their result is consistent with a simulation study I have conducted. (The discrepancy between Nelson's simulation and mine triggered the Hwang and Trietsch research.) The test can reveal the results of tampering by Funnel Rule 2. It can also reveal cyclical mixtures, such as the case depicted in Figure 5.9 with a run of 25 points in alternating pattern (if we ignore a point that is equal to its predecessor). Again, the test is nonparametric, and if two consecutive points are equal we ignore one.

Test 5: Two out of three consecutive points in A or beyond, to the same side of the centerline. This test is designed to identify process shifts from center before Test 2, but it is likely to require a larger shift. Note that two consecutive results in the same A zone suffice here; and even if one point is missing, as long as it is preceded and succeeded by points in A to the same side of the centerline, the test is activated. The *RFS* of this test, on both sides combined, is 0.0020.

Test 6: Four out of five consecutive points in B or beyond, to the same side of the centerline. This test is similar to Test 5, but requires a smaller shift. The *RFS* is 0.0034 on both sides combined.

Test 7: Twelve to fifteen consecutive points in Zone C, on either side of the centerline. 15 is recommended by Nelson. Others, including Hwang and Trietsch, are satisfied with 13 (which leads to *RFS*=0.0022), and 12 is also a reasonable choice (with 0.0032). This test is activated when the estimated standard deviation is inflated. There are, notes Nelson, two major causes for such inflated estimates: (i) the most likely explanation is arithmetical errors during the construction of the chart; (ii) another likely cause is *stratification*, or mixture; i.e., each subgroup spans several divergent sources, so the range is excessive, and therefore the control limits are too wide. Trietsch and Hwang added that the test may be activated by sampling error (which is quite likely when the control limits are based on too few data).

Test 8: Five to eight consecutive points on both sides of Zone C, but none in it. 8 was recommended by AT&T (1958), and later by Nelson. However, 6 was used by others, and induces a very small *RFS* (0.0007). Hwang and Trietsch recommended 5 (with *RFS*=0.0022). This test is triggered when the control limits are too narrow to reflect the variability of the population. This can be due to three main causes: (i) computation errors, (ii) the existence of several divergent sources that are *not* mixed in each subgroup, or (iii) sampling error. As to divergent sources, control charts *should* be based on internal variation rather than variation between sources, so this test helps identify excessive between-sources variation (mixture).[3]

---

[3]Another test for this would be two consecutive points in A, on opposite sides of the centerline. This will add about 0.0010 to the *RFS*. But it is not one of the established tests.

Test 4a:[4] 7, 8, or 9 points in a row alternating up and down while *straddling the centerline*. (Compare with Test 4 where the points are not required to straddle the centerline, but more points are needed to show a significant pattern.) This test has a theoretical *RFS* that is identical to that of Test 2. The conditions are also identical to those we stipulated in Test 2. Specifically, as in Test 2, a point *on* the median is ignored. This is because the event of alternating above and beyond the median has the same "in control" probability as that of staying on one side of the median. In the case depicted in Figure 5.9, for instance, this test would identify the mixture before Test 4.

Box 7.2 summarizes the tests, but with a single limiting value for each (as recommended by Hwang and Trietsch). The sequence is by the limiting values. The *RFS* -- on both sides combined when applicable -- and assumptions about the distribution are given in brackets.

=-
Box 7.2

Test 1:   One point outside the control limits (beyond A). [0.0027; normal]

Test 5:   Two points out of three in Zone A, on the same side of the centerline. [0.0020; normal]

Test 6:   Four points out of five in Zone B or beyond, on the same side of the centerline. [0.0034; normal]

Test 8:   5 consecutive points beyond Zone C, on both sides. [0.0022; normal]

Test 3:   A run of 6 increasing points, or 6 decreasing points. [0.0024; nonparametric]

Test 2:   A run of 9 points on the same side of the centerline. [0.0020; symmetric]

Test 4a: A run of 9 points that cross the centerline every time. [0.0020; symmetric]

Test 7:   13 consecutive points in Zone C, on both sides of the centerline. [0.0022; normal]

Test 4:   13 consecutive points with a seesaw pattern. [0.0026; nonparametric]

=-

If we practice fractional adjustment, the risk of Tests 4 and 4a may increase slightly. This only occurs if the process is perfectly stable (otherwise fractional adjustment will often

---

[4]This test is not in wide use, and is not part of the list compiled by AT&T (1958). It is likely to identify the "egg-timer effect" earlier than Test 4. It is especially effective in detecting the results of Funnel Rule 3.

reduce the risk of these and other tests). But even with a perfectly stable process, fractional adjustment with small λ will not increase the risk by much. Nonetheless, if these tests tend to activate, and there's no other explanation, we should experiment with reducing λ and even stopping the adjustment procedure. When the procedure is required, there will be altogether *less* signals with it than without.

			Test		
r	8	3	2/4a	7	4
3	0.0225	*a*	*a*	*a*	*a*
4	0.0070	*a*	*a*	*a*	*a*
5	**0.0022**	0.0139	0.0323	*a*	*a*
6	***0.0007***	**0.0024**	0.0159	0.0357	*a*
7	***0.0002***	***0.00035***	**0.0079**	0.0236	0.0410
8	***0.00007***	***0.00004***	**0.0039**	0.0157	0.0257
9	*b*	*b*	**0.0020**	0.0106	0.0162
10	*b*	*b*	0.0010	0.0071	0.0102
11	*b*	*b*	*b*	0.0048	0.0065
12	*b*	*b*	*b*	**0.0033**	0.0041
13	*b*	*b*	*b*	**0.0022**	**0.0026**
14	*b*	*b*	*b*	**0.0015**	**0.0017**
15	*b*	*b*	*b*	**0.0010**	0.0011

a $RFS > 0.05$

b $RFS < 0.001$

Table 7.1. Theoretical *RFS* for various tests and limiting values.

Since Tests 2, 3, 4, 7, and 8 have been specified with various levels by various sources, Table 7.1, out of Trietsch and Hwang, reports their *RFS*'s that fall between 0.001 and 0.05. The table assumes that one-sided tests are applied to both sides. Particular entries that are recommended in the literature are presented in **bold** print. The objective to report the *RFS* associated with published recommendations involved values below 0.001 for Tests 8 and 3: these entries are in ***bold italics***. (Including *RFS*'s of up to 0.05 is not meant as a recommendation to assume such large risks, especially when several tests are prescribed together.)

Readers are urged to pick limiting values that are compatible with the *RFS* they are willing to accept, and their assessment of how relevant each test is for their process. They may also wish to adjust the individual risk levels of each test based on how many tests they choose to employ. Nelson recommended Tests 1 through 4 for routine process maintenance, by the person who is plotting the chart. Tests 5 and 6, he suggests, should be added when additional power is desired. Tests 7 and 8 are diagnostic, and they are especially important when setting up the chart. Since he did not consider Test 4a, however, we may recommend to use it in conjunction with Test 2. Note that by adding Test 4a we essentially double the risk relative to Test 2 alone. But with runs of 9 the combined risk is below 0.004. Later we will show one more reason why it may not be very risky to add Test 4a.

Calculating the combined risk of a set of tests at different limit values is not trivial, because the tests are not statistically independent. Some of them are positively correlated -- i.e., the patterns that activate one test are likely to activate other tests as well (e.g., Tests 1, 2, 5 and 6 are positively correlated with each other, and so are Tests 4 and 4a). Other tests are negatively correlated, i.e., the appearance of one tends to reduce the likelihood of the other (e.g., Tests 2 and 4a are negatively correlated, and so are Tests 3 and 4. Test 7 is negatively correlated with any one of Tests 1, 5, 6, and 8). In spite of this difficulty, there is a way to calculate the *RFS* of various combinations of the tests, with the exception of Tests 3 and 4 (Champ and Woodall, 1987). Here, we'll discuss a much simpler approach: the use of an upper bound instead of an exact calculation.

Negative correlation has a very mild effect when signals are rare. But positive dependence may have a sizable effect on the total number of stoppages: if two signals happen together we only stop once. Therefore, specifying several tests together typically yields less signals than the sum of signals of each test alone. So the sum of the individual risks provides an *upper bound* on the combined risk. For instance, using all the tests Nelson specified together will induce *RFS* of less than 1.5%, and with the new values of Table 7.1, the risk will still be below 1.9%. In this connection, since Tests 4 and 4a are positively correlated, if Test 4a is specified in addition to Test 4, the net risk added by it is less than the upper bound suggests.

Finally, to summarize our discussion of *RFS*'s, it can be shown that although Tests 2 and 4a have the same risk when the distribution is symmetric, Test 4a is more robust against deviations from this requirement. For instance, with limiting runs of 8, if the centerline actually has 60% of the points below it and 40% above, the risk of Test 2 is 0.0175, but the risk of Test 4a is 0.0033. Comparing with 0.0039, by Table 7.1, Test 4a is not only closer, but also less risky. This suggests that we may use Test 4a for dispersion charts, such as R, s, and s^2 charts. But it also implies that this test cannot detect deviations from the mean (nor is it designed to do so).

7.1.1. *Applying the Tests to Attribute Charts*

The rules may also apply to np and c charts; p and u charts with variable control limits are less amenable. In all four cases they may be less powerful. As a rule of thumb, if the normal approximation is valid and the number of possible realizations within the control limits exceeds 20, *all* the tests will be applicable without major problems. Otherwise, Tests 1, 3, 4 and 4a apply in general without causing excessive *RFS*, and Test 2 applies if the centerline is approximately at the median. Test 3, whose marginal power is questionable even in the continuous case, is even less likely to work for a discrete distribution, where the number of likely realizations is small. For instance, suppose we have a p or np chart with $p=0.021$ and $n=100$, then the realizations that are within the control limits are 0, 1, 2, 3, 4, 5, and 6. Since 6 is much smaller than 20, this distribution cannot be considered continuous for the purpose of the tests presented here, and some rules will not be effective with it. Approximating this distribution by a Poisson, we see that the probability of falling below the centerline (at 2.1), i.e., obtaining 0, 1 or 2, is about 2/3, which is quite far from 0.5. Hence, Test 2 will not work well, and it's too risky below the centerline. Test 4a is safe, but it will be less powerful.[5] In contrast, let $p=0.1$ and $n=400$, and we can safely use the normal approximation with $\mu=40$ and $\sigma=6$. This generates 37 possible integer realizations within the control limits, and all the tests apply with full benefit.

7.1.1.1. *An example*

Figure 5.6 depicts the results of a process that we judged to be in control, and where the average results fit the experience of Deming over decades of repeating the same process. As an observer I can testify that there was almost no difference between the first three quarters and the last quarter. The only exception was that one worker dropped a batch when he saw many red beads in it. This may help explain one, but not both, of the signals that we discuss next. Indeed, analyzing the chart with our nine tests, this process would be judged out of control, in spite of the fact that there are only 17 possible realizations within the control limits. Figure 7.2 repeats Figure 5.6, with zones added.

---

[5]AT&T recommended different pattern lengths for such cases.

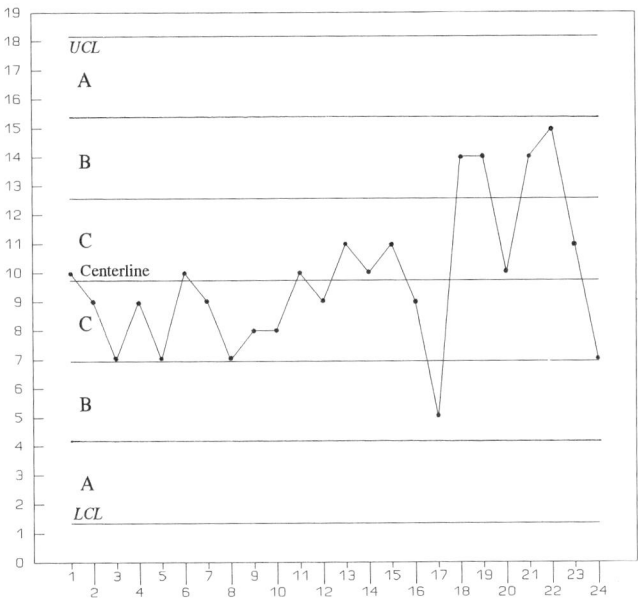

Fig. 7.2. The red beads experiment results arranged by quarters, with zones.

The first 16 points are all within Zone C, on both sides of the centerline. Therefore, Test 7 is activated (on the thirteenth point). This might have been prevented if the dropped batch would have been counted. Points 18, 19, 21, and 22 are all in Zone B above the centerline, thus activating Test 6. This is much less likely to be the result of the same mishap. Thus, there are two signals in this chart, at least one of them is false. This is what we mean when we say that increased power entails increased risk.

But this example may also serve to highlight the problem of using tests based on a continuous distribution on an attribute chart. Three points in the first run -- Points 3, 5, and 8 -- are within Zone C but very close to Zone B. Had the random variable been continuous, it might well have happened that at least one of them would fall in Zone B, thus breaking the run. The second false signal, however, would not change if we'd change the values of the four points to the next lower value. Indeed, it is likely that the second false signal is due to pure chance.

As we see, the tests can and do generate false signals. Also, the results might be different (i) if we'd change the sequence of workers within each quarter (here the sequence is reported as presented by Deming); or (ii) if we'd sequence the points based on the workers rather than based on the quarters, as we did in Figure 5.5 (where we depicted the same data starting with the four quarterly results of Linda, and then the four results of the others).

Some of our tests make no sense when the points are arranged by an arbitrary sequence, in contrast to time sequence.

7.2. Computing the Rate of False Signals (RFS)

Let p_r denote the probability that r given points will fall into the pattern associated with a test. For instance, the probability that six points in a continuous process under control will be monotone increasing is $1/6!=1/720$ (because exactly one out of 6! equally likely permutations is monotone increasing). The probability they will be monotone increasing *or* decreasing is $2/720=0.0028$ (these are two mutually exclusive patterns). Similarly, the probability nine points will fall above the centerline is p^9, where p is the probability a single point will do so, and the probability this will happen either above or below the centerline is $p^9+(1-p)^9$.

AT&T used p_r to calculate *RFS*. For instance, they stated that Test 2, with $r=8$, has $RFS=0.5^8=0.0039$ on each side, or 0.5^7 on both sides together. Nelson noted that $RFS \neq p_r$, but assumed $RFS \approx p_r$. One reason for that, perhaps, was that the computation methods for *RFS* that existed at that time -- using Markov chains -- were cumbersome and did not apply to Tests 3 and 4. Using p_r as a substitute for *RFS* is an intuitively appealing idea, but it is very inaccurate. In the case of Test 2, for example, it inflates *RFS* by about 100%! The inflation involved in Tests 4 and 7 is even higher. Only for Test 3 is the approximation roughly applicable (for $r=6$, it yields 0.0028 instead of 0.0024).

Hwang and Trietsch derived a very simple formula for *RFS* as a function of p_r for all the tests in question except Tests 5 and 6 (but including Tests 3 and 4, which the Markovian approach excludes). The results, which were established by theory, match the Markovian ones perfectly where the two methods overlap. For Tests 3 and 4 the results match extensive simulation results. They also provided efficient approximations for Tests 5 and 6.

The formula applies to families of patterns that are *nested and disjoint*. "Nested" means that a pattern of $r+1$ points contains two patterns of r (Points 1 through r and Points 2 through $r+1$). A pattern is called *proper* if it is not nested within a larger pattern. A family of patterns is disjoint if proper patterns cannot intersect each other. The patterns of Tests 1, 2, 3, 4, 4a, 7, and 8 are all nested and disjoint. But the patterns of Tests 5 and 6 are not disjoint. For example, the sequence {1, 0, 1, 0, 1} -- where 1 denotes a point in Zone A or beyond, and 0 denotes other points -- contains two proper patterns of two 1's in 3 points that would activate Test 5, but they are not disjoint. For nested and disjoint patterns, then

$$RFS = \sum_{k=1}^{\infty} \left[p_{kr} - p_{kr+1} \right] = p_r - p_{r+1} + p_{2r} - p_{2r+1} + \cdots$$

In Test 1, $r=1$ and p_j approaches zero for large j, so the formula implies $RFS=p_1$. For Tests 2, 7, and 8 the infinite series also converges, yielding the exact RFS: let p denote the probability of falling within a zone (associated with a pattern), and treating Test 2 as a one-sided test (either above or below the centerline, with $p=0.5$), we obtain

$$RFS = \frac{(1-p)p^r}{1-p^r}$$

In the case of Test 2 this has to be multiplied by 2 if the test is applied both above and below the centerline. For Test 4 we obtain a very close approximation (based on a result by Furry[6], who gave p_r for this pattern by a rapidly converging infinite series),

$$RFS[Test\ 3] = \frac{4\left(1 - \dfrac{2}{\pi}\right)\left(\dfrac{2}{\pi}\right)^{r+1}}{1 - \left(\dfrac{2}{\pi}\right)^r}$$

For the number of digits reported here, this formula yields exact results. Furthermore, if $p_{2r} \ll p_r$, then $RFS \approx p_r - p_{r+1}$. This applies to Test 3 in particular (e.g., $p_{12}/p_6 = 0.0000015$). Therefore, all the digits reported for this test, based on this approximation, are exact.

To calculate the RFS of Tests 5 and 6 exactly we can represent them by a Markov chain and solve for their first passage time (i.e., ARL). In the case of Test 5 this involves solving five linear equations, and Test 6 requires 27 of them. (See Greenberg, 1970, for the details of constructing the Markov chain, and how many states it has. But, for our purpose, there is no need to use generating functions as he suggested.) Using this method we obtain $RFS[Test\ 5]=0.0009751$ and $RFS[Test\ 6]=0.0017183$ (on each side). But our formula can be adapted for these tests approximately, and it is much easier to apply. This is important with data-based control charts. Tests 5 and 6 involve patterns of $r-1$ points out of r in or beyond a particular zone. More generally, we may look at tests involving patterns of $r-k$ points, where $k=1$ is not stipulated. To approximate RFS for any k we redefine p_r as

$$p_r \triangleq \binom{r-1}{k} p^{r-k}(1-p)^k$$

---

[6]AMS Problem 4755, *American Mathematical Monthly*, 67, 1958, pp. 533-534.

where p is the probability of falling in or beyond the zone, i.e., 0.0227 and 0.1587 for Tests 5 and 6. This definition suggests that the stopping point must be in the zone, and the previous $r-1$ points (or less, if we just started the count) should include exactly $r-k-1$ zone-points. With this definition in place, p_r-p_{r+1} is a good approximation of RFS; adding elements of the form $p_{2r}-p_{2r+1}$ etc. is marginally beneficial. When we apply this approximation to Tests 5 and 6 the results are 0.0009729 and 0.0017112, comparing very well to 0.0009751 and 0.0017183. By adding the next two elements, $p_{2r}-p_{2r+1}$, the difference in Test 5 is beyond the number of digits reported here, but for Test 6 we obtain 0.0017116 -- an inconsequential improvement. Hwang and Trietsch also present another approximation for the $k=1$ case that yields 0.009732 and 0.0017115.

There is an intuitive explanation why the formula $RFS \approx p_r-p_{r+1}$ works so well for all our tests. Suppose we stop due to a signal and look backwards. We must see a pattern of at least r points (including the last one), or we shouldn't have stopped. This event has a probability p_r. But suppose we see a longer pattern, an event with a probability p_{r+1}, then we should have stopped *before!* Therefore, to obtain the RFS we have to subtract p_{r+1} from p_r. Furthermore, if we look back and see a pattern of exactly kr points, then we should stop *now* for the kth time due to the same pattern. The elements $p_{kr}-p_{kr+1}$ in our exact formula provide the rate of additional consecutive stoppages due to such long patterns.

7.3. Mixtures, Cycles, Trends, and Erratic Points

Problems that can cause patterns on control charts include mixtures, trends, cycles, and erratic points related to nonrecurring special causes. Other patterns may be peculiar to a particular process, so process knowledge is always important.

Mixtures cause problems of two types. If we mix before sampling -- a mistake, but common enough to warrant discussion -- the result is likely to be an excessive estimate of the process variance, and too many points will be in Zone C. Test 7 is designed to detect this. If, as we should, we avoid mixing before the subgrouping, points will tend to exceed the control limits. They will also tend to be beyond Zone C (Test 8). One of the main objectives of control charts is to identify such cases, i.e., provide evidence that there are large differences between sources. Therefore, it is very important to take subgroups that are not mixed, using rational subgrouping. For instance, if a production layout has two "identical" machines supplying the same part, we should take separate subgroups from each machine. It is also a good idea to arrange these subgroups in the same sequence every time, so a seesaw pattern may emerge if there is a consistent difference between machines

(Figure 5.9). The data in Table 5.3 is organized by such rational subgrouping, recognizing that both workers and time may cause variation.

Cycles may be the result of the time of day, the day of the week, the influence of other factors (e.g., the power supply, the hydraulic pressure, whether a nearby machine is operating and causing vibrations etc. Box 7.1 discusses a case in a Japanese factory. It also speaks to leadership issues beyond SQC.

=-

Box 7.1

At specific times every day a particular machine produced defects. A team of engineers and operators studied the problem, to no avail. It was a clear "assignable cause," but not easy to diagnose.

One morning, an 18-year-old recent high school graduate, while waiting at a rail crossing just outside the factory on her way to work, noticed that her car vibrated when the train passed. She told the team about this, suggesting that vibrations due to trains might be the culprit. Indeed, it was found that the problems coincided with the timetable of the trains.

The technical solution was to dig a deep water channel between the rail and the plant: the water absorbed the vibrations. But the technical solution is immaterial. What's important is that the cyclical nature of the problems provided an important clue. And what's even more important is that an 18-year-old novice was listened to!

=-

Trends may appear due to tool wear, gradual contamination of chemicals, increasing pressure to "turn out the numbers" towards the end of the month (or the week, or the quarter), etc. The latter is so widely spread that it has a name: the hockey-stick phenomenon. Sometimes trends may be observed while new methods are gradually introduced, or new workers. Test 3 is designed to identify trends, although its power to do so is in question, since it is not likely to be the first test to provide a signal. Nonetheless, it is nonparametric, and therefore it applies even to run charts without control limits (and so does Test 4). One of the lesser reasons this test is criticized (Walker et al., 1991) is that its *RFS* has not been inflated by much in the literature, so *relatively* to other tests it seems to signal falsely too often. But this criticism is moot with our new pattern lengths. The results of Davis and Woodall (1988), however, are not based on this error, so we must conclude that Test 3 is appropriate mainly for run charts and, perhaps, for non-normal distributions (e.g., dispersion charts and individuals charts). Nonetheless, trends may trigger a run-count test that we discuss in Section 7.5, which is not impaired by the existence of other tests.

Erratic points occur when a temporary special cause is in action (e.g., a bee stung the driver so the car swerved). If the effect is large enough, it will show as a point outside the three sigma control limits. Thus, the use of the control limits is especially appropriate to discover erratic points.

Finally, basic Shewhart charts are not powerful against small deviations. Tests 2, 5, and 6 help alleviate this problem, and make the basic Shewhart chart much more competitive with *CUSUM* and *EWMA* charts. As is often the case with good things, however, power must be paid for. Here, the payment is additional complexity and increased *RFS*.

7.4. Applying the Tests to Single Charts

Our tests so far applied to continuous charts: a chart may be drawn on separate sheets, but if a pattern starts at the end of one sheet and continues on the next one, we implicitly assumed we'll identify it. In practice, control charts are often examined sheet by sheet, separately. Or the process may not run long enough to fill more than one sheet. We'll refer to each such sheet as a *single control chart*. We also made an implicit assumption that the process is monitored on a continuous basis, and stopped as soon as a point indicates lack of control (be it by itself, as in Test 1, or combined with its predecessors, as in the other tests). But control charts are not always examined in real-time. Sometimes Test 1 is used to stop the process immediately, but the other tests are administered after the fact, and this, again, is often done for each sheet separately. Deming's Red Beads experiment provides an example of a single chart. In this section and the next one we look at single charts. For convenience, we'll focus the discussion on the $\bar{x}$ chart, although the dispersion chart generates signals too.

First, let us discuss the probability that a chart with, say, N points will include at least one false signal. To differentiate this probability from our *RFS* (which relates to the continuous chart case), we'll denote it by α, or the α-risk. This usage is fairly common, although some authors also refer to our *RFS* as the α-risk.

When the signal in question is Test 1, i.e., a single point out of control, then for a process that is really in control there is a theoretical probability of 0.0027 that each single point will *show* out of control, and the complement, 0.9973 is the probability for each point to show in control. The probability of no false signals is 0.9973^N. So

$$\alpha = 1 - 0.9973^{N} \approx 0.0027N \quad (when \ N \ is \ small)$$

The approximation is reasonable for $N < 40$ (for $N = 40$, $\alpha = 0.1025$, and the approximation is $\alpha \approx 0.108$; for $N = 50$, $\alpha = 0.1264$, and the approximation is $\alpha \approx 0.135$).

Since N is often smaller than 40, for Test 1 $\alpha \approx N \cdot RFS$. This does not hold, however, for any pattern test of more than one point. For example, take a chart with $N=20$ points, and suppose we want to examine the α-risk of Test 2, where we require 9 points to be on the same side of the centerline. Any such run of points that *ends* on Points 9 through 20 will be counted, but the test will never be activated on any of the first eight points, even if they are the tail of a long run. That is, by examining single charts we ignore some legitimate runs, and this reduces both our risk and our power. Table 7.2 provides approximate α-risks for $N=20$ and $N=30$. As in Table 7.1, we use **bold**, or ***bold and italics***, type to mark the tests recommended in the literature.

	Test		
N	1	5	6
20	**0.053**	**0.034**	**0.053**
30	**0.078**	**0.053**	**0.086**

a. Approximate α-Risk for 20 and 30 Points for Tests 1, 5, and 6

	Test				
r	8	3	2/4a	7	4
5	**0.036**	0.203	0.482	-	-
6	**0.011**	0.036	0.239	0.460	-
7	*0.003*	*0.005*	**0.115**	0.317	0.482
8	*0.0009*	*0.0006*	**0.054**	0.212	0.318
9	-	-	**0.025**	0.139	0.201
10	-	-	0.012	0.090	0.123
11	-	-	-	0.057	0.074
12	-	-	-	**0.036**	0.043
13	-	-	-	**0.022**	**0.025**
14	-	-	-	**0.014**	**0.015**
15	-	-	-	**0.008**	0.008

b. Approximate α-Risk for the other tests ($N=20$)

Test

r	8	3	2/4a	7	4
5	**0.057**	0.307	0.710	-	-
6	**0.018**	**0.058**	0.374	0.625	-
7	*0.005*	*0.008*	**0.188**	0.462	0.659
8	*0.0016*	*0.001*	**0.092**	0.328	0.474
9	-	-	**0.045**	0.226	0.321
10	-	-	0.021	0.153	0.209
11	-	-	-	0.102	0.132
12	-	-	-	**0.067**	0.082
13	-	-	-	**0.044**	**0.051**
14	-	-	-	**0.029**	**0.031**
15	-	-	-	**0.019**	0.019

c. Approximate α-Risk for the other tests ($N=30$)

Table 7.2

As mentioned, for some of the tests, specifically Tests 1, 2, 5, 6, 7, and 8 (also known as "zone tests"), we can calculate exact α-risks even when they appear in combinations. This is based on representing the chart by a Markov chain. A computer program for that purpose was developed by Champ and Woodall (1990). Using this program, Walker et al. (1991) calculated the α-risk for several combinations, as provided in Table 7.3.

N	Tests: 1,5	1,5,6	1,2,5,6*
20	0.083	0.130	0.174
30	0.123	0.194	0.263

*Test 2 is specified with 8 points

Table 7.3. (Source: Walker et al., 1991).

It's instructive to observe how high the α-risk can get for some of the limiting values at the low end, although the *RFS* is less than 5% for all of them. After all, *RFS*=5% implies *ARL*=20, so we shouldn't be surprised that in 20 or 30 points α is excessive.

For the same reasons discussed before, when we combine tests together, the sum of the individual α-risks is an upper bound on the combined α-risk. Specifically, if we add the dispersion chart to the picture, and apply to it a combination of tests, such as Test 1, and, potentially, Tests 3, 4, and 4a, then it will impart an additional α-risk. Test 1 alone imparts, roughly, a risk that is up to 50% higher than that of Test 1 on the $\overline{x}$ chart, and the other tests have the same risks or lower than their counterparts (since two of them are nonparametric, and Test 4a is less risky in the presence of asymmetry).

Incidentally, some sources recommend an approximate calculation for test combinations that is based on an assumption of independence. Thus, if the risk associated with Test j is α_j, instead of using our upper bound $\alpha \leq \Sigma \alpha_j$, they recommend

$$\alpha \approx 1 - \prod_{j=1}^{k}(1 - \alpha_j)$$

In the case of signals that are generated by two separate charts, such as the dispersion chart and the $\overline{x}$ chart, when the process is under control the false signals are almost independent, and this formula is appropriate for the computation of their combined risk.

Observe that Tests 2 and 4a, when specified with a limiting value of 7, yield an α-risk of about 11%. But stopping for a run of seven points above or below the median is a popular test, and Mosteller (1941) showed that the α-risk with N=20 is below 5%. However, Mosteller assumed that we adjust the centerline to the chart's median, with exactly 10 points above it and 10 below, while our recommendation is to use the centerline without such manipulations. The basis for our recommendation is two-fold: (i) drawing the median for every chart adds complexity; (ii) suppose the chart looks in control *after* redrawing the median, but the median is far from the centerline, then do we consider the chart in control? If not, how near does it have to be?

7.5. Run-Count Tests

Without special cause, long runs are rare. Therefore, the presence of long runs can signal out-of-control situations. But during a process improvement project we may not want to invest the necessary time to obtain such long runs. In response, we can add two more tests to our arsenal. They are based on counting runs within single charts, without regard to the length: when runs are longer than average, their number is low, and vice versa. For this purpose, we count runs above and below the median, or runs up and down, and compare the result to the likely number of runs in each case.

For instance, when we have a sequence of $n=19$ points, we'll show that the expected number of runs above or below the median is 10; if we only find 3 runs, they must be longer than usual on average, perhaps due to a special cause (such as autocorrelation). Similarly, if we find 17 runs, the process is crossing the median more often than usual, and this too may be special. It may be caused by a mixture, or by tampering as in Funnel Rules 2 or 3. Likewise, if the number of runs up and down is too low it means that their length tends to be above average and there may be drift in the data. If this number is too high it may be another sign of tampering or mixture.

7.5.1. *The Number of Runs Associated with Tests 2 and 4a*

Test 2 addresses runs above or below the median. Test 4a deals with runs of points that cross the median every time. In both cases points that are *on* the median should be ignored. In our context here we count runs within given sets of n points; therefore, points on the median, if any, also reduce the count of points in the set. Let's count the number of runs above and below the centerline in Figure 7.2. The first point is above, and it constitutes a run of 1. The next 4 points are below, and they constitute one run together, followed by another run of 1 and another run of 4, etc. Table 7.4 (second column) shows the number of runs in this case.

# of points	Straight runs	Alternating runs
1	5	9
2	1	4
3	1	1
4	2	1
5	0	0
6	1	0
7 and up	0	0
Total	10	15

Table 7.4. Runs above and below the centerline.

Before we discuss whether this number is large or small, let us count the number of runs of alternating points above and below the centerline, as in Rule 4a. The first two points are indeed on opposite sides, so we have a run of 2. The third point, however, is not opposite to either its predecessor or its successor. Therefore it counts as a run of 1 by itself. The same logic applies to the following point, and then we see that Points 5, 6, and 7 constitute a run of three, followed by two runs of 1, a run of four, etc. The total count is presented in the third column of Table 7.4.

The sum of runs of both types must be $n+1$ (in our case, $24+1=25$). To see this consider that the first point counts as a run of 1 for both types. The next point either increases the number of runs on the same side of the centerline by one (if it crosses), or increases the number of alternating runs by one (if it stays on the same side). The number of runs of either type is one plus a binomial random variable with n-1 trials and $p=0.5$. Therefore, we can write the following equations for μ_{CL} and σ_{CL} (where the subscript denotes runs relative to the centerline)

$$\mu_{CL} = \frac{n+1}{2}$$

$$\sigma_{CL} = \sqrt{\frac{n-1}{4}} = \frac{\sqrt{n-1}}{2}$$

Because the number of runs related to Tests 2 and 4a are perfectly correlated with each other (with a coefficient of correlation of -1), it is enough to count runs above and below the centerline and test their number to find out all we can about both types of runs. Considering them together clarifies that the number of runs should be neither too high nor too low (a point that even respectable sources ignore sometimes). If the number of runs above and below the median is too low, it means they are longer than expected on average, and our process is probably off-center or exhibiting statistical dependence. The former is distinguishable by a high proportion of points to one side of the centerline. If the number is too high, it means that the number of alternating runs is too low, and this implies that there is a strong egg-timer effect (e.g., due to mixture or tampering).

As a rule of thumb, if we require that n be large enough to make the minimal number of runs, or the maximal number of runs, discernible based on Criterion I ($\pm 3\sigma$), we find that this test requires $n > 10$; for $n=10$ the control limits are exactly at 1 and 10, which means that the minimal and maximal number of runs possible are still (barely) in control. Larger n will provide more power, of course. Or we could specify narrower control limits, thus increasing the power *and* the α-risk.

In our example, $\mu_{CL} = 12.5$, and $\sigma_{CL} = 2.298$, yielding control limits at 5.3 and 19.7. Since we actually counted 10 runs, the result is well within control (as it should be, because the original process was in control).

7.5.2. The Number of Runs Associated with Tests 3 and 4

The analysis here is similar to the former case, and so is the interpretation of the results, with one major difference: it is much more difficult to show the distribution of the number of runs in this case. Therefore, we'll just show basic results. For more details and former references -- dating back to 1874 -- see Levene and Wolfowitz (1944).

The number of runs associated with Test 3 is simply the number of runs of points going up or down. The number associated with Test 4 is the number of runs with points alternating up and down (without necessarily crossing the centerline). Since the distribution is continuous, when we look at any two successive points, one of them is above the other. Nonetheless, in case two successive points are at the same level -- which can happen due to rounding or discrete data -- we ignore the second point. This is analogous to ignoring points that are *on* the centerline in the former case.

Let us count these runs in Figure 7.2. First note that Points 10 and 19 are at the same level as their immediate predecessors. Therefore, we ignore them, and we obtain a sequence of 22 active points. The first three points are declining, so they constitute one run down of three. This is followed by a run up of two (most end-points are counted in two runs each), a run down of 2, a run up of 2, a run down of three, a run up of three, etc. The last run up of three includes Points 8, 9, and 11 (with 10 ignored). Table 7.5 (second column) shows the total number of runs in this case.

# of points	Runs Up & Down	Alternating runs
2	9	2
3	6	2
4	0	0
5	0	1
6	0	1
7	0	1
8 and up	0	0
Total	15	7

Table 7.5. Runs up and down (egg-timer) pattern.

These two counts must add up to n: Start with the first two points. They create one run of each type, so, for $n=2$ we have two runs. Each additional point adds one run of one of the types, but not the other. For instance, in Table 7.5 the sum is 22, which, having erased Points 10 and 19, is our n. So it is enough to investigate the number of runs up and down. Too few runs up and down indicate trends and positive correlation between successive points, while too many runs indicate tampering (which often causes negative correlation between successive points), or mixtures.

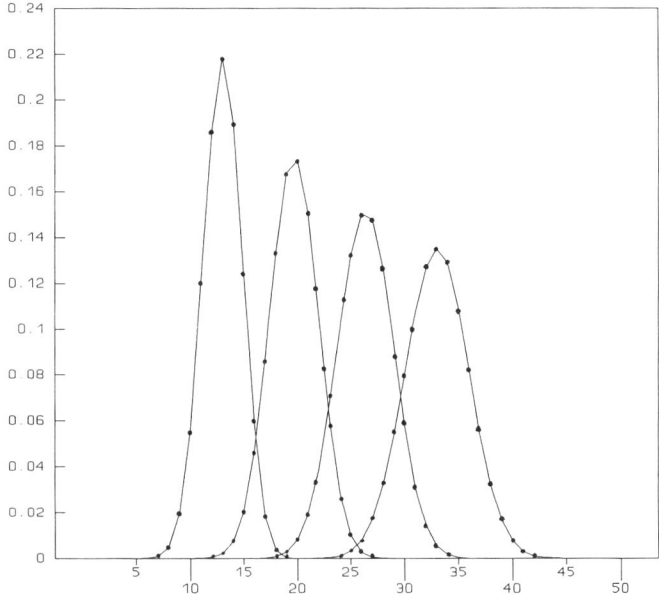

Fig. 7.3. Empirical probability mass functions for runs up and down. From left to right, $n=20, 30$, 40, and 50.

Is 15 too large or too small in this case? It's been shown by Bienaymé (in 1874) that the mean and standard deviation of the number of runs up and down, $\mu_{U/D}$ and $\sigma_{U/D}$, are given by

$$\mu_{U/D} = \frac{2n-1}{3}; \qquad \sigma_{U/D} = \sqrt{\frac{16n-29}{90}}$$

The distribution of this number is approximately normal for large n (say $n \geq 50$). Figure 7.3 depicts the empirical density function of this distribution, based on a simulation study of

500,000 "in control" sequences. The figure shows the probability mass functions for $n=20$, 30, 40, and 50. It becomes more symmetric and flatter as n increases, and the mode is approximately at $(2n-1)/3$. The same simulation study revealed that even in the region where we cannot claim that the distribution is approximately normal, the α-risk associated with using $\pm 3\sigma$ limits never exceeded 0.004.

In our example we expect the number of runs to be $43/3 = 14.33$, and the standard deviation is 1.89, yielding control limits of 8.65 and 20.01. 15 is well within control.

7.5.3. *The Robustness of the Count Method*

We've already seen that although Tests 2 and 4a have the same risk when the distribution is symmetric, Test 4a is more robust against deviations from this requirement. But in terms of run counts, as we've seen, there is no difference between Test 4a and Test 2. This suggests that run count data are also robust against deviations from symmetry. Indeed, we now show that small deviations from center do not make much of a difference here.

Since the sum of the number of runs above and below the centerline and alternating across the centerline is constant, we can investigate either type. It is slightly more convenient to calculate the distribution of the number of runs above and below the centerline, as follows. Denote the probability of falling above the centerline by p, so $q=1-p$ is the probability of falling below the centerline. The first point of the run is above the centerline with probability p, and it contributes 1 run to the count. At any stage, the last point is above the centerline with probability p, and it will cross over with a probability q, thus adding one run to the count; also, with probability q the last point will be below, and it will cross over with probability p. Thus, the complete probability of crossing over (and adding 1 to the count) is $2pq$. For $p=0.5$ this yields 0.5, which we had used in our analysis before. But small changes in p barely change the value of $2pq$ relative to 0.5. For instance, $p=0.6$ leads to $2pq=0.48$; $p=0.7$ leads to $2pq=0.42$. It would take a large n to make such small differences discernible statistically. Thus, tests based on the number of counts above and below the centerline are robust against deviation from symmetry. Consequently, they don't have much power to reveal such deviations. But they retain the power to reveal autocorrelation, both positive and negative. Positive autocorrelation implies that points are likely to be close to each other, and therefore long runs above or below the centerline are likely. Chemical processes are often positively autocorrelated. Another example is if Funnel Rule 4 is followed. Negative autocorrelation, as with Funnel Rules 2 and 3, makes crossing the centerline much more likely, and therefore it too will be revealed by this test.

7.6. Common Errors to Avoid

◆ Devising tests for control after the fact: it is often possible to argue that a particular pattern is rare, but we should select tests in advance, or the *RFS* will grow indefinitely. Nonetheless, it is valid to check whether a rare pattern repeats more than once.

◆ Using zone tests such as Tests 2, 5, 6, 7, and 8 on dispersion charts without taking into account the different probabilities that the non-normal distribution imparts. (It's legitimate, however, to adapt the zone boundaries to match the required zone probabilities, or adapt the tests for this purpose by taking into account the correct zone probabilities.)[7]

---

[7]Box 1.1 applies zone tests to an *R* chart, both above and below the centerline. See AT&T (1958), pp. 182-183 for a guide on how to devise legitimate zone tests for this purpose. Although based on an erroneous methodology for the calculation of *RFS*, it yields results that are at least roughly consistent across the board.

Supplement 7

Basic Concepts in Time Series Analysis

In Chapter 7 we've presented popular, and relatively simple, tests for statistical control. Here we mention some less popular tests. We discuss tests designed to detect and possibly to compensate for *autocorrelation*, i.e., statistical dependence between successive points. Autocorrelation may be the direct result of the use of Funnel Rules 2, 3, or 4. When this is the case, it is especially important to discover it, and then stop tampering. The knowledge that it exists *may* be enough evidence to convince one to correct the situation. But autocorrelation, especially positive (i.e., when points tend to be close to their immediate predecessors), is not always due to tampering, and it is not always correctable. For example, strong positive autocorrelation is prevalent in the chemical industry, where data are collected by automatic sensors very frequently, but the process parameters change in a much slower rate. This process change may well be due to common causes, and thus not require any intervention. When autocorrelation is unavoidable, we outline methods of control charting that allow for autocorrelation as "common" and still detects "uncommon" causes. We'll provide a basic coverage of these issues, and refer the readers to more comprehensive sources for further technical details.

Later, we present four basic time series patterns. We also show how the four basic patterns provide a framework that can fit the outcome of Funnel Rules 2, 3, and 4. This will provide us with a preliminary test to see whether it is likely that one of these rules had been active. As part of our technical presentation, we also discuss forecasting methods that may be associated with the four basic processes. In general, there is a strong connection between forecasting and control charting, since the error term of a good forecast should be a process that is in control. Therefore, when we use a forecasting technique, and monitor the forecast error, we should be able to detect assignable causes. It is important to clarify, however, that it is *not* our aim to use these relatively sophisticated forecasts for the purpose of making dynamic decisions. Instead, we simply want to be able to detect assignable causes. To understand this caveat, and why it is important, the following quote is apt

> In fact, it is quite reasonable to expect that forecasting methods will often be
> one of the factors creating system instability and then they can accentuate the
> very problems they are presumed to alleviate. [...]

In summary, forecasting methods that predict from past and present data are a mixed blessing. They may be good or bad, depending on how they interact with the remainder of the company. On the whole I am inclined to believe that present industrial forecasting attempts do more harm than good. Either way they have a powerful effect on the system and must be included in any realistic model of industrial behavior. (Jay W. Forrester, *Industrial Dynamics,* 1961, p. 338.)

That is, forecasting is too often the basis for tampering, and it causes severe fluctuations instead of preventing them.[1] But the quote also clarifies that what counts is *how* the forecast is used. In general, when dealing with systems that are difficult to improve, it is very important to use sound control limits to avoid tampering. Careless adjustment without such a signal is sometimes tampering: the only legitimate response to an unsatisfactory process that is in control is to work on the process, not its adjustment. See Chapter 4, however, where we showed that adjusting by a small fraction of the current deviation is often beneficial. Be that as it may, by using appropriate techniques we can identify special causes more reliably.

For example, many managers monitor inventory levels regularly. Inventory is supposed to fluctuate, but some managers feel uncomfortable with such fluctuations, and demand better forecasting that will make it possible to avoid them. Using such forecasts to constantly change the order points and order quantities would be tampering, and we'd probably be better off without a forecast at all. But when the inventory level is out of control in the statistical sense, *after* taking into account the expected fluctuations due to the way the system is designed, then something may indeed have to be done, and this includes, potentially, process adjustments. And if the behavior of the system is in control but unacceptable, we obtain a clear signal that we need to redesign the system. Inventory levels, incidentally, are notoriously autocorrelated, and hence this is an especially appropriate example in our context here.

S7.1. Non-Random Causes of Process Variation

Defined operationally, any cause of variation that is anticipated is not random. This

---

[1]Our discussion in Chapter 4 about fractional adjustment as opposed to using moving averages is highly relevant to this issue. Using fractional adjustment with a small λ, and not too frequently, we should expect the system to behave reasonably well, but if we use other adjustment methods, including sophisticated ones such as Box-Jenkins (which is essentially a specialized moving averages method), we may exacerbate the process fluctuations.

implies that what is non-random (or deterministic) for one may be random for another, who is not as capable of anticipating a cause or did not invest the necessary effort to do so. In this section we concentrate on causes that are in fact anticipated. The same causes, without the anticipation, could be treated as random causes. Thus, if we fail to anticipate causes that might have been predicted, the variation is operationally random for us. For example, theoretically one might be able to anticipate the results of switching raw materials from different suppliers; but they look random if we are not even aware of the switch.

But even if we do anticipate some of the variation causes and their future magnitude, we'll *always* have random variation causes superimposed on the anticipated ones. One result is that random variation can hide non-random variation. Therefore, it is impossible to measure non-random variation without statistical error (but we should know already that nothing can be measured without error).

There are two main types of deterministic variation: (i) trends; and (ii) cyclical fluctuations (e.g., seasonality). Trends, or process drift, are especially prevalent in production processes due to changes caused by the process itself. For instance, as a cutting tool wears the dimension of fabricated items may drift upwards (less cutting). This may require periodic adjustment of the process, as well as periodic maintenance (such as sharpening the tool). As the name suggests, seasonality may be measured across the seasons, but also by the days of the week or the hours of the day. For instance, hospitals may not perform elective surgery on weekends, and therefore the type and number of patients in the recovery room will differ by the day of the week. Or take precision machining, which is so sensitive to temperature that each time a worker takes a break, or a door is opened, the process may change. In such a case there may be a cyclical pattern associated with the time of day (due both to temperature changes and to breaks). But cycles are not always periodical. For example, economic cycles (boom and bust) do not have a fixed period, but they return reliably, most probably due to industrial dynamics (Forrester, 1961).

In terms of process management, trends have to be identified and either designed away economically or compensated for. Seasonality may have to be identified and handled by stratifying data (e.g., by the day of the week or the hour of the day). Shewhart control charts, as well as multi-vari charts (Seder, 1950a & 1950b), can help identify time-dependent process changes. Since both trends and cycles are time-dependent, both are identifiable by such charts.

S7.2. Statistically Dependent Causes

Random variation often involves statistical dependence. If we take our measurements too close to each other, some of the many independent underlying causes will not have had a chance to change yet, so our two readings will be statistically dependent. Past events have a delayed influence on future performance, thus creating a statistical dependence between the past and the present. Sometimes this dependence is operationally negligible, but often it is crucial. When we control-chart such a process we may find that it is out of statistical control and decide that this is due to some special cause, while it behaves as it does due to dependencies. For instance, according to Test 2, if 9 consecutive points in a Shewhart control chart are above or below the mean it is customary to pronounce it "out of control," but statistical dependence can make such events likely. As mentioned, an environment where this often happens is the chemical industry, where it may take a relatively long time for the material in the system and the system parameters (e.g., temperature, pressure) to change.

This brings us back to the connection between forecasting a time series and control charting a process. In both cases we try to describe the past data as a process that obeys some predictable statistical rules, and we may use that description to predict the future. In both cases we need to know which points "do not belong" to the regular process (special causes). But in forecasting we do not insist on perfect statistical control. For instance, we take drifts (trends), cycles (seasonality), and statistical dependence into account explicitly, rather than interpret them automatically as special problems. In a technical sense, forecasting is a generalization of control charts: the error term of an ideal forecast should be a process in statistical control. So if we use such forecasting techniques instead of regular control charts, we'll effectively isolate the predictable assignable causes from the random causes, and we'll be able to handle statistical dependencies too. Any "out of control" points that will remain will signal the need for special intervention. As long as the error term is in control, however, using the forecast results to adjust the process by Funnel Rule 2, 3, or 4 is tampering.

Without doubt, the existence of predictable causes and statistical dependence are complexities: some of us might be more comfortable in a world that is "in statistical control" in the more restricted sense that assumes i.i.d. process output. But we don't have a choice here: these complexities are part of reality. Some of the techniques necessary to deal with autocorrelation are beyond the scope of this book. The most sophisticated approach, known as Box-Jenkins (Box and Jenkins, 1976) or ARIMA (*auto*regressive *i*ntegrated *m*oving *a*verage), uses past data explicitly to estimate the autocorrelation along with other process parameters. This makes possible decomposing autocorrelation effects from random effects. In a sense, it makes the autocorrelation effects deterministic. Alwan and Roberts (1988) discussed the application of such methods to process control charts in more detail. Often, however, we can simply use *EWMA* charts (see Chapter 6) with high λ selected in such a way that the quadratic error of the sample is minimized (this may imply quite high λ values).

EWMA should be recommended whenever there is a high positive autocorrelation, due to its simplicity and effectiveness (Montgomery and Mastrangelo, 1991). On the one hand, it cannot handle negative autocorrelation (to do so would require negative λ). On the other hand, negative autocorrelation should rarely be permissible in practice; it indicates overcorrection as in Funnel Rules 2 and 3, and usually it can and should be designed away from the process. In contrast, positive autocorrelation cannot always be designed away. In the remainder of this supplement, we discuss four basic processes that can shed more light on this issue, and on the issue of forecasting in general. For each of the four there exists some *EWMA* chart that is appropriate. This explains the power of this technique for positively autocorrelated processes as well as better-behaved ones.

S7.3. The Four Basic Processes and Associated Forecasting Methods

When we analyze a time series -- which we'll denote by $\{x_t\}$, where t is the index of the period -- we should realize that there are many possible underlying models. Each such model may call for a different forecasting method. We'll discuss four basic models, and show how it is possible to identify their presence. In each case we'll also identify the best forecasting method. All our models include a noise term, ϵ_t. Throughout this supplement, we'll make the following assumptions:

1. ϵ_t and ϵ_s are identically distributed and independent for any $t \neq s$

2. $E(\epsilon_t) = 0$

3. $VAR(\epsilon_t) = \sigma^2$ for any t (this does not imply that σ is known).

S7.3.1. *The Constant Expectation Process*

Our first process, the constant expectation process, is given by

$$x_t = \mu + \epsilon_t$$

That is, the expected value of the variable, x_t, is a constant, μ (which we usually do not know), plus a noise element, ϵ_t. $\{\epsilon_t\}$ is a series of *i.i.d.* elements, so there is no interaction between any two periods. Had we known μ, our best forecast would simply be μ itself, and our forecast error would be stable (i.e., in statistical control). Since we do not know μ, we have to estimate it from data. If we want to minimize our squared error, then mathematically the best forecast is the average of as many periods as we have information about, i.e., $\overline{x}$.

The same estimate can serve as far into the future as we believe the process will remain unchanged. We may want to screen the data we use by some control chart to verify that we do not use data that does not belong to the process, i.e., data that is out of control, but for now let us assume that our data is good. Mathematically, under the (strong) assumption that the process will not change, the forecast is equally valid ten periods into the future as it is one period into the future. *This does not imply that one can rely on such a forecast ten periods into the future unless there is strong belief that the process indeed has no trend, and will not change in the future for unforseen reasons.* There is no statistical analysis on earth that can validate such a belief, but one might be justified in gambling on it if the process has been well-behaved in the past, and it seems that the correct economic decision is to make such a gamble.

An almost equally good estimate is an exponential average of the historical data, or *EWMA*, with a very low λ value. If we specify a large λ value, we introduce a large fraction of the error term into the forecast. To quantify this relationship, recall from Chapter 6 the connection between λ and the equivalent subgroup size, k_a

$$k_a = \frac{2 - \lambda}{\lambda}$$

The variance of the estimate of the process average, σ^2/k_a, is clearly increasing with λ.

How can we tell whether our process is a constant expectation process indeed? First, we expect a regression line going through the points to be flat, and when we chart the points on a control chart we expect to obtain a chart that is in statistical control. This implies, among other things, that the pattern tests will not signal any problem. Indeed, the constant expectation process is simply a regular process that is in control as defined operationally by Shewhart control charts.

For our needs here, let us introduce another method: Analysis of the process differences. The process difference in period t is defined by $\Delta x_t = x_t - x_{t-1}$. For the constant expectation process we obtain $\Delta x_t = \epsilon_t - \epsilon_{t-1}$. Similarly, $\Delta x_{t-1} = \epsilon_{t-1} - \epsilon_{t-2}$. But note now that we can use the second expression to express ϵ_{t-1} as a function of Δx_{t-1}, as follows,

$$\epsilon_{t-1} = \Delta x_{t-1} + \epsilon_{t-2}$$

Substitute this value to the expression we had for Δx_t, and we obtain:

$$\Delta x_t = -\Delta x_{t-1} + \epsilon_t - \epsilon_{t-2}$$

ϵ_t and ϵ_{t-2} are independent of each other, and the expected value of each of them is 0, therefore the expected value of $\epsilon_t - \epsilon_{t-2}$ is 0, with a variance of $2\sigma^2$. Suppose now we want to regress Δx_t by Δx_{t-1}. At first blush, it would seem as if the regression line should have a slope of -1. That is, it might seem that we should not be able to reject the hypothesis that the slope is -1. But if we try to regress such a line for a simulated process in control, the result will be a negative slope of about -0.5, and not -1. This means, operationally, that we will not be able to reject the hypothesis that the slope is -0.5. This statement holds for the standard regression model that is based on minimizing the sum of squares ("least squares"). The reason for this behavior is that the standard regression model is not really appropriate here. One of the standard assumptions is that the explaining variable is not subject to random error, but in our case both Δx_t and Δx_{t-1} are subject to errors of equal magnitudes. (Interestingly enough, if we run a regression line by eye, it is more likely to show a slope of -1 in this case!) Be that as it may, we can also see that the intercept of the regression line should be 0. Again, this just means we should not be able to reject the hypothesis that it is 0. In conclusion, we should obtain a regression line with a negative slope of about -0.5 and zero (i.e., small) intercept. Any other result suggests that the process is not really a constant expectation one.

S7.3.2. A Basic Time-Dependent Process

Let us examine now a second basic process, which differs from the constant expectation process by the influence of a deterministic cause system. Therefore, while the error terms do not change, this time the expectation is no longer constant, but rather a function of time. For example, if we have a process with a drift, we may expect the function to be a trend. And if we have a drift, but we readjust the process periodically to compensate for it (as discussed in Supplement 4), then the time function will look like the teeth of a saw. More formally, let μ_t be the expected value as a function of time, then

$$x_t = \mu_t + \epsilon_t$$

Here, unless we correct explicitly for μ_t, the process should no longer appear to be in control. But if we can identify, or at least estimate, μ_t, and deduct it from x_t, we should obtain a process in control with a centerline at 0. If we analyze the process differences, we obtain $\Delta x_t = \mu_t - \mu_{t-1} + \epsilon_t - \epsilon_{t-1}$. Similarly, $\Delta x_{t-1} = \mu_{t-1} - \mu_{t-2} + \epsilon_{t-1} - \epsilon_{t-2}$. We can use the last expression to obtain $\mu_{t-1} + \epsilon_{t-1} = \Delta x_{t-1} + \mu_{t-2} + \epsilon_{t-2}$. Substituting this value to the expression for Δx_t, we obtain

$$\Delta x_t = -\Delta x_{t-1} + \mu_t - \mu_{t-2} + \epsilon_t - \epsilon_{t-2}$$

As before, ϵ_t and ϵ_{t-2} are independent of each other, and the expected value of each of them is 0, so, again, the expected value of $\epsilon_t - \epsilon_{t-2}$ is 0, and the variance is $2\sigma^2$. If we regress Δx_t by Δx_{t-1} now, the regression line should still have a negative slope, but since $\mu_t - \mu_{t-2}$ is not zero (under our assumption), the intercept should no longer be zero. If μ_t is indeed a linear function, the intercept should be twice the slope of μ_t. If μ_t is not a linear function, however, then the difference $\mu_t - \mu_{t-2}$ itself is a function of t. In the latter case, the regression will be more messy and difficult to interpret, because these differences will behave as noise as far as the regression model is concerned.

One way to forecast such a process is by regressing μ_t. Depending on how complex this function is, this may or may not be easy. A potentially better way would be to use exponential smoothing with trend correction. Essentially, trend corrected exponential smoothing models include two elements: one to estimate the current mean, and one to estimate the current trend. The forecast k periods ahead is the current mean plus k times the current trend. Clearly the forecast quality into the future deteriorates, because small errors in the trend estimate get multiplied, and because the trend -- even if estimated perfectly -- may change. A similar observation holds for forecasts far into the future that are based on regression. This, of course, is in addition to the fact that we can't tell whether the process will change! Note that the former case, where we assumed zero trend, was equally difficult: we can never be absolutely sure that there is no trend at all.

S7.3.3. *Martingales*

The third type of process we examine is the Martingale. Here $x_t = x_{t-1} + \epsilon_t$. In other words, the process changes randomly, but its current location is the best forecast for the next location. Chemical processes often behave almost as a Martingale (e.g., see MacGregor and Harris, 1993). The readers can verify that when we analyze Δx_t by Δx_{t-1} for a Martingale we should expect a cloud centered at the origin. That is, we no longer expect a significant negative (or positive) slope.

Furthermore, when we control chart a Martingale we should *not* obtain statistical control. It should show long runs above or below the centerline. A Martingale is also more likely to show longer trends than a process in control. The reason for this is that there is a probability of 0.5 that the next point will be above the current one *regardless* of how many points are ascending already (and likewise for descending trends). Thus, the probability of a run up of, say, 9 points is the same as that of obtaining 9 points above the centerline under

Test 2 (for a process that is in control), while for Test 3 obtaining 9 points in a row is extremely rare when the process is in control. Instead, Δx_t is a process in control.

For a Martingale, the naive forecast (last period's result is this period's forecast) is best. Note that this can be treated as a special case of exponential smoothing with $\lambda = 1$. Forecasting far into the future is done by the same forecast, but it multiplies the variance of the error by the number of periods involved. For this reason this process is the least predictable of the ones we discussed so far.

S7.3.4. *Sub-Martingales*

Our final type of process is the sub-Martingale, which is a Martingale with an additional external function of time superimposed on it. For example, the Dow-Jones index is a sub-Martingale. Here, the effective market return on investment acts as the external function. After correcting for it, the process should be a Martingale. Otherwise, one could determine if it will go up or down with a high probability of success, and that by itself would have caused the index to move according to the same expectations. For a sub-Martingale the differences analysis yields a cloud, but not around the origin. Again, the best forecast is the former result, plus, when available, information based on the external function. We may want to keep an exponentially smoothed forecast of the trend, and use as a forecast the current result plus the trend correction. Clearly, as we forecast far into the future, our error compounds because we collect more error terms, the error in the trend forecast multiplies itself as well, and the external function is likely to change more and more.

S7.3.5. *Interim Conclusion*

So far, we've observed that for a process that is in control the difference sequence is such that consecutive elements are negatively correlated. Thus, when we regressed Δx_t by Δx_{t-1} we obtained a negative slope, and, in this case, zero intercept. When the process had a trend, the slope still remained negative, but the intercept was not zero any more. Martingales, in contrast, showed a zero slope and zero intercept, and when we moved to sub-Martingales the slope remained zero but the intercept was no longer zero.

Looking at control charts associated with these processes, the first is identical to a process that is in control, the second is no longer in control, but we may see the trend on the chart, and conceivably we can correct for it. The Martingale was not likely to show in control for two related reasons: First, it is likely to drift out of control; second, it is likely to remain above or below the centerline for extended periods, thus activating Test 2 (when it is used).

Our real benefit from investigating the difference sequence so far is a way to distinguish between Martingales and sub-Martingales. While a similar distinction applies to the first and second basic processes, we don't really need this type of analysis to see it, since the control chart is likely to suffice for this purpose. But this analysis may be useful to analyze the results of applying the funnel rules (see Chapter 4) to a process in control, a subject we discuss next.

S7.4. Basic Processes and the Nelson Funnel Rules

When we apply Rule 4 to a constant expectation process we obtain a Martingale. Doing the same for a time-dependent expectation process produces a sub-Martingale. Therefore, if we observe a process that tends to violate Test 2, and a difference analysis shows a cloud of points without a significant trend, one of the things we need to do is check whether Rule 4 is being applied inadvertently.

To analyze similarly for Rule 3, if the picture is not clear by itself (and the wide fluctuations are likely to be observable if we look for them), consider that under Rule 3 the series

$$\left\{-1^t(x_t - T)\right\}$$

where T is the target (recall that Funnel Rules 2 and 3 require knowledge of the target), is indiscernible from Rule 4. Thus, if this series is a Martingale, the underlying process must be a manifestation of Rule 3.

It remains to discuss Rule 2. Rule 2 may be difficult to identify because it is not as blatant as Rule 3. Tests 4 and 4a are designed to identify the results of Rule 2, and here we discuss the option of using analysis of differences for the same purpose.

If we apply Rule 2 to an adjustable process in control, the result will be

$$\left\{x_t = T + e_t - e_{t-1}\right\}$$

To see this suppose that the initial adjustment is $T + \epsilon_0$, where ϵ_0 is any value. The first item (or drop, to remain within the funnel metaphor) will be at $T + \epsilon_0 + \epsilon_1$, so our adjustment will be by $-\epsilon_0 - \epsilon_1$, yielding $T - \epsilon_1$. In a similar manner, at period t the adjustment going in is $T - \epsilon_{t-1}$, the drop is at $T - \epsilon_{t-1} + \epsilon_t$, and after adjusting by $-\epsilon_t + \epsilon_{t-1}$ the adjustment going out is $T - \epsilon_t$.

Using this result to compute Δx_t we obtain $\epsilon_t - 2\epsilon_{t-1} + \epsilon_{t-2}$. Similarly, $\Delta x_{t-1} = \epsilon_{t-1} - 2\epsilon_{t-2} + \epsilon_{t-3}$. Note now that Δx_t and Δx_{t-1} are not correlated (in contrast to the situation for the original process), since the correlation induced by ϵ_{t-1} is negated by the correlation induced by ϵ_{t-2}. It follows that if we regress Δx_t by Δx_{t-1} we should obtain a slope that is not significantly different from zero. Even if we obtain a negative slope here (when the rule is applied, but not religiously), its magnitude is likely to be smaller than 0.5, the value we expect when using the least squares regression on the constant expectation process.

S7.5. More Sophisticated Analyses

While we did not set out to cover advanced detection techniques in this supplement, we are now in a better position to understand how such techniques may be constructed. In general, if we use regression techniques to analyze a time-series, the regression output includes error estimates, e_t, which are supposed to represent the error terms, ϵ_t. If the time-series has no autocorrelation, then ϵ_t will not be a function of any former error term, ϵ_{t-k}. Suppose that we regress e_t by the former error estimates, e_{t-k}, where $k=1,2,\ldots,K$, i.e., going back K periods. If any of these terms is significant, we may suspect autocorrelation. Furthermore, we may use the relationship to account for this correlation.

The models we did present are not special cases of this approach, but they have one point in common: they are based on the relationship between the error terms at any given period and the one preceding it. Another common feature is that advanced methods, such as ARIMA, often analyze the difference sequence instead of the direct time-series itself.

The Control Chart Principle of Uncertainty: *As we collect more data our estimates are more precise mathematically, but our confidence that the process did not change during the collection decreases. Therefore it is impossible to obtain a completely reliable control chart.*

Chapter 8
Diffidence Analysis of Control Charts and Diffidence Charts

Users of Shewhart control charts are subject to confusing messages about the number of subgroups necessary for calculating control limits. Some authors gloss over this question, hoping, perhaps, that the reader will find out elsewhere. A popular rule of thumb specifies 25 routinely, 100 when exceptional precision is sought. Another rule is "20 or 30." AT&T (1958) suggested, "20 or more groups, if possible, but not less than 10." Exceptionally explicit, Wheeler (1995) is a strong proponent of small samples: in his opinion the worst that can happen is missing an out-of-control point (type II error). The position espoused here is that small samples are better than nothing, but they rarely suffice. The reason is that type I errors are also very likely, potentially leading people to chasing nonexistent causes, thus giving quality control a bad name. In contrast to Wheeler, Quesenberry (1993) reached the same conclusion we do here. His argument is that using too few data causes statistical dependence between the subsequent false signals. This is true for the population of all possible control charts, but for any given chart, once control limits are set, one way or another, a process that is in control will always generate a stream of false signals that are statistically independent of each other (Trietsch and Bischak, 1998). Therefore, the core problem is not the statistical dependence identified by Quesenberry. Trietsch and Hwang (1995) identified a more plausible culprit: the rate of false signals (*RFS*) varies too much between charts. In this chapter we use their results. We also introduce a new graphic tool -- *diffidence charts* -- that helps determine the number of samples required in each specific application. Diffidence charts can be described as control charts for control charts: they provide limits for the true control limits. Thus they help to decide whether the control chart is adequate or needs more data.

The practice of evading the question (how many subgroups are necessary?) harks back to Shewhart's landmark *Economic Control of Quality of Manufactured Product* (1931). Shewhart knew the effects of the sample size, but he chose to assume that large samples will be used. He may have refrained from specific recommendations because there is no single answer that fits all conditions, but this does not make the practical question go away. Perhaps as a result, the response was determined, all too often, too liberally. We should also consider that the cost of crunching numbers was much higher, so large samples were less economical than they are today.

Some practitioners adjust the limits based on the last 25, 50, or 100 subgroups. This policy is tantamount to using Nelson's Funnel Rule 4 ("adjust the process to the last result"). A more responsible recommendation is to use the first 25 samples to create tentative limits (*trial* limits), update them later with $m = 100$ (after collecting 75 additional subgroups), and let them be as long as the process is not changed intentionally or unavoidably. Here, we recommend this approach as the minimum necessary. But sometimes we need to sample even more, say $m = 400$, before finalizing the control chart (always using the former limits while collecting data). This may be required when there are too many points near the control signals (on either side). We'll provide a clearer criterion later, utilizing diffidence charts. But first we should study the probable results of various sample sizes, to get a better basis for economic decisions. After all, as Shewhart stressed, this *is* an economic question.

With too little data, a control chart lacks power (risking type II error), or has an excessive *RFS* (type I error). This should not surprise anyone, since in general the use of small samples leads to such results. Low power and high *RFS* are two sides of the same coin, but we'll concentrate on *RFS*. We start by discussing sources of *diffidence*, one of which is the use of small samples. We then concentrate on this particular source of diffidence, and discuss in detail the influence of using small sets of, say, 25 subgroups on the *RFS*, as compared with using sets of 100 subgroups or more. We then introduce diffidence charts, to help determine the necessary number of subgroups. "Diffidence" denotes *lack* of confidence, and yet diffidence charts are based on setting *confidence intervals* for the true location of the control limits. In a sense, what we're proposing here is to control chart the control limits themselves, because control charts may be said to provide confidence intervals for the results of processes that are in control.

The only way to decrease this source of diffidence is by sampling more. Diffidence charts can support the decision whether additional sampling is necessary in a particular case. But they also demonstrate an inherent weakness of control charts, especially when applied in a non-repetitive production environment: sometimes, a large sample is a must, but in non-repetitive environments it may be impractical to collect enough data to resolve the diffidence.[1]

It is important to state, however, that our purpose is not to *discourage* the use of control charts with small samples. Rather we aim to *encourage* the use of larger samples. When only a few data points are available, it may be most economical to use them for decision-making. On average, such a policy is quite likely to pay off handsomely. But when enough data can be collected at reasonable cost, it is potentially cheaper to do so. The theoretical foundation of diffidence charts is not complete at this writing. Specifically, the selection of the diffidence probability, and the chart's exact behavior with very small samples require further research. The aim of this chapter is to provide a *rough* quantitative estimate of the effects of small samples on the precision of control charts.

8.1. Sources of Diffidence

There are several sources of diffidence associated with control charts. Supplement 5 discusses diffidence due to extrapolating the results of an analytical study into the future, as well as diffidence about the true process distribution. Likewise, we often assume that the process, when run as designed, yields statistically independent results. Even if we check these assumptions statistically (and control charting provides such checks), we may be able to say that they are not patently false, but we can never assert that they are true. In fact, we should *know* that they are false in the strict sense: at best they are satisfactory approximations of reality that are useful in practice. Also, when analyzing complex mathematical models we often have to resort to approximations that add diffidence.

Numerical experience, including examples covered in Chapter 6 and some theory discussed in Supplement 6.2, suggests that $\bar{x}$ charts that are based on sufficient data are quite accurate for a wide range of distributions. We did not find similar reassurance with respect to dispersion charts, however. As for the problem of statistical dependence, or autocorrelation between successive items produced by a process, we discussed this briefly

---

[1]Various schemes exist to control short production runs. Some of them isolate the common process elements, e.g., machining, that apply to many products, and chart them instead of the direct measurements. This assumes that machining precision and accuracy is *not* influenced by the product itself. It is certainly a false assumption, but for products that are similar enough it may have practical value. The proof of this particular pudding is in the eating. The second approach is to give up on statistical control, and opt instead for "capability control" based on the ability of the process to hold the tolerances. A good example of this approach is *Precontrol* (Shainin and Shainin, 1988). Although it is touted to be effective for long runs as well, Precontrol is not effective for *EQL* reduction, so it should not replace Shewhart charts for long runs. Specifying the five/ten rule instead of Precontrol's qualifying procedure helps, and is recommended for short runs as well.

in Supplement 7. An important source of diffidence that we did not study previously, however, is the use of small samples. This is our main topic in this chapter. We study the behavior of control charts as a function of the sample size, to gain more insight as to how large our samples should be. We study this question for attribute charts (concentrating on np charts) and for variable charts. For the latter, we do so under a normality assumption. In reality, of course, we don't know that our process is normal. When we think we know what our distribution is (e.g., based on extensive experimentation), we may choose to perform a similar analysis for this particular distribution. But the results we obtain here may serve as a guide for any case: if we cannot accept the consequences of a small sample under the normal distribution, then it would likely be a mistake to use such a small sample when we don't even know the distribution. Most practical distributions are less well-behaved than the normal, especially with small samples.

Another source of diffidence we did not study in detail so far is our trust that the data used to devise control limits is only subject to common causes. But while we collect data we don't have yet a tool to verify this. It's impossible to control against it without risk (since it's impossible to avoid occasional errors). Trial charts are the traditional answer. Diffidence charts provide another answer, supporting the decision whether to use a data point while we are constructing the chart.

8.2. The Diffidence of Attribute Charts

In Deming's Red Beads experiment (Chapter 5), using 24 subgroups of $n=50$ each, we obtained $n\bar{p}=9.75$. According to Deming (1993, pp. 168-199), however, his long-term experience with this particular paddle showed that $n\bar{p}=9.4$ is a better estimate. Deming also reported that three other paddles, each made from different materials and different designs by different artisans, gave long-term averages of 11.3, 9.6, and 9.2. The real incidence of red beads, however, was always 20%. This proved, he said, that mechanical sampling is not identical to random sampling (which, of course, is yet one more source of diffidence). Let's check if the result obtained in November 1990 was compatible with the reported long term average. Our total number of items in the sample was $50 \times 24 = 1200$. If p would really be $9.4/50 = 0.188$, then by devising $\pm 3\sigma$ limits for the number of red beads in a sample of 1200 we'd obtain

$$1200p \pm 3\sqrt{1200p(1-p)} = 225.6 \pm 40.6 = [185, 266.2]$$

where the brackets indicate that any number between 185 and 266.2, inclusive, is within the acceptable range. That is, Deming, as a believer in control charts and an ardent supporter of the use of $\pm 3\sigma$ limits, should have accepted any result between 185 and 266 (inclusive), but might have suspected an assignable cause for results outside this range. We refer to such a range as a $\pm 3\sigma$ *confidence interval*.[2] We use a $\pm 3\sigma$ interval quite arbitrarily: arguably, a confidence interval of $\pm 2\sigma$ or $\pm 2.5\sigma$ might be more appropriate: control charts were never meant to be totally immune against statistical errors. Be that as it may, calculating $\overline{p}$ at the endpoints of this $\pm 3\sigma$ confidence interval, we obtain 0.154 and 0.222, leading to $\overline{np}$ between 7.71 and 11.08. Our result, 9.75, is certainly within this range, and thus it should not be deemed special. (Nor would it have been deemed special with a $\pm 2\sigma$ confidence interval.)

Depending on where within the range our $\overline{p}$ would happen to fall, our control limits might have been located quite differently. At one extreme we'd have

$$LCL = 50 \times 0.1542 - 3\sqrt{50 \times 0.1542(1-0.1542)} = 0.05$$

$$UCL = 50 \times 0.1542 + 3\sqrt{50 \times 0.1542(1-0.1542)} = 15.4$$

and at the other extreme

$$LCL = 50 \times 0.2217 - 3\sqrt{50 \times 0.2217(1-0.2217)} = 2.27$$

$$UCL = 50 \times 0.2217 + 3\sqrt{50 \times 0.2217(1-0.2217)} = 19.9$$

The minimal result obtained in the experiment (as reported in Table 5.3) was 5, and the maximum was 15. Both would be within the control limits at either extreme. Furthermore, when we use the same data to devise control limits and verify that they are in control, the limits tend to adjust to the data, and the *RFS* is reduced. So Deming did not take a great risk in this experiment (indeed he told us that "out of control" points were practically non-existent in his experience).

Nonetheless, this example demonstrates that the location of the control limits is random, and thus it has its own variation. Furthermore, if we calculate the *RFS* associated with these extremes, we'll obtain results that are quite far from average. Our random variable is a binomial with 50 trials and $p=9.4/50=0.188$. Exact calculations show that the

---

[2]As discussed in Supplement 5, "confidence interval" is a term Deming would not have endorsed with regard to control charts. Nonetheless, what we are doing here is devising confidence limits for $\overline{np}$. Usually, confidence intervals are labeled by the probability that they include the parameter for which they are constructed. The most popular probabilities in use are 95% and 99%. But it's also possible to label confidence intervals by the number of σ units they are based on, and this is our choice here. Trietsch and Hwang treat the same problem with probabilities (mostly for the purpose of analyzing the diffidence of pattern tests).

probability of falling outside the control limits of 0.05 and 15.4 is 0.0079, with the bulk (0.0078) falling above *UCL*. For the limits 2.27 and 19.9 we obtain *RFS*=0.0025, with the bulk falling below *LCL*. The theoretical control limits yield *RFS*=0.0016, with about 3/4 of the false signals above *UCL*. All these numbers are different from each other, and different from the often quoted 0.0027. Small wonder that Deming opposed *RFS* calculations! Too often they reflect lack of understanding of variation. Be that as it may, as is typically the case, *RFS* is lowest at the theoretical limits, i.e., the risk of type I errors increases due to diffidence.

So far we used our knowledge that the real *np* in this case, based on Deming's long-term experience, is 9.4 or very close to 9.4. To make the analysis more realistic, let us now ignore this external knowledge, and investigate the diffidence associated with the results of the experiment based only on the experiment itself.

We know that 24 subgroups, when combined, led to the estimate $\overline{np}=9.75$ (or $\overline{p}=0.195$). We also know that all these subgroups appeared "in control" based on the control limits that this average suggests. Otherwise, we might have investigated for special causes, and we might have decided to ignore some data due to the suspicion that it is not representative of the process. Let us find how small or large *p* might be in reality, such that $\overline{p}=0.195$ would be a plausible result. The operational definition of "plausible" we'll adopt here is "within $\pm3\sigma$." Again, other values, e.g., $\pm2\sigma$, might have been specified instead. Our problem is to find two limiting values, say p_L and p_U, such that

$$p_L + 3\sqrt{\frac{p_L(1-p_L)}{1200}} = 0.195; \quad p_U - 3\sqrt{\frac{p_U(1-p_U)}{1200}} = 0.195 \qquad (8.1)$$

Any *p* that is between p_L and p_U will include $\overline{p}=0.195$ within its plausible range of results. It is possible to find p_L and p_U analytically, but this involves the solution of quartic equations. It is often more convenient to solve for these values by numerical search methods. In our case, the solution (rounded to 4 significant digits) is $p_L=0.1630$ and $p_U=0.2315$. The interval is not symmetric relative to 0.195. Nonetheless, since we do not really need exact results we may opt for a much simpler approximate solution, as follows

$$p_L \sim 0.195 - 3\sqrt{\frac{0.195(1-0.195)}{1200}} = 0.1607$$

$$\qquad (8.2)$$

$$p_U \sim 0.195 + 3\sqrt{\frac{0.195(1-0.195)}{1200}} = 0.2293$$

This, by construction, is a symmetric range relative to 0.195.

For either (8.1) or (8.2), the values of p_L and p_U induce sets of control limits for our control chart that are different from those we obtained before. The limits of Figure 5.5 fall within the ranges created by these new limits. Specifically, the limits by p_L (using the approximate value) are,

$$LCL_L = 50 \times 0.1607 - 3\sqrt{50 \times 0.1607(1 - 0.1607)} = 0.24$$

$$UCL_L = 50 \times 0.1607 + 3\sqrt{50 \times 0.1607(1 - 0.1607)} = 15.8$$

and for p_U we obtain

$$LCL_U = 50 \times 0.2293 - 3\sqrt{50 \times 0.2293(1 - 0.2293)} = 2.55$$

$$UCL_U = 50 \times 0.2293 + 3\sqrt{50 \times 0.2293(1 - 0.2293)} = 20.4$$

Suppose now that we continue to monitor the performance of the workers in the future. Suppose also that we check each point against two control charts, one with control limits at LCL_L and UCL_L, and the other with control limits at LCL_U and UCL_U. Clearly any subgroup with 3 to 15 red beads will be considered in control by both charts, and therefore we should be relatively confident in pronouncing it "in control." Similarly, any result below 0.24 (i.e., 0 red beads) should be considered special by both charts, and likewise any result above 20.4 (i.e., 21 or more red beads), so we should feel relatively confident that we make the right decision there too. But what should we do if we obtain a result between 1 and 2 (inclusive), or between 16 and 20 (inclusive)? In these cases one chart signals "out of control" and the other does not. We can say that these ranges of possible results are associated with diffidence about the correct decision. For this purpose, we define a decision as "correct" if it is based on the true (and unknown) $\pm 3\sigma$ control limits. Making an "incorrect" decision implies that the risks of making type I or type II errors are not equal to those calculated without taking the diffidence into account.

The range within which a control limit is believed to belong -- be it based on $\pm 3\sigma$, $\pm 2\sigma$, etc. -- is called a *diffidence band*, or a *diffidence interval*, since we are diffident about the correct disposition of points within it. Diffidence intervals, however, also provide information about points that are clearly in or out of control: points within the inner limits are *strongly in control*, and points outside the outer limits are *strongly out of control*. "Strongly" here implies that the probability of error is less than that usually associated with control charts. Points that fall in the diffidence bands are called *indeterminate*.

In an average case, the true control limit is near the middle of the diffidence band. The area of the band above the true limit indicates that control charts based on a sample may lack power: if the control limit falls there we accept too many points. The area below reflects excessive risk: when the limit falls there we may declare points "out of control" unnecessarily. In reality, not all results are "average," so we can't tell whether we are losing power or increasing risk.

8.3. Diffidence Charts for Attributes

Suppose now that we construct a new type of control chart, where instead of regular control limits we draw pairs of control limits at LCL_L, LCL_U and at UCL_L, UCL_U, i.e., we draw diffidence bands instead of control limits. We may call the result a *diffidence chart*. Any subgroup that falls within a diffidence band makes us diffident in our decision. Figure 8.1 depicts the example we discussed (with shaded diffidence bands). Since the same data is used both to create the diffidence limits and to check the data against it, we should refer to it as a diffidence *trial* chart. Later, we'll check points based on *former* data, and we'll obtain regular diffidence charts.

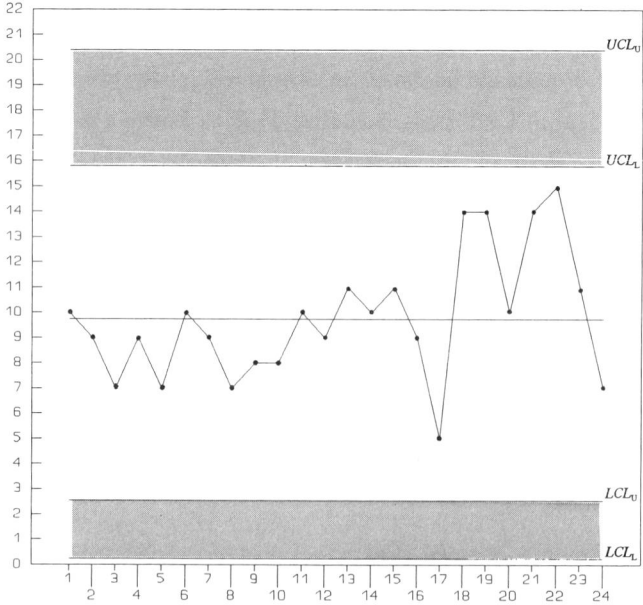

Fig. 8.1. A diffidence trial chart for Deming's red beads.

Note that in Figure 8.1 all the points are strongly in control, i.e., there are no indeterminate points. This is not a rare result, because the probability of falling within the diffidence bands is not high. Nonetheless, if we find too many indeterminate points, we may decide that the bands are too wide. There is one legitimate way to make them as narrow as we may wish: use more data. In the case of attribute charts we can even reach a state where the diffidence bands are operationally zero. For instance, if both UCL_L and UCL_U fall between 17 and 18, there can be no integer realization between them.

To clarify the relationship between the sample size and the width of the diffidence bands, let's look again at our approximate values for p_L and p_U, expressed as a function of nm (where n is the subgroup size and m is the number of subgroups),

$$p_L \approx \bar{p} - 3\sqrt{\frac{\bar{p}(1-\bar{p})}{n\,m}} \; : \quad p_U \approx \bar{p} + 3\sqrt{\frac{\bar{p}(1-\bar{p})}{n\,m}}$$

This leads to

$$p_U - p_L \approx 6\sqrt{\frac{\bar{p}(1-\bar{p})}{n\,m}}$$

For a given n, we cannot control $\bar{p}$ (which is data-generated), but we can reduce $p_U - p_L$ by increasing m. Using $\bar{p}$ as an estimate of p, we can easily compute the necessary number of subgroups to ensure that the difference will be bounded as closely as we might wish. The improvement rate is as per the square root of m, which is typical for diffidence bands. Roughly speaking, in order to reduce the width of the diffidence band by half we have to quadruple the size of the sample.

Since more data can decrease the diffidence there's a way to resolve indeterminate points. What we could do in such cases is to update the diffidence bands, based on the data collected so far and *excluding* the indeterminate point itself. It may happen that the new bands will exclude the point, and make possible a clear decision. Thus, the existence of an indeterminate point may act as a signal to update the calculations. This mechanism is not guaranteed to resolve all the indeterminate points, but it often does. *It also assures that we'll only have to update the control limits when there is a likelihood that it will help us to make a decision.* Otherwise, it is wasteful to do so.

Let us illustrate this concept by taking the results of the experiment and constructing a *dynamic* diffidence chart for them, as we go along. Our procedure will be to construct a diffidence chart after the first quarter, and if all points are strongly in control use the resulting diffidence chart without change until such time that a new point may be indeterminate. When that happens, we'll use the other points collected by that time to update the diffidence chart. Figure 8.2 shows the diffidence chart based on the first quarter, extended for the whole year. With the exception of the first quarter, this is no longer a trial chart. All the other points are judged based on previous realizations.

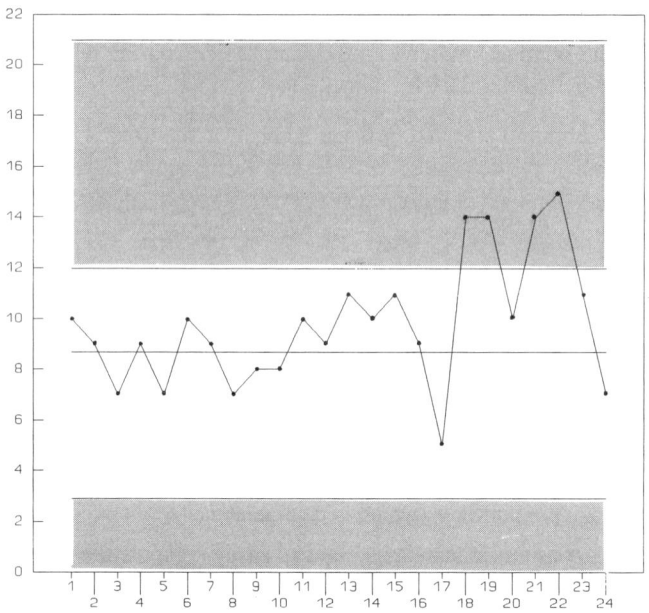

Fig. 8.2. A diffidence chart for the red beads by the first quarter data.

As it happens, the first 17 points are all strongly in control, but no less than four points thereafter are indeterminate.[3] Nevertheless, we now have more data, so we can update the chart. Figure 8.3 shows the updated chart, and now only one point (Fernando's last quarter) is indeterminate. The other high points are barely within the "strongly-in-control" range, but "barely" is operationally equivalent to "fully" in our context.

Since Fernando's last result is indeterminate, we cannot give a clear cut recommendation whether it is worthwhile to investigate his performance specifically. But we may decide to update the limits once again, based on the additional four preceding data

---

[3]In Chapter 7 we observed that the same four points trigger Test 6, and that the first 16 points are in Zone C. The latter explains, perhaps, how the results of one quarter "cover" us for almost three quarters.

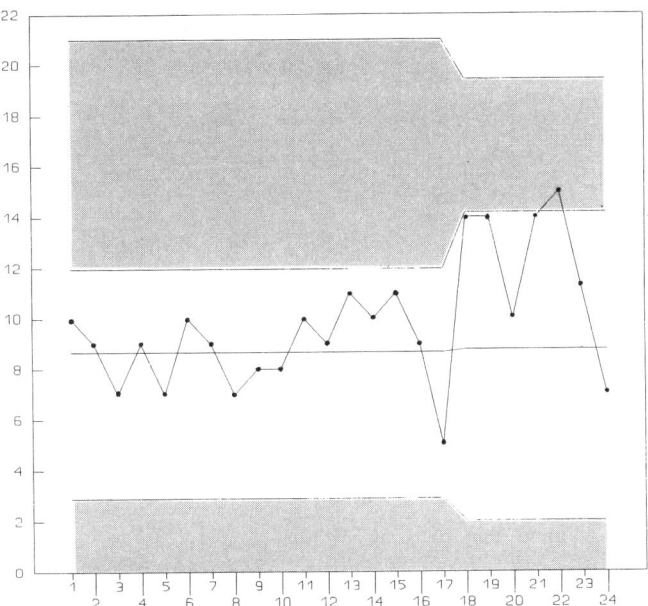

Fig. 8.3. Using 17 data points to reduce the diffidence.

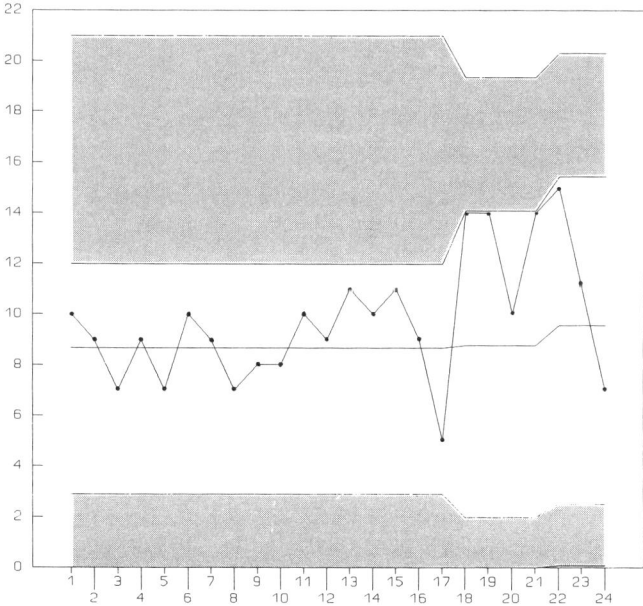

Fig. 8.4. Using four more "strong" data to reduce the diffidence further.

points that are now considered strongly in control. When we do that we obtain Figure 8.4, which shows that Fernando's performance is also strongly in control (again, barely). But suppose Fernando's output of red beads would be 16, then we'd have to continue considering his performance as indeterminate until more data would be collected. Of course, at some time we must decide whether to investigate his performance or ignore it (diffidence does not imply inaction). In the latter case, his performance should be incorporated in the $\overline{p}$ calculations. Otherwise, we will systematically exclude extreme realizations even when they belong to the process distribution.

So far we've only discussed diffidence in terms of np charts, but there is no conceptual difficulty in generalizing the concept to p charts, c charts, and u charts. We omit the details, however.

8.4. The Diffidence of Continuous Variable Charts

It is often claimed that the rate of false signal (RFS) of $\overline{x}$ charts is 0.0027. Alternately, the average run length (ARL), the inverse of RFS, is reported as 370.4. Similarly, for the most popular *dispersion control chart*, namely, the R chart with subgroups of $n=5$, the RFS is said to be 0.0046 (reducing the combined ARL to about 137). And the s chart has $RFS=0.0039$, leading to $ARL \approx 152$. These RFS values, also known as the *theoretical* values, apply under a normal distribution with *given* parameters.

The actual average RFS of Shewhart's $\pm 3\sigma$ limits when σ is estimated by data is higher in both cases. For instance, Hillier (1969) showed that when the control limits are based on twenty-five subgroups of five, and $\hat{\sigma}$, the estimate of the process standard deviation σ, is based on $\overline{R}$, the average RFS of the $\overline{x}$ chart is 0.0040 (instead of 0.0027), and the average RFS of the R chart itself is 0.0066 (instead of 0.0046); with a hundred subgroups the respective probabilities are 0.0030 and 0.0050, or roughly 10% above the theoretical values.

When viewed this way, 100 or more subgroups may be considered adequate. Even for 25, the combined average RFS is roughly 1% only. But 1% per subgroup translates to 26% when the charts are inspected 30 subgroups at a time. Here we assume that decisions are made in real time, as recommended, for example, by AT&T (1958). Depending on the frequency of sampling, 1% may still be highly excessive. Nonetheless, for our purpose we may stipulate that $RFS \approx 1\%$ is adequate. (When this is not the case we can address it by specifying wider control limits, but our analysis in this chapter would still apply. Hillier shows how to determine such wider limits.)

The rule given above, that actual average RFS is higher than typically advertized, has one notable exception: when we compute the control limits by the same data we are testing.

When we do so, the *RFS* is *lower*. As Walker et al. (1991) stated, "This is because the same data are being used to obtain the limits and therefore these 'adapt' to the observed data." We must remember, however, that the correct recommendation is to use data to estimate trial control limits *and then test **new data against them**.* Otherwise we will not be able to tell whether the process shifted significantly, and the control chart will lose most of its value. Thus, when control charts are used appropriately, the theoretical *RFS* is exceeded in practice on average. Henceforth we'll assume that the *RFS* is associated with new data that is checked against existing control limits. The only acceptable exception is during the initial data collection, and even then it may be possible to use data dynamically to judge subsequent points, as we did for the *np* chart. We'll demonstrate this for variable charts later.

Unfortunately, Hillier's results do *not* imply that if we use twenty-five subgroups to evaluate the control limits for an $\bar{x}$ and R chart we will obtain *RFS* of 0.0040 and 0.0066 in the $\bar{x}$ and R portions. Not even if the underlying distribution is normal and under control! The *RFS* is a random variable with its own variation, and each chart yields a realization of this random variable. Hillier's results reflect the *average RFS*. For any particular chart, however, the variation is an important aspect that needs to be taken into account. This is our main objective here. We will show that the variation is large. For example, with 25 subgroups, looking at the $\bar{x}$ and the R charts together, any *RFS* between 0.05% and 7% is plausible (compare with about 1% as Hillier's results suggest). We will also show how to compute a lower bound for this risk, and demonstrate that the only way to reduce it is to use larger samples. Nonetheless, because our results are computationally intensive, and considering that there is no justification to use R charts in environments that can support computationally intensive applications, we'll concentrate on $\bar{x}$ and s charts. The analysis for $\bar{x}$ and R charts is similar, and they exhibit even *more* variation (because the $\bar{R}$ statistic is less efficient than $\bar{s}$).

We will make two simplifying assumptions in this section. The first is that the process is normal. By this assumption we are not claiming that this is necessarily true in practice, or that the results cannot be used for non-normal processes. Rather, it is intended that the results we achieve for the normal case serve as an example. To be on the safe side, we might want to treat the resulting diffidence as a lower bound on the real diffidence. If the diffidence seems too large under the normal distribution, then we shall assume that it will also be too large for an unknown distribution.

Our second assumption is that we know how to adjust the process. Recall that under this assumption we can draw the centerline of the $\bar{x}$ chart at the target, where the target is the best process adjustment we can achieve methodically. As a result of this assumption the diffidence we'll obtain will be understated for those cases where the centerline has to be estimated by data. Nonetheless, our main purpose is to show that there is more diffidence here than many sources suggested. If this is true under this simplified assumption, then it is certainly true without it: not knowing the exact location of the centerline only adds diffidence. We will remove this assumption later, to make possible the construction of valid diffidence charts with μ unknown. See also Trietsch and Bischak (1998).

8.4.1. *The Variation Associated with Estimating σ from Data*

Under the assumption that the process being controlled has a normal distribution $N(\mu, \sigma^2)$, the false signals from dispersion control charts and $\overline{x}$ charts are sometimes considered independent (AT&T, 1958, p. 156). This claim is theoretically flawed: it is true that each of our three estimates of dispersion (by $\overline{s}$, s^2, and $\overline{R}$) is not correlated with the mean, but independence of false signals does not follow. For instance, suppose one unit falls far from center by chance, then it may trigger both the dispersion and the mean chart, thus constituting dependence between the two false signals. Nonetheless, we'll assume independence, as a useful practical approximation. Hence, if we know the *RFS* of both these sources, denoted by RFS_D and $RFS_{\overline{x}}$, it is straightforward to find the combined *RFS*, i.e., $RFS_{D\&\overline{x}}$. The formula for the combined *RFS* is then

$$RFS_{D\&\overline{x}} = 1 - (1 - RFS_D)(1 - RFS_{\overline{x}}) \approx RFS_D + RFS_{\overline{x}}$$

where the approximation is valid if both elements are small.

Since the location of control limits is random, *RFS* is also random. The variation in RFS_D is induced by variation in $\hat{\sigma}$ (e.g., due to variation in $\overline{s}$). In general, the variation in $RFS_{\overline{x}}$ is induced by both variation in $\hat{\sigma}$ and variation of $\overline{\overline{x}}$. Thus the variation of $\hat{\sigma}$ induces *RFS* variation in both charts. Under our simplified assumptions we know how to adjust the process, so variation in $\overline{\overline{x}}$ is immaterial, and therefore the remaining variation in $RFS_{\overline{x}}$ is only a function of variation in $\hat{\sigma}$ (signals due to bad adjustment are not false). Thus, if we study the variation of $\hat{\sigma}$, we gain information that is useful to determine the variation of *RFS* for both dispersion charts and $\overline{x}$ charts. Furthermore, $RFS_{\overline{x}}$ and RFS_D are strongly positively correlated, i.e., they vary together (even if μ is not known).

We start our analysis with the dispersion chart, for two reasons: (i) the variation should always be checked first (AT&T, 1958); (ii) the dispersion chart, when based on $\pm 3\sigma_D$, generates higher *RFS* variability, so it is more important.

8.4.1.1. *RFS variation in s charts*

Let us devise $\pm 3\sigma$ limits for $\hat{\sigma}$, σ_L from below and σ_U from above. Technically, we'll do this in terms of σ_X, as if we know it (Section 8.5 derives similar limits by the process data alone). Our study of the variation of *RFS* will be based on calculating it for these two extreme values. Defining *limiting control limits*, $LCL_{s,L}$, $LCL_{s,U}$, $UCL_{s,L}$, and $UCL_{s,U}$, where L (U) denotes the use of σ_L (σ_U), we study the *RFS* associated with the set $LCL_{s,L}$ and $UCL_{s,L}$, and the set $LCL_{s,U}$ and $UCL_{s,U}$. The former will give us a high-end value for *RFS*, and the latter, a low-end. Thus we'll obtain a $\pm 3\sigma$ confidence interval for *RFS*. Since $LCL_s = B_3\overline{s}$, $UCL_s = B_4\overline{s}$, and $E(\overline{s}) = c_4\sigma_X$,

$$E(LCL_s) = B_3 c_4 \sigma_x; \quad E(UCL_s) = B_4 c_4 \sigma_x$$

and, since $\mathrm{Var}(\overline{s}) = \sigma_X^2 (1 - c_4^2)/m$,

$$\mathrm{Var}(LCL_s) = B_3^2 (1 - C_4^2)\frac{\sigma_x^2}{m}; \quad \mathrm{Var}(UCL_s) = B_4^2 (1 - C_4^2)\frac{\sigma_x^2}{m}$$

so the limits, $LCL_{s,L}$, $LCL_{s,U}$, $UCL_{s,L}$, and $UCL_{s,U}$ are given by

$$LCL_{s,L} = B_3 c_4 \sigma_x \left(1 - \frac{3\sqrt{1 - c_4^2}}{c_4\sqrt{m}}\right); \quad LCL_{s,U} = B_3 c_4 \sigma_x \left(1 + \frac{3\sqrt{1 - c_4^2}}{c_4\sqrt{m}}\right)$$

$$UCL_{s,L} = B_4 c_4 \sigma_x \left(1 - \frac{3\sqrt{1 - c_4^2}}{c_4\sqrt{m}}\right); \quad UCL_{s,U} = B_4 c_4 \sigma_x \left(1 + \frac{3\sqrt{1 - c_4^2}}{c_4\sqrt{m}}\right)$$

Let $\lambda_{s,L}$ and $\lambda_{s,U}$ denote the *RFS* associated with the *s* chart at the two extremes. λ is a function of the *CDF* of the distribution of *s*, and of the magnitude

$$\frac{3}{\sqrt{m}}\frac{\sqrt{1 - c_4^2}}{c_4}$$

and therefore, for any given *n*, λ is a function of $3/\sqrt{m}$. Table 8.1 reports λ values for $n=5$, and $m=25, 100, 400, 1600$, and ∞, where the last value is a limiting case where $\hat{\sigma} = \sigma_X$. The computations were based on the χ^2 distribution. Similar calculations may be performed for any *n* and *m*, but Table 1 is sufficient to provide some insight into the variation that's involved in the most popular selection of *n*. The values of *m* were chosen so that the standard deviation of $\hat{\sigma}$ is reduced by half successively; the first two are associated with the prevailing rule of thumb.

    With $m=25$ any RFS_s value between 0.013% and 5.105% is plausible. The ratio between these two probabilities is about 380. Many will agree that this is excessive. Moving to $m=100$ improves the results considerably, but the plausible range is still quite wide: 0.08% to 1.56%, with a ratio of 19.5. These ratios are reported in the table. The table also

m	$\lambda_{s,L}$	$\lambda_{s,U}$	$\lambda_{s,L}/\lambda_{s,U}$	$\lambda_{s,L}-\lambda_{s,U}$
25	0.05105	0.00013	380.26	0.05092
100	0.01560	0.00080	19.543	0.01480
400	0.00800	0.00181	4.4219	0.00619
1600	0.00562	0.00267	2.1029	0.00295
∞	0.00390	0.00390	1	0

Table 8.1

records an even more important magnitude, $\lambda_{s,L}-\lambda_{s,U}$, which is the probability of obtaining a diffident result as a (decreasing) function of m, when a process is in control. For $m=25$ this probability is a whopping 5%.

Returning to $\lambda_{s,L}/\lambda_{s,U}$, an interesting feature is that as we increase the sample size four folds, the ratio is reduced by the square root function, almost exactly. This can become useful for the purpose of interpolation, e.g., if we desire to find the ratio for some m that is not listed, or if we want to know how many subgroups are needed to sample to reduce the ratio to a given value. For example, suppose we have the ratio for some m_0, r_0 (e.g., for $m_0=100$, $r_0=19.543$), and we want to know the ratio for some other m, r_m, then

$$r_m \approx r_0^{\sqrt{m_0/m}} \tag{8.3}$$

and if we want to find m to reduce the ratio to a given value it's straightforward to find the correct power and deduce m from it.

8.4.1.2. RFS variation in $\overline{x}$ charts

Variation in $\hat{\sigma}$ causes variation in *RFS* not only in the dispersion chart, but also in the $\overline{x}$ chart. Since we assume we know the centerline, we can simply compare the *RFS* at the two extremes

$$\lambda_{\overline{x},L} = 2\,\Phi\!\left(-3\left(1-\frac{3\sqrt{1-c_4^2}}{c_4\sqrt{m}}\right)\right); \quad \lambda_{\overline{x},U} = 2\,\Phi\!\left(-3\left(1+\frac{3\sqrt{1-c_4^2}}{c_4\sqrt{m}}\right)\right)$$

where $\Phi(z)$ is the area under the standard normal to the left of z.

The results, for the same values of m we used before, are given in Table 8.2. Note that the ratio obeys the same rule as that of the dispersion chart, and therefore (8.3) is also applicable here.

m	$\lambda_{\bar{x},L}$	$\lambda_{\bar{x},U}$	$\lambda_{\bar{x},L}/\lambda_{\bar{x},U}$	$\lambda_{\bar{x},L}-\lambda_{\bar{x},U}$
25	0.01894	0.00026	73.166	0.01868
100	0.00751	0.00088	8.5442	0.00663
400	0.00456	0.00156	2.9227	0.00300
1600	0.00352	0.00206	1.7096	0.00146
∞	0.00270	0.00270	1	0

Table 8.2

8.4.1.3. *Combining the results for both charts*

Table 8.3 combines the results of Tables 8.1 and 8.2, to obtain the plausible range of $RFS_{s\&\bar{x}}$. At each extreme, we combine the elements from the two tables by using the independence assumption between the two signals. We can do this because RFS_s and $RFS_{\bar{x}}$ vary with $\hat{\sigma}$ (the $RFSs$ of the two charts are dependent; the signals, by assumption, are not). For $m=25$ and a process in control, almost 7% of the points are likely to be diffident. $m=100$ is a sizable improvement, only slightly over 2% will be diffident, but to reduce the range to less than 1% we require close to 400 subgroups. As for the ratio, it no longer follows the square root as closely as before.

m	λ_L	λ_U	λ_L/λ_U	$\lambda_L-\lambda_U$
25	0.06902	0.00039	176.97	0.06863
100	0.02299	0.00168	13.685	0.02131
400	0.01252	0.00337	3.7151	0.00915
1600	0.00912	0.00472	1.9322	0.00440
∞	0.00659	0.00659	1	0

Table 8.3

8.5. Diffidence Charts for Continuous Variables

In this section we discuss the construction of diffidence charts for continuous data. We'll still assume that the process distribution is normal, but we do not necessarily know how to adjust. As with attribute diffidence charts, we'll devise data-based $\pm 3\sigma$ limits for the control limits, and see how they behave as a function of the number of subgroups in the sample. In this section we'll assume that we are still collecting data, and the limits are recalculated continuously. We'll further assume that each data point is judged against the dynamic limits based on the *former* points, and, if deemed "in control," added to the sample for the purpose of adjudging the next points. Of course, it is permissible to update by batches, as we demonstrated in the case of the attribute diffidence chart: in this sense there is no difference between the two cases. Indeterminate points that we collect en route are either investigated or set aside until they can be adjudged by more data for final disposition. It is important, however, to include these points eventually *or* declare them out of control. To just ignore them for good will cause a bias because relatively high points will be excluded systematically. Furthermore, it is important to fix the control limits at some stage, or the control chart will continuously change with possible process changes (Nelson Funnel Rule 4, again).

But we start by demonstrating how the control limits themselves vary as we add more subgroups. When control charts are supported by computer programs, it is easy to update them continuously. But this does not necessarily imply that the measurements and charting have to be automatic -- it's enough to have a computer available while we establish the control chart.

8.5.1. *Dynamic Control Limits*

Let us look again at the example based on the triangular distribution that we discussed in Chapter 6 (Figures 6.6, 6.7). Recall that depending on the choice of the sample, and its size, the number of false signals varies considerably. This is a manifestation of the variation that we are studying in this chapter. Since the underlying process distribution is not normal, we cannot make any exact claims about the magnitude of *RFS* for the charts we'll construct. But this does not imply that we are barred from using such charts. As demonstrated in Chapter 6 and in Supplement 6.1, the results are quite likely to be good for the $\bar{x}$ chart, but the *s* chart is less likely to have good control limits. Nonetheless, the bias is actually small relative to the diffidence we study here, so this should not concern us too much. Be that as it may, Figure 8.5 shows a dynamic *s* chart based on the first 50 subgroups ($n=5$). $\bar{s}$ is calculated based on all the former *s* values, never including the current one. Thus, we can continually compare the current *s* to control limit(s) based on the former ones. Note that the first point has no control limits, since there are no *previous* points that can be used for this purpose. That is, we do not use trial charting.

This dynamic chart is *not* reliable for small *m*, and thus *not* recommended here. It's just a step on our path to study diffidence. For now, let us accept it at face value, and continue. Since all the points are in control, we proceed to create the $\bar{x}$ chart for the same process, under the same continuous updating scheme (Figure 8.6). The data for calculating the control limits is based on the continuously updated $\bar{\bar{x}}$ and the continuously updated $\bar{s}$, excluding the current point.

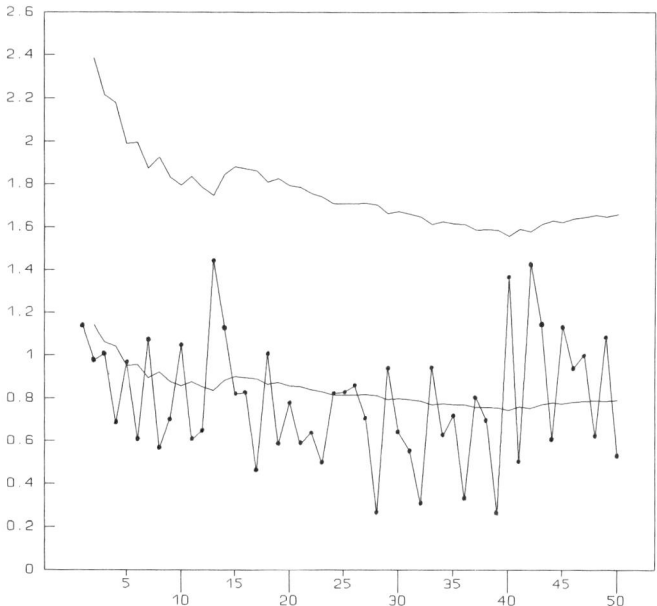

Fig. 8.5. A continuously updated *s* chart.

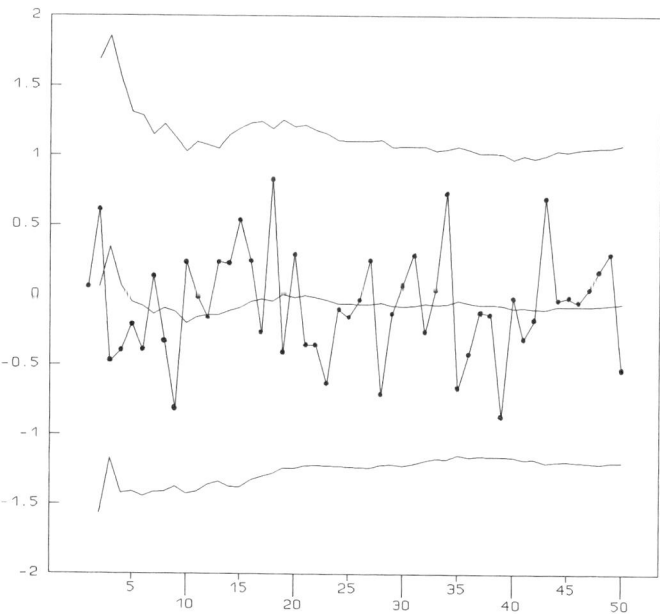

Fig. 8.6. A continuously updated $\overline{x}$ chart.

In both Figures 8.5 and 8.6 we may note that the behavior of the control limit is more erratic at the beginning (since they are based on smaller samples there), and that although they seem to stabilize, the control limits continue to fluctuate up and down throughout the figure. So we should not be too confident that we reached the correct values. To further clarify this issue, Figure 8.7 shows how the control limits of the s chart would look for four additional samples of 50, together with the one of Figure 8.5. Each line in the figure is an equally likely realization of a dynamic sequence of UCL_s estimates.

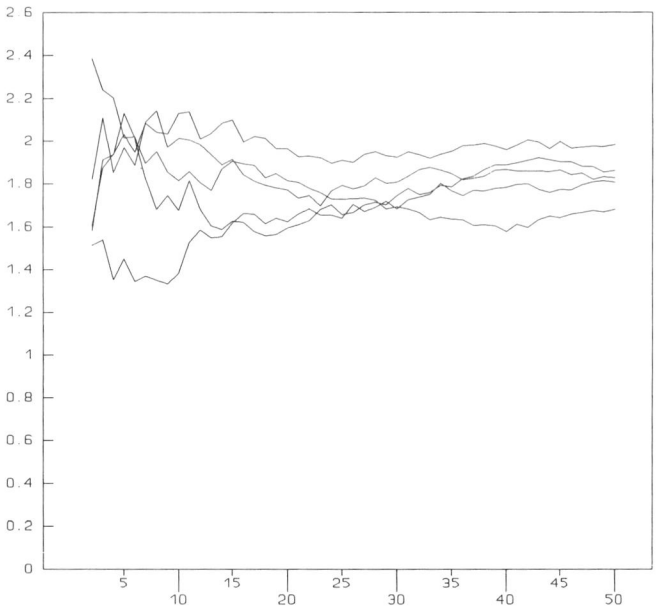

Fig. 8.7. Five random realizations of dynamically computed UCL_s values.

These five realizations were selected from a random process, without any attempt to find those that display more or less variation than others. If the picture looks a bit messy, it's because it's a realistic depiction of the variation involved in control chart estimation (except that the process here is *really* under control, while in reality even this is not certain). Even after sampling 50 subgroups $\bar{s}$ (and therefore UCL_s) does not stabilize yet, let alone after 25 subgroups. Each sequence looks progressively stable, because of the mechanism we utilize where the first points participate in all the subsequent averages, but these "stable" sequences have a long way to go until they will converge and stabilize near the true value.

A diffidence chart should show diffidence bands that are comparable to the range of variation we may expect in reality. First, let us show the limits that we might expect in this s chart, based on our knowledge of σ_X (recall that our results are based on a simulation of a process we know). At least for a normal distribution (which we assume, but do not have), this should provide a band wide enough to include most, if not all, of the sequences such as those given in Figure 8.7. Figure 8.8 depicts these limits, together with the sequences of Figure 8.5. One sequence is not fully contained within the limits. This may be due to chance, or a result of using normal-based factors with a right-triangular distribution. (Nonetheless, the overall estimate based on all 1000 subgroups is excellent -- $\hat{\sigma}_X = 0.955$, compared to the true $\sigma_X = 0.954$.)

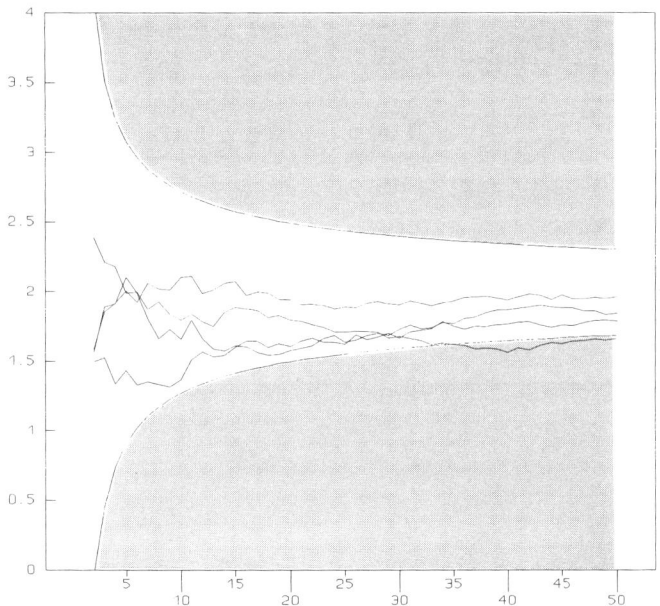

Fig. 8.8. Theoretical limits for the location of UCL_s (using the normal factors for a right-triangular distribution).

But in reality, we do not know the real process parameters. Therefore we must produce our diffidence chart by the data we collected, without assuming any prior knowledge of the process. The necessary theory is provided as follows.

8.5.2. Diffidence Charts for Dispersion

To devise diffidence limits based on data, we re-define our two limits on the real σ, σ_L and σ_U, to satisfy the following conditions:

♦ $\sigma_L < \hat{\sigma} < \sigma_U$

♦   For $\sigma = \sigma_L$, $\sigma + 3\sigma_\sigma = \hat{\sigma}$; similarly, for $\sigma = \sigma_U$, $\sigma - 3\sigma_\sigma = \hat{\sigma}$ (σ_σ is calculated for $\sigma = \sigma_L$ or $\sigma = \sigma_U$, as necessary).

For small m, σ_U may not exist, in which case we interpret it as unbounded. σ may assume any value between σ_L and σ_U (inclusive), and our realization $\hat{\sigma}$ would still be plausible. In contrast, for any potential σ value that is outside the segment $[\sigma_L, \sigma_U]$, $\hat{\sigma}$ would be an unlikely realization. Hence this segment is a confidence interval for σ. When we use $\overline{s}$ as our dispersion statistic, we have $\hat{\sigma} = \overline{s}/c_4$, and similar expressions for the other two dispersion statistics we consider in this book are given in Chapter 6. For $\overline{s}$, σ_L and σ_U can be computed by,

$$\sigma_L = \frac{\hat{\sigma}}{\left(1 + \dfrac{3\sqrt{1-c_4^2}}{c_4\sqrt{m}}\right)} ; \quad \sigma_U = \frac{\hat{\sigma}}{\left(1 - \dfrac{3\sqrt{1-c_4^2}}{c_4\sqrt{m}}\right)}$$

where if the denominator in the expression for σ_U is not positive we declare that limit unbounded. For instance, if $n=5$, then σ_U does not exist for $m=1$ because the distance from

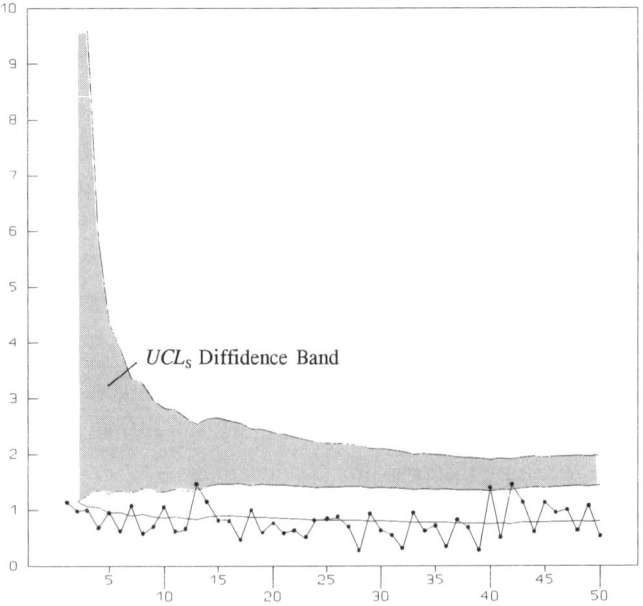

Fig. 8.9. A diffidence chart for s based on data.

the mean to 0 is less than 3 standard deviations. Operationally, this means that we suspect it might be huge.

To obtain diffidence limits for the s chart, we multiply σ_L and σ_U by B_3c_4 (which is zero in our example) and B_4c_4. Figure 8.9 depicts the results for our example (compare with Figure 8.5). A similar approach applies to other dispersion statistics that are covered in Chapter 6.

8.5.3. Diffidence Charts for $\overline{x}$

To construct a diffidence chart for $\overline{x}$ when we know μ (i.e., when we know how to adjust the process), we can utilize the same two limiting values, σ_L and σ_U that we found for the dispersion chart. We use σ_L and σ_U to develop limits $LCL_{\overline{x},L}$, $LCL_{\overline{x},U}$, $UCL_{\overline{x},L}$, and $UCL_{\overline{x},U}$, as follows,

$$LCL_{\overline{x},L} = \mu - \frac{3\,\sigma_L}{\sqrt{n}}; \quad LCL_{\overline{x},U} = \mu - \frac{3\,\sigma_U}{\sqrt{n}}$$

$$UCL_{\overline{x},L} = \mu + \frac{3\,\sigma_L}{\sqrt{n}}; \quad UCL_{\overline{x},U} = \mu + \frac{3\,\sigma_U}{\sqrt{n}}$$

But if we do not know μ, to construct a chart such as the one in Figure 8.10, we need to know the mean and the variance of LCL and UCL around their computed location at $\overline{\overline{x}} \pm 3\hat{\sigma}/\sqrt{n}$. The ideal location of the control limits is at $\mu \pm 3\sigma/\sqrt{n}$. Concentrating on UCL, It follows that the difference between the ideal location and the computed location is a random variable given by

$$\mu + 3\frac{\sigma}{\sqrt{n}} - \overline{\overline{x}} - 3\frac{\hat{\sigma}}{\sqrt{n}} = \mu - \overline{\overline{x}} + 3\frac{(\sigma - \hat{\sigma})}{\sqrt{n}} \tag{8.4}$$

By adding (8.4) to the computed location we obtain the correct location. Of course, this expression describes a random variable, but it is now clear that if we add and subtract 3 standard deviations of this expression to the computed UCL we'll obtain its valid $\pm 3\sigma$ confidence interval. A similar procedure is followed for LCL.[4]

In more detail, it is convenient to express (8.4) by the sum of two random variables, $G = \overline{\overline{x}} - \mu$ and $H = 3(\sigma - \hat{\sigma})/\sqrt{n}$. $E(G+H) = E(G) + E(H) = 0$ (because $\overline{x}$ is an unbiased estimator of μ, and $\hat{\sigma}$ is an unbiased estimator of σ), so it's appropriate to draw our limits

---

[4]The locations of $LCL_{\overline{x}}$ and $UCL_{\overline{x}}$ are dependent random variables, because deviations in $\overline{\overline{x}}$ effect them together. For the purpose of constructing a diffidence chart, this is not important. But it does cause sizable complexity if we want to estimate RFS at the two extremes, to measure its variation.

around the computed value of *UCL*. It can be shown that *G* and *H* are independent, and therefore the variance of their sum is the sum of their variances, i.e.,

$$Var(G + H) = \frac{\sigma_x^2}{n\,m} + \frac{9}{n}\frac{\sigma_x^2}{m}\frac{(1-c_4^2)}{c_4^2} = \frac{\sigma_x^2}{n\,m}\left(1 + \frac{9(1-c_4^2)}{c_4^2}\right)$$

Therefore, the standard deviation of (8.4) is given by

$$\frac{\sigma_x}{\sqrt{n\,m}}\sqrt{1 + \frac{9(1-c_4^2)}{c_4^2}}$$

Again, we look for σ_L and σ_U such that $\hat{\sigma}$ will be plausible *if and only if* σ_x is between them or coincides with one of them. This leads to

$$\sigma_L = \frac{\hat{\sigma}}{1 + \dfrac{3}{\sqrt{n\,m}}\sqrt{1 + \dfrac{9(1-c_4^2)}{c_4^2}}} \quad ; \quad \sigma_U = \frac{\hat{\sigma}}{1 - \dfrac{3}{\sqrt{n\,m}}\sqrt{1 + \dfrac{9(1-c_4^2)}{c_4^2}}}$$

where if the denominator is not positive the result is unbounded. For example, for $n=5$, we must have $m \geq 4$ to make the upper limit bounded at a finite value (compare with $m \geq 2$, which applies when μ is known). The practical implication is that (at least with $n=5$) it is

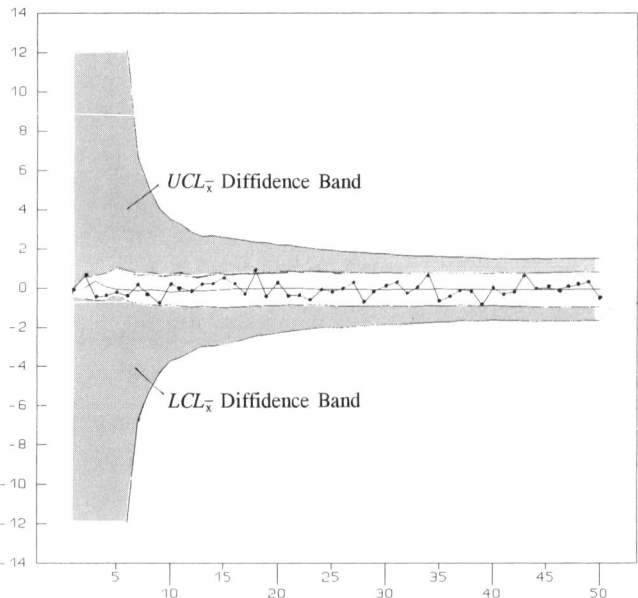

Fig. 8.10. A diffidence chart for $\overline{x}$ based on data.

practically impossible to identify out-of-control points with $m \leq 4$, or even $m=5$, at least not reliably. Any scheme that suggests otherwise -- e.g., Quesenberry (1991) -- is flawed.

As in the former case, we can then use σ_L and σ_U to develop limits LCL_L, LCL_U, UCL_L, and UCL_U,

$$LCL_{\bar{x},L} = \bar{\bar{x}} - \frac{3\,\sigma_L}{\sqrt{n}}; \quad LCL_{\bar{x},U} = \bar{\bar{x}} - \frac{3\,\sigma_U}{\sqrt{n}}$$

$$UCL_{\bar{x},L} = \bar{\bar{x}} + \frac{3\,\sigma_L}{\sqrt{n}}; \quad UCL_{\bar{x},U} = \bar{\bar{x}} + \frac{3\,\sigma_U}{\sqrt{n}}$$

Figure 8.10 depicts the results for our example (compare with Figure 8.6). In the figure, $LCL_{\bar{x},U}$ and $UCL_{\bar{x},U}$ for $m=5$ should be -164 and 164.67 (these values were suppressed for scaling reasons).

8.6. Diffidence and Pattern Tests

In Chapter 7 we introduced eight pattern tests (in addition to Shewhart's Criterion I). Of these eight tests, two (Tests 2 and 4a) are based on the centerline, and four (Tests 5, 6, 7, and 8) are based on zones whose definition presupposes knowledge of σ_X. Clearly, since we have to use $\hat{\sigma}$ to represent σ_X, the diffidence associated with $\hat{\sigma}$ is translated to diffidence

m	λ_L	λ_U	λ_L	λ_U
25	0.01237	0.00021	0.01037	0.00092
100	0.00518	0.00067	0.00611	0.00182
400	0.00323	0.00115	0.00460	0.00251
1600	0.00252	0.00151	0.00397	0.00293
∞	0.00195	0.00195	0.00342	0.00342
	Test 5		Test 6	

25	0.00025	0.00890	0.00913	0.00041
100	0.00085	0.00484	0.00463	0.00099
400	0.00141	0.00336	0.00322	0.00148
1600	0.00179	0.00276	0.00267	0.00181
∞	0.00224	0.00224	0.00220	0.00220
	Test 7		Test 8	

Table 8.4

in interpreting the results of these four tests. In general, if we remove the assumption that we know how to adjust the process, then Tests 2 and 4a also entail diffidence due to the use of data to estimate the centerline, although Test 4a is relatively robust. Tests 3 and 4 are the only ones that are not influenced by the control chart parameters at all, except in the sense that Test 3 is more likely to be activated *first* if the control limits are too far from center.

Similarly to the case with *RFS* due to Test 1, the *RFS* associated with the four tests is subject to variability because $\hat{\sigma}$ is a random variable. Table 8.4 -- similar to the one given by Trietsch and Hwang -- provides numerical results, in parallel to those of Tables 8.1 and 8.2. Note that Test 7's variation is negatively correlated with that of the other tests.

In principle there is no difficulty in devising diffidence charts with zones, so the idea of diffidence chart can also apply for the pattern tests. Readers are urged to try it, and see to what extent the diffidence zones mesh with each other for low *m* values.

8.7. Diffidence and Inaction are NOT Identical

By now, the readers should have acquired a healthy doze of skepticism about the power of control charts to detect special causes with a given *RFS*, even approximately. But this is not to say that control charts are worthless: even with very small samples (e.g., $m=20$), and thus very wide diffidence bands, there are strong arguments why control charts still have practical value. First, it may happen that the points will be strongly in or out of control, in which case we don't need more evidence. Even when that's not the case, diffidence should not cause inaction. To let it do so would be to make "perfect" the enemy of "good." In this section we argue in favor of using small samples when the alternative is either doing nothing or spending too much on collecting data. Even when we do collect much data, the arguments we present here are valid during the data collection period.

Our observations in this chapter, so far, were predicated on the behavior of a control chart devised with data that is in control. One problem that is associated with too little data is that the chart may not have power to discern points that are out of control. Wheeler (1995) comments that the worst that can happen is that the chart will not detect such a point; but if it does, in spite of the fact that the point was used to calculate the limits (and thus it is likely that the control limits will be inflated), then we can be confident that it is indeed out of control. In contrast, if we don't use the data at all, we'll certainly not identify the out of control situation. So we have nothing to lose. Although Wheeler's argument ignores the inflated probability of a false signal that we discussed in this chapter, it has merit when we take a wider perspective. Suppose we have, say, a hundred control charts, each based on small samples. The *RFS* associated with most of these charts will be close to the average value given by Hillier. Very few, if any, will give results as bad as those reported at the extremes of $\pm 3\sigma$ that we discussed in this chapter (the number of such extremes in a group of 100 is a Poisson variable with $\lambda = 0.27$). Thus, when we look at any single chart, it may be far from average, but over the large set of charts, most of the decisions we will make will be beneficial. Overall, then, we'll be much better off using charts based on few data than not using charts at all.

Also, reducing the width of the diffidence bands becomes progressively expensive as we collect more data. That is, as we spend more and more on reducing the diffidence, we obtain diminishing return on our investment. This implies that we'll have to accept some diffidence at some time. As argued above, the diffidence chart itself can support the decision whether to collect more data or not. An approximate way to interpret the data provided in Tables 8.1 through 8.4 is that the high probability listed (which is usually associated with σ_L) is the combined probability that a point that comes from a process in control will fall in a diffidence band or above. If we are willing to accept that probability, we have no problem. One thing we can do, as a policy, is to view indeterminate points as meriting investigation, but not a thorough one. In this sense they can serve as "caution limits," which some practitioners like to specify. Thus the response to an indeterminate point may be a cursory inspection of the process, and perhaps taking a couple of extracurricular subgroups as a further precaution.

Finally, to remove any lingering doubt, it is not seriously proposed here to collect hundreds of subgroups in an environment where control charts are calculated manually. This is a viable possibility only where crunching numbers is computerized. In an environment where control charts are calculated manually, the more data we collect the higher the chance that we'll make errors in recording and in computations, so the principle of uncertainty applies even if the process does not change.

In spite of rumors to the contrary, you CAN inspect quality into a product.

What we absolutely cannot prevent are errors, but we can keep those errors from generating defects. (Shiego Shingo)

Chapter 9
Inspection Theory

Inspections aim to find "unacceptable" items. Unacceptable items may be the result of common causes, when an incapable process is used, creating *out-of-tolerance* items. But defects are often the result of human error, broken tools, etc., creating *irregular* items. Irregular items need not necessarily be the result of special causes -- e.g., human error may be "part of the system" -- but they are preventable. Shingo (1986, Chapter 5), implicitly focusing on irregular items, distinguished three progressively beneficial types of inspections:

♦   *judgement inspections*, whose role is to discover defects after the fact

♦   *informative inspections*, whose role is to serve as a feedback mechanism to correct the process (e.g., control charts of output results, based on sampling)

♦   *source inspections*, whose role is to prevent defects before they happen by making sure that there are no mistakes in the process settings (sampling-based control charts of process inputs do *not* qualify as examples, but they may be better than charting outputs).

Poka-yoke -- Japanese for "error-proofing" -- is Shingo's method for keeping errors from generating defects. It involves a high level of source inspection, but at a very low per-unit cost. Some poka-yoke devices include "go/no-go" gauging that can reject out-of-tolerance parts. However, most poka-yoke's prevent errors that might have led to irregular results, or stop the process upon such errors, or alert workers to correct them. A poka-yoke device may involve cheap electronic sensors that detect occasionally recurrent abnormalities, or it may be as simple as a small dish on which a full kit of parts has to be collected before assembly so if one is forgotten, it will still be discovered in the dish, and the error can be corrected before causing significant harm down the line. Such a dish may have indentations to facilitate the kit collection and prevent mistakes there. Also, color codes could be used, especially when we have to distinguish between similar parts. Important though it is for QC, because poka-yoke is not statistical in nature, its details fall outside our scope. But studying poka-yoke principles and examples is a must for QC professionals. Shingo (1986) is the foremost comprehensive source for such a study; NKS/FM (1988) provided excellent examples. Chase and Stewart (1994) extended poka-yoke ideas to the design of service systems.

In this chapter our main concern is to inspect parts before assembly. As such, we are talking about judgement inspections that are also source inspections. They are judgement inspections with respect to the parts that are inspected, but they are source inspections with respect to the forthcoming assembly process. True, we should strive to minimize reliance on judgement inspections (moving to source inspection and error-proofing); yet, judgement inspections of parts before assembly, with or without poka-yoke devices, will have a role to play for the foreseeable future. With respect to meeting tolerances, there are two main types of such inspections. The first sorts items based on their acceptability as defined by meeting various specifications. The second is based on measuring critical dimensions and making a judgement whether their distribution is likely to be acceptable. The latter are justified only if the vendor did not use control charts for these dimensions in spite of their criticality to the customer. For this reason we do not discuss them further. Montgomery (1991) covered these plans, and listed other sources. The first type of inspection also applies to irregular items, and may be useful to prevent further damage. By nature, control charts are not an efficient tool to prevent irregularities (although they can monitor their incidence), so this type of inspection is necessary in addition to them.

9.1. Sampling Versus Deming's *kp* Rule

One of the first statistical quality control methods, developed at Bell Labs by Dodge and Romig in the twenties (Dodge and Romig, 1959), is using sampling-based inspections to decide whether to accept or reject product lots. That is, random samples are inspected, the number of defects is noted, and a decision is reached based on the count. Acceptance sampling plans include two limiting types: single and sequential samplings. In the former, known as (n, c) plans, we inspect a random sample of n items and if we find more than c defective items, we reject the whole lot. Alternatively, instead of rejecting we may inspect the lot on a 100% basis and weed out the defective items (a procedure called *rectifying inspection*). In the latter we count the defective items continually while sampling, and if the number of defects is demonstrably high we may reject the lot earlier; likewise, if the number of defects is demonstrably low, we may accept the lot earlier than under single sampling plans. Multiple sampling plans, most often *Double* sampling plans, are in between single and sequential sampling plans, and they involve a sequence of samples. After each sample we either accept, reject, or take another sample (unless the quota of samples had been reached); for example, in a double inspection plan we'll reach a final decision after the second sample at the latest, but we *may* do so after one if it provides strong evidence by itself.

Sampling inspections were adopted by the US War Department during WWII, and -- along with control charts -- they were taught widely to defense contractors. Even today, the US government specifies such plans in procurement contracts. To that end a well known military standard, MIL STD 105D, had been developed, and it is used widely not only for government contracts. In the early eighties, MIL STD 105D had been adapted, with small superficial changes, to a civilian standard, ANSI/ASQC Z1.4. (Similar standards exist for variable inspections.)

Several decades later, other experts, notably Deming and Shingo (independently and for somewhat different reasons), realized that sampling plans are usually futile.[1] Shingo opposed sampling from a practical point of view, observing that it often led to accepting high levels of defects simply because they were in statistical control, and thus "acceptable." Instead, Shingo promoted his proactive approach to quality improvement, including a source inspection function (poka-yoke). Deming grew to oppose acceptance sampling due to similar practical reasons and statistical considerations that hold for any lot size. But with the modern JIT-inspired preference for small lots, and with the modern TQ-inspired expectations for very low or even zero defect rates, the futility of sampling is compounded. That is because the samples are now likely to be almost as large as the whole lot, so they practically suggest a 100% inspection -- which, by definition, is no longer a sampling plan.

The general JIT paradigm calls for items to be so reliable that they can be accepted directly into the production process without inspection. But this does not imply that it is unthinkable in a JIT environment to inspect incoming materials. For example, during a class visit to the NUMMI plant in Fremont, CA, which is co-owned by GM and Toyota and managed by the latter, my students and I saw workers inspecting brake drums on a 100% basis. We were told that a large proportion of these drums were unusable, so they were shunted through a rectifying inspection. The plant alerted the vendor to correct the process,

---

[1]Deming readily admitted that he was party to the original drive to teach sampling inspection methods to industry, and indeed they were promoted in his earlier books.

and planned to stop the rectifying inspection as soon as better parts would start to arrive. Thus Toyota inspects items it knows are likely to cause problems before releasing them to the floor, but, as a rule, accepts the bulk of the parts directly into the production process. (Depending on the contract or the business environment, the vendor may have to send inspectors to the plant to perform the rectifying inspection, or pay for it.)

Instead of sampling, Deming supported a similar policy, called the *kp* rule. In the rule, *p* denotes the percent defective in the lot, based on a reliable estimate. $k = k_1/k_2$ where k_1 is the cost of inspecting a unit and k_2 is the cost of allowing a defective unit into the production system. The *kp* rule states that if *p* exceeds *k* we should inspect all items, but otherwise we should inspect none. The rule assumes that defective units will be replaced by good units when they are detected, whether by inspection or later on. Usually, we assume that we have a reliable estimate of *p*, a point we discuss in detail later. Also, usually, we assume that it will not be the external customer who will find the problem, but rather k_2 represents an internal failure cost. Deming stated this assumption as follows:

> We shall test the final product before it leaves the plant.
>
> If an incoming part is defective and goes into an assembly, the assembly will fail its test. If the incoming part is not defective, the assembly will not fail. (1986, p. 408.)

Note that this assumes that a defective part causes failure at the test, but Deming clarified this point later,

> A defective part is one that by definition will cause the assembly to fail. If a part declared defective at the start will not cause trouble down the line, or with the customer, then you have not yet defined what you mean by a defective part. The next step in this circumstance would be to examine the test method that declares a part to be defective or not defective.
>
> There are, of course, examples where a defect in an incoming part can be discovered in the factory only at great expense, and must be left for the customer to discover, often after some months or years. These are commonly called latent defects. Chromium plate is one example. The best solution to this problem is to avoid it by improving the process. This is also the solution to the problem of a destructive test, a test that destroys the item.

In Chapter 3 we noted that when we use the quadratic loss function the loss involved with accepting out-of-tolerance parts increases with the deviation. Thus, the potential savings by a 100% inspection is a function of the process variation and the loss function. Our focus now, however, is on irregular parts, which cause a constant damage unless we weed them by inspection. Deming's kp rule fits here: it applies only to irregular items. Although Deming did not distinguish explicitly between the two, the rule assumes a step loss function and is thus not applicable to out-of-tolerance items.

Often, the cost of letting the customer discover defects may be exorbitant. Therefore, if we cannot trust our production system to unearth the problem before shipping, we might be well-advised to assess k_2 at a very high value, often leading to 100% inspection. Some estimates show, for a range of industries, a ratio of 2,000 to 100,000 between the cost of fixing a problem at the source and the cost/loss of allowing it to cause an external failure in the field (Garvin, 1990). Obviously this means that k_2 may be huge, unless we perform a reliable test before delivery, as Deming suggested. In contrast, poka-yoke -- which is equivalent to 100% inspection -- satisfies the kp rule by reducing k_1 almost to zero.

A major question we need to answer before applying the kp rule is how to obtain a reliable estimate of p. Deming assumed that the original production process would be documented by a process control chart, and therefore we would have a long-term estimate of p. As long as the original production process was in statistical control, and we have information about the percent defective it creates on average when in control, we have all we need to know about p. In this connection, we should note that a control chart is nothing more than inspection of the behavior of processes by samples. It is true that a control chart also provides valuable information about the behavior of a process over time, but we still assume that all the items produced during a particular period are similar to the ones we sample at that period. Indeed, ideally, control charting should stop when the process becomes mature enough to be really predictable (i.e., the likelihood that it will be severely out of control is so minute that it becomes a waste to monitor against it). Poka-yoke, in contrast, is a method that allows cheap inspection of 100% of the items, so it fits the kp rule as well.

In this chapter we explain more formally why, when the kp rule's assumptions are met, sampling inspection is useless. We then discuss what we can do when the assumptions are not met. In general, sampling inspections may be necessary, at least preliminarily, when we do not know p; e.g., when we find out that the process was not in control, but we are not yet willing to scrap the whole shipment, or when the supplier is new and we do not yet know first-hand what is the quality-of-conformance of her products. Under such circumstances, we may utilize some type of sampling plan simply to estimate p, or at least determine whether p is above or below k. If we determine that p is below k, we can accept the lot into our system; otherwise, we should perform a 100% inspection, or, when that is infeasible or uneconomical to do, discard the whole lot. But if we need sampling to estimate

p, we have to discuss various sampling methods. We present several well-known methods for this purpose, and a new heuristic designed to reduce the total cost of sampling and the subsequent consequences.

When 100% inspection would otherwise be indicated but it is impossible because the testing is destructive, sampling is mandatory (Deming's solution -- improving the process -- rarely applies in the short term). In this case the idea is to verify that p is below the threshold over which we're better off scrapping the whole shipment. For example, think about products such as bombs. A bomb that does not detonate when it reaches the target represents a huge waste (depending on your point of view, that is). A bomb that detonates when it shouldn't is potentially even more damaging, but for simplicity let's concentrate on the requirement that it detonates when and where it has to.[2] The value of the bomb itself is but a minor fraction of this waste. Much more important is the value of bringing it to the target, and here we're talking about large investments in blood, sweat and materials, in that order. If we know that our technology is capable of producing bombs that detonate 90% of the time, we might decide that if a sampling plan reveals that it is likely only 85% or less of a particular shipment will detonate, we should return that shipment (to salvage raw materials, if possible). The value of the 5% duds we avoid in the field probably far outweighs the value of the 85% good bombs we discard. And we might not consider the sampling cost too high either. In contrast, we should accept lots that show evidence that 10% of the bombs will be duds. The technical jargon for this is that our *AQL* (accepted quality level) is 10%. Why accept 10% defective rate? Because, in spite of slogans such as "The only accepted quality level is zero," 10% is the best that the producer can deliver consistently with the present technology and the present process. (This does not negate the need to continually seek ways to decrease the *AQL* towards 0, however.)

9.1.1. *The Connection Between Inspection and Management By Constraints (MBC)*

MBC is a management approach, promoted by Goldratt (1990), that calls for concentrating attention on binding system constraints, and subjugating any resource that is not a binding constraint to the needs of the binding constraints. In economic terms, the

---

[2]Next to the USS Arizona memorial site in Pearl Harbor, detailed plaques list all the US Navy submarines that were lost during WWII in the Pacific Ocean, and give the known or suspected causes. A surprisingly high percentage are thought to have perished due to their own torpedoes having turned around unexpectedly. Torpedoes that detonated in the holds were equally lethal. Torpedoes that miss or don't detonate reveal the position of the submarine and open her to a counterattack. In short, it's a sad monument to the quality costs associated with defective weapon systems. But war is one big quality problem any way we look at it.

opportunity cost of non-binding constraints is zero, but that of the binding constraints [together] represents the whole system. MBC attempts to organize the production flow in such a manner that the binding constraints, or bottlenecks, will always be kept busily creating as much added value as possible, while other resources are activated to support that need by feeding the bottlenecks on time.

Inspection is also part of the production flow, especially when it is performed on items in progress on a 100% basis, or as part of control charting a process. Given that we decide that we need to inspect some of our processes, and inspect some of our work in process on a 100% basis (as per the kp rule), the question is where exactly in the production flow should we perform these inspections. When we treat this issue from an MBC point of view it becomes obvious that inspections should also serve the needs of the system's binding constraints (*bottlenecks*). Thus, they should help prevent wasting bottleneck time on items that are already defective, or permanently attaching defective items to good output of such bottlenecks. The same logic reveals that process control is more important on bottlenecks to prevent scrapping their output or the need for rework on them. Likewise, process control, in addition to the need to apply it to critical quality measurements at their source in general, is doubly important on resources that receive the output of bottlenecks as input and that are liable to damage them. Here we have to distinguish between rework and scrapping. If we can rework an item without spending bottleneck time on it any more, the situation is better than if we have to actually discard part of the bottleneck output. Allowing a process to create scrap on such bottlenecks wastes their precious time as well as materials. Allowing a process to create rework on a bottleneck is almost equally abominable. This suggests that inspections should concentrate on preventing these types of damages. For instance, before feeding a bottleneck with a raw material, we should be confident that it is not defective. Likewise, we do not want to risk running the bottleneck when it is out of adjustment, so we might want to be even more careful with bottleneck setups (but not to such an extent that it will cost us a lot of time -- the five/ten rule is handy here). And we may want to inspect carefully any subassembly that we plan to attach permanently to an item that consumed bottleneck time. In short, when evaluating k_2, we should consider the true opportunity costs.

When true economic costs are considered, there is no guarantee that k_1 will be smaller than k_2. Although this rarely happens, k_1 can be larger than k_2, leading to $k > 1$. Our decision then is simple: we should not inspect ($k > p$). One such example from my own experience occurred at Naval Air Depot (NADEP) Alameda, at a shop where jet engines were refurbished. The first step in the refurbishing process involved non-destructive testing (NDT) -- a form of inspection utilizing a fluorescent fluid that highlights cracks -- and cleaning (including cleaning the fluorescent fluid after NDT). But it so happened that both

NDT and cleaning were bottlenecks. Although some of these inspections were necessary for flight safety, and could not be avoided (to see why, apply the *kp* rule, taking into account that k_2 -- the cost of shipping a defective item and thus risking personnel -- is immense), but other NDT inspections were designed merely to avoid machining condemned parts. The reasoning was that such machining would be wasteful (which is true). But machining was not a bottleneck! Therefore, the waste involved in machining unnecessarily was not important for global performance, while the bottleneck in NDT and cleaning actually limited the system's throughput. Thus, the *kp* rule showed that many NDT operations should be eliminated. This elimination increased throughput and reduced lead-time at a negative economic cost.[3]

9.2. General Inspection Issues

Before we embark on the technical issues of this chapter, we should devote some attention to the general pitfalls associated with sampling, and to the foibles of human inspection systems. Later, we generally ignore these problems, but it's important to bear in mind that they do exist. (One of the advantages of poka-yoke is that it can help bypass such foibles.)

In this chapter we discuss sampling and inspections. It is important that we clarify some underlying issues that relate to these subjects. In general, sampling may be absolutely necessary for the enumerative study of a large population (and by population we may describe the constituents of any system, e.g., voters, iron ingots, widgets, etc.), when it is physically impossible to inspect the whole population. This can be due either to its sheer size, or because the testing itself is destructive. At other times, it may be possible and advisable to inspect a population completely. When we choose to sample, however, it is important to sample in a way that leads to unbiased results. This implies, usually, that random sampling should be utilized. In this section we elaborate on the meaning of "random" in this connection. Next, we also have to recognize that one must be very careful in organizing the inspection function, especially with human inspectors, operating in human systems with all the complexities they entail. And the first question is *who* should inspect work. This section discusses these issues in some detail.

---

[3]As the load on the inspection station is reduced, however, the load on the machining department is increased, because of occasional machining of defective items and because more units can be inducted (since we elevated a constraint by eliminating some inspections). This implies that machining *may* emerge as a new bottleneck. The next step would then be to balance the load of inspection with the load of machining by inspecting just enough items, preferably where *p/k* is largest. Such balancing will maximize the throughput of the system.

9.2.1. *On the Mechanics of Random Sampling*

One of the interesting lessons from Deming's red beads experiment (Chapter 5), is that although 20% of the beads were red, the long-term average number of defective items (red beads) was significantly different. This, Deming observed, is an example of *mechanical sampling,* which is not identical to what we usually mean when we speak of random sampling. Red beads are physically different from white beads: they have a slightly different diameter and a different texture, and they interact slightly differently with the paddle. In Deming's experience, various paddles and beads gave long term average results of 11.3, 9.6, 9.2, and 9.4 (out of 50), and they were all significantly different from the theoretical expected number: 10. Had we used Deming's experiments to estimate the number or proportion of red beads in the container, then, we would be led to significant errors. An industrial example of mechanical sampling may occur when ore is tested to determine its value. Sometimes samples are taken only from the top of the heap, where it's easy to do. More conscientious workers may try to sample, during the unloading operation, from the top, middle, and bottom, but this may still fall short of representing the whole heap without bias. What we must do is use random numbers to determine where to sample, and they should give an equal chance to each volume element in the heap. Technically, a good way to do this is to stop the conveyor belt at random times (determined by random numbers) and sample the ore at a predetermined location. Similarly, to select boxes from a shipment, pick them at random times during the unloading of the truck (which will work if the unloading is done at a fairly consistent rate).

Deming (1993, pp. 170-172) recites a case from a Japanese Steel company that switched from sampling iron ore from the top of the heap to true random sampling. Experimentation showed that the old method exaggerated the proportion of the iron in four cases out of four, by 2% to 10%. Thus, under the old method the steel company was overpaying by about 6% (although a larger sample is needed to make such a statement formally). Deming claimed that the Japanese learned the difference between mechanical sampling and random sampling after seeing his red beads experiment. New sampling standards for ore and other bulk materials were then developed based on similar principles.

A related issue is the use of polling in consumer market research (and political market research). While sampling ore to determine its concentration is an enumerative study where we wish to ascertain the properties of a particular population at the present time, polling is *not* an enumerative study. Usually we try to predict future actions based on it, and we don't really care about the present. Statistical tests are not applicable to the results of polling, at least not in terms of prediction (Supplement 5). But polling is also subject to the problem of bias. First and foremost, it involves self-selection: the respondents make a choice whether to cooperate. Second, it is often analogous to mechanical sampling. For instance, the polls before the Truman-Dewey election in 1948 were so compelling that prestigious newspapers declared Dewey as the winner. What turned out was that the polls were limited to people with phones, and at that time many Truman voters did not have phones! (Even today if we'd let the disenfranchised vote, and if they would do so, then polling by phone would have a strong built-in bias.)

What can we do when the population that is easy to poll is not fully representative of the whole universe? It is possible to represent all groups equally, but this is likely to lead to great expense, since members of some groups are more expensive to poll than others. Instead, the tool of choice here is *stratification*. We stratify the population to sub-populations -- e.g., with and without phones -- and poll each sub-population separately. The final results are calculated by a weighted average of the sub-population results. The advantage of this technique is that it allows determining the size of the sample for each sub-population separately, and thus improving the quality of the final result for a given budget. In our example we'd poll much fewer people without phones, because they were still a minority and because it is more expensive to poll them, but nonetheless we'd take their influence into account explicitly, and the result would be much better. In general, such schemes call for concentrating more resources on polling large groups that are easy to reach, but *not* to the total exclusion of the others. For more details see Cochran (1977).

In general, polling and other sampling is used to find out data about a population that exhibits diversity. At the other extreme, we find the homogeneous mixture, which is quite prevalent in the production of beverages and some other chemicals. When our product is such a homogeneous mixture, it's enough to take one sample, and it does not matter whether it's from the top of the vat, the middle, or the bottom. So, unless one pursues joy in work by sampling a particular vintage more than once, one sample is enough to represent the whole lot.

9.2.2. *Who Should Perform Inspections?*

As far as possible, the modern paradigm calls for workers to inspect their own work. That is, internal vendors are responsible for conformance. This sends a clear message that their job is to produce good items, that they are trusted to do so, and that they will be given the necessary tools. Furthermore, by such self-inspection workers have ample opportunities to learn about the types of defects that occur, which supports the real purpose of inspection: to help improve the process (Deming's Point 3). The next best choice for inspection is by the internal customer. Here a worker inspects the input before proceeding with his own production. Since he wants to produce good items, he has the necessary incentive to make sure that the inputs are acceptable. Professional inspection is the last choice, since it takes the responsibility completely away from the workers, and often creates adversary relationships between line workers and inspectors.

Nonetheless, assemblies often have to be inspected by dedicated inspectors: they may be defective in spite of having no single defect in them. This often happens due to tolerance stack: all parts may be within tolerance, and the tolerances may all be economical, and yet, by the luck of the draw, the parts can be incompatible. Today, for instance, even the leading manufacturers of automobiles and engines test each assembly, and tolerance stack is the main reason they have to do so.[4] But no single worker can prevent, or even monitor, the tolerance stack of an assembly in which his own work only plays a minor part. Such problems are not counted against any individual, however, so it should not cause adversity between line workers and inspectors.

Another important role for professional inspectors is to support workers in control charting processes. In this role the inspectors act as coaches and assistants. Note that during control charting we tend to use small batches which are less likely to lead to inspection errors due to sheer boredom. This has to do with our next subject, the reliability of inspection.

9.2.3. On the Reliability of Human Inspection Systems

Generally, in the other sections of this chapter, we assume that 100% inspection is capable of detecting 100% of all defects. In practice, when the inspection is done by humans, there is a significant chance that defects will be missed. A 20% miss rate is considered average by some experts. Deming cited miss rates of up to 50% in some cases. Furthermore, there is a significant probability that good items will be declared defective by error. Part of the problem has to do with lack of good operational definition of acceptable conformance. But the major part of the problem has to do with the "F Test," which follows. It is concerned with counting the number of times the letter "F" (capital or lower-case) appears in a given paragraph. For instance, scan the text in Figure 9.1, and count the F's. Do it just once -- most inspectors do not inspect twice. Or do it several times and see if you obtain a consistent result.

Even if you passed the F test personally, most people miss an f or two first time round, and some see f's where none exist. (I used a computer count -- because an error would be very undesirable here -- but later it took me three trials to find them all.) The point

---

[4]One of the justifications for the use of the quadratic loss function is that the likelihood of tolerance stack problems increases with the individual deviations of the parts.

When people try to count the number of f's within a text such as this one, the letters often look like a lot of buzzing insects, and it is very difficult not to err. For instance, the number of f's here is supposed to be fifteen, oops, that should be seventeen. If that's the number of f's you count (first time through, that is), congratulate yourself on belonging to a talented minority of the population.

Fig. 9.1. The F test.

is not whether a particular person got the number right the first time or not, but rather that humans make errors, especially when tasked with highly repetitive and mindless jobs. Therefore, it should not be surprising that human inspectors err too.

An especially pernicious human problem occurs when inspection systems are designed with redundancies for safety, i.e., when two or more inspectors are supposed to verify conformance. On the face of it, redundancy may look like a good solution to the problem of human error. Indeed, such redundancies are often conducive to reliability in electro/mechanical systems. But they act as "fixes that fail" when the redundant elements are humans -- unless the system is designed and managed very carefully. What happens is that some inspectors feel that others will find the defects, so they do not try very hard. Others feel that it would be embarrassing if they were the only ones to find a problem, so they refrain from pointing out defects that they think the others are likely to miss. (Deming used to say that he would not dare take a prescription that was inspected by two pharmacists.)

This problem can be solved in two ways: (i) improve the process, so we won't need the extra inspector; (ii) have one inspector *personally and alone* responsible for the results, and have two or more other inspectors reporting to him independently of each other. If the responsible inspector sees that the reports agree, and if he trusts his assistants, he may check with less care than if the reports differ. Also, if his experience shows that he can't trust his assistants, he is in a position to do something about it. This, in turn, makes each assistant -- personally and alone -- responsible for his work. In other words, as Deming might put it, they all have jobs.

Errors in clerical work are sometimes very expensive. For financial institutions, especially, computation errors are very expensive both in terms of money and customer confidence. But it is almost pointless to use inspectors to check the work: they might miss up to 50% of the errors. Far better to have the whole work done twice, completely independently, and then compare the results (preferably by a computer). Two points need to be stressed here. First, if the documents we work from are not clear (a quality defect), it is essential that the clerks be trained to stop the processing and verify the data. It is also important to go back to the source so that people there can monitor the number of times that their customer has a problem with their input, and, perhaps, improve their process. Second, if indeed the source is good, the probability of an error following two independent processes and a reliable (computerized) comparison is much lower than the product of the individual probabilities of error. The second point justifies some elaboration, as follows.

Suppose two clerks enter data from the same source into a computer, or two engineers use the same data for manual calculations. Let us assume that the probability of error of each is p, and let $q=1-p$. There is a probability of q^2 that both will come up with the same correct answer; a probability of $2pq$ that one will err, in which case our computerized check will reveal the discrepancy; and a probability of p^2 that both will err. It may seem, then, that our risk of an undetected discrepancy is p^2. But it is highly unlikely for two independent humans, *working with reliable and clear data,* to reach an exactly identical erroneous result. Almost always, their errors will be different from each other, and thus subject to detection by the comparison step. So our risk is much below p^2. Incidentally, the fact that two humans working independently rarely make the exact same error often reveals cheating in exams. If one cheats, one should be very careful who one collaborates with.

9.3. More on the kp Rule

To gain a better idea of the risks involved in making the wrong decision whether to accept or reject a lot, let us investigate the loss function associated with this decision. Generally, unless stated otherwise, we assume that rejected lots are subject to rectifying inspection, i.e., we inspect them one by one, accept the good ones, and replace the bad ones by good ones (which the vendor is obligated to supply). In some cases, however, rejection may imply returning the shipment or even destroying it, depending on the economics involved and the contract with the vendor. This would be automatically applicable, for instance, when the inspection is destructive.

First, let us investigate a special case: $p=k$. Assume that we decide to reject the hypothesis that the lot is good enough to be accepted as it is, and therefore, we inspect the items one by one at a cost of k_1 per unit. If there are N items in the lot, this will cost us $N \cdot k_1$ to do. On top of that, we'll have to induct additional items as required to replace the defective items we may find, *but note that we'll have to do that, sooner or later, with or without inspection. Therefore, the cost of replacing the bad items is totally immaterial to our decisions.* Next, assume that we decide to accept the lot into production without inspection. The result is that, on average, we will find $N \cdot p = N \cdot k$ defective items down the road, and our cost per item will be k_2. Thus, our expected cost for the whole lot will be

$N \cdot k \cdot k_2 = N \cdot (k_1/k_2) \cdot k_2 = N \cdot k_1$. Our cost, then, is the same regardless of our decision: $N \cdot k_1$ plus the hassle cost of replacing the bad items.

Suppose now that we want to measure our loss due to making the wrong decision at the point where $p = k$. But there is *no* wrong decision here: both decisions are equally good. We can say, then, that the loss due to the wrong decision at $p = k$ is 0. In general, we measure the loss associated with making the wrong decision relative to the cost of making the right decision, so a loss of zero does not imply a cost of nonconformance of zero -- just that we cannot reduce it by changing the decision.

Now suppose the fraction defective is $k \cdot (1 - x)$, where x is a positive real value between zero and one. The right decision is to accept the lot without inspection. The cost involved is $N \cdot k \cdot (1 - x) k_2 = N \cdot k_1 \cdot (1 - x)$. The wrong decision, to inspect 100%, would cost $N \cdot k_1$. Thus we lose $N \cdot k_1 \cdot x$ by making the wrong decision. Looking at the other side, suppose $p = k \cdot (1 + x)$, where x is a positive real value between zero and $(1/k) - 1$. The right decision is to inspect 100%, at a cost of $N \cdot k_1$. Accepting this lot without inspection will impart a cost of $N \cdot k \cdot (1 + x) k_2 = N \cdot k_1 \cdot (1 + x)$, thus causing a loss of $N \cdot k_1 \cdot x$. We see that by moving an absolute value of $x \cdot k$ along the p-axis the loss increases by $N \cdot k_1 \cdot x$, so the absolute slope (i.e., the directed derivative) is $N \cdot k_1 \cdot x/(k \cdot x) = N \cdot k_1/k = N \cdot k_1/(k_1/k_2) = N \cdot k_2$. Thus our loss function is

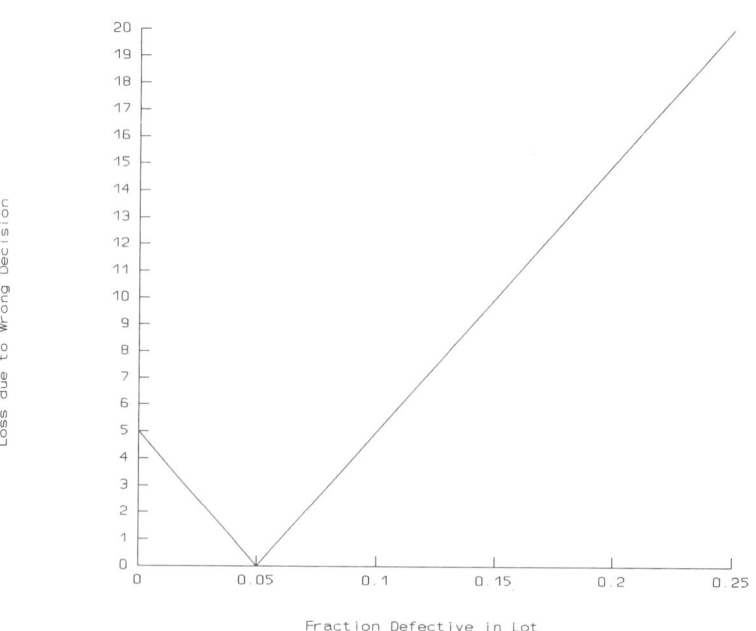

Fig. 9.2. Loss function due to wrong decision with $k = 0.05$.

$$L(p) = \begin{cases} (k-p)\cdot N\cdot k_2; & p<k \text{ and we inspect one by one} \\ (p-k)\cdot N\cdot k_2; & p>k \text{ and we do not inspect} \end{cases}$$

Since k_2 may be very large, the absolute value of the slope can be steep. Thus, we have a strong motivation not to err by much. Because the derivative of $L(p)$ has a discontinuity (at $p=k$), the loss near the minimum is more sensitive to small errors than that of the quadratic loss function, but it is less sensitive to large errors. Figure 9.2 depicts this loss function. Although the function is symmetric near k, the loss to the right is potentially higher. To the left, the maximal loss is $N\cdot k_1$ and to the left it is $N\cdot k_2$, which is almost always larger.

9.4. When Sampling is Not Futile

Suppose we know that only 90% of the lots our vendor sends us are good enough to accept as is: the bad lots cause serious loss and disruption if accepted into production as is. Had we known which type of lot had just arrived, we would either accept it as is (when good) or subject it to a rectifying inspection (when bad). When such diversity between lots exists, it may be possible to sort the lots to "good" and "bad" approximately, with the aid of a relatively small sample; e.g., we may be able to sort 95% of the good lots to the "good" pile and 90% of the bad lots to the "bad" pile. If it is economical to accept a small fraction of bad lots as is, then, we may be better off than before: instead of 90% to 10% our ratio will now be about 99% to 1%. We would rarely accept bad lots into production and we will rarely subject good lots to a full rectifying inspection. Our total cost can be much lower than by either accepting all lots (good and bad) or by inspecting all items in all lots. Alternatively, sampling is also useful when instead of rectifying inspections we simply discard suspect lots. In this case there is no alternative in the short term (until the production processes can be improved). In contrast, Deming's kp rule assumes a different scenario, where all lots come from the same population.

So, for sampling to be of value we must anticipate more than one kind of incoming lots, and we must assume that our policy with regard to the different kinds would not be identical (i.e., the percent defective in good lots must be below k and in bad lots it must either be above k or suspected to be above k). For instance, suppose that some lots come from processes that are in statistical control and produce acceptable products, but others come from processes that are out of control, and may produce more unacceptable products. Sampling plans can help sort the lots after the fact into two groups that are correlated with the real conformance they belong to. In conclusion, sampling is appropriate and possible if (i) there is a difference that sampling can detect with high probability; (ii) there is a large potential savings by accepting one population without further ado, and rejecting the other. We may also add that sampling is appropriate for the customer when there is no way to sort the lots at the source. For instance, in the case of statistical control, the vendor could and should have done the sorting upon evidence of lack of control.

The crux of the matter is that sampling is good for one purpose and one purpose only: estimating p -- the percent defective in the lot. A sample has no information beyond its size and the percent defective in it. All we can deduce from that information is an estimate of p, and the likelihood of error (a large lot provides more protection against error than a small one). Alternatively, we can present such estimates by an inequality, such as: $p > k$ with some high probability. By the time inspection is contemplated, however, we no longer know the exact sequence of production, so information about the behavior of the process over time is not available, and the count of defects is all we can get. (This is where a control chart is more informative, retaining the temporal dimension of the data.)

With this background let us discuss important cases where sampling is futile. For our discussion it suffices to assume a single sampling (n, c) plan, such that if and only if c or less items out of n are defective, the lot is accepted. If $c+1$ or more items are defective, the lot is inspected on a 100% basis, returned, or discarded. Note that $c=0$ is a viable choice, in which case we can reject upon the first defective item we find in the sample.

There are three cases we need to discuss here. The first case is when all (or the vast majority of) the lots we received from the same source in the past fell below k. We may then assume that $p < k$ again, and accept the lot without rectifying inspection. The second case is similar, but now all the lots fall above k, and our decision is clear again: inspect all items. Thus, in the first two cases the information we may expect to obtain by the inspection is useless in terms of changing our decision. And we should not invest any resources in obtaining information that is not necessary for decisions.

For our third case, suppose now that the process that creates the product is under statistical control, and therefore we have documented evidence about p. The question then is, What do we need to sample for? We already know p, so there is absolutely no point in sampling. We can simply employ the kp rule to determine whether to accept the lot or inspect 100%. Note that if p is not acceptable at all, we would not do business with this supplier. Therefore we should not return the shipment. In general, shipments may only be returned upon evidence that they are not as good as the contract calls for or not as good as they should be with the given process. Also, the parties should not contract for a level of conformance that they know cannot be delivered. If they do, and they utilize sampling inspection to accept or reject lots, they are simply entering into a complexity ridden lottery system.

There are two standard objections to this observation: one is misleading but the other has some merit (Milligan, 1991). The first is that p is only the *average* fraction defective, and we may have an especially good or especially bad lot on our hands, which sampling may reveal. This objection is based on a misunderstanding about what statistical control implies. Statistical control implies that there is no special cause that acts on all items, but rather each item is conforming or nonconforming as a result of many small independent influences. Therefore, *the probability the next item will be defective is independent of the condition of the present item.* With such independence, it follows that the number of defective items in the remainder is independent of the number of defective items in the sample. Note now that if our production process includes persistent long term autocorrelation, it does not conform to the definition of statistical control, at least not as operationally defined by Shewhart control charts. In this case, and indeed whenever the lot was not produced under statistical control, sampling may be useful (unless one of the first conditions apply and we can predict with confidence that p is below or above k in spite of the problem). The second objection is that the process might have been out of control and the vendor did not inform us. If the process is out of control, we may need to sample in order to estimate p, and make a decision about the remainder. In general, vendees that base acceptance decisions on control charting at the source require to see the control charts so they should know whether the process was in control. But such charts have been known to be falsified. This raises an issue of trust. If we do not trust our supplier then we really cannot tell whether the process was in control or not, and what defective fraction the process creates when in control. In such a case, at least until we may gain enough experience with the supplier, we may consider p to be unknown. One relevant question is whether we really must do business with suppliers that we do not trust. Note that if Deming's Point 4 is ignored, and we change suppliers frequently in a never-ending chase for a cheaper price, it is not likely that we will be able to trust them. Under such a defective system, sampling may be called for. And sampling may be called for if we have evidence that the production process was indeed out of control during the production of the lot. This should, ideally, be done by the producer, since he is responsible for the consequences of allowing a process to run out of control. (An out of control process does not yet imply that the lot should be rejected. It may be more wasteful to reject than to accept.) But as long as p is in control it's enough to know the average in order to make the decision based on the kp rule. In the long run, even though sometimes we'll err by accepting a particular lot we shouldn't have, we will be compensated for it by other times when the lot will be better than average. Under this scenario, where sampling fails to provide prediction for the remainder, it's the average that counts in the long run.

Thus, if p is likely to be above (below) k, our decision is easy: reject (accept). And if the process was in statistical control, and we can compare p to k, again we have an easy decision. Indeed, the case where we may need sampling is when the conformance of the lots we received in the past is generally good, but p sometimes exceeded k and is not in statistical control. But if p behaves wildly enough to defy describing it by a reliable distribution (e.g., if we plot p over many shipments from the supplier the chart is out of control), we take a risk by using the past average as a predictor for the future. Indeed, the single most important benefit of statistical control is that it provides predictability.

9.4.1. *Deming's Recommendations for Cases that Justify Sampling*

Deming made specific recommendations for cases that do justify sampling. The method Deming recommended most, for its simplicity more than anything else, was developed by his doctoral student, Joice Orsini, in her dissertation. The Orsini rule is as follows:

a.   For $k \leq 1/1000$, inspect 100%

b.   For $1/1000 < k \leq 1/10$, test a sample of $n=200$, and accept the remainder without further inspection if and only if there are no defects in the sample.

c.   For $k > 0.1$ accept without inspection.

Orsini's rule is an example of a particular (n, c) plan, $(200, 0)$, applied at a particular range of k; a pure policy is pursued outside this range. A more complex procedure that Deming recommends for its power to reduce the average cost better than Orsini's rule is due to Anscombe (1961). Anscombe suggested a sequential plan using an initial sample of

$$n = 0.375 \sqrt{N \frac{k_2}{k_1}} = 0.375 \sqrt{\frac{N}{k}}$$

If there are 0 defects in this initial lot, accept the remainder. Otherwise, take subsequent samples of size $n = 1/k$. Sampling is continued until the total number of defective items found is one less than the number of samples inspected. This may lead to 100% inspection when the stopping condition is not satisfied.

A point to consider here, which was not addressed by Deming or by Anscombe, is that it costs more to sample a unit based on random numbers than to check a unit as part of a 100% inspection. We need to set up a proper random number sampling system, and pick up the not-necessarily-convenient-to-get-to items. Thus, when sampling, the cost per unit may exceed k_1. Let $S \cdot k_1$ be the additional inspection cost due to random sampling, then one can safely say that, when applying Anscombe's rule, if $0.375(1+S)\sqrt{[N(k_2/k_1)]} \geq N$ we should prefer a 100% inspection. (Anscombe developed his method to help a utility company determine whether home electrical meters were functioning correctly. For a utility it is much easier to select a meter randomly from its records than to inspect it. Therefore, for Anscombe's original purpose $S \approx 0$.)

A related problem with Anscombe's method, when sampling costs are high, is that often such cases involve preparing the sample for inspection in advance. For instance, if we want to inspect items at random from a large shipment we may have to set them aside, based on random numbers, during the unloading process. Otherwise, once the items have been stored, depending on the storage arrangements, it may be too late to create a random sample. In such cases sequential sampling is not fully appropriate, although in practice some users might be willing to forego the correct randomization: it is a highly compromised principle. Depending on the circumstances, such compromise may cause serious problems, but it may also be benign -- the exact specific effects in each case are unknowable. To be on the safe side, one should not forego randomization without a good economic reason, because it involves an unknown and often unnecessary risk. But letting the need for randomization drive the production plan may be equally unreasonable. For instance, control charting is based on sampling, but usually without randomization.

Orsini's rule, when it calls for sampling, specifies $n=200$, and therefore it should be possible to prepare a random sample in this case. But Orsini's rule is quite arbitrary. For instance, it does not take into account the shipment size, N. We might be willing to accept, say, 500 units based on inspecting 200, but maybe not 5000. The simplicity offered by this is a welcome feature, but the price may be too high sometimes. The next subsection introduces a new heuristic that attempts to reduce the total expected costs of sampling and potentially making the wrong decision based on the sample. It is based on a single (n, c) plan, to avoid problems in preparing the sample.

9.4.2. *A Heuristic Approach to Reduce the Cost of Inspection and Production*

The optimization of inspection when the costs of random sampling is included is an open research problem. Nonetheless, we now present a heuristic for this purpose, which is approximately correct for large lots with relatively high k. Trietsch (1996) provides the details. The heuristic is based on a normal approximation to the binomial distribution. It is not presented as an analytic solution because this approximation is not always appropriate for realistic applications.

The formula calls for devising an (n, c) plan with

$$n = \sqrt[3]{\frac{0.04\,(N-n)^2(1-k)}{k(1+S)^2}} \approx \sqrt[3]{\frac{0.04N^2(1-k)}{k(1+S)^2}}$$

here the approximation holds if n is not large relative to N. Otherwise, a simple iterative procedure converges to a stable solution quickly. As a rule of thumb, we should use the iterative procedure if the initial n approximation exceeds 10% of N. Otherwise, the difference between successive iterations will be small. c is then given by

$$c = \lfloor n\,k \rfloor$$

that is, c is the largest integer that does not exceed $n \cdot k_1/k_2$. If the number of defective items in the sample exceeds c, we inspect the remainder one by one. Otherwise, we accept the remainder into the production process. But if $n(1+S) \geq N$, we should perform a 100% inspection right away. Furthermore, suppose we assess that the probability that we'll have to conduct a 100% inspection is f, then if $n(1+S)+f(N-n) \geq N$ we should prefer an outright 100% inspection. While it may be difficult to assess f, managers make gambles that are tantamount to assessing f every day.

Numerical Examples:
Example 1: Let $N=1000$, $k=0.1$ and $S=0.2$ (which is a relatively low value).

Orsini's rule calls for applying a $(200, 0)$ sampling plan. But if we increase k even by a tiny bit (e.g., increase k_1 or decrease k_2), Orsini's rule jumps to no inspection at all.

Anscombe's first sample is

$$n = 0.375\sqrt{\frac{N}{k}} = 0.375\sqrt{\frac{1000}{0.1}} = 37.5 \approx 38$$

and if any defective items are found it is followed by samples of 10 until the total count of the defective items falls below the number of samples. For example, if the first sample included 2 defective items, we have to sample at least two more groups of 10 (which we might as well combine) before accepting the remainder.

To apply the heuristic, using the approximation we obtain

$$n \approx \sqrt[3]{\frac{0.04N^2(1-k)}{k(1+S)^2}} = \sqrt[3]{\frac{0.04 \cdot 1000^2(1-0.1)}{0.1(1+0.2)^2}} = \sqrt[3]{250000} \approx 63$$

c is given by $\lfloor 63 \cdot 0.1 \rfloor = 6$. n is less than 10% of N, so by the rule of thumb we may leave it as is. Nonetheless, to illustrate the iterative procedure, and demonstrate that the difference is small when $n/N < 0.1$, we proceed to iterate. $N - n = 1000 - 63 = 937$. Using 937 in the formula, we obtain:

$$n \approx \sqrt[3]{\frac{0.04(N-n)^2(1-k)}{k(1+S)^2}} = \sqrt[3]{\frac{0.04 \cdot 937^2(1-0.1)}{0.1(1+0.2)^2}} = \sqrt[3]{219492.25} = 60.32 \approx 60$$

By feeding $n = 60$ back into the formula, we can see that the expression returns $n = 60$ again, i.e., it converges to $n = 60$ (with $c = 6$).

Example 2: Same as example 1, but with $N = 10000$.

Orsini's rule is not predicated on N, so we still use a (200, 0) plan to determine the disposition of the remainder.

Anscombe's rule now calls for a first sample of 119 units, followed, upon any defective items, by subsequent samples of 10 units each.

By applying the heuristic, the initial result is 292. A second iteration yields 287, which is also the stable result. Again, it does not seem necessary to bother with the second iteration at all. c is 29 if we use 292, or 28 if we use 287.

Example 3: Returning to $N = 1000$, let $k = 0.001$.

This example shows what happens at Orsini's second boundary, at or above which she recommends 100% inspection. But note that if we increase k even by a tiny bit the rule reverts to the preliminary (200, 0) plan.

Anscombe's rule calls for a first sample of 375, followed by samples of 1000 if necessary. Clearly this implies a single (375, 0) plan, since if we need a second sample the whole lot will be inspected.

Using the heuristic the first approximation yields $n = 303$. Since this is a large proportion of N, we may (or may not) decide to iterate, leading successively to $n = 238$, $n = 253$, $n = 249$, and, finally, $n = 250$. c in this case will be 0 in all cases. In this particular case (for which the normal assumption behind the heuristic is relatively unfounded, incidentally), the heuristic yields a result that is between the Orsini and the Anscombe recommendations.

Example 4: Let $N = 10000$ and $k = 0.001$.

Orsini's rule is without change: use a (200, 0) plan.

Anscombe's rule calls for a first sample of 1186 items, followed by additional samples of 1000 if necessary.

With the heuristic, the initial result is 1405 (which is above 10%). The second iteration yields 1270, the third 1284, and the fourth, finally, the stable solution: 1282. Our c value this time is 1 (1282/1000 gets rounded down to 1; the same would apply for, say, 1982, because our rule is to round down). The normal approximation is still not entirely appropriate here, but it's much better than in the former case.

In the cases where we used iterations, the final n was lower than the initial value -- a result that could be anticipated. Therefore, in a sense, a decision *not* to iterate may be described as a conservative policy. The main benefit of such a policy is a reduction in complexity.

All the examples above are based on a low value of S. By setting $S=0$ we'd obtain an even better comparison between the heuristic and the other rules (both of which implicitly assume $S=0$). In our case, had we used $S=0$, n would increase by about 13% (in all the examples). If we increase S the heuristic yields smaller samples. For instance, if we set $S=5$ instead of $S=0.2$, n will decrease roughly per the third root of $((1+5)/(1+0.2))^2=25^{1/3}=2.9$. Recall also that with high S we should always verify that we're not better off with a 100% inspection to begin with, but in the examples above changing S from 0.2 to 5 would not yet lead to samples that are too expensive (unless f, the probability of a bad lot, is high). Roughly speaking, in these cases, the cost of inspection would rise by a factor of 1.7 (since the samples are more expensive per unit, but smaller). This will also be accompanied by a higher risk, of course, and in this case the risk will also be roughly 1.7 times larger, since it's related to $\sqrt{n}$.

9.4.3. *The "First and Last" Inspection Rule*

A very efficient type of inspection applies when a process is known to produce only acceptable items when it is in control, but there is a danger that it can go out of control during the production of a batch, in which case it will produce *only* defective items. Assume that poka-yoke is not applicable, so such defective items can indeed occur.

While control charting is advocated to make possible stopping such a process before it makes further defects, it is not always economical, or even feasible, to inspect the process during production, and halt it immediately upon the production of any defect. For instance, the rate of production may be too fast for that. However, if we inspect the first and last items, and find them both acceptable, then we may assume that all the items in between were acceptable too.

If we find deterioration in the conformance of the last item, we may then decide to inspect the whole lot, to sort the bad items from the good ones. Or, if the items are arranged in the order of production, we can inspect from the last unit backwards until we find where the process started producing bad items. We can then safely accept the items produced before that time.

Note that inspecting the last items can provide similar evidence even when the process may still produce marginally acceptable items while out of control. That is, we sample a few items in the beginning, to verify that the process is in control when it starts, and a few at the end, to verify it stayed in control. In short, instead of a pure first-and-last policy involving just two items, we take two samples.

Finally, we can use the first-and-last inspection rule even when the process can produce an occasional defective item while in control, with a probability that does not justify 100% inspection, but will produce only defective items when out of control. In this case we accept the lot without 100% inspection when the first and last units indicated that it ran in control, knowing full well that it may contain an occasional defective item. The criterion for accepting such a lot is by applying the *kp* rule.

In the service industry, the first-and-last inspection rule applies to the production of multiple copies of large documents on modern copying machines. Inspecting the output on a 100% basis is extremely labor-intensive and rarely justified economically. Taking samples during production is practically impossible. But it is enough to inspect the last item, and most of the prevalent defects that may have occurred during the run will be revealed. This is especially important in organizations such as government agencies where equipment and supplies are bought by price tag alone, and defects of the following type are prevalent: (i) the copier feeds two pages of the original at once, thus one of them is missing in the output; (ii) the copier feeds an original in a crooked orientation, creating defective output. Incidentally, by monitoring the total count of copies (using the counter of the copying machine) we can verify that the first defect type did not occur, since when it does the number of copies is less than planned.

In the remainder of the chapter we discuss some classical methods of acceptance sampling (of the type Deming and Shingo called obsolete). These methods, however, are used often, and as such professionals should know about them. Furthermore, the theory covered in the next section provides insight into the problem of selecting subgroup size for attribute charts.

9.5. Devising Single Sampling (*n*, *c*) Plans

Acceptance sampling plans in general are usually described in terms of resolving conflicts between producers and customers. It is convenient to do so here too (TQ's aim to achieve win-win relationships notwithstanding). Under the conflict scenario we have a producer who wishes to have all the lots accepted by the customer, and a customer who wants to take no risk of accepting bad lots. The producer determines what constitutes good conformance, and the risk she is willing to take of having good lots rejected by error. Likewise, the customer determines what constitutes bad conformance, and what risk he is willing to take of accepting a bad lot by error. With this information in place both parties seek a sampling plan that will achieve all these ends. That is, the sampling plan is supposed to reject most of the lots that the customer considers bad and accept most of the lots that the producer considers good. Errors should be bounded by the allowed risks that the producer and the customer specified. The following conventional definitions will be used:

AQL (accepted quality level): The fraction defective that the producer commits not to exceed. Often expressed in percents. A lot with a fraction of *AQL* or less defective items is considered "good."[5]

α: The risk the producer is willing to take that a good lot will be rejected by error. Also known as *the producer's risk*.

LTPD (lot tolerance percent defective): The maximum fraction defective that the customer is willing to accept without further inspection. A lot with a fraction of *LTPD* or more defective items is considered "bad."

β: The risk the customer is willing to take that a bad lot will be accepted by error. Also known as *the consumer's risk*.[6]

In this section we are concerned with finding an (n, c) plan that, over the long run, will accept at least $100(1-\alpha)\%$ of all "good" lots and reject at least $100(1-\beta)\%$ of all "bad" lots. Furthermore, among all such (n, c) plans, we have a vested interest to minimize n, and thus reduce the sampling cost. The selection of α and β is usually arbitrary, but supposedly they should be chosen to minimize the total costs -- and sampling represents only one cost. Thus, to really select α and β intelligently we need to have information about the likelihood of "bad" lots (if it is very low we may afford high β but require low α, and vice versa if it

---

[5]If $AQL > k$, the kp rule implies 100% inspection.

[6]The customer may not be the final consumer, but the usage here is conventional.

is very high). Specifically, when we have knowledge, or when we are willing to gamble, that the fraction of bad lots is f, then a good rule of thumb is to set α and β such that $f\beta = (1-f)\alpha$. By increasing n we can decrease both of these risks, and vice versa, until the combined cost of sampling and risk seems reasonable. But to really do it right we also need information how bad a "bad" lot can be, and the probability that "good" lots are actually better than AQL. Having said that, however, we proceed to ignore the issue. Instead, we implicitly assume that α and β are given exogenously and they are not subject to change.

Many, including respectable authors, misinterpret the meaning of AQL and $LTPD$. The most important points are (i) AQL and α are within the prerogative of the producer, while, symmetrically, $LTPD$ and β are for the customer to determine; and (ii) the parties can use sampling to do business together only if $LTPD > AQL$.

One of the probable reasons why the role of $LTPD$ and β is not clearly understood is because MIL STD 105D, and its civilian counterpart ANSI/ASQC Z1.4, are predicated on AQL and α only. The standard covers single, double, and multiple sampling plans. They come in three strengths: *normal-*, *reduced-*, and *tightened* inspection. Normal plans are used initially. Tightened plans are used with vendors whose lots were rejected too often in the near past, and they specify larger samples, designed to better protect the customer. The shift back and forth between normal and tightened inspection is based on the acceptance history of the last few lots. The shift to reduced inspection requires strong evidence of conformance, including evidence that the process is running smoothly, and it is only done at the prerogative of the customer. Reduced plans use smaller samples, and as long as the real nonconformance is below AQL, they are not very likely to reject (which sometimes implies that once a product is in reduced inspection a producer has to mess up big to be shifted back). For further details on MIL STD 105D (and similar standards for variable measurements, such as MIL STD 414), see, for example, Montgomery (1991). Another possibility is to study the standard itself. (The civilian version is available from ASQC.)

The pertinent point here is that although it is possible to find the performance of the plans in terms of $LTPD$ and β, their construction and recommended selection procedures ignore these parameters completely. Since many studied acceptance sampling by being trained in the use of MIL STD 105D (or one of its former versions), it may be less surprising now why the role of $LTPD$ and β is not always understood correctly. This is unfortunate, since the errors caused by this misunderstanding are legion. For this reason, the approach of the standard is badly flawed. Here we concentrate on the version where $LTPD$ and β play a symmetric and equal role to AQL and α. Incidentally, Dodge and Romig themselves concentrated on $LTPD$ and β, which is more in line with the modern customer focus. Their charts, however, include AQL data as well.

9.5.1. *Why the Customer Should Not Dictate AQL and α*

Simply put, it's none of the customer's business what *AQL* and α the producer might elect. Ideally, by stating *AQL*, the producer is informing the customer what level of quality (in terms of percent defective) she is capable of achieving consistently with her present processes. This, incidentally, does not conflict with a continuous drive to improve conformance: it merely describes the current reality. Unfortunately, people misconstrue *AQL* to reflect *desired* conformance, and this is undeniably a negative side-effect of using sampling plans. So much so that some experts oppose sampling on this ground alone. Be that as it may, the customer need not be happy with the quoted *AQL*, but his options do not include dictating it *except by taking his business elsewhere*. The customer indicates his conformance demands by stating his *LTPD*. The problem of too low *AQL* will arise, potentially, when *LTPD* (the necessary conformance) is stricter than *AQL* (the available conformance).

Upon such a case the customer has several options, including the "no deal" alternative which should never be ignored. The customer may decide that he has to accept a higher *LTPD*, which would make it possible to do business. Alternatively, the customer may inform the producer that the competition is capable of meeting or beating his *LTPD*, or that he is not prepared to accept less. At this point the producer may choose to relinquish the business or to redesign her process (e.g., by removing causes of variation, tightening her own demands from her vendors, adding process controls and inspections). Nonetheless, whether pushed by the customer or not, the producer has to set *AQL* as per her ability to actually deliver, while the customer sets *LTPD* according to his needs.

The producer also has the right to demand any level of protection she feels she needs by specifying a low α. She should realize, however, that specifying low α is equivalent to raising the costs the customer bears, so she should consider a tight α as equivalent to demanding a higher price. Symmetrically, the customer has the right to set β as low as he may wish, but he should realize that it will inflate the sample size, and with it the sampling costs, for which he has to pay when all is said and done.

There is perfect symmetry between the roles and the rights of the producer and the customer. Still, in practice one often finds that the customer tries to dictate *AQL* (and sometimes α) to the producer, while producers usually don't try to dictate *LTPD* and β to their customers. This is why we concentrate here on the case of the customer overstepping his bounds.

Chase and Aquilano (1992, p. 200) cited an anecdote, attributed to Hewlett-Packard during their first dealings with Japanese suppliers (a generation or so ago). HP demanded

AQL of 2%. The vendor thought that he could deliver perfect products. Since the customer is king, HP won. When the shipment arrived, it included the agreed upon number of good cables, and, packaged separately, bad cables. In his letter the Japanese supplier wrote: "We have sent you 100 good cables. Since you insisted on 2 percent *AQL*, we have enclosed 2 defective cables in this package, though we do not understand why you want them." Whether this happened exactly this way, and whether it really involved HP, is not known to this author (nor, it seems, to Chase and Aquilano), but what's clear is that the level of misunderstanding in the field is so high that this could easily happen, and probably did on more than one occasion. It is of course an exceptionally severe case. Customers may try to negotiate *lower AQL* by stating a stricter *LTPD*, but they should not demand worse conformance than the producer wants to deliver.

The misunderstanding alleged in the story about HP did not lead to a real problem. But the same level of ignorance can easily lead to serious business errors. Here's one that's really common: A salesperson assures us that items are tested with a very attractive (low) *AQL* and a very low α (say 1%). This sounds impressive, and the salesperson may not even know that the information is misleading (most of them are simply not knowledgeable in statistical quality control). But the information is totally irrelevant to our needs as customers. As customers we should only be concerned with *LTPD* and β. *AQL* and α relate to the producer's risk -- not ours. For instance, if the sampling plan specifies a very high c and low n, the producer is covered in terms of α, but the customer is probably *not* covered in terms of β even if his *LTPD* is high (let alone if *LTPD* is not much larger than *AQL*).

We need to stress again that this is a common *mistake,* and usually *not* a case of intentional misrepresentation. It's just that when the producer is large and the product is not customized (say, a commodity) the producer often takes the test upon herself on behalf of all customers (and the intention is commendable). In such cases she needs to understand exactly whose interests she's supposed to protect. Since she is trying to protect the customer from excessive defect rates, she should specify tight *LTPD* and low β. If she's trying to protect herself from rejecting lots too often, she should specify lax *AQL* and low α. If she can do both, that's fine, but it's the figures she chose for *LTPD* and β that her salespersons should report to customers. In such cases, however, it is far better for the producer to monitor her conformance at the source (by control charts), and she should not have to do any further sampling unless there is evidence it is necessary (lack of control).

9.5.2. *Why LTPD Must Exceed AQL*

Clearly, unless $LTPD \geq AQL$, there can be no match between what the producer is prepared to deliver and what the customer is prepared to accept. Furthermore, a necessary condition for the application of sampling in general, and (*n*, *c*) plans in particular, is *LTPD > AQL*. That is, if *LTPD = AQL*, we can do business, but not based on sampling. If *LTPD = AQL ≥ k*, this implies inspecting all items. If *LTPD = AQL < k and* the customer trusts the vendor it is possible to accept without sampling. But otherwise, again, the whole lot has to be inspected because sampling is not applicable. Our subsequent discussion of operating curves should clarify this point.

9.5.3. *Operating Characteristics Curves for (n, c) Plans*

Suppose we decide to use a particular (*n*, *c*) plan, say (200, 3). We inspect 200 items, and if we find 3 or more defective ones, we reject the lot (or inspect it on a 100% basis, as the case may be). Figure 9.3 depicts the probability of accepting a lot based on this plan, as a function of *p*, the real defective fraction in the lot. Such a curve is called an *operating characteristics (OC) curve.* It is drawn under the assumption that the lot is much larger than the sample (which makes the binomial distribution applicable). An equivalent assumption is that *p* is not necessarily the exact defective fraction in the lot, but rather the defective fraction in the larger population to which the lot belongs (e.g., the output of the production

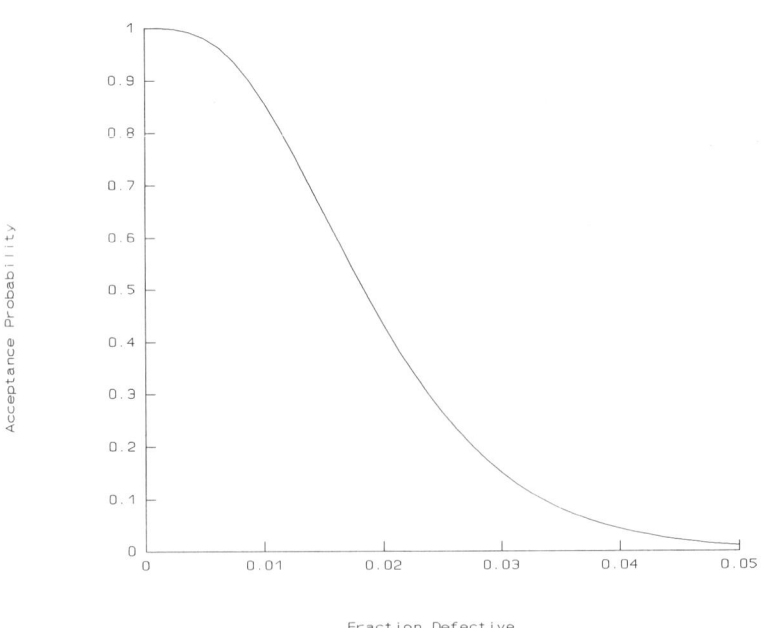

Fig. 9.3. Operating characteristic curve for (200, 3) plan.

process when in control). Without one or the other of these assumptions, the hypergeometric distribution applies, and the OC curve should be a function of n, c, and the lot size.

Given our assumption, the probability that the next item we withdraw will be defective is p, regardless of the number of defective items that we withdrew already. Under these circumstances, we can use the binomial distribution to compute the probability of having 3 or less defective items out of 200, yielding, together, the probability of acceptance that the curve depicts. For instance, for $p=0.005$, the probability of accepting is given by

$$P(accept) = \binom{200}{0}0.005^0 0.995^{200} + \binom{200}{1}0.005^1 0.995^{199}$$

$$+ \binom{200}{2}0.005^2 0.995^{198} + \binom{200}{3}0.005^3 0.995^{197} \approx 0.981$$

As another example, for $p=0.05$ the probability of accepting implied by the same OC curve is

$$P(accept) = \binom{200}{0}0.05^0 0.95^{200} + \binom{200}{1}0.05^1 0.95^{199}$$

$$+ \binom{200}{2}0.05^2 0.95^{198} + \binom{200}{3}0.05^3 0.95^{197} \approx 0.009$$

How should an ideal OC curve look? It would be 1 at least until AQL, and drop all the way to zero before reaching $LTPD$. This would satisfy both parties without risk. No sampling plan has such a curve, but by specifying very large n, we can get as close as we may wish to this ideal. Nonetheless, if $AQL=LTPD$ would be allowed, this would imply that the OC curve would have to coincide with the perpendicular line at AQL. The only way to achieve this is 100% inspection, which is why we insist on the strict inequality $LTPD>AQL$ for sampling to be feasible.

This brings to light an important characteristic of sampling plans: if the fraction of defective items is anywhere between AQL and $LTPD$, both the producer and the customer should be satisfied regardless of the decision. If we reject the lot, the producer can't complain because the fraction of defective items exceeds AQL. If we accept, the customer can't complain because the fraction of defective items is below $LTPD$. This does not imply that the customer is obligated to pay for the defective units, of course, but it does imply that he can't complain that the lot was shipped in the first place. Thus, one may refer to the range between AQL and $LTPD$ as "no-man's-land." The OC curve of a "perfect" sampling plan drops from 1 to 0 within this range.

Note now that we could have approximated the binomial distribution by the Poisson distribution. This would be especially appropriate for p=0.005, but it might also be acceptable for p=0.05. Indeed, in the former case the Poisson distribution would indicate a probability of 0.981 (compare to 0.981), and in the latter case the Poisson would indicate 0.01 (compare to 0.009). The approximation may seem worse in the latter case, which could be expected, but the difference is between two minute values, and it would not be likely to change our decisions by much, if at all. Considering that p values of 0.05 and more are becoming more and more irrelevant to sampling with the levels of conformance common today, we might be vindicated in using the Poisson approximation as a rule when calculating acceptance probabilities for sampling plans. The OC curve is simply a function that reflects many such calculations.

Suppose now that $AQL=0.006$, $\alpha=0.05$, $LTPD=0.03$, and $\beta=0.1$. Would the (200, 3) plan work for us? We will answer this question in two ways. First, we'll use straightforward calculations (utilizing the Poisson approximation). Next we'll utilize the OC curve to find out graphically whether the plan is appropriate.

To check an (n, c) plan we must make sure that it protects the producer for *any* level of defects up to AQL, and, symmetrically, that it is appropriate for the customer for *any* level of defects above $LTPD$. As we'll see presently, however, it is enough to verify the plan for the two points $p=AQL$ and $p=LTPD$. Starting with $p=AQL$, we obtain $np=200\times0.006=1.2$. Using a Poisson table for $\lambda=1.2$ we find that the probability of accepting is approximately 0.96. The producer's risk, $1-0.96$, is less than 0.05, so she is adequately protected at $p=AQL$. She's even better protected for $p<AQL$. But the same plan would not be acceptable to the producer for any $AQL>0.0067$ (approximately). As for the customer, for $p=LTPD$ the Poisson approximation has $\lambda=0.03\times200=6$, leading to a probability of 0.151, which is the consumer's risk. Since $0.151>0.1=\beta$, the customer is not adequately protected by the plan. With this particular β the (200, 3) plan would only work for $LTPD>0.0335$ (approximately).

Figure 9.4 shows how we could obtain the same result graphically. Two hurdles are shaded in the figure, one for the producer and one for the customer. For an (n, c) plan to be appropriate it must pass above the producer's hurdle and below the customer's. Ours passes above the producer's, but conflicts with the customer's. It would be okay if they just touched, but here the curve actually passes through the hurdle, and this is not acceptable. The question is how we can find a plan that satisfies both parties, and does so with as few inspections as possible. Just trying a multitude of plans is not an efficient way to go about it.

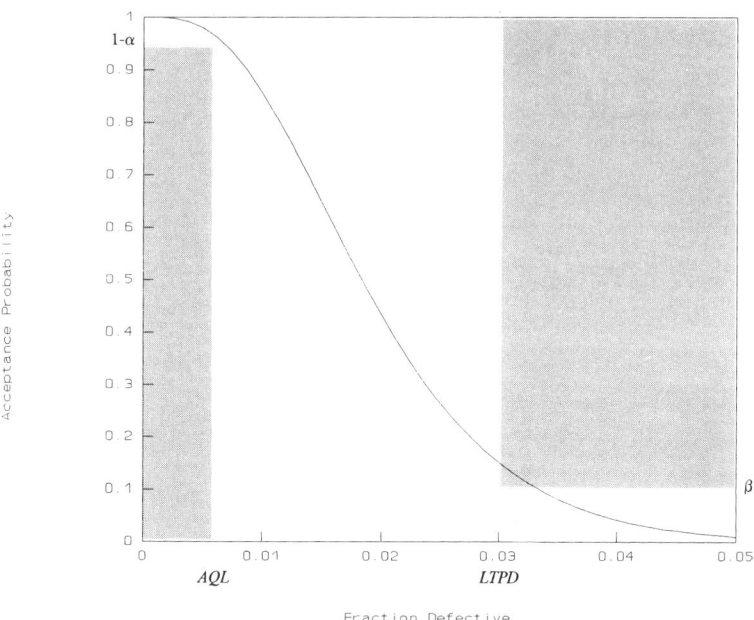

Fig. 9.4. OC curve with Hurdles at *AQL* and *LTPD*.

9.5.4. *Finding (n, c) Plans Methodically*

In general, we want to be able to devise (n, c) plans for any *AQL*, α, *LTPD*, and β, and do so with the minimal n possible. We'll do this with the help of a reversed Poisson table. (One enters a regular Poisson table with a number c and a given λ, and obtains a cumulative probability. One enters a reversed Poisson table with a number c and a cumulative probability, e.g., β or $1-\alpha$, and the table provides λ.) But we start with an important special case that does not require a table: $AQL=0$.

Suppose our producer uses $AQL=0$, like the one who sent two defective cables separately to satisfy a perceived but inexplicable customer need. Therefore, she does not need to specify α: as far as she is concerned, the OC curve of *any* sampling plan will fall from 1 to 0 to the right of *AQL*. What remains is for the customer to devise a plan satisfying his needs. This will take the form of an $(n, 0)$ plan with a large enough n to ensure that if there is no defective item in the sample (i.e., we accept because $0 \leq c=0$), the probability that the fraction of defective items will be *LTPD* or above will be β or less. *LTPD* still has to be higher than *AQL*, even in this case, or sampling will never suffice to prove adequate conformance.

Mathematically, this happens to be the simplest case to solve, with or without the Poisson approximation. First, we obtain an $(n, 0)$ plan using the binomial distribution. The probability of a binomial random variable being exactly 0 -- the only case leading to acceptance -- is $(1-p)^n$, and we need to calculate this value for $p=LTPD$. To satisfy the β-risk constraint, we stipulate $(1-LTPD)^n \le \beta$. Taking logarithms (with any base, but for convenience we'll choose the base e) from both sides of this equation we obtain $n \cdot \ln(1-LTPD) \le \ln(\beta)$ (the ln function is monotone increasing so it maintains inequalities intact). Recalling, however, that the logarithms involved in both sides of the new inequality are negative (both $1-LTPD$ and β being fractions), when we solve for n we divide two negative numbers to obtain a positive one, so we have to reverse the sign of the inequality. We obtain

$$n \ge \frac{\ln \beta}{\ln(1-LTPD)}$$

For example, let $LTPD=0.005$, and $\beta=0.1$. Then $n \ge \ln(0.1)/\ln(0.995)=459.36$, which we must round up to 460. Of course, a larger sample, say 500, or 1713, will also provide protection, but we wish to minimize n while satisfying the stipulated risk: *Not* to take on the full risk is waste. We allow the risk specifically to balance the cost of the sampling.

As a second example, it might be interesting to reverse the numbers, so $\beta=0.005$ and $LTPD=0.1$. This will lead to 50.28, or 51. As these examples demonstrate, the sample size rises for tight $LTPD$ faster than it does for a low risk.

Let us repeat the above calculations with the Poisson approximation. Our Poisson approximation for the number of defective items at $p=LTPD$ with a sample of n is $P(n \cdot LTPD)$. The probability of 0 for a Poisson variable is $e^{-n \cdot LTPD}$. Our stipulation is that $e^{-n \cdot LTPD} \le \beta$. Taking the natural logarithm of both sides leads to

$$n \ge \frac{-\ln \beta}{LTPD}$$

For small $LTPD$, $LTPD \approx -\ln(1-LTPD)$, and hence this result is an approximation of the one we obtained for the binomial. Furthermore, we now see that it's $LTPD$ that dictates the quality of the approximation. For $LTPD=0.005$ and $\beta=0.1$ this leads to 460.51, which we have to round up to 461 (compare to 460). For $LTPD=0.1$ and $\beta=0.005$ this leads to 52.98, or 53 (compare to 51). Both approximations are acceptable, but the latter is worse both absolutely and relatively. Since the Poisson approximates the binomial better for small p, and here it is $LTPD$ that plays that role, this is not surprising.

Before we continue to the more general case, let us look at one more example. In modern times the $LTPD$ requirements are becoming progressively stringent, and some customers state them in PPM (parts per million). Assume, then, that $LTPD$ is 5PPM, and let's say that we trust the vendor enough to accept a relatively large β-risk of 25%. We receive a shipment of 5,000 items (which is medium size under JIT, but will soon be considered large as our JIT systems continually approach the ideal lot size of 1). How many items should we sample?

In this case the Poisson approximation leads to $\ln(0.25)/0.000005 = 277{,}258.87$ which we should round up to 277,259. Most readers will agree that it is difficult to sample 277,259 items out of 5000, and the value of acceptance sampling in this case is highly questionable. As it happens, the model we used is *not* appropriate here, and the correct sample size in this case is "only" 4912.[7] But practically speaking it is obvious that a sampling plan that calls for sampling over 98% of the lot is not really an attractive choice. Indeed, the JIT paradigm calls for working with vendors who can be trusted to deliver directly to the production line, without acceptance inspection. As discussed before, in case a problem develops we can always create an ad-hoc 100% inspection station for items that prove to be problematic. But clearly sampling becomes less and less relevant as our conformance standards are raised and our shipments are decreased.

Referring specifically to MIL STD 105D and to Dodge-Romig *LTPD* tables (which are better geared to protect the customer), Deming wrote: "The day of such plans is finished. American industry cannot afford the losses that they cause." (1986, p. 133.) Deming also claimed that *AQL* and *LTPD* specifications are interpreted [erroneously, but very often] as permission to sell defective items, and get paid for them too. Vendors will always be found, he said, who are willing and able to sell defective items when that's what the customer wants. Thus, although he was not a supporter of ZD by any stretch of the imagination,

---

[7]The problem arises because we use an approximation beyond its relevant domain. The culprit is our assumption that n is small relative to N. Here, we should switch to another probability model. Suppose we sample n ($< N$) units and find no defective items. To keep the total number of defective items below $N \cdot LTPD$, we should be willing to accept a remainder that comes from a population with $p = N \cdot LTPD/(N-n)$. Plugging this value into the Poisson approximation we used before, we obtain a new expression

$$n \geq \frac{-\ln \beta \, (N-n)}{N \cdot LTPD}$$

which leads to the following minimal n value:

$$n = \left\lceil \frac{-N \cdot \ln \beta}{N \cdot LTPD - \ln \beta} \right\rceil$$

where, because $\ln\beta < 0$, the expression between the two ceiling signs must be strictly smaller than N. Since we round up, $n = N$ is theoretically possible, but not $n > N$.

Deming's point here is similar to one made by ZD proponents who view $AQL > 0$ as an *intent* to settle for a high level of defects. We also see now that these plans are only appropriate for large AQL and $LTPD$ values and large lots, which are inappropriate in modern industry. Thus, one doesn't have to embrace the ZD management philosophy to reject acceptance sampling in most cases.

Nonetheless, let us continue and show how to devise (n, c) plans in general. We continue to assume that the Poisson distribution is appropriate, with $\lambda = n \cdot AQL$ and $\lambda = n \cdot LTPD$ at the two points associated with the producer and the customer. Conceptually, our procedure is simple. We start with a low c value, and then seek an n that will work with this c for both producer and consumer. If c is too small, we'll fail in our effort to find such an n. We'll respond by increasing c until we find the smallest c that works. For this c we'll then select the smallest n that works for both parties.

Above, we've seen that a (200, 3) plan is not adequate for $AQL = 0.006$, $\alpha = 0.05$, $LTPD = 0.06$, and $\beta = 0.1$. Let us find a plan that will work. Our search procedure for c will be simple: we'll start with $c = 0$, and increase it by steps of 1 until we find a satisfactory plan.[8] Starting with $c = 0$, then, we want to see if any $(n, 0)$ plan exists for these data. Our first question is this: supposing $c = 0$, and given $LTPD$ and β, what is the *smallest* n that will satisfy the customer's needs? To answer this question we go to a Poisson table, and we seek the λ value that yields a probability of β in the $c = 0$ column. Using interpolation between the values $\lambda = 2$ with 0.1353 and $\lambda = 2.5$ with 0.0821 (which may be found in such a table), we see that $\lambda = 2.33$ yields a probability of 0.1 (approximately) for $c = 0$. Hence we have $n \cdot LTPD = 2.33$, leading to $n \geq 2.33/0.03 = 77.7$ which, formally speaking, we have to round *up* to 78. Thus, as far as the consumer is concerned, any plan with $n \geq 78$ and $c = 0$, would be acceptable. To avoid the complexity and error associated with our interpolation, we may prefer to use a reversed Poisson table, such as Table 9.1, where we find for the row 0.1 (i.e., where $\beta = 0.1$) and $c = 0$ the value 2.3026. Correcting for the small error we had by using 2.33 instead of 2.3026, we now see that the producer should also accept a plan with $n = 77$. But what about the producer? The producer needs n to be small, so our question now is what is the *largest* n that the producer will accept. Again, we look at Table 9.1 under $c = 0$, at the row 0.95 (i.e., $1 - \alpha$), and we find 0.0513, which means that $n \cdot AQL$ should not exceed 0.0513, leading to $n \leq 0.0513/0.006 = 8.55$, meaning that the producer will only accept $n \leq 8$, or demand that c be increased. This means that we look for a plan with at most 8 but at least 77 units: an impossibility. Hence, we must try a larger c, such as 1.

---

[8] More efficient search procedures can be devised quite easily, if desired.

Prob\c	0	1	2	3	4	5	6	7
0.010	4.6052	6.6383	8.4059	10.0451	11.6046	13.1085	14.5706	16.0000
0.025	3.6889	5.5716	7.2247	8.7673	10.2416	11.6683	13.0595	14.4227
0.050	2.9957	4.7439	6.2958	7.7537	9.1535	10.5130	11.8424	13.1481
0.100	2.3026	3.8897	5.3223	6.6808	7.9936	9.2747	10.5321	11.7709
0.250	1.3863	2.6926	3.9204	5.1094	6.2744	7.4227	8.5585	9.6844
0.500	0.6931	1.6783	2.6741	3.6721	4.6709	5.6702	6.6696	7.6693
0.750	0.2877	0.9613	1.7273	2.5353	3.3686	4.2192	5.0827	5.9561
0.900	0.1054	0.5318	1.1021	1.7448	2.4326	3.1519	3.8948	4.6561
0.950	0.0513	0.3554	0.8177	1.3663	1.9701	2.6130	3.2853	3.9808
0.975	0.0253	0.2422	0.6187	1.0899	1.6235	2.2019	2.8144	3.4538
0.990	0.0101	0.1486	0.4360	0.8233	1.2791	1.7853	2.3302	2.9061

Prob\c	8	9	10	11	12	13	14	15
0.010	17.4027	18.7831	20.1447	21.4899	22.8208	24.1391	25.4461	26.7428
0.025	15.7632	17.0848	18.3904	19.6821	20.9616	22.2304	23.4896	24.7402
0.050	14.4347	15.7052	16.9622	18.2075	19.4426	20.6686	21.8865	23.0971
0.100	12.9947	14.2060	15.4066	16.5981	17.7816	18.9580	20.1280	21.2924
0.250	10.8024	11.9139	13.0196	14.1206	15.2173	16.3102	17.3999	18.4865
0.500	8.6690	9.6687	10.6685	11.6684	12.6682	13.6681	14.6680	15.6679
0.750	6.8376	7.7259	8.6198	9.5186	10.4217	11.3286	12.2388	13.1521
0.900	5.4325	6.2213	7.0208	7.8293	8.6459	9.4696	10.2996	11.1353
0.950	4.6952	5.4254	6.1690	6.9242	7.6896	8.4639	9.2463	10.0360
0.975	4.1154	4.7954	5.4912	6.2006	6.9220	7.6539	8.3954	9.1454
0.990	3.5075	4.1302	4.7712	5.4282	6.0991	6.7824	7.4767	8.1811

Table 9.1

Repeating the same procedure for $c=1$, we find that now n has to exceed 130 but not exceed 59. Again this is infeasible, and we have to repeat the procedure for $c=2$, which calls for $n\geq178$ but ≤136. $c=3$ requires n to exceed 223 but not exceed 227, which, for the first time, is feasible. The cheapest, and thus optimal, plan that will satisfy both parties is $(223, 3).^9$ But the plans $(224, 3)$, $(225, 3)$, $(226, 3)$, and $(227, 3)$ all meet the requirements of both parties. Furthermore, if we wish to specify $c>3$ there is an unlimited number of feasible plans available, but these plans will be unnecessarily expensive.

To recap, Table 9.1 is a reversed Poisson table, arranged by rows each of which is appropriate for a particular required probability, and by columns for each particular c. Generally speaking, the upper rows, with the low probabilities below 0.5, are associated with the consumer's risk, β, and the lower ones denote potential probabilities of acceptance $1-\alpha$, which the producer requires. In our example, data are found in two rows: the $\beta=0.1$ row (fourth from the top) and the $1-\alpha=0.95$ row (third from the bottom). In the 0.1 row, under $c=0$ through 3, we find 2.3026, 3.8897, 5.3223, and 6.6808, respectively. Dividing these values by $LTPD=0.03$ and rounding up, this indicates that n should not be less than 77, 130, 178, and 223, respectively. In the 0.95 row we find 0.0513, 0.3554, 0.8177, and 1.3663. Dividing these figures by $AQL=0.006$ and rounding down, we obtain the following upper bounds on n: 8, 59, 136, and 227.

There is a recommended shortcut in the procedure to find the minimal c when using Table 9.1. Note that we divided the values of the β row by $LTPD$ and those of the $1-\alpha$ row by AQL before comparing them, and that we required the first value to be smaller than the second one. Thus what we need to do is compare the ratio between the values reported in the two pertinent rows to $LTPD/AQL$, which is constant, and see when we stop exceeding it for the first time. In our case, $LTPD/AQL=5$, and the ratio between the β row and the $1-\alpha$ row, corresponding to $c=0$ through 3, is 31.372, 8.425, 5.233 (>5), and 4.036 (<5). We see that it takes at least $c=3$ to satisfy both needs, which is what we found before.

Table 9.1 can also be used to draw operating characteristics curves for any sampling plan with $c\leq15$. To do that, divide the values given in the appropriate column by n, and use the results as p, the fraction defective, on the horizontal axis. The probabilities associated

---

[9]More elaborate schemes accept for, say, $n = 2$, and specify a side lottery to determine what to do for the next level, such as 3. This is equivalent to allowing c to be continuous. In our case that would make possible a plan with less than 223 items. We ignore this possibility because it involves unwelcome additional complexity. It is more sound economically to change α or β than to use such a scheme.

with each row are used for the vertical axis. The points may be connected by a freely drawn smooth curve.

Theoretically, there is no difficulty in extending Table 9.1 as much as we might like. We stopped at $c=15$ because at this value it becomes permissible to use the normal approximation instead of the Poisson. It is quite permissible to use the normal approximation even with much lower c, e.g., 10. We now develop this approximation.

Let z_α satisfy $\Phi(z_\alpha)=\alpha$ (where $\Phi(z)$ is the area under the standard normal curve from $-\infty$ to z. For instance, if $\alpha=0.01$, $z_\alpha=-2.33$. $z_{(1-\beta)}$ is defined similarly. For instance, if $\beta=0.05$, then $z_{(1-\beta)}=1.645$.

Taking into account the continuity correction, we have to use $c+0.5$ to represent c, because a value between $c-0.5$ and $c+0.5$ is rounded to c, and the rule is that we accept a lot with exactly c defective items. So, to protect the producer,

$$c + 0.5 \geq n\,AQL - z_\alpha\sqrt{n\,AQL(1-AQL)} \qquad (9.1)$$

And to protect the consumer,

$$c + 0.5 \leq n\,LTPD - z_{1-\beta}\sqrt{n\,LTPD(1-LTPD)} \qquad (9.2)$$

Subtracting (9.1) from (9.2)

$$n(LTPD - AQL) - z_{1-\beta}\sqrt{n\,LTPD(1-LTPD)} + z_\alpha\sqrt{n\,AQL(1-AQL)} \geq 0$$

or,

$$\sqrt{n} = \frac{z_{1-\beta}\sqrt{LTPD(1-LTPD)} - z_\alpha\sqrt{AQL(1-AQL)}}{LTPD - AQL} \qquad (9.3)$$

which gives us a first (usually non-integer) approximation for n. With this n we use (9.1) or (9.2) *as if they were equalities* to find c (the result should be the same, except for rounding errors). Usually, c is not an integer, so we round it up. Then, we have to increase n accordingly. This can be done optimally by solving a quadratic equation, but a better recommendation is to inflate n by $(\lceil c\rceil + 0.5)/(c+0.5)$, and round it to the nearest integer. Thus, if n is the result of (9.3), and c then satisfies (9.1) or (9.2) as equalities, our final sampling plan is (ROUND$[n\cdot(\lceil c\rceil + 0.5)/(c+0.5)]$, $\lceil c\rceil$).

As an example, let $\alpha=0.1$, $\beta=0.05$, $AQL=0.01$, $LTPD=0.025$. Using Table 9.1 we find that any plan between (679, 10) and (702, 10), inclusive, is appropriate. Therefore, (679, 10) is the most economical solution. We now compare this with the normal approximation, although it's neither necessary yet nor fully justified. By the normal table we obtain $z_\alpha = -1.282$, and $z_{(1-\beta)} = 1.645$. By (9.3) we now get $\sqrt{n} = (1.645\sqrt{[0.025 \times 0.975]} + 1.282\sqrt{[0.01 \times 0.99]}) / 0.015 = 25.626$, or $n = 656.7$. By (9.1), treated as an equality, we get $c = 9.34$, which implies $c = 10$. Inflating n by the ratio between $(\lceil c \rceil + 0.5) = 10.5$ and $c + 0.5 = 9.84$, we obtain $n = 700.74$, which we round to 701. Thus, we obtain the program (701, 10), which is good, but not optimal. The results are acceptable, however, and they only get better for higher c.

A good use of the normal approximation may be to show that if *LTPD* is too close to *AQL*, sampling is not effective (although it's theoretically possible). For example, let $AQL = 0.01$, $LTPD = 0.011$, $\alpha = 0.01$, $\beta = 0.05$; so $z_\alpha = -2.33$, $z_{(1-\beta)} = 1.645$, and we obtain $\sqrt{n} \geq (2.33\sqrt{[0.01 \times 0.99]} + 1.645\sqrt{[0.011 \times 0.989]}) / 0.001 = 403.4$ or $n \geq 162,740$. Clearly, such a huge sample is not practicable. Increasing the allowed risks helps, but likely not enough.

9.6. Sequential Sampling Plans

Recall that during our construction of (n, c) plans we typically found that the $(n, 0)$ plan that satisfies the customer puts the producer under excessive risk. Suppose now that, as a customer, you sample many items and find no defects. You might be tempted to accept the lot even before you complete the inspection plan. Similarly, if you collect $c + 1$ defective items before finishing the lot, or even less than that but after only sampling a few items, a temptation exists to reject forthwith. Stopping the inspection in mid-stream is called *curtailment*, and it is often done in practice. (One reason to avoid curtailment is when rejected lots are returned to the vendor, and we wish to maintain a record of the quality received. If we stop when we collect $c + 1$ defects, and claim that the percent defective is $c + 1$ over the number inspected, the result is a biased estimator, which is also likely to exhibit large variance. Rather than compensate for the bias, we might wish to finish the sampling plan. This consideration is less important when we perform rectifying inspection of the remainder, since we can collect even better data during the rectifying inspection, but then we are not really curtailing the inspection.)

In general, it may happen that a partial sample will provide enough information to make the decision, one way or the other, and only in cases the evidence of the partial sample is inconclusive, we need to sample the rest. This observation leads to the idea of multiple-sampling plans, where we take an initial sample, and based on its results accept, reject, or take another sample. This includes double-sampling, multiple-sampling, and, at the extreme, sequential plans that do not have a predetermined limitation on the number of samples taken.

Anscombe's method is such a multiple sampling sequential plan, also known as a *group sequential plan* because he recommends sampling the items in groups. It is also possible to sample sequentially on an *item-by-item* basis. In this section we discuss an item-by-item sequential sampling plan developed during WWII under the leadership of Abraham Wald (see Wald, 1947).

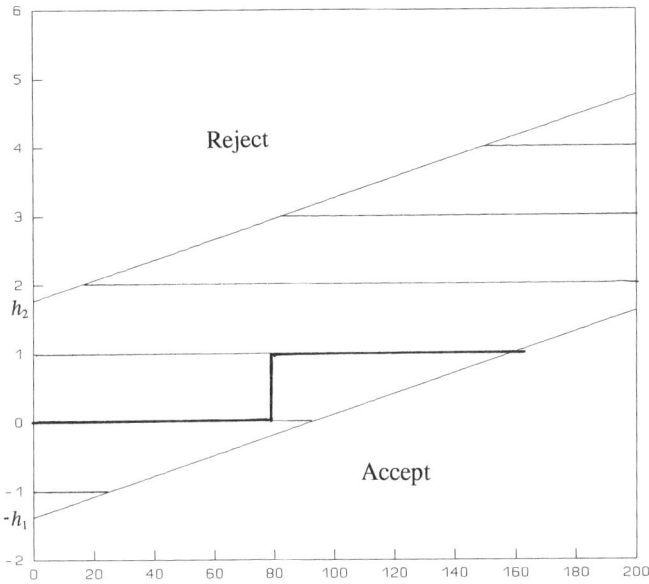

Fig. 9.5. Sequential sampling decision lines.

Figure 9.5 shows how such an item-by-item sequential sampling plan is carried out. There are two parallel boundaries which intersect the Y-axis at distances of h_1 (from below) and h_2 (from above). The two boundaries have a slope, t, such that $AQL < t < LTPD$. As we sample sequentially, we plot the current number sampled on the X-axis and the number of defective items accumulated on the Y-axis. The result is a flat line -- if all items are good -- or a series of one or more steps. As soon as this plot leaves the band between the bounds, the inspection terminates. If the plot crosses the lower bound (as the one shown in the figure), we accept the lot, and if it crosses the upper bound we reject it. (In the unlikely event where the plot is *on* the boundary we continue sampling.) An excellent lot will cross rather quickly -- at least relatively to the parallel (n, c) plan -- while a very bad lot will also terminate rapidly. But if the percent defective is close to the slope of the boundaries, it may take a long time for the program to terminate. This is only likely to happen when the conformance is strictly between *AQL* and *LTPD* (no-man's-land). In such a case, the only problem with the extended inspection is the cost of inspection itself. The conformance is likely such that we are formally indifferent between accepting or rejecting. It is useful to think of this statement in the context of destructive testing: Wald's main application was to the destructive testing of bombs. The most important cost to avoid is delivering duds to the target, so the inspection cost is a minor consideration.

9.6.1. *Constructing Sequential Sampling Plans*

Wald utilized approximations that assume low *AQL* and *LTPD*. In general, the theory behind these rules is beyond our scope, but it is based on the idea that in order to be accepted or rejected after a particular cumulated number of inspections the lot must not have been accepted or rejected before. This calls for a relatively complex conditional probability analysis to determine the overall α- and β-risks.[10] The results, however, are quite easy to implement.

What we need to devise a plan is to find three numbers: h_1 (the distance below the origin at which the lower bound intersects with the Y-axis), h_2 (the distance above the origin at which the upper bound intersects with the Y-axis), and t (the slope of both boundaries). Our data is *AQL*, α, *LTPD*, and β. The model is based on the assumption that *all* these values are small. Otherwise, the risks may not be exactly as desired. We start by calculating an interim value, Y,

$$Y = \frac{1}{\ln\dfrac{LTPD(1-AQL)}{AQL(1-LTPD)}}$$

where instead of the ln we could specify a logarithm with any other base, as long as we retain it for the subsequent calculations. Next, we use Y to obtain the results we need,

$$h_1 = Y\ln\frac{1-\alpha}{\beta}$$
$$h_2 = Y\ln\frac{1-\beta}{\alpha}$$
$$t = Y\ln\frac{1-AQL}{1-LTPD}$$

For example, let's find a sequential plan to replace the (223, 3) plan we devised

---

[10]The process can be described by a Markov chain with two absorbing states.

before for $AQL=0.006$, $\alpha=0.05$, $LTPD=0.03$, and $\beta=0.1$. The calculations here yield $Y=0.6120$, $h_1=1.3779$, $h_2=1.7690$, and $t=0.01496$.

Note that h_1, which provides protection against erroneous acceptance, is smaller than h_2 in this example. This is because we specified a larger β value. With $\alpha=\beta$ we would obtain $h_1=h_2$. t is between AQL and $LTPD$, and it is not a function of either α or β. We accept when the number of items inspected, n, exceeds $(h_1+d)/t$ for the first time without a preceding rejection, where d is the number of defects accumulated by that time. Similarly, we reject the first time d exceeds $h_2+n \cdot t$ without a preceding acceptance. In our example, setting $d=0$ we find that it takes 119 items to accept the lot even when there are no defective items. Recall that a single sampling plan with $n=77$ and $c=0$ is enough to satisfy the customer. Here, we need to sample more. First, note that in both cases we used approximations, but it is generally the case that Wald's plan requires more inspections without a single defective item than the smallest $(n, 0)$ plan that the customer would agree to. This may look like a flaw in the method, but careful study -- way beyond our scope -- shows otherwise.

9.6.2. *On Curtailment*

Anscombe (whose paper was published almost a decade after Wald's tragic death in a plane crash) attempted to minimize the total cost of inspection under a worst case scenario, and without the use of data such as AQL, α, $LTPD$, and β. Wald, in his seminal work on sequential sampling, sought a method to replace (n, c) plans such that, at least in clear cases (where the conformance is *not* in the no-man's-land), the number of necessary inspections will be smaller. Wald's plan is especially recommended for destructive testing, since in this case if the products are good they will be accepted soon, and if they are bad they will be rejected soon. But under this scenario, if the lot is questionable, i.e., in no-man's-land, it may take a while to dispose of it. Arguably, we shouldn't worry too much about wasting items in this range, since it is the range where we are indifferent whether we accept the item or destroy it. Nonetheless, inspection is not free, and some practitioners do not like the lack of clarity. For example, it may make it difficult to schedule inspection activities, since we don't know the load exactly (which is also a problem with other plans we discussed, especially those that include rectifying inspection).

Let the plan (n_1, c_1) be the optimal single sampling plan for some combination of AQL, α, $LTPD$, and β. In response to the problem discussed, some practitioners curtail Wald's continuous sampling after $3n_1$ items. When this occurs, it's theoretically difficult to determine whether to accept or reject the lot: the process did not terminate *because* that's not possible yet. The parties may agree in advance, however, to some rule; e.g., they may decide by the distance to the decision lines: if the defect count is nearer to the upper (lower) line, reject (accept). It should be understood, however, that such a plan will not maintain α and β as intended.

9.7. Average Outgoing Quality Limit (AOQL)

After subjecting all incoming lots to sampling inspection, the average conformance of the output -- denoted by $AOQL$ -- is different from that of the input. The only exception to this rule is when the incoming lots all have the same conformance and no rectifying inspection is performed. This exception, of course, applies to the case for which we should prefer the kp rule.

Although there is no conceptual difficulty in performing $AOQL$ calculations with less than perfect inspection, we'll assume here that inspection is 100% effective. This is the conventional assumption in this case. We also assume that we are operating under the ideal sampling conditions, i.e., that there are two distinct populations of lots, with good and bad qualities. In more detail, we assume that a proportion f of all lots have AQL conformance while a proportion of $1-f$ have $LTPD$ conformance. Further, we assume that the decision whether to accept or reject was reached after sampling a small fraction of the items (by any type of plan, although in the case of a single plan it is easier to remove this assumption). Finally, we assume that the producer replaces bad items with good ones, so at the end we have the amount purchased.

With rectifying inspection, after sampling we'll accept $1-\alpha$ of the good lots plus β of the bad ones, and subject the rest to 100% inspection. Therefore, our expected fraction defective will be

$$AOQL = (1 - \alpha)fAQL + \beta(1-f)LTPD$$

When inspection is destructive, or if we have a policy of returning lots that failed inspection, we still accept $1-\alpha$ of the good lots and β of the bad ones, but now we have less good items following 100% inspection. In this case

$$AOQL = \frac{(1-\alpha)fAQL + \beta(1-f)LTPD}{(1-\alpha)f + \beta(1-f)}$$

AOQL is lower when we physically accept all lots -- with rectifying inspection as necessary -- than when we return the ones judged bad. Nonetheless, the cost of rectifying inspection may be prohibitive in some cases, and it is impossible with destructive testing.

It's interesting to look at AOQL as a function of p, the percent defective in a lot. In this case the probability of accepting the lot is given by the OC curve of the sampling plan employed. Figure 9.6 shows *AOQL* for the (223, 3) plan with rectifying inspection. If n is small relative to N, AOQL is given by the product of the probability of acceptance and the fraction defective. Note that *AOQL* receives a maximum for a particular value of p, and it decreases from there. The reason is that high p increases the probability of detection, and thus reduces the expected number of defects that remain undetected. But without rectifying inspection *AOQL=p* (for those lots we accept), which strengthens the message that sampling is potentially useful only if the incoming lots do not have the same conformance.

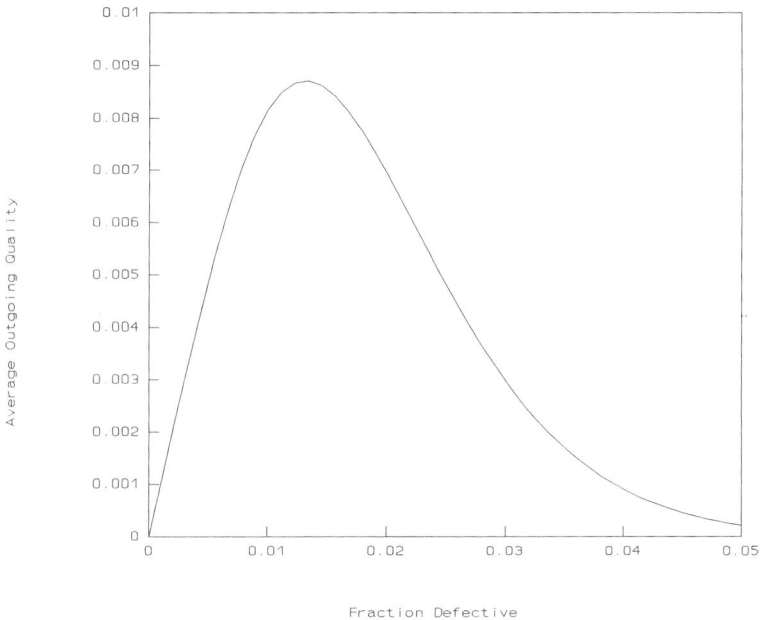

Fig. 9.6. Average outgoing quality for (223, 3) plan with rectifying inspection.

References

Adams, Benjamin M., William H. Woodall, and Cynthia A. Lowry, "The Use (and Misuse) of False Alarm Probabilities in Control Chart Design", *Frontiers in Statistical Quality Control 4* (H.J. Lenz, G.B. Wetherill, and P.T. Wilrich, Eds.), 1992, Physica-Verlag, Heidelberg.

Alwan, Layth C. and Harry V. Roberts (1988), Time-Series Modeling for Statistical Process Control, *Journal of Business & Economics Statistics,* 6(1), pp. 87-95.

Anscombe, Francis J. (1961), Rectifying Inspection of Lots, *Journal of the American Statistical Association* 56, pp. 807-823.

AT&T (1958), *Statistical Quality Control Handbook,* 2nd edition, AT&T Technologies, Indianapolis, Indiana.

Bhote, Keki R. (1991), *World Class Quality: Using Design of Experiments to Make It Happen,* Revised Edition, American Management Association, New York, NY. (Foreword by Dorian Shainin.)

Box, George E.P. (1988), Signal-to-Noise Ratios, Performance Criteria, and Transformations, *Technometrics* 30(1), pp. 1-17. [Followed by a discussion section on pp. 19-40, by various authors.]

Box, George E.P. and Gwilym M. Jenkins (1976), *Time Series Analysis, Forecasting and Control* (2nd ed.), Holden-Day, San Francisco.

Box, George E.P., Soren Bisgaard, and Conrad Fung (1988), An Explanation and Critique of Taguchi's Contributions to Quality Engineering, *Quality and Reliability Engineering International,* 4.

353

Burr, Irving W. (1967), The Effect of Non-Normality on Constants for X-bar and R Charts, *Industrial Quality Control*, May, pp. 563-568.

Champ, Charles W. and William H. Woodall (1987), Exact Results for Shewhart Control Charts with Supplementary Runs Rules, *Technometrics* 29, pp. 393-399.

Champ, Charles W. and William H. Woodall (1990), A Program to Evaluate the Run Length Distribution of a Shewhart Control Chart with Supplementary Runs Rules, *Journal of Quality Technology* 22, pp. 68-73.

Chase, Richard D. and Nicholas J. Aquilano (1992), *Production & Operations Management: A Life Cycle Approach,* 6th ed., Irwin, Homewood, IL.

Chase, Richard D. and Douglas M. Stewart (1994), Make Your Service Fail-Safe, *Sloan Management Review*, Spring, pp. 35-44.

Cochran, William G. (1977), *Sampling Techniques,* 3rd ed., Wiley.

Davis, Robert B. and William H. Woodall (1988), Performance of the Control Chart Trend Rule Under Linear Shift, *Journal of Quality Technology,* 20, pp. 260-262.

Deming, W. Edwards (1975), On Probability as a Basis for Action, *The American Statistician,* 29(4), pp. 146-152.

Deming, W. Edwards (1986), *Out of the Crisis*, MIT Center for Advanced Engineering Study, Cambridge, MA.

Deming, W. Edwards (1993), *The New Economics for Industry, Government, Education*, MIT Center for Advanced Engineering Study, Cambridge, Mass.

Dodge, Harold F. and Harry G. Romig (1959), *Sampling Inspection Tables, Single and Double Sampling,* 2nd Edition, Wiley, New York, NY.

Duncan, Acheson J. (1974), *Quality Control and Industrial Statistics,* 4th edition, Irwin, Homewood, IL.

Forrester, Jay (1961), *Industrial Dynamics,* MIT Press, Cambridge, Mass.

Gardner, Everette S., Jr. (1984), The Strange Case of the Lagging Forecasts, *Interfaces* 14(3), pp. 47-50.

Gardner, Everette S., Jr. (1985), Exponential Smoothing: The State of the Art, *Journal of Forecasting,* 4, pp. 1-28.

Garvin, David A. (1988), *Managing Quality, The Strategic and Competitive Edge*, The Free Press, New York, NY.

Goldratt, Eliyahu M. (1990), *Theory of Constraints,* North River Press, Croton-on-Hudson, NY.

Goldratt, Eliyahu M. and Jeff Cox (1992), *The Goal,* North River Press, Croton-on-Hudson, NY.

Grant, Eugene L. and Richard S. Leavenworth (1980), *Statistical Quality Control,* 5th edition, McGraw-Hill, New York.

Greenberg, Irwin (1970), The First Occurrence of *n* Successes in *N* Trials, *Technometrics,* 12, 627-634.

Grubbs, Frank E. (1954), An Optimum Procedure for Setting Machines or Adjusting Processes, *Industrial Quality Control*, July. (Reprinted in *Journal of Quality Technology*, 15(4), October 1983, pp. 186 189.)

Gunter, Berton H. (1993), Choosing and Using Statistical Software, *Quality Progress,* August, pp. 135, 137, 143-145.

Harter, H. Leon (1960), Tables of Range and Studentized Range, *Annals of Mathematical Statistics,* 31, pp. 1122-1147.

Hillier, Frederick S. (1969), $\overline{X}$- and *R*-Chart Control Limits Based on A Small Number of Subgroups, *Journal of Quality Technology*, 1(1) pp. 17-26.

Huber, P.J. (1981), *Robust Statistics,* Wiley.

Hwang, Frank K. and Dan Trietsch (1996), A Simple Relation Between the Pattern Probability and the Rate of False Signals in Control Charts, *PEIS*, 10, pp. 315-323.

Ishikawa, Kaoru (1985), *What is Total Quality Control?,* Prentice Hall, 1985.

Juran, Joseph M. (Editor-in-Chief), and Gryna, Frank M. (Associate Editor) (1988), *Juran's Quality Control Handbook*, Fourth Edition, McGraw-Hill Book Company.

Juran, Joseph M. (1988), Quality and Income, Section 3 in *Juran's Quality Control Handbook.*

Kaiser, Mark J. and Dan Trietsch (1997), The Distribution of Points in Measurement Precision Charts, *Mathematical Scientist*, 22, pp. 117-121.

Kelton, W. David, Walton M. Hancock, and Diane P. Bischak (1990), Adjustment Rules Based on Quality Control Charts, *International Journal of Production Research,* 28(2), pp. 385-400.

Leon, Ramon V, Anne C. Shoemaker, and Raghu N. Kacker (1987), Performance Measures Independent of Adjustment: An Explanation and Extension of Taguchi's Signal-to-Noise Ratios, *Technometrics* 29(3), pp. 253-265. [A central paper about S/N ratios. Followed by discussion section on pp. 266-285, by various authors.]

Levene, Howard and J. Wolfowitz (1944), The Covariance Matrix of Runs Up and Down, *The Annals of Mathematical Statistics,* 15, pp. 58-69.

Lucas, James M. (1973), A Modified V-Mask Scheme, *Technometrics,* 24, pp. 199-205.

Lucas, James M. (1982), Combined Shewhart-CUSUM Quality Control Schemes, *Journal of Quality Technology,* 14.

MacGregor, J.F. and T.J. Harris (1993), The Exponentially Weighted Moving Variance, *Journal of Quality Technology,* 25, pp. 106-118.

Milligan, Glenn W. (1991), Is Sampling Really Dead?, *Quality Progress*, April, pp. 77-81.

Montgomery, Douglas C. (1991), *Introduction to Statistical Quality Control,* Wiley, New York.

Montgomery, Douglas C. and Christina M. Mastrangelo (1991), Some Statistical Process Control Methods for Autocorrelated Data, *Journal of Quality Technology,* 23, pp. 179-193.

Morita, Akio (1987), *Made in Japan,* Collins.

Mosteller, F. (1941), Note on Application of Runs to Quality Control Charts, *The Annals of Mathematical Statistics,* 12, p. 232.

Nair, Vijayan N., editor (1992), Taguchi's Parameter Design: A Panel Discussion, *Technometrics*, 34(2), pp. 127-161. Panel Discussants: Bovas Abraham and Jock MacKay; George Box, Raghu N. Kacker, Thomas J. Lorenzen, James M. Lucas, Raymond H. Myers and G. Geoffrey Vining, John A. Nelder, Mahdav S. Phadke, Jerome Sacks and William J. Welch, Anne C. Shoemaker and Kwok L. Tsui, Shin Taguchi, C. F. Jeff Wu.

Neave, Henry R. (1990), *The Deming Dimension*, SPC Press, Knoxville, TN. (Foreword by Dr. Deming.)

Nelson, Lloyd S. (1982), Control Chart for Medians, *Journal of Quality Technology,* 14, pp. 226-227.

Nelson, Lloyd S. (1984), The Shewhart Control Chart -- Tests for Special Causes, *Journal of Quality Technology,* 16, pp. 237-239.

Nelson, Lloyd S. (1985), Interpreting Shewhart $\overline{X}$ Control Charts, *Journal of Quality Technology,* 17, pp. 114-116.

NKS/FM [Nikkan Kogyo Shimbun, Ltd./Factory Magazine] (1988), *Poka-Yoke: Improving Product Quality by Preventing Defects,* Productivity, Cambridge, MA.

Orsini, Joyce (1982), Simple Rule to Reduce Total Cost of Inspection and Correction of Product in State of Chaos, PhD dissertation, Graduate School of Business Administration, New York University. Obtainable from University Microfilms, Ann Arbor, 48106.

Quesenberry, Charles P. (1991), SPC Q Charts for Start-Up Processes and Short or Long Runs, *Journal of Quality Technology*, 23, pp. 224-231.

Quesenberry, Charles P. (1993), The Effect of Sample Size on Estimated Limits for $\overline{X}$ and X Control Charts, *Journal of Quality Technology*, 25, pp. 237-247.

Read, Robert R. (1979), Components of Student-Faculty Evaluation Data, *Educational and Psychological Measurement*, 39, pp. 353-360.

Ronen, Boaz, and Dan Trietsch (1993), Optimal Scheduling of Purchasing Orders for Large Projects, *European Journal of Operational Research,* 68, pp. 185-195.

Ryan, Thomas P. (1989), *Statistical Methods for Quality Improvement*, Wiley, New York.

Scherkenbach, William W. (1990), *The Deming Route to Quality and Productivity: Road Maps and Roadblocks*, CeePress Books/ASQC Quality Press. (Foreword by Dr. Deming.)

Seder, Leonard A. (1950a), Diagnosis With Diagrams -- Part I, *Industrial Quality Control*, January, pp. 11-19.

Seder, Leonard A. (1950b), Diagnosis With Diagrams -- Part II, *Industrial Quality Control*, March, pp. 7-11.

Senge, Peter (1990), *The Fifth Discipline,* Doubleday, New York, NY.

Shainin, Dorian, and Peter D. Shainin (1988), Statistical Process Control, Section 24 in *Juran's Quality Control Handbook.*

Shewhart, Walter A. (1931), *Economic Control of Quality of Manufactured Product,* Van

Nostrand, New York (50th Anniversary Commemorative Reissue by ASQC, Quality Press, Milwaukee, Wisconsin, 1980).

Shingo, Shigeo (1985), *A Revolution in Manufacturing: The SMED System*, Productivity Press, Cambridge, Mass.

Shingo, Shigeo (1986), *Zero Quality Control: Source Inspection and the Poka-yoke System*, Productivity Press, Cambridge, Mass.

Spiring, Fred A. (1994), A Bill's Effect on Alcohol-Related Traffic Fatalities: A Non-Manufacturing Application of the p Chart, *Quality Progress*, February, pp. 35-38. [See also letters relating to this article in the July issue, pp. 8, 11, & 12.]

Taguchi, Genichi (1986), *Introduction to Quality Engineering: Designing Quality into Products and Processes*, Asian Productivity Organization.

Tippett, L.H.C. (1925), On the Extreme Individuals and the Range of Samples Taken from a Normal Population, *Biometrica* 17, pp. 364-387.

Trietsch, Dan (1992), Augmenting the Taguchi Loss Function by the Production Cost May Invalidate Taguchi's Signal-to-Noise Ratio, AS Working Paper 92-07, Naval Postgraduate School, Monterey, CA.

Trietsch, Dan (1992a), Focused TQM and Synergy: A Case Study, AS Working Paper 92-06, Naval Postgraduate School, Monterey, CA.

Trietsch, Dan (1992b), Some Notes on the Application of Single Minute Exchange of Die (SMED), July 1992 *NPS-AS-92-019* Naval Postgraduate School, Monterey, CA (Technical Report).

Dan Trietsch (1992c), A New Recipe for a Winning Meta-Strategy: Mix Well One Deming with One Ohno and Add a Dash of Taguchi, Shingo and Goldratt, *AS* Working Paper 93-01, Naval Postgraduate School, Monterey, CA.

Trietsch, Dan (1993), Scheduling Flights at Hub Networks, *Transportation Research, Part B (Methodology)*, 27B, pp. 133-150.

Trietsch, Dan (1994), Total Quality: It's a Huge Optimization Problem, Trietsch Associates (working paper).

Trietsch, Dan (1995), Process Setup Adjustment with Quadratic Loss, *IIE Transactions* (to appear).

Trietsch, Dan (1996), An Approximate Minimal Cost Sampling Plan for a Lot with Unknown *p* When the Cost of Inspecting at Random is Larger than the Cost of Inspection in Sequence, Department of Management Science and Information Systems, University of Auckland, Working Paper No. 113, August.

Trietsch, Dan (1997), The Harmonic Rule for Process Setup Adjustment with Quadratic Loss, *Journal of Quality Technology*, 30, pp. 75-84.

Trietsch, Dan (1997-98), The Five/Ten Rule: A Constrained-Loss Economic Process Adjustment Procedure, *Quality Engineering*, 10(1), pp. 85-95.

Trietsch, Dan and Diane P. Bischak (1998), The Rate of False Signals for Control Charts with Limits Estimated from Small Samples, *Proceedings of the 33rd Annual Conference, The Operational Research Society of New Zealand*, pp. 232-241.

Trietsch, Dan, and Frank K. Hwang (1997), Notes on Pattern Tests for Special Causes, *Quality Engineering*, 9(3), pp. 467-477.

Tukey, John W. (1960), A Survey of Sampling from Contaminated Distributions, in I. Olkin et al. (ed), *Contributions to Probability and Statistics,* Stanford Press, pp. 448-485.

Tukey, John W. (1991), The Philosophy of Multiple Comparisons, *Statistical Science,* 6(1), pp. 100-116.

Wadsworth, H.M., K.S. Stephens, and A. Blanton Godfrey (1986), *Modern Methods for Quality Control and Improvement,* Wiley.

Wald, Abraham (1947), *Sequential Analysis*, Wiley, New York.

Walker, Esteban, John W. Philpot and James Clement (1991), False Signal Rates for the

Shewhart Control Chart with Supplementary Runs Tests, *Journal of Quality Technology*, 23(3), pp. 247-252.

Ware and Williams (1975), The Doctor Fox Effect: A Study of Lecturer Effectiveness and Ratings of Instruction, *Journal of Medical Education*, 50, pp. 149-156.

Wheeler, Donald J. (1995), *Advanced Topics in Statistical Process Control: The Power of Shewhart's Charts*, SPC Press, Knoxville, TN.

Wheeler, Donald J. and Neave, Henry R. (1994), Control Charts and the Probability Approach.

Woodall, William H. and Benjamin M. Adams (1993), The Statistical Design of CUSUM charts, *Quality Engineering*, 5(4), pp. 559-570.

Woodall, William H. and Frederick W. Faltin (1996), An Overview and Perspective on Control Charting, in *Statistical Applications in Process Control,* edited by J.Bert Keats and Douglas C. Montgomery, Marcel-Dekker.

Index